Comrades of Color

# Protest, Culture, and Society

General editors:
**Kathrin Fahlenbrach,** Institute for Media and Communication, University of Hamburg
**Martin Klimke,** New York University Abu Dhabi
**Joachim Scharloth,** Technical University Dresden, Germany

Protest movements have been recognized as significant contributors to processes of political participation and transformations of culture and value systems, as well as to the development of both a national and transnational civil society.

This series brings together the various innovative approaches to phenomena of social change, protest and dissent which have emerged in recent years, from an interdisciplinary perspective. It contextualizes social protest and cultures of dissent in larger political processes and socio-cultural transformations by examining the influence of historical trajectories and the response of various segments of society, political and legal institutions on a national and international level. In doing so, the series offers a more comprehensive and multi-dimensional view of historical and cultural change in the twentieth and twenty-first century.

*For full volume listing, please see back matter.*

# Comrades of Color

## East Germany in the Cold War World

Edited by

Quinn Slobodian

berghahn
NEW YORK • OXFORD
www.berghahnbooks.com

First published in 2015 by
Berghahn Books
www.berghahnbooks.com

© 2015, 2017 Quinn Slobodian
First paperback edition published in 2017

**Library of Congress Cataloging-in-Publication Data**

Names: Slobodian, Quinn, 1978– editor.
Title: Comrades of color : East Germany in the Cold War world / edited by
Quinn Slobodian.
Description: New York : Berghahn Books, 2015. | Series: Protest, culture and
society ; volume 14
Identifiers: LCCN 2015014517| ISBN 9781782387053 (hardback : alka-
line paper) | ISBN: 9781785337376 (paperback) | ISBN 9781782387060
(ebook)
Subjects: LCSH: Germany (East)—Relations. | Germany (East)—Race
relations—Political aspects. | Germany (East)—Relations—Asia. | Asia—
Relations—Germany (East) | Germany (East)—Relations—Cuba. |
Cuba—Relations—Germany (East) | African American communists—
History—20th century. | Socialism—History—20th century. | International
relations—History—20th century. | Cold War—Diplomatic history.
Classification: LCC DD284 .C65 2015 | DDC 303.48/2431008—dc23
LC record available at http://lccn.loc.gov/2015014517

**British Library Cataloguing in Publication Data**

A catalogue record for this book is available from the British Library

ISBN: 978-1-78238-705-3 hardback
ISBN: 978-1-78533-737-6 paperback
ISBN: 978-1-78238-706-0 ebook

# Contents

# Figures

# Introduction

*Quinn Slobodian*

Thousands of postcards from East Germany arriving at the prison holding
Angela Davis. The letters, "VĐ," for Vietnam and (East) Germany, on the
stone cornice of an apartment complex in northern Vietnam. An island near
Cuba's Bay of Pigs named Cayo Ernesto Thälmann. A ring road in Erfurt
named after Mao Zedong. In the four decades of its existence, East Germany's world extended far beyond Central Europe. Even after the erection
of the Berlin Wall in 1961 and the pervasive travel restrictions, people and
objects flowed in and out of the country. The spread of state socialism to
the postcolonial world, in the words of one scholar, created "an unexpected
circulation of goods, people, and information along new channels and across
discontinuous world areas."[1] Histories of the German Democratic Republic
have only recently begun to reflect this fact. This book continues the work
of exploring encounters across the borders of nation and bloc in East Germany's world. Its subjects are people of color, that is, people marked as racial
Others in the white European mind.

The book's title, *Comrades of Color,* points to a tension at its heart. What
was the status of race in a socialist world view that deemed class to be the
medium that dissolved all other differences? How did race and racialized
thinking operate in a socialist society like East Germany that had decreed
racism out of existence? What alliances were created across ethnic lines in the
German project of state socialism that had not, and could not, have existed
before? Looked at in the longer term, how can we reconcile the official anti-
racism of East Germany with the waves of racially motivated violence that
swept through the former East after 1989?

The authors of *Comrades of Color* are united by the effort to understand
how the high-minded internationalism of speeches and propaganda translated into everyday life.[2] What followed the initial moment when hands
were clasped across rifts of geography, race, and historical experience? What
did international solidarity look like beyond the frame of the official photographs? *Comrades of Color* does not strive to be a comprehensive history
of East Germany's relationship to the Global South. A range of diplomatic
histories already exist, covering the struggle of the two Germanys over the
distribution of international aid, their struggle for international recognition
before both joined the United Nations in 1972, and, more recently, pen-

etrating investigations into East Germany's arms trade.[3] Another body of scholarship exists about the use of foreign contract labor by East Germany in its last decade.[4] Drawing on material from long before the 1980s as well as after the Wall's fall, *Comrades of Color* takes a microscopic rather than panoramic perspective, homing in on the frictions of solidarity, and the moments of mismatch between the varieties of world socialism.

Historians of modern Germany embraced a scholarly trend toward transnational perspectives in the last decade. Some historians of East Germany, including contributors to this volume, have participated in this development. Following pioneering research from the Center for Contemporary History at Potsdam in the early millennium, scholars have studied East Germany's engagement with communist East and Southeast Asia, as well as the experiences of asylum seekers, contract workers, and foreign students in the GDR.[5] Studies of East Germany's official internationalism have been joined by scholarly attention to the way that campaigns of building good faith overseas were received, and remembered, by local populations.[6] While these contributions are exemplary, the dominant questions asked by historians about the GDR still remain more local ones. They ask questions about legitimacy, durability, and relative freedom: How did the Socialist Unity Party (SED) justify its own rule? How did it maintain control as long as it did? To what extent was a social existence outside of state surveillance possible?

Beyond the range of notable exceptions cited above, the glances beyond the "walled state" tend to look either westward, asking about the relative influence of West Germany and the United States as sources of information, modes of politics, and forms of mass culture; or to the aforementioned issues of foreign contract labor in the republic's final decade. Bracketed in both cases is the importance of the SED's self-understanding and self-presentation as an active member of the international community of world socialism, the importance of solidarity with the global South in its repertoire of legitimation, and empirical study of the concrete outcomes of these explicitly political North-South engagements.[7]

As in many other national histories, the inclusion of the experiences of foreigners and racial minorities often remains optional rather than obligatory. Given the centrality of international solidarity to East German self-understanding, this approach strikes this collection's authors as indefensible. Scholarly interventions are especially important as the narrative has been controlled to date by former functionaries who, though often extremely erudite, tend toward romanticizing the East German role overseas as a bright spot in an otherwise bleak record of statecraft.[8] Cultural histories of the "Second World's Third World" from the East German perspective are necessary to place the republic properly within the international field.[9]

*Comrades of Color* follows the recent work of a host of authors tracking political links between the Second World and the global South, as well as identifications between Second World actors and grassroots social movements in the First World.[10] As a collection, it makes three major contributions to the existing literature. First, it offers a representative range of examples that document the diverse breadth of interactions between East Germany and its partners in the Americas, Asia, and Africa from 1949 to 1989 and beyond. Case studies cover, among other topics, solidarity campaigns with African-American communists; film coproductions with Vietnam and China; urban planning projects in North Korea and Vietnam; and training programs for students from Mozambique.

Second, through both archival and ethnographic research, these studies establish and explore the existence of what could be called the varieties of world socialism. Although most of the interactions under study took place within the ostensibly shared ideological space of the "Second World," outcomes betrayed the influence of diverse historical experiences and local traditions in setting the horizons of political imagination. Race as a cognitive category and lived reality, dismissed by the SED as overcome in socialist society, proved far from extinct. Decolonization, the Sino-Soviet split, and the Cold War's "hot wars" inflected the traffic of ideas and actors into and out of the GDR. The overlapping geographies of region, race, and experience (of empire, world war, and colonialism) ensured that the Second World was never the homogeneous terrain implied by the Cold War analytic binary.[11]

Finally, the volume pursues the seemingly paradoxical goal of undermining the "myth of East German provincialism" (Hosek) precisely by "provincializing Germany" (Hong).[12] Viewing the GDR from a distance through the eyes and experiences of individuals from the global South challenges the historiographical framing of the two Germanys as opposites. The two republics' shared standard of living and technological prowess relative to much of the world qualified them both as members of the elite international club of industrialized nations. In some cases, actors from Asia, Africa, and Latin America used the mutual German antagonism instrumentally to secure training and aid serially from both sides. In other cases, the ideological bonds ran deeper and were reinforced through socialization in the Second World public sphere. The scholarly essays in the volume are accompanied by primary sources written from a perspective both distant and intimate, including a 1966 letter from East Germany written by South African author, William "Bloke" Modisane; an analysis of the East German university system written by a Chinese Red Guard at the height of the Cultural Revolution; and a reflection on the monuments of East German socialism by Cuban poet Victor Fowler. In a historiography that remains constrained within the terms of the German-German conversation, perspectives like these remain all but absent.[13] *Comrades of Color* begins to fill this gap and, in doing so, to reorient perspectives on East Germany's world.

## Overview of the Chapters

The following chapters make clear that postcolonial nations pursued political and socioeconomic visions not reducible to the binary alternatives of the Cold War.[14] The first chapter provides an overview of the way that race and racism were redefined in East Germany after the collapse of the Third Reich in 1945. It shows the similarities between such redefinitions on both sides of the Cold War boundary while also exploring the particularities of the modes of representing racial and cultural difference in the socialist bloc. It locates people from the global South between their status as icons and individuals in the landscape of East Germany.

The contributions to the second section "Aid *anders?*" or "aid differently?" deepen this investigation. They follow East Germans engaged in socialist projects of aid beyond the borders of Europe and ask how they differed from the frequently asymmetrical power relations involved in liberal-capitalist development assistance. At the heart of Young-Sun Hong's chapter is a confrontation between two visions of the lived space of socialist modernity in North Korea. While East Germans sought to bring Bauhaus modernity in their reconstruction of the destroyed city of Hamhung in the 1950s, Koreans sought designs appropriate to their own forms of everyday life and economic constraints. Beds, heaters, ceilings, and light-switches became objects of intense ideological debate in the confrontation between competing socialist imaginaries. Authorities wary of outside influence severed the nascent "transnational identities" developing between Germans and Koreans, in some cases leaving emotional scars as enduring side effects of geopolitical division.

Gregory Witkowski looks at the diverse ways that solidarity was defined, represented, and pitched to the East German population. He shows how the official Solidarity Committee, established in 1960, sought self-consciously to break with established conventions of North-South charity by eschewing pity-inducing images of women and children. Rather, it invoked Germans' own memories of war and reconstruction, and portrayed people in countries like Vietnam, Mozambique, and Angola as forward-looking and equipped to build socialist modernity. The Solidarity Committee competed with the lesser-known philanthropic efforts of the churches in the GDR. Witkowski demonstrates that both the Protestant and Catholic churches adhered more closely to the received script of the munificent West donating to the "deserving poor," yet they were also surprisingly forthright at times in their opposition to colonialism and their belief that charity was as important for the donor as the recipient. The solidarity efforts of both the churches and the official mass organizations created East German subjectivity in their efforts at aiding Others.

Bernd Schaefer's chapter follows the transformation of the project of "socialist modernization" in the decades-long relationship between the GDR and socialist Vietnam. East Germany was a key source of aid for the Democratic Republic of Vietnam (DRV) from 1954 through the years of the "American War" and after the establishment of the Socialist Republic of Vietnam (SRV) in 1975. Schaefer follows the traffic in experts, officials, and students between the two republics, culminating in the employment of hundreds of thousands of Vietnamese workers in East German factories in the 1980s, often under conditions unacceptable to Germans themselves. Among the more striking evidence Schaefer provides for the importance of the relationship was the printing of Vietnamese money in the GDR for two decades, the extensive training of Vietnamese intelligence services, and the seeding of a coffee industry that has made the SRV the world's second largest exporter. Schaefer reveals the bilateral relationship as a learning process, punctuated by failures, but also containing genuine successes.

The third section, "Ambivalent Solidarities," begins with a personal letter from black South African writer Bloke Modisane, who compares his special access to scarce luxury goods in East Berlin to that of a white in Johannesburg and agonizes over an encounter with an East German woman desperate to use him as a means of escape. The contributions to this section demonstrate that scholars have underestimated the delicacy involved in hosting foreigners in the GDR, even those who came as honored political guests. In a biographical essay, Simon Stevens delves into Modisane's life history to explain how his liminal existence in the GDR may have echoed his experiences in apartheid South Africa. Sara Pugach shows how received racialized tropes of the black male predator and the white German woman of "loose morals" echoed through the files of East German bureaucrats as the number of foreign students multiplied after 1960. The sexual activity of foreigners was a state concern in the GDR. A foreigner who married, or reproduced with, a German might seek to remain in the country, creating diplomatic tensions with the home nation. By staying, the foreigner upset the basic model of East German solidarity. Borders were to be crossed temporarily not permanently. Education and training were intended ultimately to be applied in one's home country.

Pugach reveals the particularity of race discourse in the situation of state socialism. She describes a bar manager criticizing the actions of certain African men for reinforcing "racist, stupid prejudices" among Germans themselves. She finds a university administrator confessing his belief in black male promiscuity privately to a colleague while noting that this could not be admitted publicly. In these contortions and concealments, we see in East Germany many of the hypocrisies and situationally selective language familiar from white majority contexts beyond the socialist world. Pugach's work gives further evidence that racial preconceptions cut across the political geographies of the Cold War blocs.[15]

Katrina Hagen's chapter on Angela Davis shows how even lionized Others were volatile political quantities. Davis was a celebrity of the highest order in the GDR and a pivotal figure in the discourse of race and racism. She became the de facto ambassador for the cause of anti-racism in 1970s East Germany. As a figurehead of the "Other America" and a card-carrying member of the Communist Party, Davis embodied the ideal object of solidarity. Yet, Hagen finds the frictions of solidarity in even this apparent fairy tale of socialist internationalism. Davis's close relationship to émigré New Left theorist Herbert Marcuse and her links to black nationalist groups like the Black Panthers placed her in questionable ideological territory for the SED. Hagen finds the SED discussing the "black racism" of the Panthers and, potentially, of Davis herself. The refusal of communists of color like Davis to dismiss race as a bugbear exterminated by socialism challenged the East German discourse head on. The appearance of the "U.S. Third World Left" in the GDR created category problems for a state party not well equipped for challenges of intersectionality.[16]

Jason Verber also finds tensions at the confluence of socialist imaginaries and the lived realities of coexistence. The East German project of building an entire school in the countryside to train young Mozambicans in 1981 was a major effort of cultural diplomacy. In practice, political rationality ran first into the obstacles of youthful sexuality with six pregnancies within the first two years of the school's existence. More seriously, internationalism collided with explicit racism in attacks on Mozambican students by far-right Germans threatening that "back in the *Führer*'s day you would have been skinned, slowly killed, and then burned." The nascent neo-Nazi movement confronted foreigners with hatred defiantly rejecting protocols of official socialist internationalism.

Verber finds the source of disagreement in the clashing "varieties of socialism" practiced by East Germans and Mozambicans. Although a large literature about the varieties of capitalism has sprung up in the past two decades, the parallel discussion about varieties of socialism in the era of the global Cold War remains thin.[17] A notable exception is in the large and growing literature about the Sino-Soviet split of the 1960s. Moving beyond former perspectives which saw China's rupture with the Soviet bloc as based on either realpolitik or ideology, new research has pursued the diplomatic but also the cultural angle, examining the transformation of an intense culture of solidarity into one of enmity in the 1960s.[18] Recent research on the Chinese influence in the global South has explained how different national histories led to identification with the Chinese and multipolar realignment of geopolitical alliances in what Jeffrey James Byrne calls the "contest of modernities."[19]

The book's fourth section, titled "Socialist Mirrors," uses two case studies to examine precisely such moments of comparison. It begins with an article from a Red Guard newspaper in Shanghai denouncing the East German university system in 1968. Working from what is likely firsthand knowledge, the author describes a rigid hierarchy designed to award careerism and punish solidarity. The GDR becomes an inverse reflection of the socialism dreamed of by the young Chinese author. This voice from the margins of East Germany's world is followed by two chapters that explore similar dialogues happening in the medium of film. I look at East Berlin's DEFA studio as a center for transnational filmmaking in the 1950s. The "world films" of Dutch documentarian Joris Ivens involved cooperation from inside and outside the socialist bloc to create cinematic analogues of the racial rainbow, depicting national realities that were parallel but rarely overlapped. I contrast this "socialist multilateralism" to the "socialist cosmopolitanism" nascent in the failed collaboration between Alex Wedding, Joop Huisken, and their Chinese partners on a feature-length documentary film in the late 1950s. Surviving only in records of heated conversations and treatments, the film project was doomed by deteriorating relations between East Germany and China and the closing of windows open briefly during the Thaw and the Hundred Flowers campaign. As in Hong's chapter, the failed coproduction reminds us of the challenges of creating outward expressions of a common socialist self-understanding across the gaps of disparate national histories.

Evan Torner and Victoria Rizo Lenshyn provide vivid illustration of similar dynamics in their exploration of the Vietnamese–East German coproduction *Dschungelzeit* (1988). The subject of the film itself was a remarkable moment of border-crossing, when German deserters from the French Foreign Legion in Indochina joined and fought with the anticolonial Viet Minh in the 1940s.[20] Torner and Lenshyn argue that the film's "transnational aesthetic" ended up containing and embodying two moments of friction: that of the postindependence 1950s, when the German defectors were compelled to leave Vietnam to "return" to the GDR, sometimes against their will, and that of the 1980s, when dissidence was becoming more widespread among cultural elites. In the film, the question of *Heimat* is called into question for the Germans who fled fascist Germany and held the firm belief that there should never be another Germany (*nie wieder Deutschland*). Through these characters, the filmmaker asks how one is expected to accept a new German nation, even one that called itself communist. Through interviews with the German filmmaker and close textual readings, Torner and Lenshyn draw out the surprising ways in which internationalist projects could be used to express doubts about East German socialism itself in the last years of the GDR.

The final section, "Internationalist Remains," begins with an essay by Christina Schwenkel describing the partial erasure of the GDR in Vietnam, where the much longer history of association with East Germany has been displaced officially by the shorter links to the Federal Republic, reinforcing the notion of the GDR as an isolated hermit republic of the Cold War. Yet, she demonstrates that the memory of East German engagement with Vietnam remains strong below the governmental level. Pointing to the importance of genuine efforts made on behalf of East German populations to aid and cooperate with the Vietnamese population both during their war with the United States and after, Schwenkel argues for the category of "affective solidarities" that escape measurement in conventional ways. She ends by pointing out how Vietnam remains a "new battleground of memory politics" between East and West Germany. The built environment of the northern city of Vinh, reconstructed with East German aid, keeps alive the possibility of an explicitly politicized form of development assistance in a neoliberal era, and a willingness to give aid the name of solidarity.

The exploration of the legacy of socialist solidarity continues in the final essay of the collection, a work of collaboration by German Studies scholar Jennifer Ruth Hosek and Cuban poet Victor Fowler Calzada. An experiment in composition and transnational conversation, the essay alternates between Fowler's search for the traces of Germany in the Cuban imaginary and Hosek's exploration of the reception of "GDR films" in Havana in recent years. Fowler's account of his grandfather hanging a portrait of the Kaiser in his home in the early twentieth century meets Hosek's account of the screening of *Goodbye Lenin!* in Havana when eager crowds broke the theater's glass doors in their enthusiasm. The uncanny sense of loss produced in Cuba by the disappearance of East Germany resonates through the essay. The Cayo Ernesto Thälmann, whose beach hosts a stone bust of the German communist leader revered in the GDR, stands as an image of a severed appendage and extraterritorial remnant of a political entity that no longer exists. Fowler and Hosek's piece reveals the material and psychological consequences of the fallen Soviet bloc for the socialist countries that survived 1989. It ends with a poetic meditation on the statues of Marx and Engels in Berlin written by

Fowler at a time when a "world had collapsed" and socialism has vanished from Germany even as it lived on in Cuba.

•  •  •

What remains of forty years of East German internationalism? A last anecdote provides one answer. In 1957, future East German leader Erich Honecker cut the ribbon of "Joint Factory 718," trumpeted as China's most modern industrial installation, built by East German architects with Chinese and Soviet funding in the northwestern suburbs of Beijing.[21] Promotional materials from the same decade showed portraits of Mao and GDR president Wilhelm Pieck above stylized images of German and Chinese workers. The men step forward to shake hands while the women stand behind them smiling, clad in the overalls and head scarves of workers. The East German–designed complex was unable to remain profitable and all but ceased operations during the period of liberalization in the 1980s. Some of its cavernous spaces were taken over by artists. By the mid 2000s, the redubbed "Arts District 798" was designated officially as a "cultural creative cluster," filled with boutiques, design stores and contemporary art galleries.[22] The former factory complex was a place to be seen for the Chinese nouveau riche. Teenagers and tourists took photos of each other in front of the remnants of the factories that echoed those decommissioned industrial sites repurposed for cultural consumption worldwide.[23] There was no trace of East Germany in the complex. Indeed, the only corporate presence in the entire district is a large cube-like office building with the logos of two German brands on it: Volkswagen and Audi. The only East German presence in the complex was a photograph from the 1980s of the two architects, now elderly, looking a little bewildered in the milieu of the Chinese *Bohème,* haunting the premises like ghosts of an earlier era.

Yet the history is not as distant as it seems. In February 2009, the Haus der Kulturen der Welt in Berlin held a conference on the "global 1989" to commemorate the twentieth anniversary of the fall of the Wall. Several Chinese intellectuals in attendance discussed the bloody denouement of the Tiananmen Square demonstrations parallel to the more peaceful events in Berlin. There had been transnational traffic in 1989, too. Chinese students from East Berlin crossed into the West to walk with protesters against the bloody crackdown on the Beijing democracy movement. A young German punk woman in Dresden called for open protest against the crackdown.[24] Dissidents in East Berlin drummed for six consecutive nights to express their own opposition.[25] In July, a band called *Herbst in Peking* (Autumn in Beijing) played a song with lyrics expressing solidarity with Chinese students, and were promptly forbidden from performing again—until after the Wall fell, at which point they achieved considerable success.[26] A letter to the state newspaper captured the effect of the events in China on one East German citizen:

> Opening my *Neues Deutschland* this morning I saw the headline "Chinese People's Liberation Army Crushes Counter-Revolutionary Uprising." As I read the article, I could only ask how a country can inform its citizens so falsely in this way. I can still see yesterday's images from television. And you want to scream in the face of as many lies as this. Let's leave aside the question of whether the demands of the students are justified or not. When a socialist country, a communist country, attacks its citizens like this, I can only wonder about this form of government. According to *Neues Deutschland*, the students' weapons of defense were "cut and thrust weapons," this is what they were attacking tanks with. I saw, and the shots were not staged or edited, how tanks simply rolled over people, how the soldiers shot at fleeing people, shot them from behind... It is amazing that film footage can still be produced under these circumstances, but it is good that it can. Because otherwise you have to believe what you are told when you are informed as one-sidedly as us. And the *Neues Deutschland*'s version, in my opinion, is not fair.[27]

The solidarity of protesters in 1989 both built on and broke with official East German internationalism. It was not of the state but against the state, mediated through troubling imagery that invoked an empathetic bond between Germans and the distant protesters. It humanized the objects of solidarity and spoke back to the government in its own language of socialism and human rights. Working as an inversion of the official rhetoric—when the GDR declared its official support for the Chinese action—it created solidarity anew, between parallel populations dissatisfied with the failure of their own governments to live up to their rhetoric.

One of the speakers at the 2009 Berlin conference was Chinese gender studies professor Ai Xioaming. She took home a copy of the poster, which featured the iconic image of a man facing down tanks at Tiananmen under the words "1989 Global Histories." She kept the poster hidden under a mattress until the anniversary of the massacre in 2013, when she affixed it to her wall, and took a photograph that she put on the internet, in her words, "to express my mourning for the dead."[28] Ai's trip to Berlin had been her last before being barred from overseas travel by the authorities. Her outspoken critique of the Chinese government cut her off from further encounters with the community of colleagues worldwide and displayed the sensitivity of some governments to alternative narratives of the past. 1989 remains alive for the Chinese state just as four decades of East German socialist republic remain alive for those Germans and foreigners who lived through them and who continue to live in the reunified Germany defined by the GDR's past in all its positive and negative aspects. Writing and recounting the history of the world from Germany, and of Germany in the world, remains a matter of intimate politics, even decades later. *Comrades of Color* seeks to continue the process of provincializing East German history and, by doing so, placing it in the larger world.

## Notes

1. João Felipe Gonçalves, "Sputnik Premiers in Havana: A Historical Ethnography of the 1960 Soviet Exposition," in *The Socialist Sixties: Crossing Borders in the Second World*, ed. Anne E. Gorsuch and Diane Koenker (Bloomington, IN: Indiana University Press, 2013), 86.

2. In general, the authors follow the methodological approach described in Katherine Pence and Andrew Zimmerman, "Transnationalism," *German Studies Review* 35, no. 3 (2012): 496.

3. Thomas PM Barnett, *Romanian and East German Policies in the Third World: Comparing the Strategies of Ceaucescu and Honecker* (Westport, CT: Praeger, 1992); William Glenn Gray, *Germany's Cold War: The Global Campaign to Isolate East Germany, 1949-1969* (Chapel Hill: University of North Carolina Press, 2003); Werner Kilian, *Die Hallstein-Doktrin: der diplomatische Krieg zwischen der BRD und der DDR 1955-1973* (Berlin: Duncker und Humblot, 2001); Ingrid Muth, *Die DDR-Aussenpolitik 1949-1972: Inhalte, Strukturen, Mechanismen* (Berlin: Christopher Links, 2000); Joachim Scholtyseck, *Die Aussenpolitik der DDR* (Munich: R. Oldenbourg, 2003); Brigitte Schulz, *Development Policy in the Cold War Era: The Two Germanies and Sub-Saharan Africa, 1960-1985* (Münster: Lit, 1995); Hans-Joachim Spanger and Lothar Brock, *Die beiden deutschen Staaten in der Dritten Welt* (Opladen: Westdeutscher Verlag, 1987); Klaus Storkmann, *Geheime Solidarität: Militärbeziehungen und Militärhilfen der DDR in die "Dritte Welt"* (Berlin: Christoph Links, 2012); Ulrich Van der Heyden, Ilona Schleicher, and Hans-Georg Schleicher, eds., *Die DDR und Afrika*, 2 vols. (Münster: Lit, 1993); Gareth M. Winrow, *The Foreign Policy of the GDR in Africa* (New York: Cambridge University Press, 1990).

4. Bernd Bröskamp, ed., *Schwarz-weisse Zeiten: AusländerInnen in Ostdeutschland vor und nach der Wende: Erfahrungen der Vertragsarbeiter aus Mosambik* (Bremen: IZA, 1993); Mike Dennis and Norman LaPorte, *State and Minorities in Communist East Germany* (New York: Berghahn Books, 2011), chap. 4; Dennis Kuck, "'Für den sozialistischen Aufbau ihrer Heimat'? Ausländische Vertragsarbeitskräfte in der DDR," in *Fremde und Fremd-Sein in der DDR: zu historischen Ursachen der Fremdenfeindlichkeit in Ostdeutschland*, ed. Jan C. Behrends, Thomas Lindenberger, and Patrice G. Poutrus (Berlin: Metropol, 2003); Annegret Schüle, "'Proletarischer International-

ismus' oder 'ökonomischer Vorteil für die DDR'?," *Archiv für Sozialgeschichte*, no. 42 (2002): 191–210; Christina Schwenkel, "Rethinking Asian Mobilities: Socialist Migration and Post-Socialist Repatriation of Vietnamese Contract Workers in East Germany," *Critical Asian Studies* 46, no. 2 (2014): 235–58; Karin Weiss and Mike Dennis, eds., *Erfolg in der Nische?: die Vietnamesen in der DDR und in Ostdeutschland* (Münster: Lit, 2005).

5. Nora M. Alter, "Excessive Pre/Requisites: Vietnam Through the East German Lens," *Cultural Critique*, no. 35 (Winter 1996–97): 39–79; Charles K. Armstrong, "'Fraternal Socialism': The International Reconstruction of North Korea, 1953-62," *Cold War History* 5, no. 2 (2005): 161–87; Jan C. Behrends, Thomas Lindenberger, and Patrice G. Poutrus, eds., *Fremde und Fremd-Sein in der DDR: zu historischen Ursachen der Fremdenfeindlichkeit in Ostdeutschland* (Berlin: Metropol, 2003); Frank Hirschinger, *Der Spionage Verdachtig: Asylanten und ausländische Studenten in Sachsen-Anhalt 1945-1970* (Göttingen: V&R unipress, 2009); Young-Sun Hong, "'The Benefits of Health Must Spread Among All': International Solidarity, Health and Race in the East German Encounter with the Third World," in *Socialist Modern: East German Everyday Culture and Politics*, ed. Katherine Pence and Paul Betts (Ann Arbor: University of Michigan Press, 2008); Jennifer Ruth Hosek, *Sun, Sex and Socialism: Cuba in the German Imaginary* (Toronto: University of Toronto Press, 2011), chap. 2; Damian Mac Con Uladh, "Guests of the Socialist Nation? Foreign Students and Workers in the GDR, 1949-1990" (Ph.D. diss., University College London, 2005); Katherine Pence, "Showcasing Cold War Germany in Cairo: 1954 and 1957 Industrial Exhibitions and the Competition for Arab Partners," *Journal of Contemporary History* 47, no. 1 (2011): 69–95; Patrice G. Poutrus, "'Teure Genossen'. Die 'politischen Emigranten' als 'Fremde' im Alltag der DDR-Gesellschaft," in *Ankunft, Alltag, Ausreise: Migration und interkulturelle Begegnung in der DDR-Gesellschaft*, ed. Christian Th Müller and Patrice G. Poutrus (Cologne: Böhlau, 2003); Patrice G. Poutrus, "An den Grenzen des proletarischen Internationalismus: Algerische Flüchtlinge in der DDR," *Zeitschrift für Geschichtswissenschaft* 55, no. 2 (2007): 162–78; Christina Schwenkel, "Post/Socialist Affect: Ruination and Reconstruction of the Nation in Urban Vietnam," *Cultural Anthropology* 28, no. 2 (2013): 252–77; Qinna Shen, "A Question of Ideology and Realpolitik: DEFA's Cold War Documentaries on China," in *Beyond Alterity: German Encounters with Modern East Asia*, ed. Qinna Shen and Martin Rosenstock (New York: Berghahn Books, 2014); Quinn Slobodian, "Bandung in Divided Germany: Managing Non-Aligned Politics in East and West, 1955–63," *The Journal of Imperial and Commonwealth History* 41, no. 4 (2013): 644–62; Quinn Slobodian, "Citizenship-Shifting: Race and Xing-Hu Kuo's Claim on East German Memory," in *Imagining Germany Imagining Asia: Essays in Asian-German Studies*, ed. Veronika Fuechtner and Mary Rhiel (Rochester, NY: Camden House, 2013); David Tompkins, "The East is Red? Images of China in East Germany and Poland through the Sino-Soviet Split," *Zeitschrift für Ostmitteleuropa-Forschung* 62, no. 3 (2013): 393–424; Denise Wesenberg, "X. Weltfestspiele der Jugend und Studenten 1973 in Ost-Berlin. Kosten und Nutzen eines 'antiimperialistischen' Jugendfestivals," *Deutschland Archiv* 36, no. 4 (2003): 651–59.

6. Celia Donert, "Whose Utopia? Gender, Ideology and Human Rights at the 1975 World Congress of Women in East Berlin," in *The Breakthrough: Human Rights*

*in the 1970s,* ed. Jan Eckel and Samuel Moyn (Philadelphia: University of Pennsylvania Press, 2014); Katrina Hagen, "Internationalism in Cold War Germany" (Ph.D. diss., University of Washington, 2008); Sophie Lorenz, "'Heldin des anderen Amerikas'. Die DDR-Solidaritätsbewegung für Angela Davis, 1970–1973," *Zeithistorische Forschungen/Studies in Contemporary History, Online-Ausgabe* 10, no. 1 (2013); Nicholas Rutter, "Look Left, Drive Right: Internationalisms at the 1968 World Youth Festival," in *The Socialist Sixties: Crossing Borders in the Second World,* ed. Anne E. Gorsuch and Diane Koenker (Bloomington: Indiana University Press, 2013).

7. A recent monograph on the frontiers of the GDR does not include a single line on foreigners crossing those borders, nor does another overview spare a sentence for internationalism. See Patrick Major, *Behind the Berlin Wall: East Germany and the Frontiers of Power* (New York: Oxford University Press, 2010); Corey Ross, *The East German Dictatorship: Problems and Perspectives in the Interpretation of the GDR* (London: Arnold, 2002).

8. Hans-Georg Schleicher and Ilona Schleicher, *Special Flights: The GDR and Liberation Movements in Southern Africa* (Harare: SAPES Books, 1998); Ulrich van der Heyden and Franziska Benger, eds., *Kalter Krieg in Ostafrika: die Beziehungen der DDR zu Sansibar und Tansania* (Berlin: Lit, 2009); Matthias Voss, ed., *Wir haben Spuren hinterlassen!: die DDR in Mosambik* (Münster: Lit Verlag, 2005). Weis describes these monographs as part of a "historiographic 'proxy war'" over the image of the East German state in today's Germany." Toni Weis, "The Politics Machine: On the Concept of 'Solidarity' in East German Support for SWAPO," *Journal of Southern African Studies* 2 (June 2011): 355.

9. David Engerman, "The Second World's Third World," *Kritika* 12, no. 1 (Winter 2011). For recent work on the Soviet Union see Julie Hessler, "Death of an African Student in Moscow: Race, Politics, and the Cold War," *Cahiers du monde russe* 47, no. 1–2 (January–June 2006); Andreas Hilger, "Building a Socialist Elite?—Khrushchev's Soviet Union and Elite Formation in India," in *Elites and Decolonization in the Twentieth Century,* ed. Jost Dülffer and Marc Frey (New York: Palgrave Macmillan, 2011); Abigail Judge Kret, "'We Unite with Knowledge': The Peoples' Friendship University and Soviet Education for the Third World," *Comparative Studies of South Asia, Africa and the Middle East* 33, no. 2 (2013); Maxim Matusevich, "Probing the Limits of Internationalism: African Students Confront Soviet Ritual," *Anthropology of East Europe Review* 27, no. 2 (Fall 2009).

10. See, e.g., Alexander C. Cook, ed., *Mao's Little Red Book: A Global History* (New York: Cambridge University Press, 2014); Robeson Taj Frazier, *The East Is Black: Cold War China in the Black Radical Imagination* (Durham, NC: Duke University Press, 2015); Anne E. Gorsuch and Diane Koenker, eds. *The Socialist Sixties: Crossing Borders in the Second World* (Bloomington, IN: Indiana University Press, 2013); Young-Sun Hong, *Cold War Germany, the Third World, and the Global Humanitarian Regime* (New York: Cambridge University Press, 2015); Robert Gildea, James Mark, and Niek Pas, "European Radicals and the 'Third World': Imagined Solidarities and Radical Networks, 1958-1973," *Cultural and Social History* 8, no. 4 (2011): 449–72; Maxim Matusevich, ed. *Africa in Russia, Russia in Africa: Three Centuries of Encounters* (Trenton, NJ: Africa World Press, 2007).

11. On the intersection of the "color lines" of race and politics in the Cold War see Heonik Kwon, *The Other Cold War* (New York: Columbia University Press, 2010); Robert J. McMahon, "Introduction," in *The Cold War in the Third World*, ed. Robert J. McMahon (New York: Oxford University Press, 2013), 2–3.

12. See also "Asia, Germany and the Transnational Turn," *German History* 28, no. 4. (2010): 515-536.

13. For an exception see the excellent collection of essays in Thomas Vogel and Thomas Kunze, eds., *Ostalgie International: Erinnerungen an die DDR von Nicaragua bis Vietnam* (Berlin: Ch. Links Verlag, 2010); see also Tanja R. Müller, "'Memories of Paradise' - Legacies of Socialist Education in Mozambique," *African Affairs* 109, no. 436 (2010): 451–70.

14. Mark Philip Bradley, "Decolonization, the Global South, and the Cold War, 1919–1962," in *The Cambridge History of the Cold War*, ed. Melvyn P. Leffler and Odd Arne Westad (New York: Cambridge University Press, 2010), 465.

15. Matthew Connelly, "Taking Off the Cold War Lens: Visions of North-South Conflict during the Algerian War for Independence," *The American Historical Review* 105, no. 3 (2000): 753–55.

16. Cynthia A. Young, *Soul Power: Culture, Radicalism, and the Making of a U.S. Third World Left* (Durham, NC: Duke University Press, 2006); see also John Munro, "The Anticolonial Front: Cold War Imperialism and the Struggle Against Global White Supremacy, 1945-1960" (University of California, Santa Barbara, 2009); Peniel E. Joseph, *Waiting 'til the Midnight Hour: A Narrative History of Black Power in America* (New York: Henry Holt and Co., 2006); Nikhil Pal Singh, *Black is a Country: Race and the Unfinished Struggle for Democracy* (Cambridge: Harvard University Press, 2004).

17. See Ronald Philip Dore, *Stock Market Capitalism: Welfare Capitalism: Japan and Germany versus the Anglo-Saxons* (New York: Oxford University Press, 2000); Peter A. Hall and David W. Soskice, eds., *Varieties of Capitalism: The Institutional Foundations of Comparative Advantage* (New York: Oxford University Press, 2001).

18. Sergey Radchenko, *Two Suns in the Heavens: The Sino-Soviet Struggle for Supremacy, 1962-1967* (Washington, D.C.: Woodrow Wilson Center, 2009).

19. Jeffrey James Byrne, "Our Own Special Brand of Socialism: Algeria and the Contest of Modernities in the 1960s," *Diplomatic History* 33, no. 3 (2009): 427–47; Thomas Burgess, "Mao in Zanzibar: Nationalism, Discipline, and the (De)Construction of Afro-Asian Solidarities," in *Making a World after Empire: The Bandung Moment and Its Political Afterlives*, ed. Christopher J. Lee (Athens: Ohio University Press, 2010), 196–234; Chen Jian, "China, The Third World and the Cold War," in *The Cold War in the Third World*, ed. Robert J. McMahon (New York: Oxford University Press, 2013); Cook, ed. *Mao's Little Red Book*; Jeremy Friedman, "Soviet Policy in the Developing World and the Chinese Challenge in the 1960s," *Cold War History* 10, no. 2 (May 2010): 247–72; Jamie Monson, "Working Ahead of Time: Labor and Modernization during the Construction of the TAZARA Railway, 1968-86," in *Making a World after Empire: The Bandung Moment and Its Political Afterlives*, ed. Christopher J. Lee (Athens: Ohio University Press, 2010).

20. See Heinz Schütte, *Zwischen den Fronten: Deutsche und österreichische Überläufer zum Viet Minh* (Berlin: Logos, 2006).

21. Jiayun Zhuang, "Factory 798: The Site of Nostalgia and Its Incontinent Dweller," *Extensions,* no. 5 (2009): 15; Jennifer Currier, "Selling Place through Art: The Creation and Establishment of Beijing's 798 Arts District," in *New Economic Spaces in Asian Cities,* ed. Peter W. Daniels, KC Ho, and Thomas A. Hutton (Hoboken: Taylor and Francis, 2012), 187.

22. Michael Keane, "The Capital Complex: Beijing's New Creative Clusters," in *Creative Economies, Creative Cities: Asian-European Perspectives,* ed. L. Kong and J. O'Connor (New York: Springer, 2009), 89.

23. The irony of this model in China is that the factories-come-museums of the West, e.g., the Tate Museum in London and the Ruhr-Museum in Bochum, are commonly understood as having been themselves "emptied out, machines packed up and shipped off to China." Hito Steyerl, *The Wretched of the Screen* (Berlin: Sternberg, 2012), 61. Arts District 798 shows the internationalization of so-called "post-Fordist" modes of cultural consumption even to regions where industrial production remains robust.

24. Oltn. Gerischer. Rapport 164/89. 10 July 1989. Die Behörde für die Unterlagen des Staatssicherheitsdienstes der ehemaligen Deutschen Demokratischen Republik (hereafter BStU) Archive, MfS, HA II, 26979.

25. Belinda Davis, "Review Essay: What's Left? Popular Political Participation in Postwar Europe," *American Historical Review* 113, no. 2 (April 2008): 371; Bernd Schaefer, "Die DDR und die 'chinesische Lösung': Gewalt in der Volksrepublik China im Sommer 1989," in *1989 und die Rolle der Gewalt,* ed. Martin Sabrow (Göttingen: Wallstein, 2012), 156.

26. Oltn. Gerischer. Rapport 157/89. 01 July 1989. BStU Archive, MfS, HA II, 26979.

27. Strobel. HA II. Abt. M. Zusammengefasster Bericht über Reaktionen der Bevölkerung zu den aktuellen Ereignissen in der Volksrepublik China. 9 Jun 1989. BStU Archive, MfS, HA II, 26.

28. Recorded talk screened at Transmediale Conference, Haus der Kulturen der Welt, Berlin, 31 January 2014.

# Bibliography

Alter, Nora M. "Excessive Pre/Requisites: Vietnam Through the East German Lens." *Cultural Critique,* no. 35 (Winter 1996–97): 39–79.

Armstrong, Charles K. "'Fraternal Socialism': The International Reconstruction of North Korea, 1953-62." *Cold War History* 5, no. 2 (2005): 161–87.

"Asia, Germany and the Transnational Turn." *German History* 28, no. 4 (2010): 515–36.

Barnett, Thomas PM. *Romanian and East German Policies in the Third World: Comparing the Strategies of Ceaucescu and Honecker.* Westport: Praeger, 1992.

Behrends, Jan C., Thomas Lindenberger, and Patrice G. Poutrus, eds. *Fremde und Fremd-Sein in der DDR: zu historischen Ursachen der Fremdenfeindlichkeit in Ostdeutschland.* Berlin: Metropol, 2003.

Bradley, Mark Philip. "Decolonization, the Global South, and the Cold War, 1919–1962." In *The Cambridge History of the Cold War,* ed. Melvyn P. Leffler and Odd Arne Westad, 464–85. New York: Cambridge University Press, 2010.

Bröskamp, Bernd, ed. *Schwarz-weisse Zeiten: AusländerInnen in Ostdeutschland vor und nach der Wende: Erfahrungen der Vertragsarbeiter aus Mosambik.* Bremen: IZA, 1993.

Burgess, Thomas. "Mao in Zanzibar: Nationalism, Discipline, and the (De)Construction of Afro-Asian Solidarities." In *Making a World after Empire: The Bandung Moment and Its Political Afterlives,* ed. Christopher J. Lee, 196–234. Athens: Ohio University Press, 2010.

Byrne, Jeffrey James. "Our Own Special Brand of Socialism: Algeria and the Contest of Modernities in the 1960s." *Diplomatic History* 33, no. 3 (2009): 427–47.

Connelly, Matthew. "Taking Off the Cold War Lens: Visions of North-South Conflict during the Algerian War for Independence." *The American Historical Review* 105, no. 3 (2000): 739–69.

Cook, Alexander C., ed. *Mao's Little Red Book: A Global History.* New York: Cambridge University Press, 2014.

Currier, Jennifer. "Selling Place through Art: The Creation and Establishment of Beijing's 798 Arts District." In *New Economic Spaces in Asian Cities,* ed. Peter W. Daniels, KC Ho, and Thomas A. Hutton, 184–201. Hoboken: Taylor and Francis, 2012.

Davis, Belinda. "Review Essay: What's Left? Popular Political Participation in Postwar Europe." *American Historical Review* 113, no. 2 (April 2008): 363–90.

Dennis, Mike, and Norman LaPorte. *State and Minorities in Communist East Germany.* New York: Berghahn Books, 2011.

Donert, Celia. "Whose Utopia? Gender, Ideology and Human Rights at the 1975 World Congress of Women in East Berlin." In *The Breakthrough: Human Rights in the 1970s,* ed. Jan Eckel and Samuel Moyn, 68–87. Philadelphia: University of Pennsylvania Press, 2014.

Dore, Ronald Philip. *Stock Market Capitalism: Welfare Capitalism: Japan and Germany versus the Anglo-Saxons.* New York: Oxford University Press, 2000.

Engerman, David. "The Second World's Third World." *Kritika* 12, no. 1 (Winter 2011): 183–211.

Frazier, Robeson Taj. *The East Is Black: Cold War China in the Black Radical Imagination* Durham: Duke University Press, 2015.

Friedman, Jeremy. "Soviet Policy in the Developing World and the Chinese Challenge in the 1960s." *Cold War History* 10, no. 2 (May 2010): 247–72.

Gonçalves, João Felipe. "Sputnik Premiers in Havana: A Historical Ethnography of the 1960 Soviet Exposition." In *The Socialist Sixties: Crossing Borders in the Second World,* ed. Anne E. Gorsuch and Diane Koenker, 84–120. Bloomington: Indiana University Press, 2013.

Gray, William Glenn. *Germany's Cold War: The Global Campaign to Isolate East Germany, 1949-1969.* Chapel Hill: University of North Carolina Press, 2003.

Hagen, Katrina. "Internationalism in Cold War Germany." Ph.D. diss., University of Washington, 2008.

Hall, Peter A., and David W. Soskice, eds. *Varieties of Capitalism: The Institutional Foundations of Comparative Advantage.* New York: Oxford University Press, 2001.

Hessler, Julie. "Death of an African Student in Moscow: Race, Politics, and the Cold War." *Cahiers du monde russe* 47, no. 1–2 (January–June 2006): 33–63.

Hilger, Andreas. "Building a Socialist Elite?—Khrushchev's Soviet Union and Elite Formation in India." In *Elites and Decolonization in the Twentieth Century,* ed. Jost Dülffer and Marc Frey, 262–86. New York: Palgrave Macmillan, 2011.

Hirschinger, Frank. *Der Spionage Verdachtig: Asylanten und ausländische Studenten in Sachsen-Anhalt 1945-1970.* Göttingen: V&R unipress, 2009.

Hong, Young-Sun. "'The Benefits of Health Must Spread Among All': International Solidarity, Health and Race in the East German Encounter with the Third World." In *Socialist Modern: East German Everyday Culture and Politics,* ed. Katherine Pence and Paul Betts, 183–210. Ann Arbor: University of Michigan Press, 2008.

Hosek, Jennifer Ruth. *Sun, Sex and Socialism: Cuba in the German Imaginary.* Toronto: University of Toronto Press, 2011.

Jian, Chen. "China, The Third World and the Cold War." In *The Cold War in the Third World,* ed. Robert J. McMahon, 85–100. New York: Oxford University Press, 2013.

Joseph, Peniel E. *Waiting 'til the Midnight Hour: A Narrative History of Black Power in America.* New York: Henry Holt and Co., 2006.

Keane, Michael. "The Capital Complex: Beijing's New Creative Clusters." In *Creative Economies, Creative Cities: Asian-European Perspectives,* ed. L. Kong and J. O'Connor, 77–95. New York: Springer, 2009.

Killian, Werner. *Die Hallstein-Doktrin: der diplomatische Krieg zwischen der BRD und der DDR 1955-1973.* Berlin: Duncker und Humblot, 2001.

Kret, Abigail Judge. "'We Unite with Knowledge': The Peoples' Friendship University and Soviet Education for the Third World." *Comparative Studies of South Asia, Africa and the Middle East* 33, no. 2 (2013): 239–56.

Kuck, Dennis. "'Für den sozialistischen Aufbau ihrer Heimat'? Ausländische Vertragsarbeitskräfte in der DDR." In *Fremde und Fremd-Sein in der DDR: zu historischen Ursachen der Fremdenfeindlichkeit in Ostdeutschland,* ed. Jan C. Behrends, Thomas Lindenberger, and Patrice G. Poutrus. Berlin: Metropol, 2003.

Kwon, Heonik. *The Other Cold War.* New York: Columbia University Press, 2010.

Lorenz, Sophie. "'Heldin des anderen Amerikas'. Die DDR-Solidaritätsbewegung für Angela Davis, 1970–1973." *Zeithistorische Forschungen/Studies in Contemporary History, Online-Ausgabe* 10, no. 1 (2013).

Mac Con Uladh, Damian. "Guests of the Socialist Nation? Foreign Students and Workers in the GDR, 1949-1990." Ph.D. diss., University College London, 2005.

Major, Patrick. *Behind the Berlin Wall: East Germany and the Frontiers of Power.* New York: Oxford University Press, 2010.

Matusevich, Maxim. "Probing the Limits of Internationalism: African Students Confront Soviet Ritual." *Anthropology of East Europe Review* 27, no. 2 (Fall 2009): 19–39.

McMahon, Robert J. "Introduction." In *The Cold War in the Third World,* ed. Robert J. McMahon, 1–10. New York: Oxford University Press, 2013.

Monson, Jamie. "Working Ahead of Time: Labor and Modernization during the Construction of the TAZARA Railway, 1968-86." In *Making a World after Empire: The Bandung Moment and its Political Afterlives,* ed. Christopher J. Lee. Athens: Ohio University Press, 2010.

Müller, Tanja R. "'Memories of Paradise' - Legacies of Socialist Education in Mozambique." *African Affairs* 109, no. 436 (2010): 451–70.

Munro, John. "The Anticolonial Front: Cold War Imperialism and the Struggle Against Global White Supremacy, 1945-1960." Ph.D. diss., University of California, Santa Barbara, 2009.

Muth, Ingrid. *Die DDR-Aussenpolitik 1949-1972: Inhalte, Strukturen, Mechanismen.* Berlin: Christopher Links, 2000.

Pence, Katherine. "Showcasing Cold War Germany in Cairo: 1954 and 1957 Industrial Exhibitions and the Competition for Arab Partners." *Journal of Contemporary History* 47, no. 1 (2011): 69–95.

Pence, Katherine, and Andrew Zimmerman. "Transnationalism." *German Studies Review* 35, no. 3 (2012): 495–500.

Poutrus, Patrice G. "An den Grenzen des proletarischen Internationalismus: Algerische Flüchtlinge in der DDR." *Zeitschrift für Geschichtswissenschaft* 55, no. 2 (2007): 162–78.

———. "'Teure Genossen'. Die 'politischen Emigranten' als 'Fremde' im Alltag der DDR-Gesellschaft." In *Ankunft, Alltag, Ausreise: Migration und interkulturelle Begegnung in der DDR-Gesellschaft,* ed. Christian Th Müller and Patrice G. Poutrus, 221–66. Cologne: Böhlau, 2003.

Radchenko, Sergey. *Two Suns in the Heavens: The Sino-Soviet Struggle for Supremacy, 1962-1967.* Washington, D.C.: Woodrow Wilson Center, 2009.

Ross, Corey. *The East German Dictatorship: Problems and Perspectives in the Interpretation of the GDR.* London: Arnold, 2002.

Rutter, Nicholas. "Look Left, Drive Right: Internationalisms at the 1968 World Youth Festival." In *The Socialist Sixties: Crossing Borders in the Second World,* ed. Anne E. Gorsuch and Diane Koenker, 193–212. Bloomington: Indiana University Press, 2013.

Schaefer, Bernd. "Die DDR und die 'chinesische Lösung': Gewalt in der Volksrepublik China im Sommer 1989." In *1989 und die Rolle der Gewalt,* ed. Martin Sabrow, 153–72. Göttingen: Wallstein, 2012.

Schleicher, Hans-Georg, and Ilona Schleicher. *Special Flights: The GDR and Liberation Movements in Southern Africa.* Harare: SAPES Books, 1998.

Scholtyseck, Joachim. *Die Aussenpolitik der DDR.* Munich: R. Oldenbourg, 2003.

Schüle, Annegret. "'Proletarischer Internationalismus' oder 'ökonomischer Vorteil für die DDR'?" *Archiv für Sozialgeschichte* no. 42 (2002): 191–210.

Schulz, Brigitte. *Development Policy in the Cold War Era: The Two Germanies and Sub-Saharan Africa, 1960-1985.* Münster: Lit, 1995.

Schütte, Heinz. *Zwischen den Fronten: Deutsche und österreichische Überläufer zum Viet Minh.* Berlin: Logos, 2006.

Schwenkel, Christina. "Post/Socialist Affect: Ruination and Reconstruction of the Nation in Urban Vietnam." *Cultural Anthropology* 28, no. 2 (2013): 252–77.

———. "Rethinking Asian Mobilities: Socialist Migration and Post-Socialist Repatriation of Vietnamese Contract Workers in East Germany." *Critical Asian Studies* 46, no. 2 (2014): 235–58.

Shen, Qinna. "A Question of Ideology and Realpolitik: DEFA's Cold War Documentaries on China." In *Beyond Alterity: German Encounters with Modern East Asia,* ed. Qinna Shen and Martin Rosenstock, 94–114. New York: Berghahn Books, 2014.

Singh, Nikhil Pal. *Black is a Country: Race and the Unfinished Struggle for Democracy.* Cambridge: Harvard University Press, 2004.

Slobodian, Quinn. "Bandung in Divided Germany: Managing Non-Aligned Politics in East and West, 1955–63." *The Journal of Imperial and Commonwealth History* 41, no. 4 (2013): 644–62.

———. "Citizenship-Shifting: Race and Xing-Hu Kuo's Claim on East German Memory." In *Imagining Germany Imagining Asia: Essays in Asian-German Studies,* ed. Veronika Fuechtner and Mary Rhiel, 34–49. Rochester: Camden House, 2013.

Spanger, Hans-Joachim, and Lothar Brock. *Die beiden deutschen Staaten in der Dritten Welt.* Opladen: Westdeutscher Verlag, 1987.

Steyerl, Hito. *The Wretched of the Screen.* Berlin: Sternberg, 2012.

Storkmann, Klaus. *Geheime Solidarität: Militärbeziehungen und Militärhilfen der DDR in die "Dritte Welt."* Berlin: Christoph Links, 2012.

Tompkins, David. "'The East is Red? Images of China in East Germany and Poland through the Sino-Soviet Split." *Zeitschrift für Ostmitteleuropa-Forschung* 62, no. 3 (2013): 393–424.

Van der Heyden, Ulrich, Ilona Schleicher, and Hans-Georg Schleicher, eds. *Die DDR und Afrika.* 2 vols. Münster: Lit, 1993.

Van der Heyden, Ulrich, and Franziska Benger, eds. *Kalter Krieg in Ostafrika: die Beziehungen der DDR zu Sansibar und Tansania.* Berlin: Lit, 2009.

Vogel, Thomas, and Thomas Kunze, eds. *Ostalgie International: Erinnerungen an die DDR von Nicaragua bis Vietnam.* Berlin: Ch. Links Verlag, 2010.

Voss, Matthias, ed. *Wir haben Spuren hinterlassen!: die DDR in Mosambik.* Münster: Lit Verlag, 2005.

Weis, Toni. "The Politics Machine: On the Concept of 'Solidarity' in East German Support for SWAPO." *Journal of Southern African Studies* 2 (June 2011): 351–67.

Weiss, Karin, and Mike Dennis, eds. *Erfolg in der Nische?: die Vietnamesen in der DDR und in Ostdeutschland.* Münster: Lit, 2005.

Wesenberg, Denise. "X. Weltfestspiele der Jugend und Studenten 1973 in Ost-Berlin. Kosten und Nutzen eines 'antiimperialistischen' Jugendfestivals." *Deutschland Archiv* 36, no. 4 (2003): 651–59.

Winrow, Gareth M. *The Foreign Policy of the GDR in Africa.* New York: Cambridge University Press, 1990.

Young, Cynthia A. *Soul Power: Culture, Radicalism, and the Making of a U.S. Third World Left.* Durham: Duke University Press, 2006.

Zhuang, Jiayun. "Factory 798: The Site of Nostalgia and Its Incontinent Dweller." *Extensions*, no. 5 (2009).

# PART I

## Race Without Racism?

# Chapter 1

# Socialist Chromatism

## Race, Racism, and the Racial Rainbow in East Germany

*Quinn Slobodian*

In August 1951, one and a half million people, including over twenty thousand foreigners, gathered in East Berlin for the third communist-organized World Festival of Youth and Students.[1] The logo of the festival was everywhere. It appeared on tickets, handbills, commemorative pins, coins, and decals, and was mounted on the side of the House of the Youth in the center of the city at Alexanderplatz. The logo depicted three young people with hands linked in a closed loop. An Asian woman in cheongsam stood in the background, smiling slightly, while a black man with a cocked head leaned away in an off-balance pose. The anchor of the composition was the white man in the foreground, standing in a spread-legged protective stance with a set facial expression, partly eclipsing the figures behind him (see figure 1.1).

The festival's second most reproduced emblem featured a ring of people linking arms around a globe crowned by Berlin's Brandenburg Gate (see figure 1.2). The smiling men and women wear traditional attire, including kimonos, fezes, berets, and thawbs. A flag in the background bore the insignia of the World Federation of Democratic Youth (WFDY), which depicted three men in profile. In the color version, the men's stylized faces are white, yellow, and black. A formally similar trio was featured on a postcard sent out as an invitation to the 1951 festival, reproduced on the cover of this volume. A publicity still from the Soviet film documentation, screened in East Germany, of the 1949 World Youth Festival in Budapest, it featured a black man and Asian woman ranged behind the foregrounded profile of a lantern-jawed blond man. As with the emblems of the festival and the WFDY, the white man was most proximate to the viewer, granting him a symbolic vanguard position that undercut the message of racial horizontality. Whether intentionally or not, the white man appeared as the first among equals.

**Figure 1.1.** Poster from 1951 World Festival of Youth and Students in East Berlin

The motifs suggest a mode of visual representation that could be called socialist chromatism. Within the larger idiom of socialist realism, socialist chromatism relied on skin color and other markers of phenotypic difference to create (overly) neat divisions between social groups within a technically nonhierarchical logic of race. Versions of the "racial rainbow" relied on conventions of numismatic portraiture and ethnography to express an earth-spanning vision of politically unified humanity through figural arche-

**Figure 1.2.** Postcard advertising 1951 World Festival of Youth and Students in East Berlin

types. These socialist chromatist images capture the paradoxical nature of race discourse in East Germany. On the one hand, East German authorities officially denounced "race thinking." On the other hand, they continued to rely on stereotypes of phenotypical and folkloric difference to illustrate themes of internationalist solidarity. At times, this mode threatened to re-instate the very dynamic of white superiority it sought to banish. Even in the officially anti-racist state, nineteenth-century racial typologies and ethnographic conventions underwrote repertoires of representing global diversity.

Historians have begun to trace the transformation of racial discourse in West Germany in the aftermath of the Third Reich's "racial state."[2] Yet communist East Germany has escaped similar scrutiny. This chapter offers a road map to changes in the categories of race and racism in East Germany as an aid to contextualizing the investigation into "comrades of color" in the chapters that follow. Moving from the reformulation of the idea of race after 1945 through the high point of the official use of the category of racism in the 1970s, it provides a brief outline of the conceptual and visual worlds of East German socialism.

# Redefining Race in East Germany after 1945

As in West Germany, reference to *Rasse* became officially taboo in East Germany after the National Socialist defeat. When a new version of the standard dictionary *Duden* appeared at the East German Leipzig Book Fair in 1947, the term *Rasse* referred only to breeds of dogs. The compound terms, "racial degeneration," "racial instinct," and "defense of the race" had all been removed, deleted abruptly from the realm of permissible discourse.[3] Race talk arose most often in efforts of debunking National Socialist ideology. The term "racism" (*Rassismus*) itself was rarely used, however. Although the term had entered English from German in the translated title of a book by sexologist and homosexual rights activist Magnus Hirschfeld published posthumously in 1938, the dominant terms in East Germany before the 1960s were "racial hatred" (*Rassenhaß*), "racial discrimination" (*Rassendiskriminierung*), and "race baiting" (*Rassenhetze*).[4] Nazi ideology was described as adhering to "racial lunacy" (*Rassenwahn*) and propagating the "racial lie" (*Rassenlüge*).

Two understandings of racism circulated in the East German discussions. The first was what would be called "scientific racism," identified most closely with Nazism, which mapped phenotypic difference onto a hierarchy of human traits of ability. The second is what would be called "cultural racism," an ideology by which certain civilizations claimed the right to rule over others. Though coded racially, cultural racism would not require a robust science of physiological difference. In 1948, East German historian Jürgen Kuczynski used the example of justifications for American expansionism based on the notion that "the Anglo-Saxon had an age-old superiority over all other peoples."[5] White supremacy, though often buttressed by scientific language, did not require it for its truth claims. This understanding of racism shared traits with the idea of "great power chauvinism" in Soviet socialist thought, which claimed that historically constituted domination of a particular nation, e.g., Russia, had to be compensated for through a conscious act of humility and the promotion of minority interests.[6]

The East German leadership felt that elites used racism in both its scientific and cultural forms as a means of misleading the majority. In 1947, Politburo Central Committee member Fred Oelssner called racial science the "ideology of tricksters and idiots," which found "psychologically fertile soil among the oppressed masses," as it transformed class resentments into the willingness for war.[7] With their vision of populations as malleable to influence from above, East German leaders saw racism as a powerful instrument of legitimation available to socialism's enemies but absent, by definition, within socialism itself.

Although heavily influenced by ideological currents from Moscow, East German discussions of race did not take place in communist isolation. Rather, they were part of an international conversation redefining the concepts of race and racism in the postwar decade. Critical reevaluations of biological concepts of race began in the 1930s as a response to fascist ideology and its expanding translation into policy. In an influential treatment from 1938, historian Jacques Barzun dismissed the idea of race as "modern superstition." The criticisms were ambivalent, however. Not all were as categorical as Barzun, even after 1945. Thinkers closer to the discipline of anthropology, in particular, including Julian Huxley and Ruth Benedict, sought to discredit racism even as they preserved the category of race as a valid way of describing inherited human traits.[8] The 1950 "Statement on Race" from UNESCO, an organization that the Soviet Union joined in 1952, reflected the postwar consensus by reaffirming the so-called three race model of mankind, providing the foundation for what one scholar calls an "egalitarian racialism," which abandoned the hierarchy of race without jettisoning the category of race wholesale.[9]

East German definitions of race were influenced by these discussions. In the postwar years, East German scholars followed the UNESCO statement in discarding racial hierarchy while preserving the kernel of hereditary racial difference. Some of the very anthropologists involved in the reconceptualization of race in the United States, including Franz Boas and his student Gene Weltfish, were cited approvingly in the East German press.[10] As an East German scientist wrote in the pages of the official newspaper, there were indeed "three great races," which he described as "white, yellow, black," or, more technically, "the equatorial or Negro-Austroloid race, the European-

Asian or Europoid race, and the Asian-American or Mongoloid race."[11] Yet these physiological differences were "historical phenomena," artifacts of human adaptation over millennia of migration that bore no relationship to modern life. Theorists of "unchanging" or "unequal" races, the author wrote, were performing acts of depoliticization. Racist thinkers sought to cloak the struggle of the "working class and the oppressed and exploited of the colonial countries against the ruling class of the imperialist states" as "natural" and borne out of permanent dynamics of race. The prescribed tactic for the East German thinker was to denounce the practice of racism even while preserving the utility of the category of race itself. On both sides of the Cold War border in the postwar years, the larger world remained divided into three primary phenotypic groups: white, black, and yellow.

## The Racial Rainbow

The racial triad of the "great races" formed the basis of the iconography of internationalism in East Germany and the broader communist bloc. As mentioned above, the logo of the World Federation of Democratic Youth, the organizer of the World Youth Festivals, used men of the "three great races" in overlapping profile from 1949 onward. The convention drew from several sources. Most proximately, the profiles reproduced the norms of numismatic portraiture as in the famous motifs of the Communist Party's founding fathers, Marx and Engels.[12] The "three races" also echoed anthropomorphic depictions of the "three continents" from earlier advertising and print culture, which itself recalled the biblical motifs of the "three wise men."[13] The racialized profiles resonated with conventions of ethnographic photography and display as well. Nineteenth century anthropology proposed the brow, nose and chin—and the "degree of prognothy," or the extent to which the lower jaw jutted forward—as a central index of racial membership.[14] Reframed in a symbolic framework of horizontal, international solidarity, the potentially negative associations of these earlier precedents seemed to have been lost on socialist designers.

The profiles of nonwhite objects of solidarity were used frequently in visual ephemera of East German internationalism, as in a solidarity stamp from the 1960s (see figure 1.3). In the late 1970s, a similar profile was used again, this time set behind bars, as part of a statement of opposition to South African apartheid (see figure 1.4).

The egalitarian racialist motif, which could be called the racial rainbow, proliferated across East German media in photographs, caricatures, and official imagery, including in solidarity stamps and photomontages (see figure 1.5).

**Figure 1.3.** Solidarity Stamp from East German trade union, Courtesy Wende Museum of the Cold War.

**Figure 1.4.** Commemorative Stamp from International Anti-Apartheid Year, 1978. Courtesy Wende Museum of the Cold War.

Other examples from visual culture included the first East German science fiction film, *Der Schweigende Stern* (The Silent Star) (1960). Led by a Soviet commander, the spaceship's crew in the film included, in addition to a Pole, an East German, and an American, a Japanese doctor, an African TV technician, an Indian mathematician, and two Chinese linguists, often composed in medium shots with one face next to the other.[15] An animated film released one year earlier featured a trio of multiracial astronauts, captured in iconic profile as they gazed through the porthole of the spaceship.[16]

The polychromatic spectrum or loop of linked hands suggested a serial equivalence of racialized national cultures. In fact, socialist chromatism propagated an image of a colored

**Figure 1.5.** Solidarity Stamp using "racial rainbow" motif. Courtesy Wende Museum of the Cold War.

world strikingly similar to the cultural pluralism being promoted by liberals in the postwar United States.[17] Despite culturally pervasive and even institutionalized racism in the United States, the two blocs in the early years of the Cold War could be said to share a formal consensus on questions of race. As with the enormously popular "Family of Man" photography exhibition at the Museum of Modern Art in 1955, the socialist world was visualized as a horizontal pluralistic community linked through metaphoric kinship of shared ideals.[18] In purely formal terms, the differences were negligible between the imagery of the 1951 World Youth Festival and Disney's "It's a Small World" amusement park ride created for UNICEF in 1964.

Socialist chromatism in East Germany was an outward extrapolation of a model that was originally an imperial, and later Soviet, mode of representing a multiethnic territory under a single administration. Consistent with nineteenth-century techniques of ethnic exhibition, Soviet pageantry relied heavily on the visual vocabulary of clothing, dance, and architecture to represent its own internal multiplicity of nations.[19] It is notable that, in the world-ethnographic model of the racial rainbow, white was a color too. Indeed, at the very time of the World Youth Festival in 1951, East German scholars were rehabilitating the respectability of German folk art (*Volkskunst*) and traditional dance within the socialist world view.[20] Folk practices became a central means of representing global unity in diversity. Lightly stylized facial features, skin color, and traditional costume became the visual repertoire of socialist internationalism. Socialist chromatism meant that markers of race were ever present even as the meaningfulness of race in establishing hierarchies of human ability was disavowed.

Soon after the establishment of the GDR in 1949, racial discrimination and prejudice were decreed as distant, either historically, in the fascist and imperial German past now identified with the Federal Republic, or geographically, in the countries of the Western bloc. While the probing examinations of German colonial history undertaken in the GDR were impressive, the inconsistency of their dichotomous position on racism was apparent early.[21] One of the Politburo members who used the work of American anthropologist Boas to denounce scientific racism publicly was Paul Merker, who wrote in 1947 that "there is neither an Aryan nor a Germanic race biologically speaking" and that "the separation of people into Aryans and non-Aryans was nothing more than dupery."[22] Merker himself provides a case study in the gap between rhetoric and reality, as his advocacy for restitution to Jewish victims of the Holocaust made him an object of suspicion in the Stalinist purges at the end of the 1940s.[23] Though not Jewish himself, he was purged along with other German Jews whose "racial" identity—and, thus, ostensible disloyalty to the "national" cause of socialism—was precisely what made them seen as potential traitors.[24] Political caricatures such as one of West Berlin mayor Ernst Reuter by Irish émigré cartoonist Elizabeth Shaw made use of long-standing anti-Semitic conventions in lampooning their subjects as sexually ambiguous and eroticized by features of hooded eyes, corpulent bodies, and full lips.[25]

## Icons and Individuals

Even as strains of cultural anti-Semitism continued to inform political culture, East German leader Walter Ulbricht declared definitively in 1950 that "there is no longer any racial hatred in the German Democratic Republic."[26] From that point on, racism was officially elsewhere. Yet even if the U.S. bloc was frequently accused of racism, it was the language of "imperialism" that was the rhetorical bludgeon of choice to attack the policies of the West Germany, France, South Africa, and the United States. The term "racism" began to surface regularly only in the 1960s, when the United Nations began to pass resolutions opposing racial discrimination to which the East German state responded with resolutions of its own.[27]

It was around this time that people of color began to speak on their own behalf in the East German public sphere. African-American singer Paul Robeson made his first appearance in East Germany in 1960, reminding the audience that there were "two Americas" and decrying injustice in the so-called Free West. In the same year, a photograph of African-American singer and émigré to the GDR, Aubrey Pankey, appeared in Neues Deutschland with the headline "I know racial hatred!" Pankey wrote that, "as an artist who had traveled through many countries in the world, I have seen and experienced fascism, anti-Semitism and racism first hand."[28] The year 1960 also saw the Sharpeville Massacre of unarmed black protesters in South Africa, a catalyzing event in East German awareness of racialized oppression overseas that helped launch fund-raising solidarity efforts.[29]

It was symptomatic of the frictions of solidarity that Pankey complained about the racial tokenism prevalent in the GDR even as he became a celebrated eyewitness to racism.[30] Even as the socialist bloc adopted the language of racism and anti-racism formally, between 400 and 500 African students a year left Soviet and Eastern European universities for West Germany in 1963 and 1964, many with the complaint that they were not permitted to organize into independent, pan-African student unions.[31] East German authorities supervised national associations for African students tightly, and placed clear constraints on free political expression.[32]

On vanishingly rare occasions, East German officials would acknowledge potential pitfalls in their strategy of anti-racist solidarity. In 1959, a member of the SED central committee commiserated with Pankey about "the pseudo-sympathetic voices for negroes, behind which in reality racist attitudes are concealed," and criticized the "uncritical cult" around certain individuals.[33] In general, however, producing uncritical cults was precisely the tactic chosen to inoculate the population against what was often called the racist "poison." Toni Weis locates a contradiction at the core of the state-socialist concept of solidarity, which perceived foreigners as "moral constructs" rather than individuals, turning people of color into heroes even as it regulated and restricted contact between East Germans and foreigners in everyday life.[34] After a period of relatively frequent contact with ordinary East Germans, for example, Vietnamese students in the late 1960s were forbidden contact with Germans by their own government, even as they were paraded on stage at solidarity demonstrations.[35]

The Vietnamese were an extreme case, and many other foreigners had more common everyday interactions, and even friendships, with East Germans. Yet the number of foreigners in the GDR remained very small. For many East Germans, it was difficult to see foreigners and people of color beyond their status as two-dimensional icons of the dominant state ideology. In many cases, they became lightning rods for resentment against the regime itself.[36] Andrew Port describes the disgruntlement of ordinary workers at making contributions to Solidarity Funds for Vietnam in the 1960s, believing that the funds would only prolong the war and detracted from more pressing domestic concerns.[37] As Weis argues, moral and professional pressure often made such donations effectively obligatory even if they were technically voluntary.[38]

While these arguments have validity, several of the chapters in this volume show that they cannot be taken to exhaust the experience of solidarity in the GDR. The authors in this collection give evidence of the depth of empathy felt by East German citizens for those struggling against invasion, occupation, and racialized oppression, and the salience of a moralized sense of differentiation from the U.S.-led bloc.[39] Additionally, not all contact was mediated through two-dimensional symbols. Young-Sun Hong and Christina Schwenkel show how solidarity and aid campaigns created situations that allowed for genuine interaction and often created abiding transnational bonds. Personal connections created both with, and in spite of, state efforts constituted important vectors of exchange.

Yet for the great majority of the East German population, icons, and contributions rather than personal experience remained the means of engaging with the global South and activists of color. Next to imprisoned South African revolutionary Nelson Mandela, the most visible icon of anti-racism in East German history was the African-American philosopher and activist

Angela Davis, discussed by Katrina Hagen below. Davis's visits to East Germany in the early 1970s coincided with an enormous increase in the use of the term "racism" as it moved to the center of SED rhetoric. Key turning points were the UN declaration of a Decade to Combat Racism in 1973, and the increased focus on solidarity with opponents of apartheid regimes in Southern Africa, including the meeting of the UN Special Committee Against Apartheid in East Berlin in 1974, a committee to which the GDR was elected a member in 1975.[40] Discussions of racism in the East German public sphere peaked in the International Anti-Apartheid Year in 1978 and the year after, when the GDR was most proactive as a "junior partner of the Soviet Union" in building connections to partners in Mozambique, Zimbabwe, and Namibia, a focus it moved away from in the 1980s because of economic constraints and a realignment on issues of international security and disarmament in Europe itself.[41] As Witkowski points out in his chapter, mentions of "solidarity" itself also peaked in this period, only to decline thereafter, suggesting that the particularity of the 1970s as a pivotal decade remains an understudied aspect of East German history.

Notwithstanding its brief peak in the late 1970s, racism became the most serious issue for the GDR after its official demise. The years of 1991 and 1992 saw thousands of right-wing-related attacks, including hundreds of arson attacks and dozens of deaths.[42] Racism could no longer be described as existing elsewhere. The attacks led to a rush of publications, motivated by a justifiably panicked search for the roots of the violence.[43] To some extent, recent publications, including this one, remain invested in the understanding of racism underlying these investigations, not in its scientific definition, but as a set of both conscious and unconscious preconceptions that link certain social, psychological, and behavioral qualities to phenotype. This book also uses an understanding of racialization as a social process and not a biological reality, usually but not always imposed by the majority group, by which "difference is registered and invested with heightened negative social meaning."[44]

Socialist chromatism in East Germany was an ambivalent mode of anti-racism. It broke definitively with the Third Reich's hierarchical associations between phenotype and ability. Yet the visual repertoire of race and racism in the GDR reproduced many of the exaggerated and even offensive stereotypical depictions of people of color. The right of representation also remained in the hands of white Germans, producing the effect, arguably subconsciously, of either the prioritizing of the white leadership role or the presentation of the nonwhite person as icon rather than individual.

In recent decades, people of color in Germany have seized the right of self-definition in a series of organizations and publications, creating new social formations and categories such as "Afro-German" and *"Asiatische Deutsche"* designed to confront and undermine dominant paradigms of understanding.[45] This process puts the power of definition back in the hands of people of color themselves after a long history of being ventriloquized in the German public sphere. In the category of "comrades of color," this book seeks to make its own small contribution to recovering experiences often considered unimportant to the white German storyline of post-1945 history as a way of illuminating ongoing difficulties, and potential rewards, of forging alliances across the socially constructed (but no less resilient) boundaries of nationality and race.

**Quinn Slobodian** is associate professor of history at Wellesley College and author of *Foreign Front: Third World Politics in Sixties West Germany* (Duke, 2012).

## Notes

1. For the number of attendees see Joël Kotek, "Youth Organizations as a Battlefield in the Cold War," in *The Cultural Cold War in Western Europe, 1945-1960,* ed. Giles Scott-Smith and Hans Krabbendam (Portland: F. Cass, 2003), 144.

2. Rita Chin and Heide Fehrenbach, "Introduction: What's Race Got to Do with It? Postwar German History in Context," in *After the Racial State: Difference and Democracy in Postfascist Germany,* ed. Rita Chin et al. (Ann Arbor: University of Michigan Press, 2009), 24; Bruce David Baum, *The Rise and Fall of the Caucasian Race: A Political History of Racial Identity* (New York: New York University Press, 2006), 176–91; Michelle Brattain, "Race, Racism, and Antiracism: UNESCO and the Politics of Presenting Science to the Postwar Public," *American Historical Review* 112, no. 5 (December 2007); Michael Burleigh and Wolfgang Wippermann, *The Racial State: Germany 1933-1945* (New York: Cambridge University Press, 1991). For one influential example see Heide Fehrenbach, *Race after Hitler: Black Occupation Children in Postwar Germany and America* (Princeton: Princeton University Press, 2005).

3. Hans Bauer, "Der entbräunte Duden," *Neues Deutschland,* 27 February 1948.

4. George M. Fredrickson, *Racism: A Short History* (Princeton: Princeton University Press, 2002), 162.

5. Jürgen Kuczynski, "Was verstehen wir unter Amerikanism," *Neues Deutschland,* 29 October 1948.

6. Yuri Slezkine, "The USSR as a Communal Apartment, or How a Socialist State Promoted Ethnic Particularism," *Slavic Review* 53, no. 2 (Summer 1994): 415–18.

7. Fred Oelssner, "Die Rassenlüge der Nazis," *Neues Deutschland,* 24 April 1947.

8. Robert Miles, "Racism as a Concept," in *Racism,* ed. Martin Bulmer and John Solomos (New York: Oxford University Press, 1999): 345–46.

9. Baum, *The Rise and Fall of the Caucasian Race,* 189; Glenda Sluga, *Internationalism in the Age of Nationalism* (Philadelphia: University of Pennsylvania Press, 2013), 112.

10. "Die Amerikanerin Gene Weltfish kämpft für Menschlichkeit und Frieden," *Neues Deutschland*, 25 January 1951. See Baum, *The Rise and Fall of the Caucasian Race*, 179.

11. Joachim Heidrich, "Wie die Menschenrassen entstanden sind," *Neues Deutschland*, 25 August 1956.

12. The use of "multiple aligned figures in profile" had origins in Renaissance conventions later revived by Louis XIV and Napoleon. Peter J. Schwartz, "The Ideological Antecedents of the First-Series Renminbi Worker-and-Peasant Banknote or What Mao Tse-tung May Have Owed to Dziga Vertov," *Transcultural Studies* 1 (2014): 52.

13. David Ciarlo, *Advertising Empire: Race and Visual Culture in Imperial Germany* (Cambridge: Harvard University Press, 2011), 65.

14. Allan Sekula, "The Body and the Archive," *October*, no. 39 (1986): 22–23; Andrew Zimmerman, *Anthropology and Antihumanism in Imperial Germany* (Chicago: University of Chicago Press, 2001), 89–90, 165.

15. On the film see Sebastian Heiduschke, *East German Cinema: DEFA and Film History* (New York: Palgrave Macmillan, 2013).

16. *Gleich Links hinterm Mond* (1959).

17. See Christopher Shannon, *A World Made Safe for Differences: Cold War Intellectuals and the Politics of Identity* (Lanham: Rowman & Littlefield Publishers, 2001); Fred Turner, *The Democratic Surround: Multimedia & American Liberalism from World War II to the Psychedelic Sixties* (Chicago: University of Chicago Press, 2014).

18. Eric J. Sandeen, *Picturing an Exhibition: The Family of Man and 1950s America* (Albuquerque: University of New Mexico Press, 1995).

19. See Greg Castillo, "Peoples at an Exhibition: Soviet Architecture and the National Question," in *Socialist Realism without Shores*, ed. Thomas Lahusen and EA Dobrenko (Durham: Duke University Press, 1997), 91–92; Francine Hirsch, *Empire of Nations: Ethnographic Knowledge and the Making of the Soviet Union* (Ithaca: Cornell University Press, 2005), chap. 5.

20. Teresa Brinkel and John Bendix, "Institutionalizing Volkskunde in Early East Germany," *Journal of Folklore Research* 46, no. 2 (2009); Jan Palmowski, *Inventing a Socialist Nation: Heimat and the Politics of Everyday Life in the GDR, 1945-1990* (New York: Cambridge University Press, 2009), 51.

21. Katrina Hagen, "Internationalism in Cold War Germany" (Ph.D. diss., University of Washington, 2008), 87–88, 103.

22. Paul Merker, "Der Arier-Schwindel," *Neues Deutschland*, 3 September 1947.

23. Jeffrey Herf, *Divided Memory: The Nazi Past in the Two Germanys* (Cambridge: Harvard University Press, 1997), 86.

24. Ibid., 114–22; Josie McLellan, *Antifascism and Memory in East Germany: Remembering the International Brigades, 1945-1989* (New York: Oxford University Press, 2004), 59.

25. Elizabeth Shaw, "You Can Call Me at Midnight Anytime," *Neues Deutschland*, 15 December 1951.

26. "Brüderlichkeit," *Neues Deutschland*, 15 März 1960.

27. See "DDR-Erklärung an die UNO. Für Beseitigung aller Rassendiskriminierungen," *Neues Deutschland*, 2 November 1963.

28. Aubrey Panke, "Ich kenne den Rassenhaß!," *Neues Deutschland*, 14 January 1960.

29. Hans-Georg Schleicher, "GDR Solidarity: The German Democratic Republic and the South African Liberation Struggle," in *The Road to Democracy in South Africa*, ed. South African Democracy Education Trust (Pretoria: Unisa Press, 2004), 1103.

30. Michael Rauhut, "The Voice of the Other America: African-American Music and Political Protest in the German Democratic Republic," in *Between the Avant-Garde and the Everyday: Subversive Politics in Europe from 1957 to the Present*, ed. Timothy Scott Brown and Lorena Anton (New York: Berghahn Books, 2011), 100.

31. Quinn Slobodian, "Bandung in Divided Germany: Managing Non-Aligned Politics in East and West, 1955–63," *The Journal of Imperial and Commonwealth History* 41, no. 4 (2013): 654.

32. Ibid., 653.

33. Quoted in Rauhut, "The Voice of the Other America: African-American Music and Political Protest in the German Democratic Republic," 100.

34. Toni Weis, "The Politics Machine: On the Concept of 'Solidarity' in East German Support for SWAPO," *Journal of Southern African Studies* 2 (June 2011): 366.

35. Anlage 4. Einschätzung der politisch-ideologischen Situation im Ausländerstudium. 25 September 1967. SAPMO, BArch, DY 30-1V A 2/9.04/466.

36. On this dynamic in the case of a single biography see Quinn Slobodian, "Citizenship-Shifting: Race and Xing-Hu Kuo's Claim on East German Memory," in *Imagining Germany Imagining Asia: Essays in Asian-German Studies*, ed. Veronika Fuechtner and Mary Rhiel (Rochester: Camden House, 2013).

37. Andrew Port, *Die rätselhafte Stabilität der DDR: Arbeit und Alltag im sozialistischen Deutschland* (Berlin: Christoph Links, 2007), 160.

38. Weis, "The Politics Machine," 360.

39. Gerd Horten, "Sailing in the Shadow of the Vietnam War: The GDR Government and the 'Vietnam Bonus' of the Early 1970s," *German Studies Review* 36, no. 3 (October 2013).

40. Schleicher, "GDR Solidarity," 1135.

41. Ibid., 1145; Gareth M. Winrow, *The Foreign Policy of the GDR in Africa* (New York: Cambridge University Press, 1990), 187–88.

42. Paul Hockenos, *Free to Hate: The Rise of the Right in Post-Communist Eastern Europe* (New York: Routledge, 1993), 28–29.

43. Eva-Maria Elsner and Lothar Elsner, *Ausländerpolitik und Ausländerfeindschaft in der DDR (1949-1990)* (Leipzig: Rosa-Luxemburg-Verein, 1994); Marianne Krüger-Potratz, Georg Hansen, and Dirk Jasper, *Anderssein gab es nicht: Ausländer und Minderheiten in der DDR* (New York: Waxmann, 1991); Andrzej Stach and Saleh Hussain, *Ausländer in der DDR: Ein Rückblick* (Berlin: Die Ausländerbeauftragte des Senats, 1993). On the debate see Rita Chin and Heide Fehrenbach, "German Democracy and the Question of Difference, 1945-1995," in *After the Racial State: Difference and Democracy in Postfascist Germany*, ed. Rita Chin, Heide Fehrenbach, Geoff Eley, and Atina Grossman (Ann Arbor: University of Michigan Press, 2009), 126–29.

44. The phrase is from Chin and Fehrenbach, "Introduction: What's Race Got to Do With It?," 4.

45. Fatima El-Tayeb, "Vorwort," in *Mythen, Masken und Subjekte: kritische Weissseinsforschung in Deutschland*, ed. Maureen Maisha Eggers et al. (Münster: Unrast, 2005),

7–9; Kien Nghi Ha, ed. *Asiatische Deutsche: Vietnamesische Diaspora and Beyond* (Berlin: Assoziation A, 2012); May Opitz, Katharina Oguntoye, and Dagmar Schultz, eds., *Showing Our Colors: Afro-German Women Speak Out* (Amherst: University of Massachusetts Press, 1992); Peggy Piesche, "Black and German? East German Adolescents Before 1989: A Retrospective View of a 'Non-Existent Issue' in the GDR," in *The Cultural After-Life of East Germany: New Transnational Perspectives,* ed. Leslie Adelson (Washington, D.C.: AICGS Humanities, 2002).

## Bibliography

Baum, Bruce David. *The Rise and Fall of the Caucasian Race: A Political History of Racial Identity.* New York: New York University Press, 2006.

Brattain, Michelle. "Race, Racism, and Antiracism: Unesco and the Politics of Presenting Science to the Postwar Public." *American Historical Review* 112, no. 5 (December 2007): 1386–413.

Brinkel, Teresa, and John Bendix. "Institutionalizing Volkskunde in Early East Germany." *Journal of Folklore Research* 46, no. 2 (2009): 141–72.

Burleigh, Michael, and Wolfgang Wippermann. *The Racial State: Germany 1933-1945.* New York: Cambridge University Press, 1991.

Castillo, Greg. "Peoples at an Exhibition: Soviet Architecture and the National Question." In *Socialist Realism without Shores,* ed. Thomas Lahusen and EA Dobrenko, 91–119. Durham: Duke University Press, 1997.

Chin, Rita, and Heide Fehrenbach. "German Democracy and the Question of Difference, 1945-1995." In *After the Racial State: Difference and Democracy in Postfascist Germany,* ed. Rita Chin, Heide Fehrenbach, Geoff Eley, and Atina Grossman. Ann Arbor: University of Michigan Press, 2009.

———. "Introduction: What's Race Got to Do with It? Postwar German History in Context." In *After the Racial State: Difference and Democracy in Postfascist Germany,* ed. Rita Chin, Heide Fehrenbach, Geoff Eley, and Atina Grossman. Ann Arbor: University of Michigan Press, 2009.

Ciarlo, David. *Advertising Empire: Race and Visual Culture in Imperial Germany.* Cambridge: Harvard University Press, 2011.

El-Tayeb, Fatima. "Vorwort." In *Mythen, Masken Und Subjekte: Kritische Weissseinsforschung in Deutschland,* ed. Maureen Maisha Eggers et al. Münster: Unrast, 2005.

Elsner, Eva-Maria, and Lothar Elsner. *Ausländerpolitik Und Ausländerfeindschaft in Der DDR (1949-1990).* Leipzig: Rosa-Luxemburg-Verein, 1994.

Fehrenbach, Heide. *Race after Hitler: Black Occupation Children in Postwar Germany and America.* Princeton: Princeton University Press, 2005.

Fredrickson, George M. *Racism: A Short History.* Princeton: Princeton University Press, 2002.

Ha, Kien Nghi, ed. *Asiatische Deutsche: Vietnamesische Diaspora and Beyond.* Berlin: Assoziation A, 2012.

Hagen, Katrina. "Internationalism in Cold War Germany." Ph.D. diss., University of Washington, 2008.

Heiduschke, Sebastian. *East German Cinema: DEFA and Film History.* New York: Palgrave Macmillan, 2013.

Herf, Jeffrey. *Divided Memory: The Nazi Past in the Two Germanys.* Cambridge: Harvard University Press, 1997.

Hirsch, Francine. *Empire of Nations: Ethnographic Knowledge and the Making of the Soviet Union.* Ithaca: Cornell University Press, 2005.

Hockenos, Paul. *Free to Hate: The Rise of the Right in Post-Communist Eastern Europe.* New York: Routledge, 1993.

Horten, Gerd. "Sailing in the Shadow of the Vietnam War: The GDR Government and the 'Vietnam Bonus' of the Early 1970s." *German Studies Review* 36, no. 3 (October 2013): 557–78.

Kotek, Joël. "Youth Organizations as a Battlefield in the Cold War." In *The Cultural Cold War in Western Europe, 1945-1960,* ed. Giles Scott-Smith and Hans Krabbendam, 138–58. Portland: F. Cass, 2003.

Krüger-Potratz, Marianne, Georg Hansen, and Dirk Jasper. *Anderssein gab es nicht: Ausländer und Minderheiten in der DDR.* New York: Waxmann, 1991.

McLellan, Josie. *Antifascism and Memory in East Germany: Remembering the International Brigades, 1945-1989.* New York: Oxford University Press, 2004.

Miles, Robert. "Racism as a Concept." In *Racism,* ed. Martin Bulmer and John Solomos, 343–55. New York: Oxford University Press, 1999.

Opitz, May, Katharina Oguntoye, and Dagmar Schultz, eds. *Showing Our Colors: Afro-German Women Speak Out.* Amherst: University of Massachusetts Press, 1992.

Palmowski, Jan. *Inventing a Socialist Nation: Heimat and the Politics of Everyday Life in the GDR, 1945-1990.* New York: Cambridge University Press, 2009.

Piesche, Peggy. "Black and German? East German Adolescents before 1989: A Retrospective View of a 'Non-Existent Issue' in the GDR." In *The Cultural After-Life of East Germany: New Transnational Perspectives,* ed. Leslie Adelson. Washington, D.C.: AICGS Humanities, 2002.

Port, Andrew. *Die rätselhafte Stabilität der DDR: Arbeit und Alltag im sozialistischen Deutschland.* Berlin: Christoph Links, 2007.

Rauhut, Michael. "The Voice of the Other America: African-American Music and Political Protest in the German Democratic Republic." In *Between the Avant-Garde and the Everyday: Subversive Politics in Europe from 1957 to the Present,* ed. Timothy Scott Brown and Lorena Anton, 92–110. New York: Berghahn Books, 2011.

Sandeen, Eric J. *Picturing an Exhibition: The Family of Man and 1950s America.* Albuquerque: University of New Mexico Press, 1995.

Schleicher, Hans-Georg. "GDR Solidarity: The German Democratic Republic and the South African Liberation Struggle." In *The Road to Democracy in South Africa,* ed. South African Democracy Education Trust, 1069–1153. Pretoria: Unisa Press, 2004.

Schwartz, Peter J. "The Ideological Antecedents of the First-Series Renminbi Worker-and-Peasant Banknote or What Mao Tse-Tung May Have Owed to Dziga Vertov." *Transcultural Studies* 1 (2014): 8–94.

Sekula, Allan. "The Body and the Archive." *October,* no. 39 (Winter 1986): 3–64.

Shannon, Christopher. *A World Made Safe for Differences: Cold War Intellectuals and the Politics of Identity.* Lanham: Rowman & Littlefield Publishers, 2001.

Slezkine, Yuri. "The USSR as a Communal Apartment, or How a Socialist State Promoted Ethnic Particularism." *Slavic Review* 53, no. 2 (Summer 1994): 414–52.

Slobodian, Quinn. "Bandung in Divided Germany: Managing Non-Aligned Politics in East and West, 1955–63." *The Journal of Imperial and Commonwealth History* 41, no. 4 (2013): 644–62.

———. "Citizenship-Shifting: Race and Xing-Hu Kuo's Claim on East German Memory." In *Imagining Germany Imagining Asia: Essays in Asian-German Studies*, ed. Veronika Fuechtner and Mary Rhiel, 34–49. Rochester: Camden House, 2013.

Sluga, Glenda. *Internationalism in the Age of Nationalism*. Philadelphia: University of Pennsylvania Press, 2013.

Stach, Andrzej, and Saleh Hussain. *Ausländer in der DDR: Ein Rückblick*. Berlin: Die Ausländerbeauftragte des Senats, 1993.

Turner, Fred. *The Democratic Surround: Multimedia & American Liberalism from World War II to the Psychedelic Sixties*. Chicago: University of Chicago Press, 2014.

Weis, Toni. "The Politics Machine: On the Concept of 'Solidarity' in East German Support for Swapo." *Journal of Southern African Studies* 2 (June 2011): 351–67.

Winrow, Gareth M. *The Foreign Policy of the GDR in Africa*. New York: Cambridge University Press, 1990.

Zimmerman, Andrew. *Anthropology and Antihumanism in Imperial Germany*. Chicago: University of Chicago Press, 2001.

# PART II

# Aid *anders?*

# Chapter 2

# Through a Glass Darkly

## East German Assistance to North Korea and Alternative Narratives of the Cold War

*Young-Sun Hong*

The Korean War played an important role in the postwar history of the two Germanys. The war accelerated West Germany's integration into the Western alliance, helped jump-start the economic miracle, and enabled East Germany to play an important role in Soviet efforts to give real substance to its ideology of proletarian internationalism and fraternal solidarity. The Korean War also led the West German government to launch its first humanitarian assistance to the developing countries. During his first diplomatic trip to Washington, D.C., in April 1953, West German chancellor Konrad Adenauer suggested that West Germany take over the army hospital that the U.S. military had been operating in the city of Pusan. The following year, eighty German doctors, nurses, lab technicians, and mechanics arrived in the city as part of West Germany's first state-organized foreign aid mission.

East Germany's most important aid program for North Korea was the reconstruction of the city of Hamhung. During the 1954 Geneva conference on Korea and Indochina, East German prime minister Otto Grotewohl told a North Korean delegate that his country would be willing to help rebuild one of the cities that had been destroyed in the war. Kim Il Sung, the head of the country, chose Hamhung, a major industrial city that had been totally destroyed during the war, to be the beneficiary of this East German largesse.[1] The histories of Hamhung and Pusan were linked in a curious way during the 1950s. Just before Hamhung was bombed, the United States had evacuated over 100,000 people from Hamhung to the Pusan area. While the former city became a ghost town, the population of Pusan exploded due to the influx of refugees. Once the armistice was signed in July 1953, Hamhung and Pusan emerged as competing sites of German-German competition within the broader East-West Cold War conflict. This time the weapons deployed were not guns, but aid money and technology, and at the center of this competition was the idea of goodwill diplomacy by and for ordinary citizens of the two divided countries.

This article focuses on the East German reconstruction program for the Hamhung area and the conflicts that it generated. As I show in greater detail below, these conflicts revolved around the respective visions of socialist modernity that East Germany and North Korea wanted to express in and through the built environment of Hamhung. The first section surveys what the socialist camp called fraternal solidarity actions on behalf of North Korea. In the second section, I outline the differences in the development policies pursued by East Germany and North Korea and show how these differences gave rise to persistent conflicts over the allocation of resources and architectural style. In the conclusion, I briefly explore the afterlife of the personal connections between East German and North Korean workers that were forged in Hamhung in the 1950s. Ultimately, through a more finely grained, more discriminating analysis of the Cold War in the global South, I hope to show that this struggle constituted a multipolar, transnational field, rather than a space that was defined and exhausted by the conflict between the two superpowers, their allies, and their clients.

## "Solidarity Is Might"

The Korean War in the north was especially devastating, not only because of the immense loss of life and the displacement and separation of millions of families.[2] Indiscriminate American bombing also destroyed most of the infrastructure, industrial facilities, farmland, and irrigation systems. By the end of the war, 75 to 100 percent of the factories, schools, and hospitals in the north had been destroyed, about 75 percent of residential dwellings lay in ashes, and the land was virtually denuded of livestock.[3] The reconstruction of Pyongyang began immediately after the armistice with the help of Soviet and Hungarian architects and engineers, and the well-known Soviet screenwriter Arkadi Perventsev came to Pyongyang to produce a color film on the reconstruction of the city.[4]

The Korean War presented governments in both West and East with the opportunity to accelerate rearmament and marginalize political opponents. In East Germany, there were spontaneous demonstrations of solidarity with North Koreans. Soon after the outbreak of the war, for example, workers' collectives in the pharmaceutical industry volunteered to work overtime to produce medicine for the North Koreans. But such spontaneous demonstrations represented the thing that the Stalinist governments of Eastern Europe feared most: political activity that was not under their control and guidance. North Korea's constant appeals for assistance, however, put pressure on East German officials, who ultimately decided to favor solidarity donations, rather than direct government loans, but also concluded that it would be better if such initiatives were controlled by the state.[5] A few weeks later, the National Front of Democratic Germany, which was an umbrella organization of the political parties and official mass organizations, declared East Germany's solidarity with the people of Korea, and, in September 1950, a Korea Aid Committee was created. The Committee sponsored documentary films, slide shows, and exhibitions on the situation in Korea. By the end of 1954, the Committee had collected approximately DM 40 million on behalf of North Korea.[6]

In terms of geopolitics, East German aid actions on behalf of North Korea were made possible by a reorientation of Soviet policy after Stalin's death in March 1953. As a first step in this direction, Khrushchev began to provide large amounts of financial aid and technical assistance to China, and, following the armistice in Korea, granted 1 billion Rubles in assistance to North Korea.[7] The East German commitment to the rebuilding of Hamhung needs to be understood within this larger context of Sino-Soviet friendship and international socialist solidarity. In 1953 East Germany agreed to convert the 30 million Ruble credit that it had offered North Korea the previous year into an outright grant and to provide an additional 30 million Rubles.[8] For its part, China provided North Korea with cotton, coal, and food. In addition, 295 Chinese technicians were sent to North Korea, along with ten thousand Chinese People's Volunteers, who worked in the rice fields, repaired bridges and railways, and built dikes and factories.[9] By the end of 1953, other socialist countries in Eastern Europe had signed similar aid agreements, which were to complement the resources that the North Koreans were expecting to generate through their 1954–56 Three Year Plan. The Sino-Soviet bloc countries also admitted North Korean children and students for education and workers for technical training.[10]

This fraternal help was generally embedded in a complex web of credits and trade agreements among socialist bloc countries. The basic modes for the provision of development assistance to states in Asia and Africa were (a) credits that were to be used to purchase capital equipment and manufactures from the donor country and that were to be repaid through the export of finished or intermediate goods produced using local natural resources and labor, and (b) the direct exchange of industrial equipment for primary products. For example, 40 percent of Soviet aid to North Korea was to be provided in the form of industrial equipment, machines and spare parts for hydroelectric power, steel, and fertilizer plants, as well as canneries and the renovation of a large hospital in Pyongyang.[11]

Soviet bloc engineers, architects, agronomists, and journalists were surprised to see so many foreign specialists on the same planes and trains heading toward Pyongyang and to hear so many different languages being spoken in the newly built International Hotel in Pyongyang. And even where such mutual affection might not have been completely spontaneous or genuine, the illusion was maintained by a constant stream of films, publications, and rituals performed by all of the communist countries. Yet beneath the surface of genuine goodwill and official ideology there were real differences both within and between countries as to the best path to socialist modernity. And these differences became increasingly clear as the situation evolved from helping North Korea meet the immediate postwar needs of its people to the formulation of longer-term programs for the construction of socialism.

The ties between the Eastern and Western members of the communist community appeared to be growing tighter by the day. In December 1954, the East German Solidarity Committee for Korea and Vietnam sent a delegation to North Korea. The well-known writer Max Zimmering, who headed the delegation, remarked that North Korea had come to epitomize an "era when all norms of life are rapidly changing." A mere decade ago, he noted, Korea had been virtually unknown to most Germans. Now, however, "[w]e suddenly became intimate with each other like twin brothers." "To write about Korea now," he noted, "means to write about fraternal love which unites many peoples of the camp of peace. ... Korea is an example of proletarian internationalism. The freedom of Korea is the freedom of the entire working people, her struggle is the struggle of peace-loving youth the world over. Hence the development of Korea constitutes the common cause of the people who want to live on their own and who hate war."[12]

While it would be wrong to dismiss the rhetoric of international socialist solidarity in the struggle against imperialism simply as a fig leaf for Soviet attempts to extend their domination into Asia and Africa, I argue that proletarian internationalism also represented a strategy for integrating Third World countries into a socialist world system. Khrushchev envisioned a division of labor within the socialist bloc in which the socialist and pro-socialist Third World countries were to serve as producers of primary products and as markets for Soviet and East European manufactures. For example, as part of their technical aid, the Soviet Union, which needed to import food from abroad, helped the North Koreans build factories for canning food, and between 1956 and 1959 Korean food exports to the Soviet Union jumped by 1,600 percent. East Germany, which suffered from a perpetual shortage of hard currency and sought to limit its imports from non-socialist countries, valued North Korea as a source of a variety of primary products (including mineral resources, tobacco, peanuts, and honey), which it hoped to procure from the North Koreans through the barter arrangements that were the typical mode of exchange among COMECON countries.[13]

In North Korea, however, such plans evoked memories of colonial rule by the Japanese.[14] In the 1950s, Kim Il Sung was first and foremost an anticolonial nationalist whose highest priorities were national unification and economic autarchy. Like many first generation leaders of postcolonial states, Kim pursued an authoritarian approach to national development that borrowed selectively from both the Soviet and Chinese models.[15] Kim insisted that the construction of socialism in North Korea could not be separated from the reunification of the entire peninsula and that the country had to follow single-handedly a special economic path in order to liquidate the legacy of colonial rule and secure the economic independence of the nation. As Kim explained in his address to the Third Party Congress in April 1956, this was the goal of the 1957–61 Five Year Plan: "The colonial lopsidedness of our industry left by the prolonged heinous rule of the Japanese imperialists should be eliminated and the foundations for socialist industrialization of our country be laid" by giving priority to heavy industry.[16]

As in North Vietnam, the North Korean struggle for national liberation and efforts to recast the emergent nation in a socialist mold were two facets of a single, convulsive process. And, like Ho Chi Minh, Kim was convinced that neither of these goals could be achieved without first securing the unification of his country. Kim's doctrine of autarchy and self-reliance (*juche*) was both a central policy goal and a rhetorical compensation for the failure to achieve either economic independence or long-term economic self-sufficiency.[17] When Kim traveled to Eastern Europe in 1956, however, it became clear that his understanding of socialist internationalism was quite different from that of the Soviets and the other socialist countries of Eastern Europe. In his meeting with East German Politburo on 8 June 1956, Kim explained to his hosts that his top priority was to build "an economic foundation for Korean reunification."[18] But the East Germans were willing to provide assistance to North Korea as part of a coordinated economic and foreign policy to promote the interests of the Soviet-led bloc. This difference in policies led to constant friction with the socialist countries whose assistance was crucial to achieving the goals set by Kim. The remainder of this chapter analyzes the Hamhung reconstruction project from 1955 until the end of the decade, when East Germany, amid the deepening Sino-Soviet conflict over leadership of the communist bloc, decided to wind down its assistance to North Korea.

# Fraternal Help in Practice:
# East Germany in the Global South

Hamhung and Hungnam, located on the northeast coast of the peninsula, were North Korea's second and third largest cities, respectively, after the capital Pyongyang. The Hamhung region was the center of the country's nitrogen chemical and hydroelectric power industries first developed in the late 1920s by the Japanese corporation Noguchi and then further expanded in the 1930s with the support of the Japanese military. During the Korean War, the region was also the scene of intense fighting. By the time of the armistice, some 90 percent of the houses and industrial plants in the region had been destroyed, and reconstructing this industrial center was no less important to building socialism than the rebuilding of the capital.[19]

After the Politburo had approved Grotewohl's proposal for the reconstruction of Hamhung in July 1954, East Germany established the Korea Construction Staff (Baustab Korea) in Berlin to manage the project. In view of the political, economic, and symbolic significance of the project, the Construction Staff reported directly to Deputy Premier Heinrich Rau, who was also minister for construction (and later minister of trade).[20] In March 1955, the Council of Ministers approved DM 204 million to fund the project from 1955 to its planned completion in 1964.[21] The East German remit was vast as they agreed to rebuild the entire city, including housing, office buildings, streets, and all other necessary infrastructure. In 1956, the East Germans also agreed to expand their massive civil engineering project to include the reconstruction of industrial plant and infrastructure of Hungnam and the nearby city of Bongun, which was a major center of the chemical industry. The guidelines for the Hamhung project had been set out in a bilateral agreement between North Korea and East Germany. For their part, the North Korean government created a Commission for the Reconstruction of the City of Hamhung in March 1955; it was headed by vice premier and chairman of the state construction committee, Bak Uiwan.[22] Each year, the Korean state planning commission prepared both a budget for the Hamhung project and a detailed list of items to be purchased from East Germany so that the East German and North Korean planning processes became intermeshed with each other.

Kim Il Sung emphasized that his top priority was to use the reconstruction of Hamhung as a vast training shop to help North Korea make the transition from artisanal to mechanized construction. He asked the East Germans to send architects, engineers, and master artisans organized in a self-contained work brigade equipped with modern machines and tools so that Korean workers could emulate their organization and work methods.[23]

Technical assistance—including vocational training—was the second pillar of East German aid to North Korea and the other countries of the Third World. In its constant struggle with West Germany for international recognition and legitimacy, East Germany placed particular emphasis on the role of technical advisers as goodwill ambassadors from the land of socialist modernity. The East German government was eager to dispatch technical advisers who—in addition to their professional qualifications—also possessed exemplary character and personality.

Several waves of East Germans arrived in Hamhung in 1955. By the end of the year, 132 German engineers, architects, machinists, and artisans were working there. Collectively, they were called the German Work Group Korea (Deutsche Arbeitsgruppe Korea, DAG). The actual construction labor was carried out by North Korea's "Construction Trust No. 18."[24] German master artisans, machinists, and other skilled workers gave these Koreans on-the-job training in precision work, and by the end of 1956 about 200 Koreans had qualified as skilled workers.[25] Other Korean workers were taught how to operate machines and construction vehicles,[26] and, in less than six months, the Construction Trust No. 18 was able to undertake certain assignments independently.[27] By 1956, the workers and technicians of Construction Trust No. 18 were capable of taking over less complicated tasks like the construction of apartment buildings. It was due to this delegation of duties that,

**Figure 2.1.** Members of the German Work Group (DAG) in front of their living quarters (ca. 1956)

while the surface area of the East German projects increased fivefold in 1956, the size of the German team could remain more or less the same.[28]

Because of the sheer size of the DAG and its seven-year presence in North Korea, the Hamhung project offers an unusual opportunity to examine North Korean and East German understandings of socialist modernity and "fraternal help" and patterns of conflict and cooperation between the East German and North Korean teams. For the mission to North Korea, the East Germans insisted that these technicians have the imagination as well as the leadership and organizational skills needed to solve independently the problems that they were expected to face in a strange and distant land. The guidelines for the recruitment of technical advisers specified that the persons selected should be intelligent enough to communicate to the Koreans "the basic, routine activities of [their] specialized area[s] without an interpreter," that they have the leadership skills needed to motivate their foreign colleagues, rather than simply to command them, and, most important of all, that they not be inclined to arrogance or expressions of "racial superiority."[29] These experts were supposed to be the embodiment of the new socialist personality and agents of international solidarity. They were also supposed to be goodwill ambassadors who could repair Germany's damaged reputation by showing that Germany, or at least its Eastern part, could no longer be associated with National Socialism. In the words of Erich Selbmann, the first director of the DAG, "it is to be expected that, after a very long period, in which the name of Germany was associated with destruction and annihilation, and a brief intermediate period, in which Germany could only passively participate in the international field, the German Democratic Republic can participate in this worldwide process of establishing peace."[30]

To judge from the list of people who worked there, the Hamhung project was a prestigious position. Selbmann was the brother of Heavy Industry Minister Fritz Selbmann. The chief architect and deputy director Hans Grotewohl was the son of the East German prime minister. Several of the other architects involved in the project were also prominent in their field. Hartmut Colden and Peter Doehler had won the 1952 competition together to design the new headquarters for the official East German newspaper, *Neues Deutschland*.[31] Landscape architects Hugo Namslauer and Hubert Matthes played an important role in "Architektenkollektiv Buchenwald," the group that had been commissioned by the Ministry of Culture to design the memorials at the former concentration camps Buchenwald, Ravensbrück, and Sachsenhausen.[32] Konrad Püschel would later become a professor at the Bauhaus in Dessau. And Horst Präßler, who succeeded Selbmann as director, later became a high-ranking official at the Construction Ministry.[33] Many of the Germans who returned from North Korea in 1956 and 1957 acknowledged that they had learned a great deal from their work in Hamhung. These people would later become the directors of East German development programs in North Vietnam, Zanzibar, and Yemen.[34]

## Becoming *Hamhunger*: Connecting East Germany and North Korea

In October 1955, East Germany decided to allow leading specialists of the DAG to bring their wives and children to Hamhung and to give these women jobs doing such tasks as secretarial and bookkeeping work, teaching at the school for the German children, supervising the Korean service personnel, and organizing social and cultural events.[35] One rare exception to this pattern was Madeleine Grotewohl, the wife of chief architect Hans Grotewohl, who herself was employed as an architect on the project. As many of the other specialists resented the fact that only a few experts were allowed to bring their family members to Korea, however, this initial policy was soon changed. At the end of 1956, a total of 125 Germans were living in Hamhung, including twenty children and twenty-six women.[36] Through 1957, this privilege was further extended to all married specialists working on the project.[37]

On the whole, the members of the German team seemed to have enjoyed living in North Korea. They traveled freely and extensively in the country, something that would be unimaginable in present-day North Korea. There were beach resorts near Hamhung as well as mountains with ancient temples and pavilions. The DAG organized excursions outside the province, and the high point for many of the East Germans was a tour of Beijing on their way back to Berlin. The group also organized many social and cultural gatherings with Soviet, Czech, and Polish aid workers, though the East Germans preferred to socialize with the Czechs more than either the Soviets or the Poles, whom they considered to be too conservative. The Germans also paraded together with the local population in major celebrations such as May Day, the anniversary of the 1917 Russian Revolution, and the celebration of North Korean independence.[38]

The Germans working in Hamhung did not live in a ghetto, but rather interacted with the North Koreans on a regular basis and at a number of different levels. At the leadership level, the Germans and Koreans—including architects and urban planners—consulted and negotiated with each other through the entire construction process. Below them were the skilled craftsmen, machine operators, masons, and carpenters who were responsible for training Koreans in their respective specialties. It was this middle level of

**Figure 2.2.** "Long Live International Solidarity," September 1957

contacts that the North Korean and East German governments packaged as the embodiment of fraternal help and disseminated to their citizens for political education. But there were also other, less formal levels of contact that were less amenable to state regimentation. In comparison to the two states' focus on work, technology, and socialist modernity in their official representations of the program, the ordinary Germans in Hamhung tended to highlight their personal contacts with Koreans. In fact, both the Korean and German authorities sometimes warned against becoming "too friendly" with their foreign co-workers, both male and female.[39]

In one respect, such contacts were indispensable because the Germans had to rely on Korean cooks, translators, and other assistance to meet their everyday needs. To improve living conditions for the Germans, the Korean authorities provided cleaners, cooks, maids, barbers, and seamstresses. The canteen offered many opportunities for more personal contacts between the North Koreans and the East Germans. In the newsletter, *Hamhunger Heimat-reportage,* which was distributed to the former members of the DAG to keep them abreast of the development of "our child Hamhung," there are many references to familiar Korean faces in the canteen as well as to the Korean food, alcohol, and cigarettes that the East Germans enjoyed in Hamhung. One example read: "The cook 'Müller' is still at his job along with the *Süße* Pak-*dongmu* [*dongmu* is the Korean word for comrade], Kim-*dongmu*—the sweet Korean women who always took care of our needs in a friendly manner. When we're thirsty and pour ourselves a Chinese beer, then everything tastes better. We decide to eat Korean food. There is *Omreis* [fried rice with an omelet on top] and other delicacies as well."[40]

The East Germans developed a sense of transnational identity based on their living and working experiences in Hamhung; they created their own collective identity as the *Tokils* (*Tokil* is the Korean word for Germany) and as *Hamhunger*. Neither the North Koreans nor the members of the DAG emphasized that they were East Germans. For many Germans there, it was often informal contact and daily experience that helped them appreciate the local culture and customs that they remembered with fondness for years to come. While our knowledge of these international aid programs is often pre- or over-determined by state-enforced, ritualized ideologies and practices, we need to be sensitive to those experiences that escaped and exceeded the more rigid intentions of the states that sponsored these programs and ask how East Germans and their Korean counterparts constructed their own experience of international socialist solidarity.

Of course, not everything was this harmonious. Although the DAG emphasized the importance of German-Korean cooperation in every aspect of the work, neither the collaboration nor the training went as smoothly as hoped.[41] There was a pervasive problem with excessive drinking, which led to verbal altercations, fistfights, absenteeism, and instances of sexual abuse of the Korean women—some of which resulted in pregnancy—by German specialists and skilled workers.[42] Racial tensions surfaced regularly in the ear-

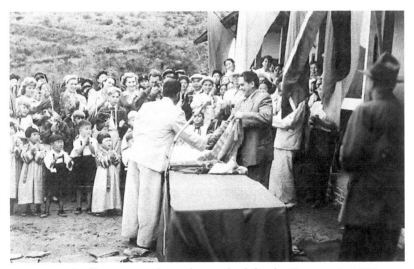

**Figure 2.3.** Präßler opening the orphanage built by the Germans in 1957

lier years. Some of the Germans were so arrogant and authoritarian that, as one DAG member reported, the North Koreans complained that Germans made the former Japanese rulers pale in comparison.[43] Some Koreans drew the connections between the autocratic manners of the Germans and "Hitler's fascism."[44] A number of people were sent home for "moral misconduct" with North Korean women.[45] Sometimes these liaisons had to be resolved politically. In one instance, a German man wanted to marry his North Korean lover, and when his request was turned down by the German authorities, he tried—in vain—to become a North Korean citizen.

At a different level, the simple act of asking their North Korean coworkers how well they themselves were being fed was problematic because the question itself was seen as an affront to the country's leadership. North Korea was heavily dependent on food imports from China, and the food crisis was particularly acute in 1955 because of the poor harvest the year before, the acceleration of collectivization, and excessive requisitioning.[46] Selbmann explained to the Germans that their task was to teach their hosts "the newest technical and economic knowledge" in the construction field, and he warned them not to attempt to change the existing local conditions "through any measures of help that do not concern us."[47] It was clear to all that the East Germans, who enjoyed an ample supply of foods, cigarettes, alcohol, and other consumer goods, lived much better than their North Korean co-workers. Some of the East Germans gave leftovers from the canteen or parties to the Koreans, and some of them even invited their Korean friends to parties at the DAG compound, where they could enjoy the food and drink.

The issue became more pressing in 1957 when the regime began to discourage unofficial contacts with foreigners and issued a more or less formal prohibition on visits by North Koreans to the Construction Group compound.[48] The East Germans had long been uncertain just how friendly they could be with their Korean counterparts without arousing the suspicion or ire of the Korean authorities. This mutual suspicion also altered the parameters of interaction between the Germans and the Koreans. The North Koreans became more cautious and reserved in their personal interaction with the East Germans than they had been in the previous years. The DAG began to require that all invitations of Koreans to private gatherings be approved in advance by the director.[49] Both Korean and German officials also sought to discourage the Germans from giving small gifts, such as food, clothing, and other items, to the Korean colleagues. The DAG also instituted a policy prohibiting staff from giving the Koreans any items purchased in the canteen or in other shops operated by the group. The earlier, more intimate conditions, which had allowed for the construction of transnational identities, were being eroded slowly by official decree.

## Build Faster and Cheaper! The Post-Stalinist Paradigm of Socialist Modernity

In addition to closer trade relations with Korea and the promised economic benefits, the East Germans had agreed to take on the Hamhung project because of its symbolic importance.[50] The reconstruction of the Hamhung industrial region was to be both a demonstration of East German technological achievements for the world to see and a mirror in which the East Germans could see their own future reflected. The project involved the construction of a vast urban-industrial complex that would embody the socialist vision of modern urban space and show how such a complex could be built through the use of modern construction technologies to achieve the most efficient use of workforce, machines, and materials. The East Germans desired to demonstrate the virtues and possibilities of the German socialist modernism that had recently triumphed as the official architectural ideology of the state.

From the very beginning, what the East Germans were proposing to do in Hamhung was measured against what the Soviets had already accomplished in Pyongyang. The East German team desired to construct buildings whose quality would have exceeded that of the buildings constructed by the Soviets and the Hungarians in the capital Pyongyang. In a 1957 report to Rau, the DAG described the ways in which the houses that were being built in Hamhung were superior to those that had been built in Pyongyang. In addition to the fact that they were standardized, prefabricated buildings

**Figure 2.4.** Präßler speaking to a planning meeting with Korean translator and bilingual instructions

constructed using modern machinery, the report emphasized the superior quality of the building and its interior fixtures, as well as the uniform design of the entire housing complex, whose impressive exterior appearance magnified the political symbolism of the project.[51]

The reconstruction of Hamhung was as much a social as a civil engineering project. Like the leftist Bauhaus architects of the Weimar years, the DAG directors were convinced that living in more modern, functional housing would educate the residents to a more modern, functional—and socialist—way of life. Traditional Korean dwellings were single-story buildings, and the Germans complained that the Koreans were culturally challenged by modern urban life, especially the idea of living in multistory apartment buildings. Although they knew that the Koreans had been critical of the apartment buildings that the Hungarians had built in Pyongyang, the DAG felt that they should refuse to compromise and, instead, try to persuade the Koreans of the virtues of their vision of the socialist city.

Debates over architectural style and construction technology were central to the socialist transformation of Moscow and Berlin in the mid 1950s. The major points of contention in the rebuilding of East Berlin were whether the real needs of the laboring classes could be best satisfied, and the identity of the new socialist state best represented, by historicism, Stalinist-era socialist realism, or Bauhaus modernism, and how these different architectural styles would help mold the new socialist personality.[52] Although the East Germans opted for a combination of socialist realism and historicism, the atmosphere shifted perceptibly after Stalin's death. In his December 1954 speech to the All Union Conference of Builders and Architects Khrushchev denounced Stalinist style and instead called for the industrialization of construction, that is, the use of prefabricated modules and other construction materials and methods to maximize labor productivity and minimize costs and materials.[53]

Khrushchev's proposal for the mechanization of construction methods quickly became the dominant post-Stalinist paradigm of architecture and urban planning in the Soviet bloc, where it became the symbol of socialist modernity and a recipe for the rapid, cost-effective means of meeting the needs of the laboring classes. From Moscow to Berlin the fortunes of architects and bureaucrats rose and fell depending on their position on this crucial question, and these same issues also led to controversy in North Korea. In April 1955, East German authorities took over Khrushchev's call to build "better, faster and cheaper" as their own motto.[54] In January 1956, North Korea held its first conference of architects and builders.[55] The discussions there echoed recent debates in Eastern Europe clearly. Following the conference, the Construction Ministry was criticized sharply for failing to adopt the mechanized construction of prefabricated buildings, and the ministry was ordered to adopt these modern methods on a large scale.[56]

## …While Visions of Socialist Modernity Danced in Their Heads: Building a Socialist Metropolis in North Korea

The DAG had long argued that their advanced construction technologies would yield enough efficiency to enable them to escape the political and budgetary constraints that were tightening around them. Their confidence seemed justified in the light of productivity on the Hungnam project, which increased by 130 percent in the first quarter of 1956 in comparison to the paltry 6 percent increase in productivity recorded by the Soviets, who were rebuilding a fertilizer plant in the region.[57] In view of the extent to which Korean officials were promoting the mechanization of construction, the DAG directors believed that they were on the right path. The East Germans thought that their technology could help the North Koreans meet ambitious production goals laid out in the plan. As Präßler noted, "with the help from the DAG, the Hamhung project is not only in terms of form, [and] architectural picture … but also in the question of the application of norms, standards, and mechanization quite exceptional."[58] However, the success of this showcase project depended not only on overcoming the limitations of the East German planned economy, but also on the cooperation and capacity of the North Koreans. Initially, the DAG felt that they "should refuse to collaborate in making technical and economic mistakes."[59] However, such purism would have required them to abandon the Hamhung project. In practice the subsequent history of their work there became one of halting, unsatisfactory compromises between modernist ideology and North Korean realities.

By 1957, the construction of these public buildings had advanced to the stage where the DAG was ready to begin installing the heating, electrical, and plumbing systems (including such things as showers and toilets). It was at this point, at the latest, that the latent differences between the East Germans and the North Koreans came into the open. When the DAG directors met with the Korean Planning Commission to finalize the materials to be shipped from Germany in 1958, the latter objected to a number of interior fixtures that the East Germans felt were indispensable to preserve the distinctly East German character of the buildings. For example, although the Construction Group insisted on installing automatic light switches in corridors and stairwells and putting electrical outlets in every room in the residential buildings, the Korean authorities objected to the proposal, arguing that such items cost too much (₩170 in comparison to the ₩100 that they had paid for similar items in Pyongyang) and that they would encourage the unnecessary use of electricity. They also raised similar objections to East German standards for the size and ceiling height of the apartments. Whereas deputy premier Bak had originally asked the East Germans to install toilets in each flat, this idea was scrapped as a luxury later in 1958.[60]

The DAG feared that the North Korean policy threatened the viability of their own plan for the reconstruction of Hamhung. Präßler was concerned about the cumulative effect of the changes demanded by the North Koreans, and he felt that it was important to demand that the North Koreans live up to their original financial commitments. Präßler proposed that the East German ambassador warn that the Hamhung project would otherwise cease to be politically tenable for East Germany and that the North Koreans would lose face with the "socialist camp as a whole."[61] Despite pressures to reduce costs, the DAG insisted on maintaining the quality of the buildings and their interior fixtures not only because the Hamhung project was of such great symbolic importance for East Germany. They also saw how other communist countries were using their development aid to lay the foundation for future exchange agreements with the North Koreans. Präßler argued that the East Germans should do the same, and he hoped that the use of East German furniture and fixtures in such public buildings as cultural clubs, department stores, and theaters would encourage the North Koreans to desire more goods made in East Germany.[62]

By that point, the on-site concrete plant was producing prefabricated concrete slabs that speeded up construction, as did the widespread mobilization of "volunteer" workers to clear rubble for street construction and do pick-and-shovel work for the water supply and sewage systems. The first Korean Five Year Plan involved the all-out mobilization of the population for the construction of the heavy industrial foundations of economic independence. There was also a greater reliance on unskilled, forced labor. North Korea suffered from an acute labor shortage due to the loss of life during the war and the migration of so many people to the south. To compensate for this shortage, all able-bodied people—officials, skilled and unskilled workers, farmers, housewives and children—were mobilized for construction work.[63] As such, the Korean plan bore many similarities to both the first Soviet Five Year Plan and the contemporary Chinese Great Leap Forward, even though it was intended to ensure the independence of North Korea from both of the communist superpowers. In every socialist country, plans for rapid socialist transformation led to conflicts within the ruling party and purges of those left holding the short end of the political stick. In North Korea, construction policy became quickly one of the main ideological battlefields within the

North Korean regime and between the North Koreans and the East Germans. Although the party leadership increased wages and lowered the prices of some consumer goods, any benefits of these measures were offset by the overall rise in the cost of living, and people had to live in an environment of fear and insecurity as the government resorted to punitive measures to sustain the ideological mobilization of the populace. The DAG was skeptical of all of these measures, and asked provincial party officials not to approve any hurried resolutions regarding construction methods that would impact its work. The Germans in Hamhung were concerned that Koreans at every level were afraid that anything they said would conflict with the party line. According to an East German report, the situation was "especially bad for those lower-level cadres who work with us, because we give them technical instructions and advice that appear to go against the party line and other higher authorities."[64]

In October 1958, when the Five Year Plan had only been underway for eighteen months, the North Koreans announced an ambitious plan to accelerate the completion of the plan in only three and a half years. This was known as the Chollima Movement. The movement was named after a legendary winged horse that could travel 1,000 li (a bit more than 300 miles) in a day. The name was chosen to describe the frenetic pace at which the country was to be rebuilt, and it ultimately led to a parting of the ways between the North Koreans and the East Germans. With the institution of the Chollima Movement, increased speed and decreased costs became the sole criterion by which the success of the project was measured, and the North Koreans gave up any pretext of achieving European construction standards. Leading members of the party traveled to production sites across the country to educate workers and farmers about the urgency of higher productivity and cost savings.

## Pyongyang Hour

The intense, chaotic, and ideologically charged atmosphere of the time is captured in the novel *Pyongyang Hour* by Choi Hak Su, who was later awarded the Kim Il Sung Prize for his literary labors.[65] The novel, which opens in November 1957, provides a fictionalized and highly idealized account of real developments in the construction field in 1957–58. The main characters are three young men who have just been discharged from the army and who arrive in Pyongyang to help with the reconstruction of the fatherland. One of the men, Rhee Sang Chul, was a native of Pyongyang, where he had spent a miserable, impoverished childhood under Japanese rule. His brother-in-law

Mun Ha Rin was the director of urban planning for the city. However, Mun had become politically suspect because he had been trained in a European architectural tradition, which, it was claimed, prevented him from grasping the importance of the Five Year Plan and the Chollima Movement. In the novel, and in reality, Kim Il Sung had denounced such people as reactionaries, claiming that their blind adherence to foreign doctrines betrayed both a secret loyalty to other powers and a lack of confidence in "our own power, wisdom and ability." Mun and his superiors were denounced in due course for their architectural and political failings, and his rehabilitation depended on his ideological conversion.

In the novel, Kim delivers a rousing fictionalized speech in which he calls on architects to build more housing at a lower cost and abandon foreign aesthetic values for a revolutionary emphasis on meeting the basic needs of the laboring masses efficiently. Mun sees the light and recognizes the virtues of traditional building practices. He becomes a convert to the traditional *ondol* (subfloor heating, which had been rejected by foreign builders, even though it was cheaper than Western electrical heating), and he asks himself how anyone would conceivably wish to introduce Western-style beds, which wasted precious iron without being superior in any way to sleeping on mats on *ondol*-heated floors. Mun even criticized the adoption of Western dimensions in housing design because they seemed to thoughtlessly take over foreign standards without giving any thought to the traditional norms that were best suited for the needs of the Korean people:

> The ceilings are also high like the houses in foreign countries. They lack style and coziness. In the past, our ancestors knew just how high ceilings should be... [Now] ceilings are so high that the space appears empty. Was it really necessary to make them so high?... How high was the ceiling in traditional *Choson* [Korean] homes? What is the average height of the *Choson* people? What is the optimal height for temperature, ventilation and light? When he was trying to find the right number, he was shocked to realize that he was ignorant of the average height of the *Choson* people. Without knowing such a thing, how could he have designed a house for them?... In the past he had imitated what others had done, and he had not succeeded in truly designing anything, which would be appropriate for our country and its people.[66]

After reflecting on these questions, Mun threw himself back into his work, designed a prototype standardized apartment building, which he regarded as the "most solid path" to the construction of mass housing at minimal cost, and continued the culture war against foreign influence by claiming that the methods used to prefabricate and mechanically assemble standardized housing units on a mass basis were Korean inventions.[67]

In the novel one of the other characters exclaimed "isn't it such a source of pride and joy to be an architect?… Construction! Something truly worthwhile. Soon there will be a fierce battle in that field."[68] The reader is given a detailed account of how plants were built at construction sites to produce the building materials needed for the project, and the novel follows the emergence of new construction specialists, such as assemblers and welders, who became the heroic protagonists in the struggle for self-reliance. The assembly brigade in which Rhee is employed developed new techniques for assembling buildings, which ultimately reduced the amount of time it took to put up the walls of a simple flat down to a mere sixteen minutes. This new assembly method was sixty-one times faster than conventional methods, and the application of this new method to all of the new housing in the fictional Pyongyang led to the overfulfillment of the construction quota for 1958. This rapid pace of such furious transfiguration of tradition as the achievement of socialism came to be known as "Pyongyang speed."

## DAG and Kim Il Sung

In real life, Kim Il Sung had predicted in January 1958 that the coming year would mark a turning point in the construction campaign. At the end of January 1958, Kim Il Sung asked the DAG directors to meet with him and other high officials responsible for the Hamhung-Hungnam reconstruction project.[69] At the meeting Kim demonstrated a surprisingly detailed command of costs and construction methods. According to Kim, the cost per square meter for residential construction had increased from ₩3,580 in 1957 to ₩4,500–4,800 in 1958. The construction teams in Pyongyang had managed to push the cost down to ₩3,100 in response to a party decree issued in October of the previous year. But this was not enough, and the advisory teams dispatched by the party to design offices and construction sites pushed the figure down to ₩1,685. These savings had been achieved, Kim explained, by reducing the size of the apartments, eliminating individual bathrooms in favor of communal toilets and showers, reducing kitchen space by 50 percent (down to 5 square meters), and lowering the ceiling height to 2.2 meters. These alterations resulted in a reduction of 50 percent of the cement and steel, 70 percent of the piping, and 38 percent of the labor that would have been required by the original plan. These savings made it possible to increase the 1958 plan target from 2,750 to 5,100 housing units, and Kim hoped to increase the number to 10,000 through the use of volunteer labor. Kim then asked the DAG to apply these same standards to the housing that it was building in Hamhung. The East Germans were naturally reluctant to go along with this proposal. After all, they had not come halfway around the world just to build cheap housing that could hardly serve as a model of socialist modernity. Kim made a partial concession on this point, establishing a unitary cost for housing construction in both cities, but allowing Hamhung provincial officials to include the German amenities if they wished to pay for them. However, it is not clear whether these provincial officials availed themselves of this option.

In mid 1958, moreover, the party leadership set new and even higher plan targets for the Five Year Plan, and the Korean Council of Ministers decreed that 65 percent of all housing constructed would have to use prefabricated materials—with the figure rising to 80 percent for the following year.[70] Korean planners and architects were hard pressed to meet these goals, and it was increasingly doubtful whether there was any constructive role left for the East Germans. For example, when Korean architects designed a 48-unit apartment building for Hamhung in 1958, they included sixteen communal lavatories and one communal washing area with two showers. While the Koreans could not ignore state construction guidelines, the East Germans could not in good conscience consent to a plan that deviated in such essential respects from their own mandate "to build a modern socialist city" in Korea.[71] The East Germans were also becoming increasingly exasperated with the chronic shortages of basic construction materials and skilled workers.

At a different level, the DAG had its own problems. First, as the Korean workers acquired more and more knowledge, the East Germans had to bring in specialists who were themselves increasingly highly trained if they were to be able to continue to fulfill their mission of transferring technical knowledge. As one German working in Hamhung noted, the German specialists could no longer get by giving simple instructions like "the machines must be placed over there and the stones must be placed here…" Since the more skilled Koreans were increasingly able and willing to criticize the work of the East Germans, the DAG wrote back to the Construction Staff that Berlin needed to send over "really qualified" planners and engineers who understood the complex issues involved in planning for an entire region and who were capable of managing highly complicated civil engineering projects.[72] Second, the responsibilities of the East Germans became both more extensive and more complex as the East Germans began to execute more complicated, large-scale infrastructure projects, such as the central heating plant, streets, and the installation of underground utility lines and piping, and the construction of special-purpose public buildings, such as a hotel, a hospital, and a technical college. These projects were so complex that they were beginning to challenge the expertise of the German engineers who had come in the first wave of specialists. For example, the engineers who were supervising the construction of the plant to make clay piping were unable to insulate the furnace foundation properly, and the Work Group asked—repeatedly, and in vain—the Berlin Construction Staff to send a special engineer to solve the problem.[73] By 1958, the size of the DAG had dropped to approximately thirty-five people, primarily architects and engineers employed in the declining number of industrial projects still underway.[74]

The persistence of chronic problems of such magnitude made it clear that it was not a problem of bureaucracy or individuals, but of fundamentally conflicting priorities. The East Germans intended to employ modern methods in the rebuilding of Hamhung, as Kim himself had requested, but it became clear that the aims and priorities of the East Germans differed in important respects from those of the North Koreans. North Korea lacked the infrastructure, machinery, and skilled workers needed to emulate East German construction methods on such a scale, and the increased reliance on the ideological mobilization of unskilled labor could not make up for these shortcomings. Mutual disaffection had grown up between the two countries as they pursued their own paths to communism. In 1960, the East German government decided to reduce its aid to North Korea sharply, despite protests from the Berlin Construction Staff.[75] In a letter to Kim, the East Germans blamed their decision to cut back their commitments in Hamhung on West German militarism, though this was probably only a fig leaf for a decision that was taken on very different grounds. Kim replied to Grotewohl in equally empty language that "we are firmly convinced that the fraternal friendship and cooperation between the Korean and German peoples on the foundation of the principles of proletarian internationalism will continue to be further strengthened…"[76] The project ended on 15 September 1962 with a ceremony in which a high-ranking East German delegation officially turned over the "Ten Thousand Hurrahs Bridge" in Hamhung to the Koreans.[77] In the end, East Germany only spent 63 percent of the money that it had budgeted for the project.[78]

## Conclusion

In this chapter, I have tried to uncover some of the entangled connections between two divided nations—Germany and Korea—that have been ignored in the main narratives of the history of Cold War Germany. It is only within the past decade that the topic has reemerged thanks to a wave of literary works by Korean-Germans, the opening of a "German Village" in South Korea, and the intensified interaction between Germany and South Korea that have followed in the wake of corporate investment by Samsung in Germany. All of these activities are a sure sign of accelerating globalization. To a large degree, however, these transnational links have been kept alive over the past half century in the private memory of the individuals who were directly involved in these projects.

In 2005, the 75-year-old Wilfried Lübke reminisced about his time in Hamhung nearly a half-century earlier. "I was elated… I could travel. In my mid-twenties, I escaped from the East German prison."[79] In 1956, he arrived in Hamhung to help with the construction of the city's water works. His wife Helga joined him a year later. In 1960, shortly after their return to East Germany, they fled to West Berlin. They felt that they were being mistrustfully watched everywhere they went in East Germany. After their experience of the wider world during their stay in Korea, they could no longer bear the "narrowness" of East Germany. But despite his antipathy toward East Germany, he remembered the enthusiasm with which he had gone to North Korea originally to build a better, communist society: "In Hamhung I thought for the first time that communism could actually work. … Here, far away from my homeland, an almost American spirit prevailed among the East Germans, few party bigwigs, flat hierarchies. Many East German citizens worked here with genuine idealism. We wanted to build up after Germany had brought so much destruction to the world."

During their time in Korea, the Lübkes also made friends with two Koreans, a female graphic designer named Park and a translator named Zang. We get glimpses of the two Koreans in Helga's diary, which reports how one icy winter evening at the home of Park's parents, four Koreans and three Germans had no difficulty carrying on "a lively conversation" in broken Korean and German. Although the general deprivation was evident in the fact that old newspapers served as wallpaper, there were still "many small, delicious, but spicy foods" that she tried—for the first time in her life—to eat with chopsticks. Wilfried Lübke remembered fondly "the exquisite supply of foodstuffs and first-class construction materials" that were available in North Korea. But these casual, everyday contacts were partially overshadowed by his encounters with Kim Il Sung, "who frequently sat together with the Germans in their living quarters and debated for hours with the leader of the work group. The personality cult that we have today didn't exist then. One time he shook my hand and said 'Keep it up, comrade!'"[80] The Lübkes often related their Korean experiences to their daughter Britta-Susann, who grew up with these stories as well as photos of Buddhist temples, Eight-Dragon-

Mountain, and Thousand-Moon-River. In 2002, she accompanied her father on a trip back to North Korea, which she documented carefully for Radio Bremen. Their former Korean acquaintances Park and Zang were no longer alive, and the country did not have the same dynamism that Lübke remembered. It was like "returning to an empty house."[81] The story of the *Hamhungers* and the *Tokils* had become a chapter in the history of two countries that no longer existed.[82]

The history of East Germany's brief presence in Hamhung was in the news again in 2008 as a reminder of the pain caused by the Cold War division of the world. The same year that the first team of East Germans arrived in Hamhung, a twenty-year-old North-Korean student named Ok Geun Hong arrived in East Germany. While studying chemistry at Friedrich Schiller University in Jena, he met eighteen-year-old Renate Kleinle. The two were married in February 1960. Their first child was born in June of that year, and a second pregnancy soon followed. However, in April 1961, Hong and 350 other Korean students were recalled—with only two days' notice—to North Korea. The couple corresponded until early 1963, when he was no longer allowed to write. Renate's repeated efforts to maintain contact with her husband went nowhere until early 2007, when the North Korean government finally informed the German embassy in Pyongyang that her husband was still alive and living in Hamhung.

Although the North Korean government initially refused to allow the couple to meet, in August 2007 Renate Hong traveled to Seoul, hoping that the couple's case would be discussed at the second summit between the North and the South, which was to be held in Pyongyang in October 2007. She asked the president of South Korea to deliver her letter to Kim's son and successor, Kim Jong Il. In the letter, she pleaded premier Kim "I wish my husband, Hong Ok-gun, would have a chance to see his two sons, who are now grown-ups... If it is impossible for my husband to come to Germany, I would be more than happy to visit to meet him. Can I expect support from you, Mr. Chairman?"[83] Finally, in July 2008—after a separation of forty-seven years—Renate Hong, then seventy-one, arrived with her two sons in Pyongyang to meet seventy-four-year old Hong Ok Geun. It is astonishing to see the many different levels—the local, the national, the global, and the human—intersecting in this story of East German assistance to Hamhung, of the two divided countries, and of the global Cold War. The history of this one couple is part of a much larger story—in this case, the story of the Sino-Soviet split that ended the relationship between North Korea and East Germany and, almost half a century later, of the efforts of the two Koreas to overcome the legacy of the Cold War and of the two Hongs to heal the wounds it left.

Dr. **Young-Sun Hong** is Associate Professor of History at State University of New York-Stony Brook. She is the author of *Welfare, Modernity and the Weimar State* (Princeton University Press) as well as *Cold War Germany, the Third World, and the Global Humanitarian Regime* (Cambridge University Press).

# Notes

1. Kim Il Sung to Otto Grotewohl (1 July 1954), BAB NY/4090/481. See also Notes (7 July 1954), BAB DL2/4423. For speculation on the exact origins of East Germany's Hamhung project, see Rüdiger Frank, "Lessons from the Past: The First Wave of Developmental Assistance to North Korea and the German Reconstruction of Hamhùng," *Pacific Focus* 23, no. 1 (2008): 55–57.
2. When Ho launched the first Three Year Plan, Kim Il Sung visited Hanoi, where he spoke on economic development in North Korea to some seventy thousand Vietnamese who had gathered at Ba Dinh Square, where Ho's mausoleum now stands. After Kim's speech, Ho rallied the crowd by asking "Workers, peasants, armymen, intellectuals and youth, are you resolved to launch a friendly emulation with the Korean people?" After a receiving a resounding "Yes!" Ho and the audience all sang "Solidarity Is Might." "Hanoi Mass Rally Welcomes Korean Government Delegation," in *Everlasting Friendship Between Korean, Chinese and Vietnamese Peoples: Documents on Goodwill Visits of the D.P.R.K. Government Delegation to China and Viet-Nam* (Pyongyang: Foreign Languages Publishing House, 1959), 219.
3. *Postwar Rehabilitation and Development of the National Economy of D.P.R.K.* (Pyongyang, 1957), 8.
4. Arkadi Perventsev, "A Few Weeks' Stay in Korea," in *Korea through the Eyes of Foreigners,* ed. n.a. (Pyongyang: Foreign Languages Pub. House, 1957), 42.
5. Frank, "Lessons from the Past," 46–74. Frank's interviews revealed that many East Germans felt that "it never was the same again as in the early days of the Korea aid program," Ibid., 52, n. 16. See also Rüdiger Frank, *Die DDR und Nordkorea: Der Wiederaufbau der Stadt Hamhung von 1954-1962* (Aachen: Shaker Verlag, 1996).
6. Korea-Hilfsausschuß, "Überblick" (9 June 1952), BAB NY/4090/481. In November 1954 the Koreahilfsausschuß was renamed the "Solidarity Committee for Korea and Vietnam."
7. Walter Ulbricht to Grotewohl (6 August 1953), and Anton Ackermann to Grotewohl (11 August 1953), in BAB NY/4090/481. See also Charles K. Armstrong, "'Fraternal Socialism': The International Reconstruction of North Korea, 1953-62," *Cold War History* 5, no. 2 (2005): 161–87; Odd Arne Westad, *The Global Cold War: Third World Interventions and the Makings of Our Times* (New York: Cambridge University Press, 2007), 66ff.; Deborah A. Kaple, "Soviet Advisors in China in the 1950s," in *Brothers in Arms: The Rise and Fall of the Sino-Soviet Alliance, 1945-1963,* ed. Odd Arne Westad (Washington, D.C.: Woodrow Wilson Center Press, 1998).
8. "Die ökonomischen Beziehungen der Koreanischen Volksdemokratischen Republik zu den Ländern des sozialistischen Lagers," BAB NY/4090/481.

9. "Materialzusammenstellung über die Hilfe der befreundeten Länder für den Wiederaufbau der Volkswirtschaft in der KVDR," (24 January 1956), AAA MfAA, A/7013, and Fischer, "Aktenvermerk, betr. Visite beim … Kim Ir Sen," (5 August 1954), AAA MfAA, A/5575.

10. Fendler, "The Korean War (1950-1953), 49–60, especially 55. For example, approximately 900 Korean workers were sent to Czechoslovakia, and 1,000 children and students were sent to Hungary, though they were recalled immediately after the 1956 uprising there.

11. The terms of trade contained in these agreements invariably favored the donor country. On this last point see Martin Rudner, "East European Aid to Asian Developing Countries: The Legacy of the Communist Era," *Modern Asian Studies* 30, no. 1 (1996): 1–28, and Jude Howell, "The End of an Era: The Rise and Fall of G.D.R. Aid," *The Journal of Modern African Studies* 32, no. 02 (1994): 305–28. Kim refused to join COMECON because he regarded unequal terms of trade as a sign of dependency.

12. Max Zimmering, "As a Guest to the Land of Mountains and Rivers," in *Korea through the Eyes of Foreigners,* 16, 22.

13. "Informationsmaterial über die Handelsbeziehungen" (1952–56), BAB NY/4090/ 481, "Delegationsleiter Protokoll" (January–February, 1956), BAB DL2/4407, "Aktennotiz" (15 July 1957), BAB DL2/1686; Balázs Szalontai, "'You Have No Political Line of Your Own:' Kim Il Sung and the Soviets, 1953-1964," *CWIHP Bulletin,* no. 14/15 (Winter 2003–Spring 2004): 93.

14. Kim's suspicions of foreign powers were reinforced by his experiences with the Soviet Union and China in the fall of 1950, when both Stalin and Mao threatened to abandon North Korea and leave the country to face UN forces alone. See Kathryn Weathersby, "Stalin, Mao and the End of the Korean War," in Westad, ed., *Brothers in Arms.*

15. Joshua Barker, "Beyond Bandung: Developmental Nationalism and (Multi)Cultural Nationalism in Indonesia," *Third World Quarterly* 29, no. 3 (2008): 521–40; Balázs Szalontai, *Kim Il Sung in the Khrushchev Era: Soviet-DPRK relations and the Roots of North Korean Despotism, 1953-1964,* in Cold War International History Project Series (Stanford, CA: Stanford University Press, 2005); Sumit Sarkar, "Nationalism and Poverty: Discourses of Development and Culture in 20th Century India," *Third World Quarterly* 29, no. 3 (2008): 429–45.

16. Kim Il Sung, Report of the Central Committee of the Workers' Party of Korea to the Third Party Congress (held in April 1956), in *Postwar Rehabilitation and Development of the National Economy of D.P.R.K.* (Pyongyang, 1957), 10. See also Kim, *Report on the 10th Anniversary of the 15 August Liberation of Chosun by the Glorious Soviet Army* (Pyongyang, 1955).

17. Heonik Kwon, "North Korea's Politics of Longing," *Critical Asian Studies* 42, no. 1 (2010): 2–25; Heonik Kwon, *The Other Cold War* (New York: Columbia University Press, 2010), 48–53, 90–116; Bernd Schaefer, "Weathering the Sino-Soviet Conflict: The GDR and North Korea, 1949–1989," *CWIHP Bulletin,* no. 14/15 (Winter 2003–Spring 2004); Szalontai, "'You Have No Political Line of Your Own'."

18. Stichwortprotokoll (8 June 1956), BAB NY/4090/481.

19. On the rebuilding of Pyongyang, see Armstrong, "'Fraternal Socialism'," 171–76.
20. Meloh/Baustab Korea, "Informationsmaterial über die Durchführung der Hilfe der Deutschen Demokratischen Republik beim Aufbau der Stadt Hamhung" (1955), BAB NY/4090/481.
21. Hafrang to Heinrich Rau (14 January 1955), BAB, DL2/4423, Minutes of a Baustab Korea meeting (28 March 1955), BAB DL2/4398, and Baustab Korea to Präsidium des Ministerrats (27 June 1962), BAB DL2/4408.
22. "Verordnung des Ministerkabinetts über die Bildung einer Kommission für den Wiederaufbau der Stadt Chamchyng [sic]" (7 March 1955), AAA MfAA A/10211.
23. Fischer, "Aktenvermerk, betr. Visite beim … Kim Ir Sen am 5. August 1954" (5 August 1954), AAA MfAA, A/5575.
24. In January 1957, the Construction Trust No. 18 consisted of some 3,300 primarily female workers. Chair of the Korean Democratic Women's Organization of the Construction Trust No. 18 to Frauenbund des VEB Bau-Union Hoyerswerda (21 January 1957), and director of Ham Nam Bautrust to director of VEB Bau-Union (22 June 1957), both in BAB DY/30/IV2/6.06/21.
25. Secretary of the Korean Workers' Party at the construction trust No. 18 to his counterpart at the VEB Bau-Union Hoyerswerda (21 January 1957), BAB DY/30/IV2/6.06/21.
26. Präßler, Quarterly Report (April 1956), BAB DY36/1176, and Minutes of a staff meeting (12 May 1955), BAB DL2/4398.
27. Minutes of a staff meeting (29 October 1955), BAB DL2/4398.
28. Präßler, Quarterly Report (April 1956), BAB DY36/1176.
29. Vorschlag für deutsche Kader: Strukturplan "Bauindustrie…" (3 January 1955), BAB DL2/1686.
30. Selbmann, Jahresbericht für 1955, BAB DL2/4411.
31. "Erinnerung. Hartmut Colden (1915-1982)," authored in January 1979, BAB Sgy30/2222. Doehler was one of the persons accused of moral misconduct. He was recalled to East Germany, but then sent back to North Korea, where he was once again accused of misconduct toward Korean women and toward Koreans in general. Protocol (26 May 1955), DL2/4398, and DAG to ambassador Fischer (6 May 1957), BAB DL2/4402. The fact that both Selbmann and Grotewohl were related to high-level politicians created the impression among team members that management was immune to criticism and that grievances, especially on the part of skilled workers, would not be looked on favorably.
32. Hubert Matthes, "Hugo Namslauer zum Gedenken," *Studienarchiv Umweltgeschichte* 5 (1999): 31–32; http://www.arbeitskreis-konfrontationen.de/Kunst_als_Zeugnis/Erinnerungskulturen/Ravensbrueck (accessed 12 June 2012).
33. http://www.hermsdorf-regional.de/ehemalige/praessler-horst/start.html (accessed 12 June 2012).
34. Wolfgang Bauer, Reportage: "Die letzte Stadt der DDR. Ein Besuch in Hamhung," http://www.wolfgang-bauer.info/pages/reportagen/nordkorea/nordkorea.html (accessed 12 June 2012).
35. Präßler, Note (14 May 1956), BAB, DL2/4402.
36. "Entwicklung der DAG Hamhung," BAB, DL2/4402.

37. Minutes (3 October 1955), BAB DL2/4398, Baustab, Note (25 October 1955), BAB DL2/4422, and "Collective Resolution" (1 August 1957), and DAG to Guhlich (8 August 1957), BAB DY/30/IV2/6.06/21.

38. Rechenschaftsbericht (8 July 1955), BAB DY36/1176, Report to Tille (12 July 1956), BAB DY36/1176, Stasch to Josef Lux (13 July 1957), BAB DY/30/IV 2/6.06/20, and Präßler, Jahresschlußbericht für 1957 (20 January 1958), BAB DL2/4397.

39. Jahresbericht der DAG Hamhung für 1955, BAB DL2/4411, Rudi Guhlich, Memo (25 October 1955), BAB DL2/4422, and Minutes of Belegschaftsversammlung (3 April 1957), BAB DL2/4398.

40. Hamhunger Heimatreportage, No. 2 (26 October 1959), BAB DL2/4421.

41. Minutes of a staff meeting (12 May 1955), BAB DL2/4398.

42. Minutes of DAG staff meetings (26 May 1955, 1 and 3 October 1955), BAB DL2/4398, Baustab, Notes on interviews with the Germans who had just returned from Korea (18 and 25 October 1955), BAB DL2/4422, and Minutes of meeting (3 April 1957), BAB DL2/4398.

43. Frank, *Die DDR und Nordkorea*, 35–36.

44. Quoted in Kim Myun, "East Germay's Hamhung Construction Project," *Minjog* 21 (1 June 2005), http://www.minjog21.com/news/read.php?idxno=1815.

45. Among the extensive materials documenting these problems, see Minutes of direction meetings on 24 and 27 June, 6 November 1955, all in BAB DL2/4398.

46. Farmers were subjected to "excessive forced deliveries" of up to 50 percent of the crop in 1955. Both domestic pressure and urging from Moscow forced the North Korean government to invest more in agriculture. See reports by the Hungarian embassy in Hamhung to the Hungarian Foreign Ministry (13 April 1955, 10 May 1955, and 17 August 1955), *CWIHP Bulletin,* no. 14/15 (Winter 2003–Spring 2004): 107–10, and Szalontai, "'You Have No Political Line of Your Own'," 90.

47. Minutes of staff meeting (10 June 1955), BAB DL2/4398.

48. Guhlich, Note (25 October 1955), BAB DL2 /4422.

49. Minutes of staff meeting (3 April 1957), BAB DL2/4398.

50. Guhlich to Präßler (2 September 1957), BAB DL2/4402.

51. DAG to Rau (10 July 1957), BAB DL2/4416.

52. Manfred Nutz, *Stadtentwicklung in Umbruchsituationen* (Stuttgart: F. Steiner, 1998), 75.

53. Christine Hannemann, *Die Platte: Industrialisierter Wohnungsbau in der DDR* (Wiesbaden: Vieweg, 1996), 61ff.

54. Nutz, *Stadtentwicklung in Umbruchsituationen,* 72.

55. Report on the First Baukonferenz (no date, but presumably February 1956), BAB DL2/4426.

56. DAG, "Gedankenkonzeption" (18 December 1956), BAB DL2/4416.

57. DAG, Quarterly Report, 1. Quarter 1956 (April 1956), BAB DY36/1176, and Präßler, "Expose der Deutschen Arbeitsgruppe Hamhung über Erweiterung der Aufgaben auf die Städte: Hungnam—Bongun" (10 January 1956), BAB DL2/4416. These figures quietly glossed over the greater degree of complexity involved in the construction of the Soviet plant.

58. DAG to Rau (10 July 1957), BAB DL2/4416.
59. Protokoll über die Parteileitungssitzung (23 November 1957), BAB DY/30/ IV2/6.06/20.
60. Präßler, Jahresschlußbericht (20 January 1958), BAB DL2/4397.
61. Präßler, "Gedankenkonzepten zum Beschluss des Zentralkomitees der Partei der Arbeit Koreas…," (18 December 1956), BAB DL2/4416.
62. DAG, Quarterly Report (April 1956), BAB DY36/1176.
63. Szalontai, *Kim Il Sung in the Khrushchev Era*, 121–23.
64. "Protokoll der Parteileitungssitzung vom 3.12.1957" (4 December 1957), and Stasch to ZKdSED (6 December 1957), both in BAB DY/30/IV2/6.06/20.
65. Choi Hak-Su, 평양시간 (Pyongyang Hour) (Pyongyang, 1976).
66. *Pyongyang Hour,* 157–58.
67. *Pyongyang Hour,* 127, 156–58.
68. Ibid., 37, 179.
69. Protocol of a meeting with Kim Il Sung (1 February 1958), BAB DL2/4416.
70. The Polish embassy, "Note" on the Korean Five Year Plan (18 June 1958). WWC, North Korea International Documentation Project. Document Reader. "New Evidence on North Korea's Chollima Movement and First Five-Year Plan (1957-1961)," ed. James Person (February 2009).
71. Foerster to Fischer (1 July 1958), DL2/4416; Förster, Semi-annual report (28 July 1958), DL2/4397 (Teil 1).
72. Präßler to Gulich (24 May 1957), DY/30/IV2/6.06/21. Leitung-Kollektiv, DAG to Guhlich (24 June 1957), and DY/30/IV2/6.06/21. Guhlich to Lux (Abt. Bauwesen beim ZKdSED) (29 June 1957), BAB DL2/4402.
73. Management Collective DAG (Präßler, Stasch, Hessel) to Rudi Guhlich (24 June 1957), DL2/4402.
74. Data on the makeup of the East German mission taken from annual reports, 1956-59, in BAB DL/4397 and BAB DL2/4416.
75. Baustab Korea, IA, to Guhlich, director of the Baustab Korea (8 November 1960), BAB, DL2/4399.
76. Letter of 5 November 1960, cited in Schneidewind to Schwab (11 November 1960), WWC.
77. Baustab Korea to the Präsidium of Ministerrat (27 June 1962), BAB, DL2/4408.
78. Baustab Korea to the Presidium of the Ministerrat (27 June 1962), DL2/4408.
79. Wolfgang Bauer, Reportage: "Die letzte Stadt der DDR. Ein Besuch in Hamhung," http://www.wolfgang-bauer.info/pages/reportagen/nordkorea/nordkorea.html (accessed 20 July 2012).
80. Ibid.
81. Britta-Susann Lübke, "Das Märchenland meiner Kindheit. Die Rückkehr meines Vaters nach Hamhung (2002)," in *Nordkorea. Einblicke in ein rätselhaftes Land,* ed. Christoph Moeskes (Berlin: Ch. Links, 2004), 138, 144.
82. http://www.koreaverband.de/kultur/film/filmTip.html, "Nordkorea—eine Wiederkehr. Der Traum vom Tausend-Mond-Fluß," broadcast on 30 June 2003 (22.10—23.40 on arte). Ein Film von Britta Lübke (Eine Produktion von Radio Bremen für Arte D/Nordkorea 2003).

83. The couple's story was widely covered in the press. See, for example, Jack Kim, "After 46 years, couple hope to meet again in North Korea," *The Guardian* (24 August 2007), and Cho Sang-Hun, "German Woman Seeks Reunion with North Korean Husband," *New York Times,* 22 August 2007. See also Ryu Kwon-ha, "North Korean Husband of German Woman is Alive," *JoongAng Ilbo* (13 February 2007); Wieland Wagner, "Eine Liebe damals in Jena," *Der Spiegel* 36 (2007): 134; "Couple Reunited in North Korea after 47 years"; *New York Times* (6 August 2006), "North Korea Allows a Separated Couple to Reunite after 47 years," *JoongAng Ilbo* (5 August 2008). Hong Ok Geun was remarried and had three children in Hamhung.

## Bibliography

Armstrong, Charles K. "'Fraternal Socialism': The International Reconstruction of North Korea, 1953-62." *Cold War History* 5, no. 2 (2005): 161–87.

Barker, Joshua. "Beyond Bandung: Developmental Nationalism and (Multi)Cultural Nationalism in Indonesia." *Third World Quarterly* 29, no. 3 (2008): 521–40.

Frank, Rüdiger. *Die DDR und Nordkorea: Der Wiederaufbau Der Stadt Hamhung Von 1954-1962.* Aachen: Shaker Verlag, 1996.

———. "Lessons from the Past: The First Wave of Developmental Assistance to North Korea and the German Reconstruction of Hamhùng." *Pacific Focus* 23, no. 1 (2008): 46–74.

Hannemann, Christine. *Die Platte: Industrialisierter Wohnungsbau in Der DDR.* Wiesbaden: Vieweg, 1996.

Howell, Jude. "The End of an Era: The Rise and Fall of G.D.R. Aid." *The Journal of Modern African Studies* 32, no. 02 (1994): 305–28.

Kaple, Deborah A. "Soviet Advisors in China in the 1950s." In *Brothers in Arms: The Rise and Fall of the Sino-Soviet Alliance, 1945-1963,* ed. Odd Arne Westad, 117–40. Washington, D.C.: Woodrow Wilson Center Press, 1998.

Kwon, Heonik. "North Korea's Politics of Longing." *Critical Asian Studies* 42, no. 1 (2010): 3–24.

———. *The Other Cold War.* New York: Columbia University Press, 2010.

Lübke, Britta-Susann. "Das Märchenland Meiner Kindheit. Die Rückkehr Meines Vaters Nach Hamhung (2002)." In *Nordkorea. Einblicke in ein rätselhaftes Land,* ed. Christoph Moeskes, 88–98. Berlin: Ch. Links, 2004.

Nutz, Manfred. *Stadtentwicklung in Umbruchsituationen.* Stuttgart: F. Steiner, 1998.

Perventsev, Arkadi. "A Few Weeks' Stay in Korea." In *Korea through the Eyes of Foreigners,* ed. n.a., 106. Pyongyang: Foreign Languages Pub. House, 1957.

Rudner, Martin. "East European Aid to Asian Developing Countries: The Legacy of the Communist Era." *Modern Asian Studies* 30, no. 1 (1996): 1–28.

Sarkar, Sumit. "Nationalism and Poverty: Discourses of Development and Culture in 20th Century India." *Third World Quarterly* 29, no. 3 (2008): 429–45.

Schaefer, Bernd. "Weathering the Sino-Soviet Conflict: The GDR and North Korea, 1949–1989." *CWIHP Bulletin,* no. 14/15 (Winter 2003–Spring 2004): 25–38.

Szalontai, Balázs. *Kim Il Sung in the Khrushchev Era: Soviet-DPRK Relations and the Roots of North Korean Despotism, 1953-1964.* Cold War International History Project Series. Stanford, CA: Stanford University Press, 2005.

————. "'You Have No Political Line of Your Own': Kim Il Sung and the Soviets, 1953-1964." *CWIHP Bulletin,* no. 14/15 (Winter 2003–Spring 2004): 87–103.

Weathersby, Kathryn. "Stalin, Mao and the End of the Korean War." In *Brothers in Arms: The Rise and Fall of the Sino-Soviet Alliance, 1945-1963,* ed. Odd Arne Westad, 90–116. Washington, D.C.: Woodrow Wilson Center Press, 1998.

Westad, Odd Arne. *The Global Cold War: Third World Interventions and the Making of Our Times.* New York: Cambridge University Press, 2007.

## Chapter 3

# Between Fighters and Beggars

## Socialist Philanthropy and the Imagery of Solidarity in East Germany

*Gregory Witkowski*

While East Germany officially rejected the colonial past of imperial Germany, the government and its people continued to define themselves in a national and racial hierarchy in juxtaposition to the developing world. One can see this clearly in the campaigns of socialist philanthropy and solidarity across the forty years of the GDR's history. The following article examines three major East German charitable collections for the developing world: the state-directed "Solidarity Fund," (*Solidaritätsfond*), the Protestant "Bread for the World," (*Brot für die Welt*), and the Catholic "Need in the World" (*Not in der Welt*). The Solidarity Fund attempted to overcome the traditional power relationship between donor and recipient through the narrative of solidarity. Yet the concept of solidarity was common to both Christian and communist ideology, and the churches drew upon it themselves in their own rhetoric. Indeed, all three collections declared a common cause with recipients that respected their needs and saw aid as a way of unifying a community, as well as overcoming the divides of distance and wealth that separated people.

Portrayals of need are important in compelling donations to charitable collections. The images used in the campaigns provide a good measure of the type of portrayals that appealed to East German authorities who approved them and individual citizens, who donated money. As such, they represent both official and unofficial views of the developing world. These collections, especially the church ones, appealed to a broad public, in contrast to many international interactions that were primarily led by youth.

This essay begins by following patterns of giving to the Solidarity Funds and unpacking the imagery used in campaigns. The rhetoric of the Solidarity Funds invoked memories of war and reconstruction for German populations and sought to transcend (not always successfully) the established visual conventions of Western charity. The Christian collections adhered more to the symbolic vocabulary of need and deprivation in the nonwhite world, while augmenting their calls for donations with attention to the legacies of colonialism and the need to recompense for aspects of German history. All groups involved were surprisingly frank about the function of charity not only for the receiving population but also as a means of building internal solidarity within the GDR itself.

## The Solidarity Fund: Moral Barometer and Tool of Foreign Policy

The communist Solidarity Committee developed out of the working groups created in the 1950s to raise awareness about specific communist independence movements and international struggles, most notably in North Korea (see Hong's contribution in this volume).[1] The SED's Secretariat initiated a more formal structure with a directive in January 1960 that required the mass organization "National Front" to organize the collection of workplace donations to support leftist national and independence movements in Africa and elsewhere. Seven months after the first collection, the SED formed a specific committee on which all of the major mass organizations had representatives. Consisting of a seven-person Secretariat and a forty-person committee, the solidarity committee drew together representatives from state ministries, mass organizations, and party members.[2] Drawing upon traditions of working class solidarity that stretched back to the nineteenth century, this committee aimed to support independence movements in the developing world and to secure the "united anti-imperialist front of the nations." The "Statute of the Afro-Asian Solidarity Committee in the GDR" declared that it sought "the continuing deepening of ties between the population of the GDR and the peoples of Africa and Asia in the spirit of international solidarity and friendship among peoples."[3]

The mission statement reflected the Marxist-Leninist world view of East German leaders. It linked global poverty with "imperialist" economic and political exploitation and called for solidarity with those in need. This ideological position saw an improvement in this global system through an increase in public consciousness and the development of international solidarity. What is perhaps surprising is that the statutes dictated that such a change in consciousness needed to occur in the GDR. That is, the change needed to happen among donors and not recipients. One of the key tasks of the committee was that it should "advance and develop the population of the GDR's thoughts of solidarity with the people of Africa and Asia fighting for freedom and national independence."[4] While the statutes go on to add a

Cold War character and include "all of Germany" in its target audience, they clearly emphasize educating donors as well as helping recipients.[5]

The Solidarity Committee organized collections in factories or streets and the purchase of stamps or other small memorabilia, which required public displays of approval and therefore included greater public pressure. As the official GDR "political dictionary" defined it, solidarity meant "mutual support and commitment, the willingness to help and sacrifice," which was "a basic principle of the working class and all progressive forces."[6] Posters and other advertisements placed in factories and public places also called for bank transfers of money to the fund, which could be done privately. These calls were part of a much larger media effort related to the call for solidarity. A search for the term "solidarity" in a database of the official SED newspaper, *Neues Deutschland,* shows that from 1961 through 1989, the term appeared in at least 600 different articles annually. The high point of usage came in 1973 when it appeared in 2,207 articles.[7] Given the government's coordination of all media, similar emphases are likely to be found in radio and television broadcasts. As the Solidarity Committee presented its appeal, East Germany was saturated with calls for solidarity with those in need.

In fact, the early success of the collection came from more general reporting. The outrage incited by the Sharpeville Massacre in 1960, when South African police shot at defenseless black protesters, helped garner support for the program immediately. The trade union (FDGB) took a leadership role in this regard. It reported on Africa in its daily newspaper *Die Tribüne* regularly and declared that all of the money collected in Solidarity stamps in April 1960 would go to support Africa. FDGB campaign imagery depicted Africa as a space of both tradition and modernity. One of the stamps included a woodcut image of a smiling dark-skinned man drumming in front of a field of crops with distant figures, one with a child on her back, apparently pounding yam next to a grass hut. Another from the same era showed a black woman in a wrap walking with a book in front of a backdrop of modern functionalist high-rise apartment buildings. After the first wave of decolonization in the early 1960s, the imagery was less violent and confrontational than a stamp from 1959, which showed balled black hands in chains hovering over a silhouette of the African continent.

Donations from the FDGB to the fund remained considerable. For instance, in 1962, the FDGB donated 1.75 million East German Marks to the Solidarity Fund. By comparison, only 146,000 Marks were collected from individuals.[8] While there was a bank account to which people could transfer money, most donors gave at the workplace. Like with all such collections, workers felt pressure to donate. This demand was, of course, not limited to the GDR. Other workplace-giving collections likewise placed demands on workers to donate but the degree of pressure and feeling of compulsion was much greater in East Germany.[9] As one activist said, as an SED member it was "out of the question" not to donate.[10]

It would be wrong to assume, however, that there was not a feeling of concern for the developing world or a desire to create solidarity. Evidence of this can be found not only in the Solidarity Fund efforts but also in both church and later student efforts to collect for the developing world. By 1989, the Solidarity Fund had reportedly collected a total of 3.7 billion East German Marks for causes throughout the world.[11] In fact, the fund was so successful that the SED Secretariat reduced the amount that the trade union and others should donate in 1982 and lowered the denominations of the stamps sold by the Solidarity Committee. East Germans continued to give money at a high rate despite this change designed to lower collections.[12] There are a number of possible explanations for this trend. Donors may have simply continued to give the same amount out of habit. The declining East German economy in the 1980s provided fewer options for consumers to spend their money and so giving was less of a sacrifice because consumers found few goods worth buying. These seem plausible as explanations of the giving patterns but I would argue that the Solidarity Fund's literature also succeeded in raising people's feeling of social responsibility and sense of solidarity with those in need. This sense of social justice, which was also increasing in regard to human rights within the GDR, led many to continue to donate even as requests for donations declined.

The Solidarity Committee used the funds collected to support African, Asian, and Latin American partner governments as well as insurgents. It focused especially on Cold War hot spots including Vietnam, Nicaragua, Chile, Angola, and Mozambique. In doing so, the committee supported areas of international conflict, on the one hand, and established donations as a moral barometer, on the other. In this way, the committee's work was as much about its influence at home as its work abroad. The committee sought to construct an identity of donors (and the GDR) on the side of moral righteousness.

In terms of a domestic sense of righteousness, the focus on Southeast Asia seems particularly noteworthy. With the onset of large-scale American intervention in Vietnam, the Solidarity Committee established a special commission for Vietnam. Sending support to Vietnam was a useful propaganda tool for the GDR as it linked the West German government with the United States and the destruction of the war.[13] The commission was successful in garnering support for its activities. From its inception in 1965 through 1968, the Solidarity Committee sent goods valued at 75 million East German Marks to Vietnam. These figures increased after the Tet Offensive in

1968.[14] After the war, the Solidarity Fund continued to support Vietnam, emphasizing the buildup of infrastructure and reminding East Germans of the destruction that the West had caused in that nation.

## The Imagery of the Solidarity Fund: War Memories and Reconstruction

Images serve a significant function in collection campaigns. The imagery used in campaigns for Vietnam and other nations helps us to see the particularity of the East German approach to international solidarity, even as they distinguished themselves by not appealing directly for contributions. For example, the Solidarity Committee sponsored a competition among artists in 1967 to create posters that emphasized the resolve, righteousness, and optimism of the Vietnamese. Artists were told explicitly not to show war victims, crying children, or mothers. No weapons were to be depicted either. Finally, and perhaps most importantly, the artists were told not to directly solicit from donors. Instead, these posters were designed to inform and educate. In the end, the Solidarity Committee strayed from these constraints in other campaigns, including weapons, crying children, and mothers in need in its campaigns. In this sense, the creation of a distinct socialist aesthetic faced the challenge of overcoming inherited visual conventions of charity. Even still, two constants remained: the messages that the human spirit of the recipients was not daunted by their task and that the Solidarity Fund was more about connecting an ideology with a cause than about soliciting donations for that cause.[15] The following section analyzes the publications of the Solidarity Committee to see how they illustrated need and sought to educate East Germans about the Committee's priorities for support. The campaigns emphasized points of connection whenever possible even as they created an image of the recipients as essentially different and distant.

The committee played on the recent German experience of destruction during the Second World War in its displays of support for the Vietnamese. One poster from 1972 shows a map of Vietnam, Laos, and Cambodia. The remainder of the space is occupied by images and text, all illustrating the point of the slogan that "Solidarity aids victory!" Among the texts is a newspaper clipping that carries the headline "Continuous American Attacks." Another image illustrates the tonnage of American bombs dropped on Vietnam during that conflict as well as the much smaller number of bombs dropped in Europe during the Second World War. Finally the poster juxtaposes photos of American warplanes over the map of Southeast Asia with two anguished children hugging each other in the lower right-hand corner.[16]

Another poster from 1972 is powerful in its simplicity. It depicts a young Vietnamese girl wearing a helmet that is clearly too large for her head (see photograph in Schwenkel's chapter below). The size of the girl and the helmet are emphasized by placing the girl at the bottom of the poster and only showing her from the shoulders up. Her face expresses clear concern. At the top of the poster appears the slogan again: "Solidarity aids victory."[17] The image gestures clearly at the effects of the war on children. In 1971, about 14 percent of the East German population had experienced the Second World War as children.[18] These posters drew upon these powerful formative experiences with war to convince them that the war in Vietnam was equally horrible. In all of these posters, the Solidarity Committee had to walk a fine line. Clearly, many older East Germans would have still associated the war with the vicious fighting on the Eastern Front. As such, the images did not portray ground combat. Instead, they emphasized bombing, which in the German experience was carried out more by the Americans and British than the Soviets. The concentration on children and women was part of a larger narrative too but seemed especially appropriate here given the German experience of war. Through these images, the Solidarity Committee established a clear contrast between the destruction of Southeast Asia caused by "U.S. aggression" and West German "neo-colonialism," on the one hand, and East German donors and the GDR, which would help rebuild the region, on the other.[19]

In general, philanthropic organizations use portrayals of recipients to generate donations. In its portrayal of Vietnam, the Solidarity Fund was able to draw, all at once, on the emotional connection that East Germans would have with those suffering from war, highlight the role of the common enemy (the United States, Federal Republic, and Western capitalism) in creating that destruction, and claim the moral high ground as the German state that was helping these victims. Of course, the Solidarity Fund played only one part in a much larger East German narrative about Vietnam. One of the earliest images of support for Vietnam came in a 1966 film made by DEFA about blood donation, *400cm³*. This film wove together shots of East Germans donating blood with the wounded in Vietnam, linking them literally through bodily fluid. It received national and international attention.[20] *Neues Deutschland* linked Vietnam and calls for solidarity regularly. From 1965 to 1980, the SED mouthpiece published over 5,600 articles that discussed both Vietnam and solidarity.[21]

In collections for areas that were not directly suffering through war, portrayals of devastation and humanitarian need still formed an integral part of donor campaigns. Despite its declared position, in its publications the Solidarity Committee tended to feminize need or attribute it to the helplessness of children. A series of posters by the photographer Thomas Billhardt illustrates this trend. For instance, one poster is a photograph of an African woman wearing a traditional head wrap. She is holding her blanket-covered child up to her shoulder. As she looks over the baby at the viewer, one can make out a slight smile on her face. The background is out of focus but it is clear that she is outside. Superimposed are the words "Solidarity is Life for the African Peoples," forsaking national context or specificity for a vague reference to the continent as such.[22] The series by Billhardt included portrayals of Africa, Asia, Latin America, and the Middle East. Four of five posters featured women cradling babies in their arms adorned in traditional dress, marking them as culturally distinct from contemporary Europeans. All standing in the open air, the women peer directly at the viewer, showing resolve but also imploring for help. The last poster depicts a shirtless Latin American man holding a baby. In this case, the innocent baby rather than the man looks at the viewer.[23] The imagery evokes the helplessness of the developing world. It is not the man seeking help but rather the child.

Images of women and children in need conform to long-established conventions of humanitarian appeal. Yet the Solidarity Committee's posters also depicted stronger, often masculine, individuals ready to build socialism if given the chance. Indeed, it is in these images of men that East German publications deviate from norms of philanthropic representation in liberal capitalist contexts. The GDR had a different narrative of need, namely, the need for masculine fighters to bring about socialist revolution. The Solidarity Campaign generally avoided reproductions of weapons in its appeals but wanted to show strength. One placard had the slogan "Our Solidarity makes the People of Africa stronger." A number of men stand together in the image. The faces of young and old are firm and defiant and a young man in front stands with his arms on his hips.[24] A more specific call for help to Angola declared that the "Fight goes on." In this case, a young man whose face shows similar determination as the men depicted in the other posters gazes at the viewer. He is clothed in what appears to be a military uniform complete with a cap. Behind him one can see rows of similarly outfitted men.[25] While portrayals of Africans in Germany had shown the supposed dangers posed by black African men in the past, this new imagery is much more empowering for men. Also, unlike African women, men are not shown in traditional garb. Rather their attire indicates their commitment to modernity, which for the Solidarity Committee meant support of socialism. It is perhaps not surprising that the communists, who themselves had a tradition of fighting (from the KPD) that emphasized masculinity, would portray African fighters in a similar fashion. Still it is clear that these portrayals are much different from the traditional narratives for charitable donations rooted in portraits of despair and poverty. These individuals were poised to bring about change themselves.

Further images appealed to the possibility of rebuilding and the willingness of recipients to do so. For instance, an appeal from 1975 declares "Vietnam, Solidarity right now!" The image is a photograph of a young, happy Vietnamese couple standing in a field. A dirty shovel slung over a man's shoulder resembles the rifle he may have once carried. It is caked in mud, indicating that he had been working. The man engages the viewer by looking directly at the camera and smiling. One sees happy socialist workers here in the tradition of socialist realism. This couple is prepared to rebuild Vietnam through their hard work. Their modern dress also pointing to a new, more modern Vietnam even as their means of production remain more primitive.[26] Another poster draws on the German recollection of the so-called "women of the rubble," German women who gathered the remnants of buildings and rebuilt many structures after the Second World War. It depicts a bombed house with a Vietnamese woman framed in the middle. This example from 1973 called for solidarity to rebuild Vietnam.[27] Even in the Bilhardt series mentioned above, one sees essentially happy recipients (mother and child), who are not facing the extreme poverty depicted in Western and church literature.

The posters played on recent German experiences of war and destruction. They provided an opportunity for East Germans to show that they were now a rebuilt country that could aid other lands. Given public pressure to donate, it is difficult to determine the efficacy of such images in generating gifts, but these appeals were likely designed less to stimulate donations and more to educate donors. The vast majority of the donations came from organized giving through the FDGB so that the Solidarity Committee did not need to appeal to donors for funds. Their narrative thus reflected the educational goals in their mission statement. The Cold War provided the lens through which the Solidarity Committee portrayed global problems. While relating them back to experiences of Germans during the war, the Committee aimed to provide a vision of a socialist struggle against the aggression and imperialism of the West. Solidarity was the slogan through which they both separated themselves from the West and engaged with the world.

## Christian Solidarity: Dire Need and Christian Responsibility

The two major church collections, the Protestant "Bread for the World" and the Catholic "Need in the World," followed more traditional narratives of need but, like the Solidarity Committee, sought to use moral responsibility as a means to educate and engage East Germans. The collections emerged out of efforts in the FRG and followed a path similar to that of West German religious offerings, emphasizing the need of the recipient and the Christian obligation to help the poor. The East German funds remained separate from the West German collections and the church leadership downplayed any political overtones in their efforts. Still, a separation occurred between the Catholic and Protestant efforts in the West that may have been mirrored in the East.

East German churches primarily struggled to resist the encroachment of a political system with totalitarian aims and church leaders worried rightfully that any challenge in foreign affairs might lead the government to clamp down on them and doom their efforts. At the same time, the leadership of both the Catholic and Protestant institutions remained aware that their policy decisions in East Germany would affect their constituents in West Germany and beyond.[28] In implementing these campaigns for the developing world, the Catholic and Protestant churches did not cooperate extensively but rather each sought to defend its own prerogatives. The following section dissects the goals of two mainstream religious collections, arguing that they too were highly concerned with domestic mobilization as well as granting aid in the developing world.

During the Lenten season of 1959, the Catholic Church began to collect money in the FRG to combat poverty in developing nations under the name "Misereor." Protestant church officials met shortly thereafter to discuss similar efforts.[29] They wanted to demonstrate their concern for the poor and felt it important to show that the two confessions had similar priorities in terms of social service.[30] Although both the Catholic and Protestant churches had bishoprics that extended across the border separating East and West Germany, they took different approaches to this partition. The Catholic Church limited its campaign to the FRG. From the beginning, however, in the fall of 1959, the Protestant bishops from both sides of the intra-German border met in Berlin to complete initial plans for a collection in East and West Germany.[31] The East German representatives felt that their participation was critical and that they had much to offer even as all acknowledged the difficulties of cross-border collaboration. They realized that they needed to be careful, however, to keep their collection focused on benefactor need and not politics.

The Protestant churches placed a great deal of emphasis on choosing the apolitical name "Bread for the World." As Church Councilman Christian Berg described later: "One could bring this slogan to the Christian public as well as the critical and questioning world." The term bread had both a religious connotation (Christ having said: "I am the bread of life") but also fulfilled a fundamental human need for sustenance. In this way, the collection signaled that it was fulfilling both a basic and religious need. Its goal was to look throughout the "world," anywhere where there was need, a reality that was certainly possible when one combines the East and West German collections. For Berg, the smallest of the words, "for" was critical as well. It was "positive, helpful, constructive; the collection was not directed against anyone; completely and totally without an 'anti.'"[32] In this way, the collection was designed to mollify critics, including communist ones.

The ideology behind the campaign was one of equals or of solidarity. In fact, two other names, one that referenced the biblical beggar at the door, "Lazarus at Europe's Door," and the other that spoke of direct need, "Your Brothers are Hungry," were rejected as sounding too much like begging.[33] The mission statement for the campaign emphasized instead that the collection was partially out of thanks for the help received after the Second World War. It was a recognition of "collective responsibility" and a "practical show of Christian solidarity."[34]

Much like the Solidarity Fund, Bread for the World aimed to educate Germans and inspire their participation in church activities as well as raise money for the developing world. At the first organizational meeting, Church Councilor Christian Berg began by listing the goals of the campaign and its effects in Germany. These included educating East and West Germans about world hunger and providing an example to both German governments that German Protestants were willing to work to help the needy. This emphasis continued in the following years as the collection helped keep the church community active. As the Protestant bishops told their Catholic counterparts, "Concern for the needs of those outside (the GDR) increases the community's willingness to sacrifice and thereby their willingness to secure internal needs."[35] Thus, the collection served to mobilize church support within the GDR both in terms of active participation as well as increased donations for things such as church upkeep.

Bread for the World was highly successful at engaging donors. The first collection in 1959 garnered 4.8 million East German Marks, an impressive success given that the collection took place exclusively in the churches during the advent season. In fact, if one uses the official 1:1 exchange rate, this yield represented a greater amount per capita than in the FRG.[36] Over the first three years of Bread for the World in the GDR, it collected 11.8 Million DM East yet was able to distribute just over 4 million DM East in that same time.[37] For a few years, the church did not call officially for support for the collection in the GDR, but it still organized collections every other year even as it accumulated more money than it could distribute. Bread for the World thus became a symbolic collection for a time as it could not grant most funds, an unusual situation for charitable collections. Mobilization of parishioners, however, was an important goal that could be accomplished even without distributing the funds.

Church leaders faced a number of difficulties distributing donated funds. They could not transfer money as the East German Mark was not hard currency and a transfer to West German Marks was ruled out as too provocative. Thus, the Diaconia needed to cooperate with the state, which controlled the economy, in order to organize purchases and shipments of goods. This process required months of negotiation. State officials enlisted the aid of the East German Red Cross, a government-aligned agency with ties throughout the world via the International Red Cross, in order to maintain control of the shipments. The Diaconia and East German Red Cross agreed to mutually decide where to send donations. Recipients had control over how to use the goods they received.[38] In practice, the East German Red Cross sent donations only to states that maintained good relations with the GDR and rebuffed all other requests for aid. Church leaders seemed concerned to fund projects only in areas where Protestant representatives could assure them that the goods were received. While nonprofits generally are concerned with accountability in terms of verifying the use of goods by recipients, the worry in this case seemed to be as much about the state taking the goods as about the recipients misusing the aid.

Despite these hurdles, monies collected in the GDR for Bread for the World supported 38 projects in its first three years, from 1959 to 1962, including immediate assistance for catastrophes as well as long term developmental aid. Bread for the World supported disaster assistance after floods in Algeria. They sent blankets to Skopje, Yugoslavia, after an earthquake and materials to set up a hospital to help victims. They likewise supported a hospital in Peru.[39] They also sent medicine and other support to India. After an earthquake in Iran, they both delivered initial relief and helped with redevelopment by rebuilding a village. In virtually all cases, aid was reserved for communist and nonaligned countries. In total, Bread for the World funded fourteen projects in Asia, twelve in Africa and five in Latin America with the rest unnamed in its first three years.[40]

For its part, the Catholic Church was so concerned about any potential problems with the East German government that it rejected a collection in the East initially as too logistically complicated and too controversial domestically and internationally. In 1958, it began its collection, Misereor, only in the FRG. Catholic leaders were impressed with their returns in the FRG and watched the Protestant campaign in the GDR closely. In 1964, the bishops examined Bread for the World to consider whether it should start a similar campaign in the GDR. It discovered that the Diaconia found "noticeably positive effects" from the collection.[41] Despite this analysis, contradictory information and conflicting views among Catholic leaders meant that it would still take a number of years to begin a collection in the GDR. East German bishops argued that they did not want to be dependent on the Red Cross. Furthermore, they collected money and goods for needy Catholics in Eastern Europe already, including book collections sent to a Polish archdiocese. As such, there was less need for East Germans to take part in either of the Misereor or Adventiat collections started in the FRG.[42] Here too the primary interest seems to have been the donors as much as the recipients.

In the end, a combination of internal as well as external factors played key roles in the formation of the collection Need in the World. Externally, the church sought to assist the needy, primarily in colonies that had large Catholic congregations but that became nonaligned or communist in the postwar period (Algeria, Vietnam, India). This focus fit with SED hopes to gain diplomatic recognition or support for East Germany. Internally, lay Catholics, parish priests, and some church leaders (especially Msgr. Otto Gross) pressured the hierarchy for a collection.[43] In this, they were likely helped by the changes taking place in the Vatican under Pope John XXIII calling for more direct contact with parishioners' needs and with aid for the developing world.

After years of debate and negotiation, the East German Catholic Bishops began the collection in March 1968. They organized this effort separately from Misereor, clearly signifying the distinction by calling their East German collection "Need in the World."[44] In this way, they eliminated the direct biblical reference (and use of Latin) of Misereor and focused instead on the idea of providing help to the needy. The Catholic Church was less direct in its mission statement than the Protestant churches in setting goals for its donors but at a conference before the collection, the bishops discussed their goals. They declared that "Through this new collection our believers are given the opportunity to bear responsibility for the need in the world and at the same time to provide a return on the considerable aid that they themselves have received and receive."[45] In this case, the collection allowed donors to "repay their debts" by helping someone else instead of the person that helped them—thus "paying it forward," to invoke more recent terms. Here too the effort was placed on the donors. According to church leaders, this collection allowed East German Catholics to free themselves of a sense of responsibility through their serial reciprocity. It is an interesting statement in that East German churches and even individuals continued to receive donations from West Germans up until the end of the GDR, institutionally for the churches and for individuals in the ubiquitous packages sent by West

German relatives. This example of reciprocity fits with emphasis that church leaders placed upon East German donors in this effort.

The Catholic Church organized every aspect of the campaign including the purchase and shipment of goods with the money donated. Unlike the Protestants' campaign, Catholic relief efforts were free from the interference of the Red Cross or any other intermediary. The aid would be sent "from church to church" through the Catholic missions, Caritas. For the church, this appearance of independence was critical and one of the final obstacles to starting the collection. Archbishop Alfred Bengsch, whose Berlin diocese included both East and West Berlin, was especially concerned with appearing too close to the East German state.[46] In theory the state limited them to purchasing factory surpluses and Caritas in East Germany initially had difficulty finding goods. Catholic leaders, however, quickly secured needed goods by establishing personal connections with factory directors and paying cash for all deliveries.[47] Even as the economy contracted in the 1980s, their warehouse remained stocked.

## The Imagery of Christian Solidarity: Anti-colonialism and the Helpless Poor

The Catholic "Need in the World" raised 83 million DM East in twenty-one years, an impressive figure in that the Catholic population in the GDR hovered between 1 and 1.5 million, or around 10 percent of the total population.[48] Bread for the World collected 180 Million DM East over thirty years, a lower per capita rate but still substantial given that in the early years, collections were not publicized every year. The government limited advertising of the collections to within the churches and only permitted campaigns for collections during Advent. These collections were public to the extent that the donor could be observed giving money but generally donations were made in envelopes so that the amounts were unclear. In addition, individual donors contacted church officials with offers to give to the campaign, in some cases donations that equaled thousands of East German Marks.

While these figures were themselves impressive, the collections served as important factors in mobilizing donor support. To do so, the two campaigns initially emphasized the twin themes of need and helplessness, which they often attributed to women and children. Their depictions of need showed individuals in far more desperate situations than the imagery employed by the Solidarity Fund. It was a moral responsibility for Christians to help those in such desperate straits. An analysis of these images will indicate this trend. Unlike with the Solidarity Fund, the images available for these two collections are much less comprehensive so I focus on the few available. The analysis is compounded by the reality that in the 1980s, many of the posters were produced in the Federal Republic and sent to the GDR but it is not clear exactly which images were used. For Bread for the World, Western television and radio advertisements would also have been heard by the many East Germans who got their news and entertainment from Western stations.

When the East German Diaconia launched Bread for the World in 1959, it published a pamphlet to distribute at churches. In it, the missions declared that many of the 50 million children born each year worldwide died because of undernourishment. The pamphlet argued that "Christian Europe" had a responsibility for this problem because of its legacy of colonization.[49] The extent to which either government censors or communist views of colonialism influenced this message is not clear. Either way, it was a significant point of distinction from the West German collection. The West German collection appealed simply to the plight of the poor everywhere, comparing such suffering to the West German experience with poverty immediately after the Second World War. Anti-colonialism was a theme that Protestant publications in the GDR continued to employ. An editorial in one of the regional church newspapers pointed to the continued exploitation of the developing world even after the end of the colonial era. It spoke specifically of the German proclivity before the Second World War to buy what were referred to by Germans as "colonial goods" or items produced in the former colonies. The editorial used this tendency to link Germans to the continued exploitation of these lands well after Germany lost its colonies.[50] In employing this concept, Protestant leaders emphasized an interpretation similar to those of the SED that "imperialism" was to blame for the problems of the global South. While the collections employed Christianity as the common reason for donating to the needy, its call for solidarity likewise placed its narrative in line with that of the state.

Despite criticizing colonialism, some Protestant publications perpetuated a view of Africans as clearly in need of European material and technological support. For instance, the 1959 pamphlet produced by the Diaconia discussed above sported a photo on the front cover of a harvester driving across a wheat field juxtaposed with an image on the back cover of a naked baby. The baby, clearly marked as non-European by skin color, was thin and tall with a bandage on his side. A nurse carries the baby with one hand on the bottom and another lifting an arm to show the bandage. While the nurse's face is not shown, the baby stares at the viewer with ruffled hair. These images idealized East German modernity and wealth as many East German farmers still relied on animals to plant and harvest crops and the GDR remained on rations into the late 1950s. At the same time, by focusing on a thin, bandaged baby, this image stripped recipients of markers of individuality other than that of need. Essential in this and other posters was the idea of the "deserving poor," that is, those who were in need not because of a moral failing (e.g., laziness, inability, poor choices) but who required assistance through no fault of their own. The construct of the deserving poor can be traced back to Christian ideology from the Middle Ages and remained prevalent in these images too.[51] These portrayals of the poor remained strong into the 1970s, when in the West, they were replaced by a mixture of smiling, hopeful recipients with those in more desperate need.[52] These changes to Bread for the World in the FRG may have influenced portrayals in the East but it is not clear which of the images were used. Catholic efforts, on the other hand, remained focused on extreme poverty in both East and West Germany.

The motif of helplessness persisted in "Need in the World." For instance, a poster from the 1980s under the slogan "Our Help—Hope for Others" emphasized the inability of aid recipients to help themselves. In one poster, a young black woman stands in an open doorway of a wooden home. She wears a dress but no shoes. A shovel leans near the doorway to the hut but the woman's arms cannot be seen. The image seems to suggest two things: she is willing to work but is incapable of even reaching out for the most basic of tools. Instead she stands within the protection of the home staring out at the viewer. Because there are no windows in the home, the doorway is the one inlet to the home and she is there alone. Her only hope, according to the slogan, is "our help."[53]

Another poster depicts two children, possibly in a refugee camp, pulling down a metal mesh fence so they can peer over it. One boy wears a coat and no pants while the other has a sweater and pants. The absence of adults who could care for these boys underscores their vulnerability and need for assistance. The poster's impact lies in the children tugging down on the fence, trying to see out of the enclosure and, at the same time, eliminate the barrier between the viewer and themselves, between the need of the encampment and the wealth of the viewer.[54]

The images discussed above indicate a manifestation of a hierarchical view, portraying Africans as helpless without European aid. It is a racialized world view, which normalized the East German experience, including the GDR among the world's advanced nations, even as it ratified a separate existence for the developing world that could only change with European aid. In following this narrative, "Need in the World" aligned with many Western portrayals of need. In many of these cases, the images did not emphasize the real needs of the recipients but rather those conditions most likely to elicit support.[55] In this way, philanthropic gifts were as much about conceptions of the "other," in this case, the recipients, as about the needs being addressed. The posters portrayed the deserving poor, primarily women and children, who did not have the means to help themselves without external help. In this way, the collections were most interested in mobilizing donations immediately.

Under pressure from SED policies, the churches faced potential social marginalization with a diminishing number of parishioners. The campaigns explained above exemplified the types of activities that the churches used in the GDR in order to continue to attract support from the population of an officially atheist state. The collections featured prominently in church newspapers for parishioners. Generally, these newspapers would publish a call for giving followed by a report on the collection itself, and, in some cases, a declaration of the amount donated. Finally, follow-up articles showed the grateful recipients. Though small, these articles illustrated the continuing global engagement and thus, the relevance, of the Catholic and Protestant Churches even within the communist system. Taken alone, the collections could not do much to stem the tide of secularization occurring as a result of SED policies and the general trend in modern European views of religion. Yet they did help to engage those who remained in the churches and maintain activism among parishioners, not least among youths who, in some cases, started their own collections for the needy.[56] Although these groups separated themselves from the mainstream church collections, they still worked with church officials. They remained a means for the clergy to reach a demographic that, in East Germany and elsewhere, it was increasingly losing.

The collections of the Solidarity Fund and the churches reveal a great deal about the ways in which East Germans engaged international concerns. Given the physical separation between donor and recipient, philanthropic institutions linked these two groups. In doing so, they defined the needs of the recipients for the donors and chose the type of aid given. Whether emphasizing socialist or Christian solidarity, the campaigns of the Solidarity Fund, "Bread for the World," and "Need in the World" sought to educate East Germans and mobilize them to action.

In the case of the Solidarity Committee, this "educational process" was to take the form of an increased awareness of poverty and of the need for support for communist-aligned populations. In this way, the committee stressed solidarity with those of the developing world in a common socialist revolution. To do so, they portrayed the recipients as clearly different but also capable of helping themselves. The regime hoped that these campaigns would emphasize the moral responsibility of the GDR as well as the necessity of continuing to support socialist movements.

For the churches, their collections were important means to engage constituents in a state that left them relatively few opportunities to foster interest in church affairs. They emphasized Christian solidarity and provided the opportunity for individuals to free themselves from the emotional obligation of having been aid recipients through their participation in the collection campaigns. Overall, they focused most on the extreme poverty of the developing world and pictured women and children as the recipients. In contrast with what the socialist narrative held, these individuals could not help themselves but rather needed Western aid.

The collections also offered distinctly different solutions. For the Solidarity Committee, modernization through socialism provided the means while, for the churches, European aid constituted the recipients' only hope. Neither of these approaches embraced an understanding of cultural difference as a positive attribute. In this way, the mediating agencies emphasized the superiority of the donor as much as the bond of solidarity between donor and recipient. As such, they perpetuated a racialized and hierarchical world view.

As Toni Weis has argued, solidarity was as much about East Germans defining themselves as about aiding recipients.[57] In this way, philanthropic giving became a reflection of the donor's values, mediated by the collection organization's goals more than the recipients' needs. Their donations could cross borders and have an impact—even as they themselves could not visit those places. In this way, the mainstream collections both empowered and placated the population, allowing donors to place themselves in a larger world view but one that catered to their own understanding of aid, need, and solidarity. Collections provided East Germans a measuring stick for their national development. While the Federal Republic is often viewed as the primary point of comparison, the collections tied East Germans to a much larger world. East Germans thus placed themselves clearly in the "advanced world" with the resources and concern to be donors to the global community.

**Gregory R. Witkowski** is Associate Professor of Philanthropic Studies. After eight years as a professor of history, Witkowski became the Director of Graduate Programs at the then Center on Philanthropy in 2010 and helped transform it into the Indiana University Lilly Family School of Philanthropy, the world's first school focused on the scholarly study of societal impacts of giving and best practices of philanthropy. His research focuses on grassroots interactions, including state power and popular activism. This essay is part of a larger project exploring the relationship between philanthropy and civic engagement in the former GDR. His research has been supported by the Fulbright Commission, the Social Science Research Council, the Alexander von Humboldt Foundation, and other agencies.

# Notes

1. Ilona Schleicher, *DDR-Solidarität im südlichen Afrika: Auseinandersetzung mit einem ambivalenten Erbe* (Berlin: SODI, 1999).

2. "Protokoll der 1.Sekretariatssitzung des Komitees der Solidarität mit den Völkern Afrikas vom 14 July 1960" Bundesarchiv Berlin (hereafter BA) DZ 8 7413.

3. *Die afro-asiatische Solidaritätsbewegung* (Berlin: Staatsverlag der DDR, 1986), 23.

4. Ibid.

5. For more on the role of the Solidarity Fund in state efforts for legitimacy see Gregory Witkowski, "'Unser Tisch ist besser gedeckt': Ostdeutsche Philanthropie und Wohltätigkeit, 1959-89," in *Stifter, Spender, und Mäzene. USA und Deutschland im historischen Vergleich,* ed. Thomas Adams, Gabriele Lingelbach, and Simone Lässig (Stuttgart: Steiner 2009), 305–25.

6. As cited by Toni Weis, "The Politics Machine: On the Concept of 'Solidarity' in East German Support for SWAPO," *Journal of Southern African Studies* 2 (June 2011): 357.

7. Database "http://zefys.staatsbibliothek-berlin.de/ddr-presse" (accessed 30 March 2014).

8. Komitee der DDR für Solidarität mit den Völkern Afrikas "Haushaltsplanvorschlag 1963" undated, SAPMO-Barch DZ 8 7416.

9. For an example of workplace giving in the Western context, see Eleanor L. Brilliant, *The United Way: Dilemmas of Organized Charity* (New York: Columbia University Press, 1990), 164–69.

10. As cited by Weis, "The Politics Machine," 360.

11. Hans-Joachim Döring, *Es geht um unsere Existenz: die Politik der DDR gegenüber der Dritten Welt am Beispiel von Mosambik und Äthiopien* (Berlin: Links, 1999), 209.

12. For lists of annual donation numbers see Schleicher, *DDR-Solidarität im südlichen Afrika.*

13. See for instance the pamphlet, *The West German Government Involved in Vietnam,* 1966. On East German solidarity with Vietnam see Gerd Horten, "Sailing in the Shadow of the Vietnam War: The GDR Government and the 'Vietnam Bonus' of the Early 1970s," *German Studies Review* 36, no. 3 (October 2013): 557–78.

14. Günter Wernicke, "The World Peace Council and the Antiwar Movement in East Germany," in *America, the Vietnam War and the World,* ed. Andreas Daum, Lloyd C. Gardner, and Wilfried Mausbach (New York: Cambridge University Press, 2003), 309–10.

15. "Notiz über die Vorbesprechung zum begrenzten Plakatwettbewerb Vietnam am 21 December 1967," BA DZ 8 7619.

16. Image from German Historical Museum, Plakate Inventar Nr. 90/1340. Published on CD-ROM, Deutsches Historisches Museum, Plakate der SBZ/DDR: Politik, Wirtschaft, Kultur, Diskus CD-Reihe, 1999.

17. Image from German Historical Museum, Plakate Inventar Nr. 90/1345. Published on CD-ROM, Deutsches Historisches Museum, Plakate der SBZ/DDR: Politik, Wirtschaft, Kultur, Diskus CD-Reihe, 1999.

18. *Statistisches Jahrbuch der DDR, 1972* (Berlin: Staatsverlag der DDR, 1971), 430.

19. Publications of the Solidarity Committee include *The US Aggression in Vietnam: Protocol of the International Vietnam Conference* (Berlin: Vietnam Commission of the Afro-Asian Solidarity Committee of the GDR, 1969) and Afro-Asian Solidarity Committee, *The Neo-Colonialism of the West German Federal Republic* (n.p.: Afro-Asian Solidarity Committee in the German Democratic Republic, 1965).

20. Nora M. Alter, "Excessive Pre/Requisites: Vietnam Through the East German Lens," *Cultural Critique,* no. 35 (Winter 1996–67): 50.

21. Database http://zefys.staatsbibliothek-berlin.de/ddr-presse (accessed 30 March 2014).

22. Image from German Historical Museum, Plakate Inventar Nr. 90/1292 Published on CD-ROM, Deutsches Historisches Museum, Plakate der SBZ/DDR: Politik, Wirtschaft, Kultur, Diskus CD-Reihe, 1999.

23. Image from German Historical Museum, Plakate Inventar Nr. 90/1292, 90/1293, 90/1294, 90/1295, 90/1346, Plakate der SBZ/DDR.

24. Image from German Historical Museum, Plakate Inventar Nr. 90/1300 Published on CD-ROM, Deutsches Historisches Museum, Plakate der SBZ/DDR: Politik, Wirtschaft, Kultur, Diskus CD-Reihe, 1999.

25. Image from German Historical Museum, Plakate Inventar Nr. 90/1327. Published on CD-ROM, Deutsches Historisches Museum, Plakate der SBZ/DDR: Politik, Wirtschaft, Kultur, Diskus CD-Reihe, 1999.

26. Image from German Historical Museum, Plakate Inventar Nr. 90/1323. Published on CD-ROM, Deutsches Historisches Museum, Plakate der SBZ/DDR: Politik, Wirtschaft, Kultur, Diskus CD-Reihe, 1999.

27. Image from German Historical Museum, Plakate Inventar Nr. 90/1258. Published on CD-ROM, Deutsches Historisches Museum, Plakate der SBZ/DDR: Politik, Wirtschaft, Kultur, Diskus CD-Reihe, 1999.

28. For an introduction to the complicated relationship between the churches and the communist regime, see Robert F. Goeckel, *The Lutheran Church and the East German State: Political Conflict and Change under Ulbricht and Honecker* (Ithaca: Cornell University Press, 1990); Bernd Schaefer, *Staat und katholische Kirche in der DDR* (Cologne: Böhlau, 1999).

29. For more information on the foundation of Misereor and "Bread for the World" in the West see Annett Heinl and Gabrielle Lingelbach, "Spendenfinanzierte Private Entwicklungshilfe in der Bundesrepublik Deutschland," in *Stifter, Spender und Mäzene: USA und Deutschland im historischen Vergleich,* 287–311.

30. Christian Berg, "Die Entstehung der Aktion BfdW in Berlin 1959," Archiv des Diakonischen Werk der Evangelischen Kirche Deutschlands (ADW), BfdW DDR 1, page two of document.

31. "Kurzprotokoll über die Arbeitssitzung Bread for the World," on 23 September 1959 in Berlin-Charlottenburg, ADW BfdW DDR 1, page six of protocol.

32. Christian Berg, "Die Entstehung der Aktion BfdW in Berlin 1959," Archiv des Diakonischen Werk der Evangelischen Kirche Deutschlands (ADW), BfdW DDR 1.

33. Ibid.

34. "Leitsätze für die Arbeit der Aktion BfDW der Evangelischen Landes- und Freikirchen in der DDR," undated, ADW, BfdW DDR 1.

35. Bemerkungen zum Bericht Bread for the World, 1 April 1964, Bistumarchiv Erfurt ROO Vors./Sek. D. BOK/ BBK A I 16.
36. Uwe Kaminsky, "Nothilfe über die Grenzen hinaus. Die Entstehung von Brot für die Welt in der DDR." In *Diakonie im geteilten Deutschland*. ed. Ingolf Hübner and Jochen-Christoph Kaiser. (Stuttgart: Kohlhammer Verlag, 1999), 183.
37. "BfdW Information" Nr. 5, 20 Mai 1963 in Landeskirchliches Archiv Schwerin (LKAS) LB Beste 104.
38. Untitled agreement, 23 July 1960 ADW BfdW DDR 68.
39. "Vorschlag Bekanntmachung...BfdW Weihnachten 1963," LKAS LB Beste 104.
40. "BfdW Information" Nr. 5, 20 Mai 1963 in LKAS LB Beste 104.
41. Bemerkungen zum Bericht Bread for the World, 1 April 1964, Bistumarchiv Erfurt ROO Vors./Sek. D. BOK/ BBK A I 16.
42. Letter Alfred Bengsch to Cardinal Döpfner, 17 January 1966, Bistumarchiv Erfurt, NidW Vorgeschichte und Westkorrespondenz, nicht eingeschlossen.
43. Letter from Aufderbeck to Bengsch, 20 February 1967, Bistumarchiv Erfurt ROO Vors./Sek. D. BOK/ BBK A I 16. For more on the formation of the collection see Witkowski, "'Unser Tisch ist besser gedeckt'," 316–19.
44. Höllen, Document 621, 71.
45. "Protokoll der Berliner Ordinarienkonferenz vom 31 August-1 September 1967," Bistumsarchiv Erfurt ROO Vorsitzender/Sekretariat der BOK/BBK 1965–67.
46. Höllen, Document 576, 3.
47. Bishop Braun, "Bericht über die Anfänge des Bischöflichen Werkes Need in the World," Diözesanarchiv Berlin Ia/15-1, p. 2 of report.
48. Religious affiliation in the 1970s and 1980s is difficult to measure but the number of East Germans claiming religious affiliation clearly declined. For more, see Detlef Pollack, "Von der Volkskirche zur Minderheitskirche. Zur Entwicklung von Religiosität und Kirchlichkeit in der DDR," in *Sozialgeschichte der DDR*, ed. Hartmut Kaelble, Jürgen Kocka, and Hartmut Zwahr (Stuttgart: Klett-Cotta, 1994), 272.
49. Pamphlet published by Evangelische Verlagsanstalt, 1959. ADW HGSt 3199.
50. Mecklenburgische Kirchenzeitung, "Bread for the World. Der eine Zentner," 15 December 1968.
51. Gabriele Lingelbach, *Spenden und Sammeln: der westdeutsche Spendenmarkt bis in die 1980er Jahre* (Göttingen: Wallstein, 2009), 187. For the longer history see Larry Frohman, *Poor Relief and Welfare in Germany from the Reformation to World War I* (New York: Cambridge University Press, 2008).
52. Lingelbach, *Spenden und Sammeln: der westdeutsche Spendenmarkt bis in die 1980er Jahre,* 10–11.
53. Poster from Bistumsarchiv Erfurt, Need in the World. This collection is not yet catalogued.
54. Posters from Bistumsarchiv Erfurt, Need in the World. This collection is not yet catalogued.
55. For church images in the FRG see Lingelbach, *Spenden und Sammeln: der westdeutsche Spendenmarkt bis in die 1980er Jahre.* For additional examples outside of Germany see John F. Hutchinson, *Champions of Charity: War and the Rise of the Red Cross* (Boulder: Westview Press, 1996). For backwardness see Egon Mayer, *The*

*Production of Philanthropy: A Case Study of the Imagery and Methodology of Jewish Fundraising* (New York: Center for the Study of Philanthropy, 2001).

56. For a communist analysis of the success of nontraditional religious activities to maintain popular support, see "Einschätzung der Entwicklung der Art und Weise und der Methoden der religiös politischen Beeinflussung der Bevölkerung durch die evangelischen Landeskirchen mit Schlußfolgerungen." SAPMO-Barch DY 30 IV A2/14/9, 68–82.

57. Weis, "The Politics Machine."

# Bibliography

Afro-Asian Solidarity Committee. *The Neo-Colonialism of the West German Federal Republic.* n.p.: Afro-Asian Solidarity Committee in the German Democratic Republic, 1965.

Alter, Nora M. "Excessive Pre/Requisites: Vietnam through the East German Lens." *Cultural Critique,* no. 35 (Winter 1996–67): 39–79.

Brilliant, Eleanor L. *The United Way: Dilemmas of Organized Charity.* New York: Columbia University Press, 1990.

Döring, Hans-Joachim. *Es geht um unsere Existenz: die Politik der DDR gegenüber der Dritten Welt am Beispiel von Mosambik und Äthiopien.* Berlin: Links, 1999.

Frohman, Larry. *Poor Relief and Welfare in Germany from the Reformation to World War I.* New York: Cambridge University Press, 2008.

Goeckel, Robert F. *The Lutheran Church and the East German State: Political Conflict and Change under Ulbricht and Honecker.* Ithaca: Cornell University Press, 1990.

Horten, Gerd. "Sailing in the Shadow of the Vietnam War: The GDR Government and the 'Vietnam Bonus' of the Early 1970s." *German Studies Review* 36, no. 3 (October 2013): 557–78.

Hutchinson, John F. *Champions of Charity: War and the Rise of the Red Cross.* Boulder: Westview Press, 1996.

Kaminsky, Uwe. "Nothilfe über die Grenzen hinaus. Die Enstehung von Brot für die Welt in der DDR." In *Diakonie im geteilten Deutschland.* ed. Ingolf Hübner and Jochen Christoph Kaiser, 180–93. Stuttgart: Kohlhammer Verlag, 1999.

Lingelbach, Gabriele. *Spenden und Sammeln: der westdeutsche Spendenmarkt bis in die 1980er Jahre.* Moderne Zeit. Göttingen: Wallstein, 2009.

Mayer, Egon. *The Production of Philanthropy: A Case Study of the Imagery and Methodology of Jewish Fundraising.* New York: Center for the Study of Philanthropy, 2001.

Pollack, Detlef. "Von der Volkskirche zur Minderheitskirche. Zur Entwicklung von Religiosität und Kirchlichkeit in der DDR." In *Sozialgeschichte der DDR,* ed. Hartmut Kaelble, Jürgen Kocka, and Hartmut Zwahr, 271–94. Stuttgart: Klett-Cotta, 1994.

Schaefer, Bernd. *Staat und katholische Kirche in der DDR.* Cologne: Böhlau, 1999.

Schleicher, Ilona. *DDR-Solidarität im südlichen Afrika: Auseinandersetzung mit einem ambivalenten Erbe.* Berlin: SODI, 1999.

*The US Aggression in Vietnam: Protocol of the International Vietnam Conference.* Berlin: Vietnam Commission of the Afro-Asian Solidarity Committee of the GDR, 1969.

Weis, Toni. "The Politics Machine: On the Concept of 'Solidarity' in East German Support for Swapo." *Journal of Southern African Studies* 2 (June 2011): 351–67.

Wernicke, Günter. "The World Peace Council and the Antiwar Movement in East Germany." In *America, the Vietnam War and the World,* ed. Andreas Daum, Lloyd C. Gardner, and Wilfried Mausbach, 299–320. New York: Cambridge University Press, 2003.

Witkowski, Gregory. "'Unser Tisch ist besser gedeckt': Ostdeutsche Philanthropie und Wohltätigkeit, 1959-89." In *Stifter, Spender, und Mäzene. USA und Deutschland im historischen Vergleich,* ed. Thomas Adams, Gabriele Lingelbach, and Simone Lässig, 305–25. Stuttgart: Steiner 2009.

Chapter 4

# Socialist Modernization in Vietnam
## The East German Approach, 1976–89

*Bernd Schaefer*

## The GDR and Early Reconstruction of Socialist Vietnam

East German support for socialist Vietnam was a remarkable feature of "socialist internationalism." Though lagging understandably in volume behind the programs of the Soviet Union, the GDR's contributions to the socialist modernization of Vietnam, including bilateral economic, military, and intelligence relations, were both conventional and innovative.[1]

Hanoi and East Berlin began with the shared challenge of representing the socialist part of a divided nation with a capitalist adversary at its borders. When the Democratic Republic of Vietnam (DRV) was unified with the former Republic of Vietnam in the South as the Socialist Republic of Vietnam (SRV) in 1975–76, it was the GDR among all Soviet allies that developed a truly close bond with its fellow communists in Hanoi and Ho Chi Minh City/Saigon. The close relationship between DRV/SRV and GDR was greatly facilitated by the fact that neither of the two partners was willing or able to dominate the other and both showed a certain respect for their counterpart. The GDR honored what it perceived as Vietnam's astounding resilience and revolutionary-military credentials during the war against the United States and the American-backed South. The SRV, in turn, admired East Germany's state of economic development and technological prowess within the socialist world. Unlike the asymmetric and often patronizing relations between the Soviet Union and other socialist states in both the Second and Third World, the East German capacity to contribute to the modernization of "fraternal countries" in the Third World was smaller in scale but significant in substance. The GDR offered poorer partners not only options of development but also avenues of reciprocity, however symbolic those might have been.

Vietnam suffered from constant warfare, both internally and against foreign powers, between 1945 and 1954, and again from the late 1950s to 1975. After 1954, the DRV in the North was industrialized through Soviet-style imports of entire factories from all over communist Europe to force rapid modernization. Massive U.S. bombing between 1964 and 1968 rendered most of these sites dysfunctional. Reconstruction resumed for a brief period between 1969 and 1971 with the aid of an East German economic advisory and consulting team. Solicited and appointed by Hanoi's Prime Minister Pham Van Dong, the team traveled and operated on-site all over the DRV. Then the Northern 1972 "spring offensive" and the subsequent, truly massive American bombing campaign destroyed more of North Vietnam within four months than during four years of intense warfare in the 1960s. By the time of the Paris Peace Agreement with the United States in January 1973, Vietnamese production had fallen far below 1964 figures for everything except rice. The country was plagued by a very basic war economy, lack of infrastructure, worker shortages, and endemic corruption.

In the period after the First Indochina War, the GDR had been engaged primarily in practical "solidarity" through material aid organized by the state-run GDR "Solidarity Committee" and supported by more or less solicited donations from all segments of East German society at workplaces and in educational institutions (see Witkowski's chapter in this volume).[2] With the end of the Korean War, the solidarity committee for North Korea was expanded to cover Vietnam in November 1954 and remained operational until 1958. By the end of the 1950s, it had provided the financial and material means for a hospital, a school, and an orthopedic workshop in the DRV. With the full entrance of the United States into the Vietnam War in 1965, a dedicated "Vietnam Committee" was established within the state-run solidarity framework of the East German mass organization "National Front."[3] For a considerable time, Vietnam became the centerpiece of large East German solidarity donation campaigns like "Bicycles for Vietnam," "Blood for Vietnam," "Sewing Machines for Vietnam," and "Kali for Vietnam" that mobilized almost the entire GDR society and economy. Special annual programs like "Notepads for Vietnam's Children" or "Fly Red Butterfly, Fly" even engaged children at East German elementary schools. In that time, a total of 143 small workshops for craftspeople were established by solidarity funds to train young Vietnamese in various professions. In all cases, the GDR Solidarity Committee solicited and collected donations, organized transportation, and worked with local partners in Vietnam.

Two projects stood out in the early years of GDR support for Vietnam. Between 1956 and 1958, East Germany helped to build and support the printing house of the ruling Vietnamese Workers Party's (VWP; Lao Dong

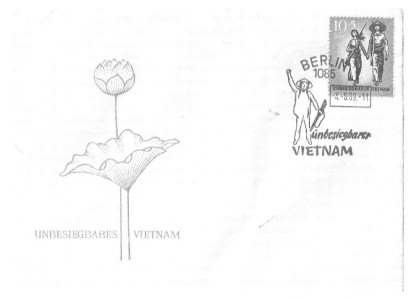

**Figure 4.1.** Stamps and seals expressing East German solidarity with "Invincible Vietnam"

Party), Tien Bo in Hanoi, which printed the Communist Party's central newspaper and other official periodicals and publications. Also, in 1958, a joint Vietnamese-GDR friendship hospital took over an older hospital from 1906 with forty buildings. This medical facility was to play a major role in providing care to the Vietnamese elite and later to victims of American bombings. The GDR Solidarity Committee and the East Berlin university hospital Charité, as well as the Berlin-Friedrichshain Urban Hospital, were steady suppliers of equipment. The two medical institutions also sent their specialists to Hanoi for frequent, short-term stints and trained Vietnamese doctors in the GDR.

In another demonstrative example of East German solidarity for Vietnam and a highly symbolic act, in 1955 a group of 350 Vietnamese children of VWP cadres between the ages of ten and fourteen traveled by train to the GDR, where they were to live for about three years. They were educated in East German schools, colleges, and factories in the Saxon cities of Dresden and Moritzburg. The "Moritzburger" became a well-known network in Vietnam up to the present, acting as lobbyists for the education and training of Vietnamese in East Germany.[4] In a sense, the Moritzburger opened the later constant flow of young Vietnamese students to the GDR and also acted as early pioneers of the large educational training and contract worker program for Vietnamese launched and implemented in the 1980s under different circumstances during Vietnam's severe economic crisis.

Propelled by East Berlin's propagated self-image, the GDR was seen as a highly industrialized, technologically sophisticated showcase of socialism with high living standards by the socialist countries of the Second and Third World. The partial truth behind this image combined with the relentless trumpeting of East German achievements in overseas propaganda resulted in expectations and demands from Vietnamese partners that were often excessively high. In the 1980s, when the GDR was increasingly unable to meet those expectations due to its own economic problems, East Berlin's ambassador in Hanoi viewed his own country's propaganda as unhelpful and even as "counterproductive."[5]

Without a doubt, however, the GDR had the deserved reputation of providing complimentary and excellent vocational, college, and university education to students from "fraternal" countries. While the GDR provided this education to tens of thousands of foreigners in the German language overall, it created networks in certain Third World countries that maximized East German cultural and political influence. The numbers for Vietnam were the highest among developing countries. By 1989, 5,435 Vietnamese students had graduated from GDR universities and colleges, almost all of them in engineering, natural, and medical sciences. 960 of them acquired a doctoral degree. In addition, 14,450 specialized workers (*Facharbeiter*) had been trained in East German businesses and factories. After the end of the "American War," Vietnam advanced into a prime focus of GDR international aid, easily surpassing other recipients of East German aid and support like Mozambique, Angola, Ethiopia, Cuba, Mongolia, and later Nicaragua.[6]

## Attempting to Stabilize Socialist Vietnam

East German contributions to the socialist modernization of the DRV gathered steam after the end of hostilities in North Vietnamese territory in 1973 and the establishment of the SRV in 1975. Following approval by the respective Communist Party politburos and councils of ministers, the State Plan Commissions of the GDR and SRV signed detailed five-year agreements planning for the periods of 1976–80, 1981–85, and 1986–90. A bilateral Committee for Economic and Scientific-Technological Cooperation, in short, "Economic Committee," was to deal with issues arising between these respective five-year periods.[7]

East Germany's early contributions to the construction of socialist Vietnam did not diverge from the Soviet-style modernization practiced since the 1950s in various parts of the socialist, or socialist-aspiring, Third World. Rapid industrialization and the creation of a factory workforce were considered the bedrock for the establishment and construction of socialism leading to the ultimate implementation of communism. This entailed deliveries of complete production sites on the basis of interest-free credits that indebted recipient countries heavily. In the case of Vietnam, floods of such interest-free credits were awarded after the end of the American War in 1973, the Unification War in 1975, and, to lesser degree, after the Chinese military intervention of 1979. In addition, exports of Vietnamese products to the GDR received a 30 percent bonus increase that went directly into SRV budgets.

The GDR built a cannery in Hanoi, a glass factory in Hai Phong, and a cooking oil refinery in Ha Bac in this manner. All those projects had been started before 1963 and 1967 respectively, but were interrupted and damaged during the American War. Newer industrialization projects included a steel factory in Bac Thai begun in 1975, a brewery in Hanoi in 1981, and later a tropical juice factory in Nghia Dan in 1984. In all these cases, GDR specialists designed the factories and delivered all the material. Vietnamese personnel were to receive some qualifications in the GDR before the entire actual construction on site was passed into the hands of Vietnamese workers. Such massive projects ran into a multitude of problems and ultimately proved largely inefficient for economic development. Problems included highly deficient or entirely missing infrastructure, the lack of a sufficient number of trained Vietnamese specialists, grave shortages of electricity, and the supply of raw material and spare parts. Hermann Schwiesau, who was the GDR's ambassador to the SRV between November 1982 and November 1986, recalled a telling anecdote about his visit to a textile factory in Hanoi that produced clothes and garments for export to the GDR in order to provide some compensation for GDR aid to Vietnam. He wanted to pay just a short two-to-three-hour visit to the site not far from the GDR embassy, while the director of the factory implored him to stay there for a full day including lunch and cultural performances. Schwiesau happily relented when he found out the real reason behind this request: his visit as a foreign dignitary guaranteed the factory an uninterrupted flow of electricity for the entire length of his stay and thus a full day of actual work.[8]

When combined with local shortcomings and Vietnam's climate, which could be forbiddingly hot and humid, enforced socialist modernization from abroad turned out to be highly inefficient and unsatisfactory. It became a costly waste of resources for all sides involved. Of more durable and lasting effects were only certain small-scale projects like the Orthopedic Technology Center in Ba Vi near Hanoi erected between 1973 and 1984 or a school for mechanics in Pho Yen developed between 1973 and 1981. Both projects were funded through donations from the GDR Solidarity Committee.[9]

On a different scale, any coordination of Vietnam support and modernization as envisaged by the Soviet-bloc "Council for Mutual Economic Assistance" (COMECON), of which the SRV had become a full member in 1978, did not yield desired results despite numerous declarations and meetings. Second World efforts to achieve Vietnamese modernization remained rather isolated and bilateral affairs. According to a GDR participant in many COMECON meetings where the issue of Vietnam was on the table, proposals made in those settings were too grand and unrealistic. Funding was just delegated to individual states without proper evaluation and, last but not least, COMECON members had highly divergent interests. They were hardly able to act in a joint and coordinated fashion, with Romania being particularly obstructive in various ways.[10] In overall quantitative terms, Soviet credits and commitments to Vietnam dwarfed those of other COMECON members by far. The GDR, however, constantly maintained a clear second position ahead of the other socialist European states with regard to the support of Vietnam.

## The Rebuilding of the City of Vinh

In this pattern of socialist modernization, the grand project of reconstructing the provincial capital city of Vinh in North Vietnam between 1973 and 1980 proved to be one of the more lasting effects of East German aid (see Schwenkel's contribution to this volume).[11] As in the case of the completely destroyed North Korean City of Hamhung during the 1950s about twenty years earlier (see Hong's contribution to this volume), and following on the heels of a bilateral GDR-DRV government agreement from October 1973, the GDR took up the task of rebuilding a mostly war-destroyed and uninhabitable mid-size provincial city. On a rotating annual basis, forty East German specialists went to Vinh to direct the reconstruction of a new city under formal Vietnamese guidance. In an enormous logistical and managerial cooperation effort, new apartment and public facilities in the "Quang Trung" quarter were built for a population of ten thousand people over the course of seven years.

Interestingly, the GDR took strong exception to Vietnamese requests of a complete industrial serial construction with all materials imported from East Germany. Instead the GDR concept of using only local construction material produced by a Vietnamese workforce on site carried the day and was highly appreciated in the end. For that purpose, the GDR advisers trained Vietnamese construction experts and helped to build or modernize an entire set of industrial factories for all products needed to construct buildings and apartments (concrete, stone, sand, water, shingles, repair facilities). Overall, the pre-1989 reconstruction effort of Vinh remained limited to this one quarter. Unrelated to urban reconstruction, a cotton factory was also being built in Vinh with East German aid in 1975. It was not completed until 1986 and never evolved into a productive enterprise.

As a result, Vinh, now a much enlarged city in Northern Central Vietnam's Nghe An province, features an East German–style residential quarter. It was always viewed as a GDR implant (albeit welcome) by the Vietnamese side. When East German Ambassador Schwiesau visited Vinh in the early 1980s, three years after the quarter's completion, it already displayed some wear and tear. He pointed this out to his Vietnamese hosts and asked them to take somewhat more care. His Vietnamese interlocutors agreed and suggested the GDR itself should do more for "its" quarter. After all, this would also be about the reputation of the GDR in Vietnam.[12] While Quang Trung subsequently suffered from an increasingly marginal and neglected fate after 1990,[13] those Vietnamese directly involved in the reconstruction project of Vinh maintain a nostalgic, romantic, and affectionate perspective on the project.[14]

## Other Fields of East German Support

In contrast to the massive Soviet commitments and those of other East European countries, East German military support lagged behind due to the comparatively low level of arms production capacities in the GDR. Between 1965 and 1985, East Berlin provided free military aid to Vietnam of less than USD 35 million. The major bulk of this was supplied up to 1975 and during the Sino-Vietnamese War of 1979. It consisted mostly of light weaponry, grenades, mines, and ammunition, besides all sorts of engines, spare parts, generators, and medical supplies. After 1975 the GDR also indulged in symbolic acts like equipping the Vietnamese army's brass ensemble and training its soccer team in the GDR. More substantial contributions were the military training of about 400 Vietnamese military cadres in GDR officer schools and the procurement of complimentary equipment for the Vietnamese Army Officers' School in Ho Chi Minh City worth about USD 700,000.[15] During the military conflicts with Cambodia and China in 1978–79, complimentary aid was also bolstered with material support for nominally civilian purposes that were nonetheless related to war efforts.

One sector stands out in GDR support for united Vietnam right after the 1975 military victory so admired by East German power elites. This was the close cooperation in intelligence and related technology, which became an ever expanding enterprise. The extent to which the GDR's Ministry for State Security (MfS or Stasi) contributed to Vietnam's "socialist modernization" in this way may be disputable. Nevertheless, the large SRV Ministry of Interior (Ba Cong An) benefited to high degree from external aid in its surveillance and pursuit of "internal enemies," of which, according to Vietnamese communist definitions, there were legions after the country's reunification. In diverse areas like SRV counterespionage activities, internal control of Vietnam's administrative and economic apparatus, issuance of official and unofficial documents, border checks at airports and harbors, or the development of interrogation and prison systems, East German technology and advice had an impact.

Technological cooperation between MfS and Cong An dates back as early as 1959, picked up during the "American War" between 1965 and 1973, and intensified after 1975. Until 1979, all GDR deliveries in the intelligence sector were complimentary and taken from the Stasi international "solidarity fund." Afterward the SRV had to pay for those intelligence technology products the Stasi itself had to acquire for hard currency in Western capitalist countries. One form of Vietnamese reimbursement in this regard consisted in clandestine acquisition of Japanese-made technology elsewhere in East Asia in which the MfS was interested.

In concrete terms, the GDR support in the intelligence field consisted of material aid for document production, electronic technology, chemical substances, signal communications, and various sorts of surveillance devices and technology. Furthermore, the MfS proved to be helpful in analyzing and cataloguing the massive caches of mostly light weaponry obtained or confiscated by the North Vietnamese from the Americans and especially the defeated South Vietnamese Army. Stasi and Cong An held regular high-ranking and cross-section delegation exchanges in both the GDR and the SRV. There were a significant number of Vietnamese cadres in East Germany for training and GDR specialists in Vietnam for advice and gaining experience on a rotating basis. In 1978, an Institute for Criminal Technology, funded and equipped by the MfS and built by a special GDR construction brigade, was opened in a Cong An complex in Vinh Yen. It included laboratories and the signal and electronics department of the SRV Ministry of Interior and was supplemented in 1980 by a "special paper factory" (*Spezialpapierfabrik*) for document production at the same location. A telling indication for extremely cordial relations between the two ministries is this 1985 episode: for its fortieth anniversary the Cong An had produced a propagandistic movie named "Turtle Lake" after a lake in Saigon. It was to be aired in Vietnamese movie theaters to hail and commemorate communist intelligence achievements. As it turned out, Cong An embarrassingly ran out of film rolls and could not acquire them in the SRV. The MfS was asked for help and organized the production of sufficient rolls at the East German *Orwo* factory in Wolfen discretely. They were flown to Vietnam and handed over without a word uttered about this action in order not to hurt local pride.

A much larger "fraternal" action in a similar vein had transpired earlier, also respecting Vietnamese pride by maintaining total secrecy. After the military victory of 1975, North Vietnam lacked the capacity to manufacture its own new currency to be introduced with upcoming unification. During the American War, North Vietnamese money was produced by Chinese specialists who were now no longer available since the souring of relations between Hanoi and Beijing. In June 1975, the DRV government therefore discretely requested help from the GDR. MfS and Cong An were commissioned to launch and operate a secret multiyear operation ("Aktion VAU," named after the letter "V") to manufacture Vietnamese banknotes and coins in East Germany and transport them back to Vietnam camouflaged as weapons deliveries (SRV and GDR intelligence officers involved in the operation were to wear regular army uniforms when acting on Vietnamese territory). Altogether 580 million Vietnamese coins and 837 million banknotes went into production in a special paper factory in Leipzig and the state mint in East Berlin between October 1975 and February 1979. As the entire operation lasted well into 1986, those numbers may have more than doubled. During this period of ten years, about 100 to 120 Vietnamese workers came to the GDR annually for currency production and worked in shifts in Berlin and Leipzig guarded by Cong An and MfS officers.

## Innovative Concepts for Mutual Benefit

From the early 1980s, the GDR explored multiple means of mutual-benefit cooperation with Vietnam both out of enlightened self-interest and of insight into the SRV's mounting problems. In 1981, for instance, the GDR had provided roughly USD 250 million in "development aid" to socialist countries in the Third World and "national liberation movements" altogether. This figure represented 0.78 percent of the GDR gross "national income" and was a substantial drain on the economy.[16]

In the socialist Third World proper, gross deficiencies in production efficiency and the accumulation of debts from Second World credits to build industrialization projects seemed to create a vicious cycle and reduce the developing socialist partners to bottomless pits. In the case of Vietnam, the economic situation had deteriorated massively since the late 1970s both as a result of the war and ideologically motivated, severely misguided economic and agricultural decisions. The SRV was almost in free fall by the mid 1980s with high inflation, widespread rationing, and sinking living standards. A focus on industrialization had diverted resources from other sectors and the former capitalist South Vietnamese economy became hardly manageable due to American and regional embargos. Industries worked at barely 50 percent capacity.[17] With ongoing battles in Indochina and constant, unenlightened retribution against real and imagined internal enemies, defense- and intelligence-related costs were exceedingly high and remained a major obstacle to the much-needed transformation into a civilian economy. Ultimately, the Vietnamese Workers Party made bold moves toward political and economic reform at its 6th Party Congress in December of 1986 together with a reassessment of its regional foreign policy. The "new era" of *Doi Moi* was set to replace the dreary *Bao Cap* period, which was defined as a "subsidy economy." Up until 1989, however, results were still nascent and tentative and did not affect the major picture of relations between the socialist Second and Third Worlds.

In the case of the GDR, a rethinking had emerged concerning how to conduct bilateral economic relations with the Third World. In East Berlin "internationalist aid" was no longer viewed as the solidarity obligation of a rich socialist country to give freely and generously to the poorer fraternal socialists of the Third World, as the latter preferred, if not expected. It was calculated that Vietnam might be roughly USD 150 million in debt to the GDR by the end of the 1980s. Therefore, more innovative forms of "internationalist" cooperation were considered in East Germany out of domestic economic strains and the widening economic gap with the capitalist countries of Western Europe.[18] The GDR had to straddle maintaining the still much-desired, traditionally cordial relations with Hanoi and its own dwindling economic capabilities to provide the level of aid to which Vietnam had become accustomed.[19] SRV representatives had demanded even forcefully that its GDR counterparts meet the "obligations" of a rich socialist partner at times.[20]

In the case of Vietnam, a concept of "mutual benefit" gained traction ultimately in the GDR in order to enable the SRV to build export capacities for indigenous products and therefore create prospects for a long-term repayment of its accumulated external debt to East Germany. In theory, this new approach had the potential to contribute to more development in Vietnam, albeit in incremental fashion and only with plenty of time on hand. In the early 1980s, GDR experts expected these exports to have an effect by 1991 and last for twenty years until full repayment could be achieved by 2011. On an additional level, the SRV was now also expected to "export" temporary workers to the GDR as another way of indirect debt repayment. Finally, some shoe and textile production capacities for exclusive export to the GDR were set aside in Vietnam to relieve the East German workforce and further contribute to Vietnamese repayment abilities.

## Vietnamese Contract Workers in the GDR and Seeds of Racism

In 1979, bilateral government agreements established a large Vietnamese guest worker program, which peaked in the late 1980s, while similar agreements on smaller scales were also signed by the GDR with Mozambique, Angola, and Cuba. The program provided minor relief to SRV domestic economic problems and bolstered GDR production of those goods designed for export against hard currencies from capitalist states like the Federal Republic of Germany. Between 1980 and 1986, about twelve thousand Vietnamese settled in the GDR for both work and educational training temporarily. The recruitment of Vietnamese workers spiked between 1987 and 1989 when roughly sixty thousand additional SRV citizens entered the GDR to join its workforce for short- and long-term stints. At the end of 1989 about 58,000 Vietnamese contract workers were based in the GDR. Unlike their fellow workers in previous years, those who had arrived since 1987 hardly received any training and qualification. Instead, they had to work three shifts within 24 hours in East Germany's lagging industry. At the time, GDR workers were no longer willing to work such around-the-clock shifts. In order to maintain social stability during the 1980s, the East Berlin government did not consider it politically prudent to force the East German labor force into shift work.

Overall, this program seemed like a perfect win-win situation to mutually benefit the sharply contrasting needs of both socialist countries. From the GDR perspective, the guest workers made up for the growing East German shortage of worker supply and the comparatively low morale of its own German workforce. The Vietnamese not only had to work harder and longer, but also incurred much lower labor costs. While the limited compensation and benefits were extraordinarily high by Vietnamese standards, the contract workers' eagerness to labor harder for what East Germans viewed as dumping wages did not enamor them to their GDR co-workers who often harbored resentments against foreign contract workers.

For Vietnam, this program not only alleviated slightly the steady and rapid population growth at home. The Vietnamese families, whose members were selected to participate in the program, were considered fortunate and benefited significantly from what their relatives netted abroad and returned in remittances. High bribes were paid to officials in Vietnam to be included in this program,[21] and those who made it recall their experiences in often glowing light as they were able to trade the dire economic situation in the SRV during the 1980s for life in a comparatively prosperous socialist country.[22] The GDR paid the social insurance of the contract workers directly to the Hanoi government, as well as 12 percent of their respective wages. This netted the SRV about 200 million GDR Marks annually (roughly about USD 35 million).[23] The workers were allowed to transfer about 60 percent of their wages to their families and dependents in Vietnam. Many of them bought East German goods scarce in the SRV and, despite strict GDR regulations limiting shopping sprees, shipped them on a massive scale. Almost all items were shipped by air, straining the capacities of the GDR airline Interflug. Vietnamese workers in the GDR refrained from sea shipments, as they were aware of the large scale of corruption and graft by Vietnamese harbor workers and officials, all the way from the East German Baltic Sea harbor of Rostock to the harbors in Vietnam where many deliveries "disappeared."[24] The most popular items were disassembled motorcycles, bicycles, sewing machines, electronics, fabrics, sugar, and soap. Moreover, Vietnamese contract workers engaged in production and small-scale merchant business within East Germany that bordered on the illegal before, and then massively after, German unification.[25] All of this did not fail to create internal squabbles and fights among highly entrepreneurial Vietnamese rings of sellers and producers, and between South and North Vietnamese, as had become common in Vietnam proper throughout the 1980s.

Among some East Germans, in particular those with xenophobic and conservative law-and-order leanings, the Vietnamese presence in the GDR also led to resentments and expressions of racism. The contract workers from Southeast Asia were derogatorily referred to as "Fidschis", a generic GDR term for Asians that was clearly meant to be a racial slur. While on the one hand GDR citizens benefitted from Vietnamese handicraft and fabricated "Jeans", and willingly bought items from Vietnamese sellers on impromptu markets all over the GDR, often the same people decried what was viewed as Vietnamese hoarding and "buying-up" of GDR items for shipments back home to Vietnam. Younger Vietnamese men sometimes got in violent trouble with East Germans when trying to socialize with young East German women. Various incidents and outbursts of racism during the 1980s were expressions of deep unease and insecurity on the side of some East Germans. They were brought up and used to living in a completely homogenous society without much travel options, when they suddenly had to manage limited cohabitation with other races, i.e. contract workers from Vietnam, but also from Mozambique, Angola, and Cuba. Unlike Asian or African students concentrated in university housing and near campuses, the contract workers were distributed all over the GDR according to production needs and location of selected factories. As a result, in their cities and towns of residence, those contract workers were usually segregated from East Germans in isolated apartment blocks and buildings. With the East German Stasi and police presence evaporating after December 1989, from 1990 onwards anti-foreigner incidents in East Germany became more frequent and violent, resulting also in some murders or murderous attempts. In August 1992, for instance, riot attacks occurred against an apartment complex inhabited, among others, by Vietnamese workers and their families in the Rostock city suburb of Lichtenhagen near the Baltic coast.

## Laying the Foundations of Vietnamese Coffee Power

In addition to the contract worker program, the GDR decided to support the SRV by boosting export capacities with the launch of coffee, natural rubber, pepper, and coconut oil production in 1980. All those products were expensive and of low quality in the GDR proper, where they had to be imported at world market prices. Furthermore, the availability and quality of coffee was a fetish as well as a source of discontent in the GDR that caused repeated headaches for the East German politburo, notably during the domestic "coffee crisis" of 1977–78.[26] With Vietnamese-made products the GDR government hoped to satisfy domestic consumer demands and obtain quality coffee beans in the long term at much lower costs than by buying them for "valuta" currency on the world market.[27]

Along with the imported sophistication and efficiency of the SRV Ministry of Interior shown above, coffee was another important and successful East German contribution to Vietnamese modernization that outlasted the collapse of communism in Europe and the Soviet Union. While the GDR disappeared too early to reap the benefits of cheap Vietnamese coffee imports beyond tentative beginnings, the SRV has become the world's second largest coffee exporter thanks, in part, to the East German plantation starter kit.

French colonialists had cultivated coffee in the Southern highlands of Dac Lac province in Vietnam since 1926. With the departure of the French, however, many plantations were abandoned and production fell to a mere trickle. By 1980, in socialist Vietnam only six thousand hectares in total were still cultivated with coffee plants. Ten percent of these fields were in a location near Buon Ma Thuot in Dac Lac, with rather intransigent minority populations, which the GDR scouted out in 1980 for a grand-scale development project called "Kaffee-Kombinat Viet-Duc" [Vietnamese-German]. In two bilateral government agreements between GDR and SRV in the years 1980 and 1986 East Germany laid the foundations for the import of quality coffee beans and Vietnamese debt repayment. Over a period of twenty years, the SRV was expected to reserve 50 percent of its entire production in Dac Lac province for the East German domestic market and its consumption.

In return, the GDR stated its willingness to invest about USD 20 million to jump-start Vietnamese coffee production. Most of the money allocated was spent to build a 12-megawatt water power plant in nearby Dray Linh to provide the energy needed for the plantations. Furthermore, the GDR provided all the necessary equipment including trucks, vehicles, and sprinklers. About ten thousand workers with their families were resettled from the Southern Vietnamese coastline to the highlands to mitigate the impacts of local indigenous people opposing the coffee project. For the new settlers, the GDR built basic housing, schools, hospitals, and stores. Three to five GDR experts living in the former French plantation owner residences stayed on-site on a rotating basis to provide Vietnamese workers with advice and assistance. SRV specialists were sent to the GDR temporarily to be trained to run the plantation. The GDR solidarity movement sent complimentary fabrics, medical, and school supplies to Buon Ma Thuot and Dray Linh.

By 1989, the "Kombinat Viet-Duc" had grown into the largest Vietnamese coffee plantation by far, from 600 to 8,600 hectares of plants, thereby surpassing the overall SRV coffee-cultivated area of 1980. From 1986 onward, about five thousand tons of coffee beans were exported to the GDR, though products still lacked in quality. Management and supply problems were a factor, but another factor was the comparatively short time in which Vietnamese experts and workers had to be trained to cultivate a difficult crop like coffee beans. Ultimately, however, it was the GDR for whom the clock was running out in 1989–90. Nevertheless, Viet-Duc in Dac Lac evolved into the nucleus of the SRV coffee industry that thrived in the 1990s with further foreign technological assistance from united Germany and elsewhere. It catapulted Vietnam into the astonishing position of becoming the second largest global coffee exporter behind Brazil and before Colombia as of 2008; a position it would have taken considerably longer to reach, if at all, without the GDR launch in Dac Lac during the 1980s.[28] About 15 percent of the world's green coffee is harvested in Vietnam and it is the country's second most important export article after rice. Ironically, the largest importer of Vietnamese coffee beans with about 13 percent of the overall harvest is the reunified Germany.[29]

# Conclusion

The rather inadvertent East German contribution to the capitalist Vietnamese coffee success story cannot disguise the fact that socialist modernization in Vietnam was bound to fail, notwithstanding certain innovative "Second World" concepts. Economically, the "Second World" was inherently flawed. It became significantly weaker during the last decade of the Cold War, when the gap with the "First World" widened. GDR approaches regarding Vietnam during the eighties were driven by domestic necessities and realistic insights. They marked a clear deviation from the conventional large, ineffective, and heavy-handed Soviet-style industrialization efforts and credit handouts. The new East German concepts of cooperation oriented toward mutual benefits were highly appreciated by Vietnam itself and were certainly innovative within the narrow socialist framework. Overall, however, they remained without major effects given Vietnam's daunting economic, social, and regional problems. The SRV subsidy economy reached the brink of a collapse in 1986, which was only averted by economic reforms that reversed course and deviated from the orthodox socialist path. For tactical reasons and political expediency, Vietnamese *Doi Moi* pretended to have been inspired by Soviet *perestroika,* but in fact it was incited to no small degree by the successful development of Chinese capitalist economic reforms during the 1980s in Vietnam's region. The Chinese connotations of *Doi Moi* could be admitted more openly when it was implemented with more force in the 1990s. The GDR faded into history, but it remained a highly positive memory in the SRV, not the least among those roughly 100,000 Vietnamese able to speak or understand German due to previous stays in the GDR or work with East German experts. Nostalgia has its limits, however. Relations with socialist Europe and the former "Second World" remind Vietnam of the dire economic times and hardships of the 1970s and 1980s, a period that appears to the current aspiring generation of Vietnamese as wholly surreal.

**Bernd Schaefer** is a Senior Scholar with the Woodrow Wilson International Center's Cold War International History Project (CWIHP) and a Professorial Lecturer at George Washington University, both in Washington, D.C. He holds a Ph.D. from the University of Halle in Germany and a MPA from the Harvard Kennedy School. Recent publications include *1965—Indonesia and the World* (Gramedia, Jakarta, 2013), *Coming to Terms: Dealing with the Communist Past in East Germany* (Stiftung Aufarbeitung, Berlin), *The East German State and the Catholic Church, 1945-1989 (*Berghahn Books) and *Ostpolitik, 1969-1974: Global and European Responses* (Cambridge University Press, ed. with Carole Fink).

# Notes

1. See Bernd Schaefer, "Die DDR und Vietnam: Ein besonderes Verhältnis," in *Deutsch-Vietnamesische Beziehungen: Tagungshand zum 35jährigen Jubiläum der diplomatischen Beziehungen zwischen der Bundesrepublik Deutschland und der Sozialistischen Republik Vietnam,* ed. Goethe Institut Vietnam, Vietnam National University, and Auswärtiges Amt (Hanoi/Berlin: 2010), 13–19. This volume is completely bilingual and also contains this article in Vietnamese.

2. See Achim Reichardt, *Nie Vergessen—Solidarität üben!* (Berlin: Kai Homilius, 2006), 45–46, 64–68; Günter Wernicke, ""Solidarität hilft siegen!" Zur Solidaritätsbewegung mit Vietnam in beiden deutschen Staaten," *Hefte zur DDR-Geschichte,* no. 72 (2001).

3. Willi Zahlbaum, "'Solidarität hilft siegen' (Autobiographisches Dokument von 1989)," in *Die DDR und Vietnam: Berichte-Erinnerungen-Fakten, Teil I,* ed. Ilona Schleicher (Berlin: Verband für Internationale Politik und Völkerrecht e.V, 2011), 75–85.

4. Mirjam Freytag, *Die "Moritzburger" in Vietnam: Lebenswege nach einem Schul- und Ausbildungsaufenthalt in der DDR: Vermitteln in interkulturellen Beziehungen* (Frankfurt: IKO-Verlag für Interkulturelle Kommunikation, 1998). In 2005 some of the Vietnamese "Moritzburger" repeated their train journey from thirty years ago and returned to Saxony for an emotional visit. The president of the German Parliament (Bundestag) officially received the group.

5. Hermann Schwiesau, "Erfahrungen und Einsichten: Als Botschafter der DDR in Vietnam," in *Die DDR und Vietnam: Berichte-Erinnerungen-Fakten, Teil I,* ed. Ilona Schleicher (Berlin: Verband für Internationale Politik und Völkerrecht e.V, 2011), 14.

6. GDR Ministry for Economic Cooperation (Ministerium für Wirtschaftliche Zusammenarbeit/MWZ), Report of Countries Division, 2 October 1990. The author thanks Dr. Walter Molt, adviser to the MWZ, for a copy of this extensive report outlining the global spectrum of GDR development aid. The report was finalized one day before German unification abolished both the GDR government and the MWZ.

7. For a comprehensive overview rich in facts compiled during the 1990s see Dieter Knöfel, "Hilfe und Zusammenarbeit—die Wirtschaftsbeziehungen zwischen der DDR und Vietnam," in *Die DDR und Vietnam: Berichte-Erinnerungen-Fakten, Teil I,* ed. Ilona Schleicher (Berlin: Verband für Internationale Politik und Völkerrecht e.V, 2011), 20–38.

8. Hermann Schwiesau, "Erfahrungen und Einsichten: Als Botschafter der DDR in Vietnam," 16.

9. Reichardt, *Nie Vergessen—Solidarität üben!,* 66–67.

10. Author's interview with Dr. Dieter Knöfel, former member of the GDR State Plan Commission and Secretary of the GDR-Vietnamese Committee for Economic and Scientific-Technological Cooperation. Berlin, 5 February 2005.

11. The author wants to thank Dr. Dieter Knöfel, former member of the GDR State Plan Commission and Secretary of the GDR-Vietnamese Committee for Economic and Scientific-Technological Cooperation, for a copy of his extensive May 2004

German-language documentation "On GDR Support of the SRV Concerning Design and Construction of the City of Vinh."

12. Schwiesau, "Erfahrungen und Einsichten," 18.

13. See the excellent article by Christina Schwenkel, "Civilizing the City: Socialist Ruins and Urban Renewal in Central Vietnam," *Positions* 20, no. 2 (Spring 2012), 437–70.

14. Union der Freundschaftsorganisationen, Die vietnamesisch-deutsche Freundschaftsgesellschaft der Provinz Nghe An, and Das Volkskomitee der Stadt Vinh, *Spuren der Geschichte Vietnamesisch-Deutscher Freundschaft beim zeitigen Wiederaufbaus der Stadt Vinh in den Jahren 1973-1980* (Hanoi: The Gioi Publishing, 2011). This 156-page publication prepared by a committee of five Vietnamese veterans involved in construction during the 1970s, and translated by Dipl.-Ing. Nguyen Van Luc in excellent GDR-style German, was published in German(!) by Vietnam's Foreign Language Press government publisher.

15. Rudolf Oelschlägel, "Vietnamesische Offiziere an der Militärakademie 'Friedrich Engels' in Dresden: Erinnerungen eines Lehrers und Betreuers," in *Die DDR und Vietnam: Berichte-Erinnerungen-Fakten, Teil I*, ed. Ilona Schleicher (Berlin: Verband für Internationale Politik und Völkerrecht e.V, 2011), 70–90.

16. Decree of SED Politburo, 28 September 1982. Die Bundesbeauftragte für die Unterlagen des Staatssicherheitsdienstes (BStU), Zentralarchiv (ZA), SdM 1697, p. 471.

17. For many interesting details see Schwiesau, "Erfahrungen und Einsichten," 6–9.

18. GDR Council of Ministers, Decree on the Report of National Economy Plan Coordination for 1981 to 1985 between the GDR and the Socialist Republic of Vietnam, 11 June 1980. BStU, ZA, SdM 1661, 424–36.

19. Schwiesau, "Erfahrungen und Einsichten," 13.

20. Ibid., 15.

21. Ibid., 17.

22. For a welcome recent focus on Vietnamese experiences based on oral history see Christina Schwenkel, "Rethinking Asian Mobilities: Socialist Migration and Post-Socialist Repatriation of Vietnamese Contract Workers in East Germany" *Critical Asian Studies* 46, no. 2 (2014), 235–258, especially p. 246–253.

23. This aspect of East German–Vietnamese relations has been one of the few researched so far, albeit mostly focusing on the GDR itself and the working and living conditions of the Vietnamese workers. See Karin Weiss and Mike Dennis, eds., *Erfolg in der Nische?: die Vietnamesen in der DDR und in Ostdeutschland* (Münster: Lit, 2005); Karin Weiss, "Vietnam: Netzwerke zwischen Sozialismus und Kapitalismus," *Aus Politik und Zeitgeschichte,* no. 27 (2005): 24–30; Nguyen Van Huong, "Die Politik der DDR gegenüber Vietnam und den Vertragsarbeitern aus Vietnam sowie die Situation der Vietnamesen in Deutschland heute," in *Materialien der Enquete-Kommission "Überwindung der Folgen der SED-Diktatur im Prozess der deutschen Einheit"*, ed. Deutscher Bundestag (Baden-Baden: Nomos, 1999), 1301–63.

24. Schwiesau, "Erfahrungen und Einsichten," 17.

25. GDR Customs Administration, Information, undated [ca. 1988]. BStU, ZA, HA VI, 15192, p. 51–55.

26. Stefan Wolle, *Die heile Welt der Diktatur: Alltag und Herrschaft in der DDR 1971-1989* (Berlin: Ch. Links, 1998), 199–201.

27. "On GDR-SRV Cooperation Concerning the Production of Coffee Beans." For an excellent summary and compilation of facts, see Siegfried Kaulfuss, "Die Entwicklung des Kaffeeanbaus in Vietnam," in *Die DDR und Vietnam: Berichte-Erinnerungen-Fakten, Teil I*, ed. Ilona Schleicher (Berlin: Verband für Internationale Politik und Völkerrecht e.V, 2011), 39–51.
28. See http://www.ico.org/profiles_e.asp?section=Statistics (accessed 1 April 2014).
29. Kaulfuss, "Die Entwicklung des Kaffeeanbaus in Vietnam," 50.

## Bibliography

Freytag, Mirjam. *Die "Moritzburger" in Vietnam: Lebenswege nach einem Schul- und Aus-bildungsaufenthalt in der DDR: Vermitteln in interkulturellen Beziehungen*. Frankfurt: IKO-Verlag für Interkulturelle Kommunikation, 1998.
Huong, Nguyen Van. "Die Politik der DDR gegenüber Vietnam und den Vertragsarbe-itern aus Vietnam sowie die Situation der Vietnamesen in Deutschland heute." In *Materialien der Enquete-Kommission "Überwindung der Folgen der SED-Diktatur im Prozess der deutschen Einheit"*, ed. Deutscher Bundestag, 1301–63. Baden-Baden: Nomos, 1999.
Kaulfuss, Siegfried. "Die Entwicklung des Kaffeeanbaus in Vietnam." In *Die DDR und Vietnam: Berichte-Erinnerungen-Fakten, Teil I*, ed. Ilona Schleicher, 39–51. Berlin: Verband für Internationale Politik und Völkerrecht e.V, 2011.
Knöfel, Dieter. "Hilfe und Zusammenarbeit—die Wirtschaftsbeziehungen zwischen der DDR und Vietnam." In *Die DDR und Vietnam: Berichte-Erinnerungen-Fakten, Teil I*, ed. Ilona Schleicher, 20–38. Berlin: Verband für Internationale Politik und Völk-errecht e.V, 2011.
Oelschlägel, Rudolf. "Vietnamesische Offiziere an der Militärakademie 'Friedrich Engels' in Dresden: Erinnerungen eines Lehrers und Betreuers." In *Die DDR und Vietnam: Berichte-Erinnerungen-Fakten, Teil I*, ed. Ilona Schleicher, 70–90. Berlin: Verband für Internationale Politik und Völkerrecht e.V, 2011.
Reichardt, Achim. *Nie Vergessen – Solidarität üben!*. Berlin: Kai Homilius, 2006.
Schaefer, Bernd. "Die DDR und Vietnam: Ein besonderes Verhältnis." In *Deutsch-Viet-namesische Beziehungen: Tagungsband zum 35jährigen Jubiläum der diplomatischen Beziehungen zwischen der Bundesrepublik Deutschland und der Sozialistischen Repub-lik Vietnam*, ed. Goethe Institut Vietnam, Vietnam National University and Auswär-tiges Amt, 13–19. Hanoi/Berlin, 2010.
Schwenkel, Christina. "Civilizing the City: Socialist Ruins and Urban Renewal in Cen-tral Vietnam." *Positions* 20, no. 2 (Spring 2012): 437–70.
Schwenkel, Christina. "Rethinking Asian Mobilities: Socialist Migration and Post-Social-ist Repatriation of Vietnamese Contract Workers in East Germany." *Critical Asian Studies* 46, no. 2 (2014): 235–258.
Schwiesau, Hermann. "Erfahrungen und Einsichten: Als Botschafter der DDR in Viet-nam." In *Die DDR und Vietnam: Berichte-Erinnerungen-Fakten, Teil I*, ed. Ilona Schleicher. Berlin: Verband für Internationale Politik und Völkerrecht e.V, 2011.
Union der Freundschaftsorganisationen, Die vietnamesisch-deutsche Freundschafts-gesellschaft der Provinz Nghe An, and Das Volkskomitee der Stadt Vinh. *Spuren*

*der Geschichte Vietnamesisch-Deutscher Freundschaft beim zeitigen Wiederaufbaus der Stadt Vinh in den Jahren 1973-1980.* Hanoi: The Gioi Publishing, 2011.

Weiss, Karin. "Vietnam: Netzwerke zwischen Sozialismus und Kapitalismus." *Aus Politik und Zeitgeschichte* no. 27 (2005): 24–30.

Weiss, Karin, and Mike Dennis, eds. *Erfolg in der Nische?: die Vietnamesen in der DDR und in Ostdeutschland.* Münster: Lit, 2005.

Wernicke, Günter. ""Solidarität hilft siegen!" Zur Solidaritätsbewegung mit Vietnam in beiden deutschen Staaten." *Hefte zur DDR-Geschichte* no. 72 (2001).

Wolle, Stefan. *Die heile Welt der Diktatur: Alltag und Herrschaft in der DDR 1971-1989.* Berlin: Ch. Links, 1998.

Zahlbaum, Willi. "'Solidarität hilft siegen' (Autobiographisches Dokument von 1989)." In *Die DDR und Vietnam: Berichte-Erinnerungen-Fakten, Teil I,* ed. Ilona Schleicher, 75–85. Berlin: Verband für Internationale Politik und Völkerrecht e.V, 2011.

# PART III

## Ambivalent Solidarities

# William "Bloke" Modisane to Margaret Legum, 1966

Sunday

It's been a long time and I have lost count of how many times this letter was begun.[1] The details of the safari can only be told verbally, but it is perhaps interesting that the climax, in the sense of re-education, should have come from East Germany. I've learned so much about my life by having been in Potsdam. It was like being back in South Africa with the roles reversed in a kind of Kafka nightmare. It was like an English tourist visiting in Sophiatown. It's a bit complicated and I might not even be telling it properly. One sort of understood imploring white friends to buy one liquor because one was not permitted to do so oneself. One was actually asking somebody to break the law, and one used the condition of one's fluid life as a weapon of blackmail. I can see this today, and know also if the friend in Johannesburg had expressed thoughts of fear of getting into trouble with the police, I would probably have accused him of indifference to my "oppressed" state. I tremble at the thought that—I'm not even sure I ought to say it, or can in a way which would reduce the utter shame I feel. Did one perhaps not make friends in order to secure the supply of contraband luxuries? How much of this has motivated all friendships? When I wrote Blame Me the consciousness had not insinuated itself too clearly, or if it did, with what consciousness did I disguise this?

All the explanation begins to sound like a rationalization, to justify my actions which I am profoundly ashamed of, because I was afraid of getting into trouble with the Police. Once again East Germany returned to me the fear of the Police—and believe me, Margaret, this is not Cold War politics. Not that they did anything, but their overwhelming presence, the sight of so many uniforms and signs of prohibition somehow did this to me. It's all a bit confused, but I shall try to tell it as best I can.

It has been said that prohibition places a premium on goods. There is in East Berlin a thing called Intershop where foreigners are allowed to engage their beaugeous [sic] state by being able to buy Western goods and food at re-duced rates—cheaper than in London or New York, and these can only be paid for in foreign currency. I realize that these Eastern countries must earn hard currency, but I think the system is vile. Whiskey costs DM 12.00 about £1.20; in the open shops Johnny Walker cost 80.00 Marks, about £8. So it is with other goods—cigarettes, chocolates, coffee. Outside this shop are scores of East Germans imploring people—particularly Africans and other obvious strangers, to buy them one thing or the other, offering to pay double or whatever in East marks. This is forbidden and the shop is full of plainclothes Policemen.

The young people one can refuse in exchange for hostile looks and comments, but it is the older people, women in particular: "My daughter has a small child, could you buy me chocolates, coffee?" And people sort of stop to look, and some of them look like Police. So one explains that it is dangerous, and the look of disappointment is so great I give her a bar of my own chocolate, in full view of everybody, and then very expansively refuse to take the money pushed at one. I couldn't possibly, I reasoned, be arrested for making a present. Once when I could not give away a pound of Maxwell Coffee the old gentleman spat at me. I resolved then not to enter that shop again.

Then the Landlord who runs this constant-running cold water Hotel was having guests for dinner, and I suppose that since he must obviously brag of being able to secure Western goods because of the foreigners in his hotel, he asked me to buy him a few things. I had been classed as a Third Category tourist who must exchange 28 shillings a day, which gave me rather a small room. When I asked for a larger room, or at least one not cluttered with furnisher [sic] I was moved into a large room at the extra cost of EM 2 a day which he requested me to pay in West marks at the official rate of one to one. And all told, with the breakfast he wanted WM 10, which of course it's illegal for him to have and me to give him. So explained that in West Berlin one WM is exchanged for 2.90 EM. He pretended surprise. All my foreign money must be exchanged only at the bank, and included in the 28 shillings was money to be spent on food. Anyway, the arrangement for the larger room was a private deal which the Travel Agency, which arranges all accommodation for foreigners, was not to know about. It was for ten days and I agreed to pay him in WMarks. So come the day of his dinner party, he asks me to use the money to buy him things at Intershop. I was due to go to West Berlin that morning to post and collect me mail; so he offers to drive me to East Berlin which is two hours by train from Potsdam.

In the shop this man takes over the buying—ordering goods in excess of the WM20 due to him and proceeds to put the things in his bag. By this time I'm so terrified I'm speechless and all I wanted was to get away from him very fast. We part company and I begin walking to customs when this very nice man, apologizing profusely, asks to see my passport. "Why?" He shows me his Police identity. "That was Böttge, wasn't it." he said. Yes. "How much money did he give you?" Nothing. Why? "May I see your declaration?" He requests to see all the money I have on me. I give it to him. There were WM7 unaccounted for. "Where's the rest of the money?" Maybe it's change which I might have left at the hotel. "Why did you buy those things for Böttge?" He's my landlord, he's only carrying them home for me. I'm going to West Berlin and might be too late to find Intershop open. I didn't have more money than I was supposed to have or much less—which would have meant that I had disposed of my money illegally, like buying blackmarket East marks. He didn't believe my story and he was disappointed he couldn't substantiate irregular practice.

This prepared me, rather unfavorably, for what was to follow. Of course, I never went to Intershop again.

I had been eating at his restaurant—the food was reasonable in spite of the beer, but it was mainly to look at the waitress who was the best I had seen in my entire four weeks in East Germany. In any case all my illusions about German girls, particularly in this socialist country, had been shattered. In East Germany, particularly in Potsdam where Africans are pointed, stared at, and giggled at like curiosities, the girls seem to be on a crash programme for the title: Miss Virginity 1966. But there was this waitress whom I could look at and curse the socialist reconstruction of morals in the seven-year plan. One evening whilst serving me she invited me to wait for her to finish work. It was all terribly discreet and everything and the next time round she asked me to follow her at a respectable pace. Don't argue, I told myself, you might be lucky. Four weeks is four weeks.

I followed her to the apartment and once inside she began undressing. All done with me sweating on the chair, she informed me, quite coldly, that she would do anything I wanted. She standing in front of me celebrating her victory repeating: "I will do anything you want." Why? You are a foreigner, if you marry a woman you can take her with you. In West Germany you can divorce me on any grounds you like. I will stay with you as long as you like if you take me to West Germany. The temptation to promise anything and get what I was dying for became increasingly difficult to resist. It was the most difficult moment of my life. During one moment I said: Scrupples [sic] to hell, Bloke. Don't be a fool. I'm not proud of myself, Margaret, but I couldn't do it. I was too honest or too afraid—the latter, most likely. I refused the lady—which was not very gallant. I tried to reason with her, explained why I couldn't. And she sat on my lap, very nude, and begged me with tears in her eyes.

I can still see the tears in her eyes, and I keep asking myself, Why? On the way home I moved the scene to Sophiatown. What if somebody could have helped me to get out of Sophiatown and did not? What thoughts would have turned in my mind? I'm driving myself mad. Should I have done it? What real danger would there have been for me? What could they have done if they found out? Now that I declined to do it I'm searching for reasons to ease an ill conscience. I so desperately want somebody to say I was right. I have tried to find fault with her approach—then I say, why not? It depends how desperate you are. Why the blackmail? She could have done it another way. Rationalizations all. But hell, what can I do? She was entitled to use whatever method seemed persuasive.

Even in telling it to you I try to make light, but what a burden on my conscience. But it's behind me and this week-end I shall be in London and after the ordeal of looking for a flat I might even commit this thing into a deeper past of forgetfulness. On June 17 I finished the work in Potsdam after reading eleven volumes which were 80% in German Gothic. The four months of intensive German at Achenmühle did not include learning the Gothic alphabet, which I learned to read myself. I went and bought a German grammar, locked myself in for 48 hours and learned it. Then I returned to the archives to be driven mad by individualist characteristics of the handwriting. That took another 48 hours to feel comfortable. But I managed to read them all with difficulties here and there.

I'm at the stage where I read better than I speak, but this will be re-ad-justed soon. I've also been rather ambitious by buying a recording of Goethe's Faust which I listen to all the time, and before I leave I want to buy Thomas Mann reading from his work. This will speed up my speech. In the meantime I have till Friday to do all the work here then fly to London from Bonn on Friday or Saturday. I shall telephone you Saturday or Sunday. I'll probably be living in one of those Europe on $5 a Day hotels in Russel Square—which by the way is a myth. I'm dying to see the children, and hope to do so soon.

On Friday I picked up Colin's letter and was amused by your reported comments about my writing to you. Absolutely justified of course, and you are too dear a friend to completely forget even if I might let you suffer my carelessnesses of extended silences.

Love
Bloke

## Notes

1. The source of the Modisane letter is BC1329, Colin Legum Papers, University of Cape Town Libraries Special Collections. Thanks are due to the archive for permission to reproduce the letter.

Chapter 5

# Bloke Modisane in East Germany

*Simon Stevens*


"It's a long way from Johannesburg, although East German[y] conjures up several memories of Sophiatown. It's terribly depressing." William "Bloke" Modisane wrote these words in May 1966, in a letter to a friend, the London-based South African journalist Colin Legum.[1] It was a subject he took up at greater length in a letter to Legum's wife Margaret the following month, which is reproduced above.

Bloke Modisane was a leading member of the "*Drum* generation" of black South African writers, which also included Arthur Maimane, Es'kia Mphahlele, Nat Nakasa, Lewis Nkosi, and Can Themba. During the "fabulous decade" of the 1950s it was this close-knit group of writers and journalists who made *Drum* magazine, as Paul Gready puts it, "the symbol of a new urban South Africa, centered on and epitomized by Sophiatown."[2] Sophiatown—"the most cosmopolitan of South Africa's black social igloos" as Modisane himself characterized it—was a freehold "suburb" west of Johannesburg that, until its destruction, was one of the few areas of apartheid South Africa where Africans had legal property rights.[3]

Like most of the other members of the *Drum* generation, Modisane both published short fiction in the magazine and worked for it as a journalist, writing regular social and entertainment columns. Nkosi remembered him "dark-suited, bow-tied, the dandiest writer on the paper; to the delight of other members of the staff he signed his articles Bloke 'Debonair' Modisane."[4] In addition to writing, Modisane participated in late 1950s in the nonracial "African Theatre Workshop." In 1957–58 he and Nkosi worked with the visiting American director Lionel Rogosin, cowriting the script for Rogosin's film *Come Back, Africa,* and also appearing in it. For Modisane, the film was "the first authentic cinematic record of the system of apartheid in South Africa."[5] *Come Back, Africa* became a staple of anti-apartheid meetings around the world in the 1960s: in 1966 student activists arranged for it to be shown in West Berlin as part of an informational evening opposing the gruesome Italian documentary about postcolonial Africa, *Africa Addio.*[6]

Modisane would later describe himself as "an alien situated between the scorn and the hatred of both the white and the black world." His one-room Sophiatown shack in the 1950s was "a fly-over which connected the two worlds," filled with books, art, and sound recordings from Europe and North America. He was a voracious reader. Before being recruited to *Drum*, he had worked at the radical Vanguard Bookshop, owned and run by a "fierce and fanatical Trotskyist."[7] It was at the bookshop that Modisane first encountered the work of Franz Kafka, which would be a major influence on his writing. Kafka's attraction, he later explained, was that "this man could create a night-mare."[8] Nkosi recalled spending hours in Modisane's room, "holding intense discussions, listening to his formidable collection of jazz and classical records of Mozart, Beethoven, Bártok, and Stravinsky, and listening spellbound to the recorded monologues of Olivier's Richard III and Brando's Mark Anthony," much as Modisane would later improve his German by listening to a recording of Goethe's *Faust*.[9]

Modisane had also "arranged and furnished [his Sophiatown room] for the purposes of seduction." Sex for him was a form of escapism and his exploits were legendary among his friends. In his efforts "to effect a quick and successful seduction," it became, he recalled, "a most important challenge to set records, to actually work within a time limit, setting the clock and proceeding to operate on the reluctant Miss. I became inconsolately depressed and frustrated by the presence of an immovable blouse, it was an affront to my ego, and as a last resort I would fall back on the 'I love you' hypocrisy. If this did not work then there was something decidedly wrong with the woman."[10]

The fact that freehold Sophiatown lacked the regimented control that characterized townships built and owned by the government made it a target for the apartheid regime in the 1950s. Officials relocated Sophiatown residents to townships elsewhere in the course of the decade and eventually bulldozed the neighborhood to make way for a new all-white suburb. Modisane refused to leave Sophiatown until the last possible moment, and did not wish to stay in South Africa after its destruction. His autobiography opened with the declaration that "Something in me died, a piece of me died, with the dying of Sophiatown." The South African government, however, refused to issue Modisane a passport. The South African security police sought to blackmail him to inform against his *Drum* colleagues in return for permission to leave the country. Eventually in March 1959, Modisane left South Africa illegally on a train to Bechuanaland (now Botswana) dressed not in his usual debonair attire but as a migrant laborer. Having made his way north to Dar es Salaam in Tanganyika (now Tanzania) he cabled Lionel

Rogosin, then editing *Come Back, Africa* in New York, who arranged a plane ticket for him to London.[11]

Modisane spent the next few years as a "struggling artist" in London. In 1960, he wrote to the African-American writer Langston Hughes that he was "drift[ing] from job to job, working my guts out by day and writing by night."[12] Increasingly he took acting parts on the stage, on radio, and on television. He also wrote TV and radio plays and programs himself. Modisane remained close to other members of the small South African exile community in Britain. Back in South Africa, he had been a member of the African National Congress (ANC) Youth League in the early 1950s before becoming alienated from the Congress movement. At the end of the decade, he had found himself in "mental accord" with—but did not join—the breakaway Pan Africanist Congress (PAC), which was critical of what PAC leaders perceived to be the domination of the ANC by white communists. In London, Modisane appears to have interacted with a diverse range of South African exiles. He played poker with the leading white communist Joe Slovo, for instance, and was close to Colin and Margaret Legum, white South Africans known in anti-apartheid circles for their anti-communism.[13]

In September 1963, *Blame Me on History,* Modisane's autobiography, was published to considerable acclaim. He subsequently began applying to various foundations for funding to continue his writing. It was this that ultimately took Modisane to East Germany, after the self-described "bum writer with pretensions about writing books on history" received a grant from the Rockefeller Foundation to research and write a book on the Maji Maji resistance against German rule in East Africa in 1905–07. Modisane spent most of 1965 in Tanzania, conducting archival research and oral history interviews and visiting the places where fighting had taken place.[14] In late 1965 or early 1966, he traveled to Germany and spent four months intensively studying German in Bavaria in West Germany before continuing his archival research. In the 1920s, the records of German colonial administration had been transferred to the Reich Archive in Potsdam, and they remained there, under East German control, after the division of Germany. In May 1966, therefore, Modisane crossed through Checkpoint Charlie and spent several weeks researching in Potsdam.

Modisane visited East Germany at a time of increasing ties between the GDR and South Africans opposed to apartheid. The ANC had established an "External Mission" immediately after the Sharpeville Massacre in March 1960, and quickly expanded its international presence and activities. There were already long-standing links between the Socialist Unity Party (SED) and the South African Communist Party (SACP). In the 1960s, the increasingly close alliance and overlapping memberships of the SACP and the ANC ensured that the ANC too became a recipient of GDR support. In July 1960, the SED had established a Committee for Solidarity with the Peoples of Africa (later renamed the Solidarity Committee of the GDR), which was responsible for maintaining relations and support for the ANC and other liberation movements. The Solidarity Committee also mobilized anti-apartheid campaigns inside East Germany, organizing rallies and other protests, for instance, during the Rivonia Trial of Nelson Mandela and his co-accused in 1963–64, and during the trial of SACP chairman Bram Fischer in March–May 1966, around the time of Modisane's visit. In addition, the Solidarity Committee provided scholarships for South African students to study in East German educational institutions. There were five ANC students studying in the GDR in 1962, a number that increased over the subsequent decades to around a hundred South African students at any one time by the late 1980s.[15]

The first major ANC delegation visited the GDR in December 1963. Duma Nokwe (Secretary-General of the ANC and a member of the SACP Central Committee) and Moses Kotane (Secretary-General of the SACP and Treasurer of the ANC) led the delegation, which received a pledge of goods worth 100,000 GDR Marks, the first installment of material aid from the Solidarity Committee to the ANC. Aid would continue at substantial levels until the end of the GDR although material rather than financial aid was provided, due to the GDR's persistent shortage of hard currency. Most notably, *Sechaba*, the new "official organ" of the ANC, was printed in the GDR at the Solidarity Committee's expense from 1967 onward.

East Germany also provided training. In 1961–62, SACP member Mac Maharaj, who subsequently played a leading role in Umkhonto we Sizwe (MK), the ANC's armed wing, spent nearly a year being trained in the GDR, first in printing, and then in sabotage. From 1969 onward, individuals and small groups of MK cadres underwent training in the GDR in propaganda and underground work before attempting to infiltrate back into South Africa.[16] Around the same time, as the historian Stephen Ellis has recently emphasized, the Stasi began to provide security training to the ANC's newly established department of intelligence and security, which would later be responsible for the notorious abuses of dissidents and suspected spies in the ANC's camps in Angola in the 1980s. Stasi instructors, Ellis records, taught ANC trainees that "security depended on respect for 'states of real socialism.'"[17]

Bloke Modisane's position in East Germany in 1966 as a South African who was not aligned with the ANC or the SACP was thus an unusual one. His account of his time there hints at themes that have so far received little attention in the historiography of East German relations with opponents of white minority rule in southern Africa. The great strength and the great limitation of the literature on international solidarity with the struggle against apartheid is that until very recently it has been written primarily by former participants. The monumental series on *The Road to Democracy in South Africa* produced by the South African Democracy Education Trust, for instance, which includes a two-part, 1,300-page volume on *International Solidarity*, proclaims that the chapters of that volume are "written by activist scholars with deep roots in the movements and organizations they are writing about."[18] For communist countries, this means primarily former diplomats or members of state-sponsored solidarity committees. The chapter on the GDR and the South African liberation struggle is by Hans-Georg Schleicher, a former GDR diplomat in Africa and at the UN, who is also the co-author (with his wife Ilona Schleicher) of the only book-length study of the subject in English.[19]

Schleicher frames his chapter in *The Road to Democracy* as an effort "to do justice to the real achievements of GDR solidarity."[20] Just as one instrumental purpose of East German solidarity with the struggle against apartheid was, as Toni Weis argues, "to reflect back on the GDR and shed a favorable light on it in the eyes of its population," there is a sense in which much of what has been written on this topic since the end of both apartheid and of East German communism is intended to shed a more favorable light on the GDR in the eyes of history.[21] The achievements of GDR solidarity with opponents of apartheid were of course very real, and present a stark contrast to the policies of most Western governments toward South Africa. But generally absent from a literature that has, understandably, focused on the *activities* of the struggle against apartheid, wherever that struggle took place, are the kinds of tensions hinted at in Modisane's letter. As Hugh Macmillan has pointed out in his recent work on the ANC in exile in Zambia, there has been remarkably little scholarly study of "the ANC and the South African *experience* of exile."[22] In the East German case, the "solidarity" actions on which the historiography has focused did not generally involve official encouragement of personal contacts between East Germans and southern Africans: in Weis's words, the GDR government emphasized "solidarity between peoples at the cost of solidarity between people."[23] The nature of the personal contacts that occurred nevertheless, and of South Africans' experiences and perceptions of the actually existing socialism in East Germany, remain topics for further research.

Modisane's fearful account of the "overwhelming presence" of the East German police contrasts starkly, for example, with Maharaj's recollection that during his training in the GDR in 1961–62 "there was no sign... at the level of ordinary people's lives that the state was a repressive force; there was no sign of a secret police spying on people. To the extent that it existed or was noticed, it was seen as a benign defensive force." Indeed, for Maharaj, "In 1961, the GDR was on the march. Reconstruction of the economy was taking place side by side with social and medical services, and free education for everybody. Unlike London [where Maharaj had previously been studying] where if you couldn't afford it you were left behind." Whereas Modisane's time in the East Germany left him feeling depressed, Maharaj's experiences there served to reinforce his unconditional commitment to communism.[24]

Writing to Langston Hughes from Berlin in May 1966, Modisane compared the experience of being black in a small town in East Germany to "being caged in a zoo with children giggling at one and having parents drawing their children's attention to you saying Nieger [sic]—which sounds dangerously like Nigger."[25] But in Modisane's letter to Margaret Legum, it is not such racial microaggressions that he stresses, but rather the privileged position in which his foreign citizenship placed him relative to ordinary East Germans. One theme that had run through his 1963 autobiography was how, amid the numerous restrictions placed upon African life under apartheid, "prohibition places a high premium on restricted goods," whether those "goods" were interracial sex (prohibited in apartheid South Africa by the "Immorality Act"), the home brews illegally sold by Modisane's mother in her shebeen (speakeasy), or the martinis, wine, and after-dinner drinks that Modisane had served to guests at the elaborate dinner parties he hosted in his Sophiatown room, despite the illegality of Africans consuming "European" liquor.[26] In East Germany, it was the "signs of prohibition" that stood out to him and that led him to draw parallels with South Africa. His letter to Margaret Legum focuses above all on his experiences arising from two forms of prohibition: first, the prohibition on East German citizens possessing foreign currency and shopping in the *Intershops,* the stores that sold Western-produced or Western-quality products to foreign visitors in order to earn hard currency for the state, and, second, the prohibition on citizens leaving the country, a restriction that perhaps recalled Modisane's own difficulties escaping South Africa.[27]

Whether Bloke Modisane ever returned to the GDR after his "terribly depressing" experiences there in 1966 is unclear. We know very little about his life in exile.[28] His research on German East Africa was never published, but he maintained links with Germany. During his 1966 visit, he appears to have made connections that enabled him subsequently to write for West German television.[29] In the context of rising anti-immigration sentiment in Britain, Modisane wrote in the early 1970s that his "sense of rejection is waxing, and the search for another country to live in is on the way up."[30] He subsequently married a German woman, and moved with her first to Rome and then to Dortmund in West Germany. He continued to live in Dortmund after his wife left him, and it was there that he died in 1986, at age sixty-two. It was, as his former editor at *Drum* wrote, "a sorrowfully miserable end, for by this time he was living quite on his own in that cold, cold room in that cold German city, with only his bottles of whisky for company."[31]

**Simon Stevens** is a Max Weber Postdoctoral Fellow at the European University Institute. He completed his doctorate in international history at Columbia University. His dissertation was entitled "Boycotts and Sanctions against South Africa: An International History." Stevens has also been a Dissertation Fellow at the Center for the United States and the Cold War at New York University and a National Fellow at the Miller Center for Public Affairs at the University of Virginia.

## Notes

1. Bloke [Modisane] to Colin [Legum], letter, 28 May [1966], File B13.43, Colin Legum Papers (Collection BC1329), Manuscripts and Archives Department, University of Cape Town Libraries, Cape Town, South Africa.
2. Paul Gready, "The Sophiatown Writers of the Fifties: The Unreal Reality of Their World," *Journal of Southern African Studies* 16, no. 1 (1990): 144. See also Lewis Nkosi, "The Fabulous Decade: The Fifties," in Lewis Nkosi, *Home and Exile and Other Selections,* expanded ed., Longman studies in African literature (London; New York: Longman, 1983), 3–25; Michael Chapman, ed., *The 'Drum' Decade: Stories from the 1950s* (Pietermaritzburg: University of Natal Press, 1989).
3. Bloke Modisane, *Blame Me on History* (London: Panther, 1965), 18.
4. Nkosi, "The Fabulous Decade," 8.
5. Bloke Modisane, untitled contribution to Lionel Rogosin, *Come Back, Africa* (Johannesburg: STE Publishers, 2004), 133.
6. On the opposition to *Africa Addio,* see Quinn Slobodian, *Foreign Front: Third World Politics in Sixties West Germany* (Durham, NC: Duke University Press, 2012), 137–46.
7. Sylvester Stein, *Who Killed Mr. Drum?* (Bellville, South Africa: Mayibuye Books, 1999), 80; Modisane, *Blame Me on History,* 83–89.
8. Liz Gunner, "Exile and the Diasporic Voice: Bloke Modisane's BBC Radio plays 1969–1987," *Current Writing: Text and Reception in Southern Africa* 15, no. 2 (2003): 53, 55.
9. Lewis Nkosi, "Bloke Modisane: Blame Me On History," in *Still Beating the Drum: Critical Perspectives on Lewis Nkosi,* ed. Lindy Stiebel and Elizabeth Gunner (New York: Rodopi, 2005), 300.
10. Modisane, *Blame Me on History,* 215–16.
11. Ibid., 7, 272–85, 294–95, 299–301, 306–18; Stein, *Who Killed Mr. Drum?,* 146; Rogosin, *Come Back, Africa,* 126.

12. Shane Graham and John Walters, eds., *Langston Hughes and the South African Drum Generation: The Correspondence* (New York: Palgrave Macmillan, 2010), 113.

13. Gready, "The Sophiatown Writers of the Fifties," 152; Modisane, *Blame Me on History*, 255; Michael Chapman, "More than Telling a Story: Drum and Its Significance in Black South African Writing," in *The 'Drum' Decade: Stories from the 1950s*, ed. Chapman, 202–6; Stein, *Who Killed Mr. Drum?*, 167; Dennis Herbstein, "Margaret Legum: Exiled Economist Who Returned to Help Shape the New South Africa," *Guardian*, 15 November 2007, 41.

14. Graham and Walters, *Langston Hughes and the South African Drum Generation*, 169, 173, 176–77, 181.

15. Hans-Georg Schleicher, "GDR Solidarity: The German Democratic Republic and the South African Liberation Struggle," in *The Road to Democracy in South Africa*, vol. 3, pt. 2, *International Solidarity*, ed. South African Democracy Education Trust (Cape Town: Zebra Press, 2004), 1092–94, 1110–17, 1126; Hans-Georg Schleicher and Ilona Schleicher, *Special Flights to Southern Africa: The GDR and Liberation Movements in Southern Africa* (Harare: SAPES Books, 1998), 41–50. On the posters produced by the Solidarity Committee to express and mobilize solidarity with the struggle against apartheid, see Heike Hartmann and Susann Lewerenz, "Campaigning against Apartheid in East and West Germany," *Radical History Review*, no. 119 (2014): 191–204.

16. Schleicher, "GDR Solidarity," 1103–04, 1118–21, 1123–32; Schleicher and Schleicher, *Special Flights*, 34, 50–55, 61–62; Padraig O'Malley, *Shades of Difference: Mac Maharaj and the Struggle for South Africa* (New York: Viking, 2007), 87–92.

17. Stephen Ellis, *External Mission: The ANC in Exile, 1960–1990* (London: Hurst, 2012), 78, 152, 159, 184–85, 216–17. See also Schleicher and Schleicher, *Special Flights*, 62–63.

18. South African Democracy Education Trust, *The Road to Democracy in South Africa*, vol. 3, parts 1 & 2, back cover.

19. Schleicher, "GDR Solidarity," 1069–53; Schleicher and Schleicher, *Special Flights*.

20. Schleicher, "GDR Solidarity," 1070.

21. Toni Weis, "The Politics Machine: On the Concept of 'Solidarity' in East German Support for SWAPO," *Journal of Southern African Studies* 37, no. 2 (2011): 363, 353–55.

22. Hugh Macmillan, "The African National Congress of South Africa in Zambia: The Culture of Exile and the Changing Relationship with Home, 1964–1990," *Journal of Southern African Studies* 35, no. 2 (2009): 303–5 (emphasis added); Hugh Macmillan, *The Lusaka Years: The ANC in Exile in Zambia, 1963–1994* (Auckland Park, South Africa: Jacana Media, 2013).

23. Weis, "The Politics Machine," 366.

24. O'Malley, *Shades of Difference*, 90–92; Mac Maharaj, interview by Padraig O'Malley, 4 November 2002, http://www.nelsonmandela.org/omalley/index.php/site/q/03lv0 3445/04lv03689/05lv03714/06lv03742.htm.

25. Graham and Walters, *Langston Hughes and the South African Drum Generation*, 182. Maharaj recalled similar "curiosity" about his color in the small East German village where he trained in printing, but he also remembered the GDR as "the first country where I did not feel I was being discriminated against because I was a black man,"

unlike both South Africa and Britain. See O'Malley, *Shades of Difference*, 90–91; Mac Maharaj, interview by Padraig O'Malley, 18 September 2002, http://www .nelsonmandela.org/omalley/index.php/site/q/03lv03445/04lv03689/05lv03714/0 6lv03731.htm.

26. Modisane, *Blame Me on History,* 219, 37, 260.
27. On the history of Intershops in East Germany, see Jonathan R. Zatlin, *The Currency of Socialism: Money and Political Culture in East Germany* (New York: Cambridge University Press, 2007), 243–85.
28. Gunner, "Exile and the Diasporic Voice," 49–50; André Landman, "Serendipitous Discoveries: The Elusive Bloke Modisane in the Colin Legum Papers," *Social Dynamics* 36, no. 3 (2010): 453–56.
29. On Modisane's connections with "German TV people" during the period he was back living in London in the 1970s, see Stein, *Who Killed Mr. Drum?,* 211, 202–03.
30. Landman, "Serendipitous Discoveries," 455.
31. Stein, *Who killed Mr. Drum?,* 231.

# Bibliography

Chapman, Michael, ed. *The 'Drum' Decade: Stories from the 1950s.* Pietermaritzburg: University of Natal Press, 1989.

———. "More than Telling a Story: Drum and Its Significance in Black South African Writing." In *The 'Drum' Decade: Stories from the 1950s,* ed. Michael Chapman, 183–232. Pietermaritzburg: University of Natal Press, 1989.

Ellis, Stephen. *External Mission: The ANC in Exile, 1960–1990.* London: Hurst, 2012.

Graham, Shane, and John Walters, eds. *Langston Hughes and the South African Drum Generation: The Correspondence.* New York, NY: Palgrave Macmillan, 2010.

Gready, Paul. "The Sophiatown Writers of the Fifties: The Unreal Reality of Their World." *Journal of Southern African Studies* 16, no. 1 (1990): 139–64.

Gunner, Liz. "Exile and the Diasporic Voice: Bloke Modisane's BBC Radio Plays 1969–1987." *Current Writing: Text and Reception in Southern Africa* 15, no. 2 (2003): 49–62.

Hartmann, Heike, and Susann Lewerenz. "Campaigning against Apartheid in East and West Germany." *Radical History Review,* no. 119 (2014): 191–204.

Landman, André. "Serendipitous Discoveries: The Elusive Bloke Modisane in the Colin Legum Papers." *Social Dynamics* 36, no. 3 (2010): 453–56.

Macmillan, Hugh. "The African National Congress of South Africa in Zambia: The Culture of Exile and the Changing Relationship with Home, 1964–1990." *Journal of Southern African Studies* 35, no. 2 (2009): 303–29.

———. *The Lusaka Years: The ANC in Exile in Zambia, 1963–1994.* Auckland Park, South Africa: Jacana Media, 2013.

Modisane, Bloke. *Blame Me on History.* London: Panther, 1965.

Nkosi, Lewis. "Bloke Modisane: Blame Me On History." In *Still Beating the Drum: Critical Perspectives on Lewis Nkosi,* ed. Lindy Stiebel and Elizabeth Gunner, 297–310. New York: Rodopi, 2005.

———. *Home and Exile and other Selections.* Longman studies in African literature. Expanded ed. London; New York: Longman, 1983.

O'Malley, Padraig. *Shades of Difference: Mac Maharaj and the Struggle for South Africa.* New York: Viking, 2007.

Rogosin, Lionel. *Come Back, Africa.* Johannesburg: STE Publishers, 2004.

Schleicher, Hans-Georg. "GDR Solidarity: The German Democratic Republic and the South African Liberation Struggle." In *The Road to Democracy in South Africa,* vol. 3, pt. 2, *International Solidarity,* ed. South African Democracy Education Trust, 1069–153. Pretoria: Unisa Press, 2008.

Schleicher, Hans-Georg, and Ilona Schleicher. *Special Flights to Southern Africa: The GDR and Liberation Movements in Southern Africa.* Harare: SAPES Books, 1998.

Slobodian, Quinn. *Foreign Front: Third World Politics in Sixties West Germany.* Durham: Duke University Press, 2012.

South African Democracy Education Trust. *The Road to Democracy in South Africa.* Vol. 3, Cape Town: Zebra Press, 2004.

Stein, Sylvester. *Who Killed Mr. Drum?* Bellville, South Africa: Mayibuye Books, 1999.

Weis, Toni. "The Politics Machine: On the Concept of 'Solidarity' in East German Support for SWAPO." *Journal of Southern African Studies* 37, no. 2 (2011): 351–67.

Zatlin, Jonathan R. *The Currency of Socialism: Money and Political Culture in East Germany.* New York: Cambridge University Press, 2007.

Chapter 6

# African Students and the Politics of Race and Gender in the German Democratic Republic

*Sara Pugach*

In 1967, a Zambian official at his country's embassy in Moscow held a meeting with East German diplomats. They discussed the official's concern that there were several Zambian students in the German Democratic Republic who wanted to marry local women, or indeed already had. The Zambian official was unhappy with this development, since "there are still many difficulties to overcome in Zambia, and apart from the effort that it would take their husbands to care for them, the women would have trouble accustoming themselves to the country." He suggested that he would be pleased if the GDR found a way to prevent these marriages. The response of his East German counterparts was swift, decisive, and unequivocal: the GDR would not prevent foreigners from marrying its citizens, nor would it attach any race-based conditions to such marriages.[1]

The East German reaction to the Zambian request echoed the general GDR policy on race. The GDR presented itself as a nonracist, anti-imperialist state, and contrasted itself with the West, which the GDR considered the inheritor of Nazi racism and imperialism.[2] As Toni Weis has argued, the GDR imagined Africa through the lens of solidarity. According to Weis, this meant that the GDR and its African partner states would work together toward the goal of socialist harmony and economic development. While the GDR was more economically advanced in terms of Marx's historical epochs, the two sides were still equal and would support each other in the struggle to create forward-thinking socialist states.[3]

On the ground however, East German attitudes toward interracial relationships or marriages were not as liberal as the Zambian official was led to believe. African students who came to the GDR between the 1950s and 1970s found themselves in a place where the professed anti-colonial, anti-racist dogma of the ruling Socialist Unity Party frequently came into conflict with the realities of everyday racism. Racial and sexual stereotypes remained remarkably consistent with those of the pre-1945 era, even as government officials and ordinary citizens alike struggled to dispel them. The GDR was more a site of ambivalence and inconsistency than tolerance when it came to questions of race.

The idea of the lascivious African man and his counterpart, the promiscuous German woman, so prominent in imperial Germany, continued especially to shape perceptions of African-German interactions in the GDR.[4] The SED was committed to demonstrating that its leaders had resisted Nazism; East German doctrine held that while fascism continued to survive in and even define the neighboring Federal Republic, the GDR had expunged all its traces.[5] The anxiety surrounding African men who consorted with white women make it clear, however, that even if racial biases were denied on an official level, bigotry nonetheless endured and complicated other efforts to integrate foreigners into the GDR.

The inseparable realities of the Cold War and decolonization defined GDR attitudes toward Africans living in the state, though these attitudes did shift as the Cold War progressed. Soviet ideology was anti-imperial, and as a satellite of the USSR East Germany had to position itself as an ally to Africa in the broader fight against late colonialism. Additionally, the Soviets wanted to attract as many allies from recently decolonized nations as possible to compete with the United States. The GDR and other Soviet bloc countries were to assist in the mission of supplying aid to states that were nonaligned or leaning toward socialism. However, the GDR was not only interested in fostering bonds to emergent African states because of its relationship with the Soviet Union. The GDR also hoped to combat the West German Hallstein Doctrine, which held that the FRG was the only actual German state. From 1955 through 1972, the FRG used the Hallstein Doctrine to punish any state that recognized the GDR's political existence by threatening to sever diplomatic and economic ties with the offender.[6] In crafting cultural and education exchange agreements with newly independent African nations such as Guinea,[7] the GDR thus challenged the doctrine and asserted itself as a legitimate political entity.

The prejudices that African students confronted undercut the GDR's claim to defend international solidarity and racial equality against Western imperialism. Life as an international student in East Germany was not easy. In some cases, such as among the Zanzibari medical trainees, whom Young-Sun Hong has discussed, African students were purposefully separated from the general public and lived in substandard housing in smaller East German towns like Quedlinburg.[8] Whatever educational institution they attended, their teachers and fellow students subjected them to constant political education, and they were inundated with Marxist ideology.[9] This education was, moreover, intended not only to mold their political opinions, but also to contribute to their moral, including sexual, improvement. Finally, they encountered an East German population that was deeply conflicted about race. On the surface, university officials such as those from Leipzig's Karl Marx University (KMU) were supportive of African students and their right to live and pursue an education in the GDR. At times, however, the private statements that these officials made about African men and their white girl-friends or wives belied their supposedly neutral, anti-racist attitudes.

At the same time, the presence of African students also became routine. They either lived in the same dormitories as German students,[10] or in international dorms, which housed exchange students from countries around the world.[11] According to Ginga Eichler, an East German who lived in an international dorm during the 1960s, the reason that dorms for international students were established was relatively mundane: during the annual *Leipziger Messe,* or trade fair, Leipzig dormitories were repurposed to house *Messe* guests. While German students usually went home for the holidays during the *Messe,* international students did not have that option. Thus dormitories where international students could continue to live even during the *Messe* were created.[12]

Archival records also indicate that relationships between African male students and East German women were fairly commonplace. Many personal files from the KMU in Leipzig reveal such relationships. Perhaps most indicative of the prevalence of interracial unions, however, was the existence of an illegal "abortion ring" in the 1960s. According to accounts from the Leipzig District Court, a Nigerian agriculture student was the middleman facilitating contact between African students with pregnant East German girlfriends and a woman who performed abortions for financial compensation. The accounts show that the woman, who was also East German, carried out at least 60 abortions between 1962 and 1965, primarily on women who had been "impregnated by an African student."[13] The following chapter will discuss the ways in which the case was handled, and its more complex implications for the history of Afro-German relationships. What the court case first confirms, however, is that relationships between Africans and Germans were unexceptional. They became points of political debate, and were freighted with long-held stereotypes of black sexuality. Nonetheless, they occurred frequently.

Despite this partial integration of African students into East German life through dormitories and romantic relationships, everyday racism persisted both on the street and in private political exchanges. Indeed, racism remained a major problem for East German officials in the Ministry of Foreign

Affairs, Ministry of Education, and other federal institutions, and one that they needed to suppress. To contest the Hallstein Doctrine, it was crucial that the GDR cement ties with African countries. Offering scholarships and other means of support to African students was one way of doing so. Recently decolonized states needed individuals trained in specific, usually practical, subjects, such as tropical or veterinary medicine, that would concretely contribute to national development.[14] In the case of Guinea, which lost access to significant financial and material aid when its population voted to become independent from France in 1958, higher education in Soviet bloc countries replaced metropolitan schooling in colonial capitals like Paris.[15]

African students were not simply pawns of Cold War politics. Degrees obtained overseas could bring heightened status at home, and study in the GDR was sometimes the first step to travel and settlement elsewhere, often in the West.[16] While Africans who lived in Germany prior to 1945 had little recourse to help when confronted with racism, Africans in the GDR could turn to their own embassies and governments. They could, and did, threaten to leave East Germany if their demands went unmet. Since East Germany wanted to project a positive image in independent Africa, universities were sensitive to the appeals of African students, and worked to accommodate them, not drive them out. African students were now honored guests, not colonial subjects, and the appearance of overt racism could damage the GDR's status on the international stage. The ambivalent attitude toward sex and race at all levels, however, threatened the GDR's status as a brother in anti-imperial solidarity.

## African and German Sexuality in the GDR

There were subtle shifts in how Germans dealt with sexual relationships between white women and black men over time. In the imperial and Weimar era, African carnal desires were seen as a threat, and in the Nazi period they were to be expunged through measures such as sterilization.[17] Throughout, the idea that African male and German female sexuality constituted an explosive combination was relatively consistent. It would have been surprising, then, if this belief had not persisted in the GDR. Indeed, a 1959 report concerning international students by the Vice Rector for Student Affairs at Leipzig's KMU suggests how little the hypothesis about the relationship between black men and white women had changed from the early twentieth century. In a section of the report labeled "the moral situation," the Vice Rector commented that, "from time to time there are some students—especially those from African countries—who make themselves vulnerable to complaints because of their association with questionable women." He continued: "We are convinced that this state of affairs will be improved through the strengthening of our cultural work with these international students."[18] In other words, the Vice Rector thought that immoral German women were enticing African men. Moreover, he saw socialist morality as the answer to the problem of sexual impropriety.

Some Africans overstepped the moral bounds of the GDR so completely that they put themselves in danger of being expelled from the country. In 1963 the director of a dormitory in Leipzig complained that a Malian vocational student's promiscuity was causing problems for other residents. The man usually did not come home until at least 1 A.M., and was always in the company of a different woman. He had rejected all attempts to dissuade him from this behavior. The director did not consider him worthy of receiving career training in the GDR, and recommended sending him back to Mali.[19] The process whereby the GDR would have ejected the student was, however, very dissimilar to a colonial expulsion. Removal could only take place after lengthy examination of an individual case, and in consultation with Mali or another African partner state.[20] There was no summary expulsion. Under the political circumstances, the GDR tread cautiously, unwilling to upset relations with any African nation.

The East German "corrective" to aberrant African behavior was thus different from that of earlier eras. Rather than expelling or deporting perceived offenders, GDR officials hoped to take another tack. They were optimistic that the East German example of morality would save African students from their own worst impulses. To this end, Leipzig's Vice Rector even recommended that dormitory directors "work patiently and doggedly" on the issue of appropriate sexuality with African students.[21] Sexual conditioning was apparently part and parcel of the general East German goal of Marxist (re)education. A good Marxist not only hewed to a specific ideology; he was also able to exercise self-control over his baser impulses. There were occasional expulsions on moral or sexual grounds as, for example, with the Nigerian who helped women procure abortions, or a Ghanaian medical student who admitted to raping an East German colleague. But students were more commonly allowed to remain in the belief that they could be rehabilitated.[22]

African women, too, were subject to East German moral education. In the 1960s, four Guinean women came to Leipzig as part of a special training program at the *Deutsche Hochschule für Körperkultur* (DHfK). All were working toward degrees that would enable them to return to Guinea as coaches or gym teachers for girls. Two of the Guineans were assigned to be roommates, but did not get along. The school's director of international affairs alleged that they had almost come to blows, but would not approve their request for single rooms. Instead, the women were cautioned to heed the rules of their dormitory.[23] While the director never explicitly mentioned race when discussing the conflict, it was likely in the subtext. Elsewhere, he had advised all four Guinean women that they needed to improve their conduct. He said, "You have been warned to adhere more closely to school rules concerning cleanliness, morality, and local customs, as well as to maintain good mutual relationships amongst yourselves."[24] The stereotype of African lasciviousness that adhered to African men does not seem to have extended to African women. There was little fear that female African students would become involved with white men. Nonetheless, as with the men, their morality was suspect and needed correction.

The morality that the East German political and educational institutions hoped to impart to their African male and female students closely echoed SED leader Walter Ulbricht's 1958 speech "Ten Commandments of Socialist Morality." As Jennifer V. Evans has argued, while there is a rich historiography on the conservative ethics of the postwar West, including the FRG, there has been less emphasis on the similarly staid morality of the 1950s and 1960s GDR.[25] This conservative, family-centered morality was reflected in Ulbricht's speech, as he urged East German citizens to behave in an upright, virtuous manner. His call to moral decency was also intended as a blow to the FRG, which he depicted as a hotbed of sin completely under the control of the debauched United States.[26] Josie McLellan's work on love in the GDR also shows the extent to which the state remained conventional in its attitudes toward sex and the family at least in the 1950s and 1960s, allowing for some sexual liberation but largely within the framework of traditional heterosexual pairings.[27] In this context, Africa can be viewed not only as a political battleground but also a moral one, where those students who were trained in socialist countries would become models of responsibility, while Westerners fell deeper into depravity.

Ulbricht envisioned a properly moral GDR, where citizens were decent and hardworking. At the same time, the GDR was also narrated as an anti-racist, anti-imperial bastion. In reality, though, fear of African sexuality continued. Conflict over racial biases and the extent to which they should be allowed to exist persisted alongside that fear, since it was clear that prejudice weakened the GDR's image as a racially neutral society. In 1963, for example, a bar brawl in Leipzig brought the debate on both African-German relationships and the GDR's anti-racist commitment into sharp relief. The manager of the pub where the incident occurred reported that a large group of African students had fought with a handful of Eastern Europeans. The fight began inside the restaurant, surged into the foyer and cloakroom, and ended on the streets of Leipzig. As the brawl moved from place to place, more Africans joined.[28]

The bar manager used the event as a platform to make commentary on the goings-on at his café, and his impressions of the general problem with African students and sexually available German women. He claimed that many such women frequented his establishment, and lowered its reputation. One of these women had even been the catalyst for the fight. Additionally, the manager maintained that Africans were essentially the only exchange students who caused him difficulties. Indian, Chinese, Japanese, Korean, and Arab students were not disruptive. Neither, he intoned, were *most* Africans, but when troubles did occur, Africans were usually the culprits.[29]

While he denigrated his African clientele, the manager also held himself up as a properly anti-racist East German citizen. He said that he and his staff always treated their African clientele in a friendly manner, and that neither his employees nor his other customers had ever made a bigoted remark in their presence. African impropriety only concerned him because of the effect it might have on the broader Leipzig public. When Africans misbehaved in front of Germans, he fretted that they reinforced preexisting "racist, stupid prejudices." The conduct of a minority of African students would therefore harm the entire African community as Germans would not differentiate between the troublemakers and the larger population. Moreover, if discrimination became rampant, it "would not serve the continuous struggle of honest socialists the world over for the abolition of racial antagonism."[30]

The manager's report on the fight became a general commentary on his African customers. It reflected broader inconsistencies and contradictions in GDR attitudes toward race. He asserted that his staff and patrons were not overtly racist, but worried about the overall effect of African aggression on an *already* racist East Germany. The manager's personal prejudices were also on display. He placed himself on the side of the international socialists who condemned racism, but still assumed that it was the African students, not their Eastern European counterparts, who were responsible for the brawl. Further, he insinuated that Africans upset racialized and gendered orders in the GDR. If anyone shared culpability for the brawl, the manager took for granted that it was immoral white women. Together, African students and libertine German women destabilized a moral hierarchy in which German females were not meant to seduce or form connections with African males.

The manager envisaged a GDR that prized equality and reflected tolerance, but still prohibited African-German unions. He was not alone in conceiving of a GDR that was at once inclusive *and* exclusive. In the mid 1960s, the head of the Malian students' organization in the GDR accused a representative from the KMU's office of international affairs of viciously slandering a fellow Malian. He was charged with telling the man's German wife that her African husband would probably cheat, because he believed that Africans were only in East Germany to have children with as many women as possible.[31] The representative's superior at the KMU upbraided him for making such an uncouth, racist remark, and warned him that he would have to watch his language in the future. Yet the superior also made it clear that he shared his subordinate's suspicion of African men who had relationships with German women. He even agreed that Africans would likely stray from monogamous relationships. However, he confided, he did not want the Malians to know his true opinion.[32] Officially, he hoped to portray the GDR as a paragon of racial equality to its African students, who were esteemed guests. In private, he doubted African morality and fidelity.

The Malians were not the only Africans who remarked on the prejudice that they encountered in the GDR, or its equation to their relationships with white women. In 1965, representatives of the Union of African Students in the GDR addressed a letter to Ulbricht about the racial discrimination they had encountered in East Germany. The missive discussed growing tensions between African and East German citizens, which had devolved into physical violence in some instances. Cultural misunderstanding played a role in these cases, but so did entrenched racism. This racism was especially evident in attitudes toward African men who went out with German women. The drivers of the Leipzig Taxi Association were particularly guilty in this respect. The Union's letter related that "here we see arrogance, jealousy, and perhaps even hatred. Maybe some individuals think it is disgraceful to drive Africans—and there are many who will not serve us at all when they see girls in our company."[33] Discrimination made everyday activities like going out for the evening challenging. The writers of the letter, who self-identified as communists, intoned that if something was not done about racism, there would be more conflicts. These might reach the Western press and prove embarrassing for all involved.[34]

The governmental response to the letter was to send officials from the Ministry of Education to speak with African students in Leipzig and Rostock. In these meetings, the GDR representatives emphasized that the Union was responsible for policing the behavior of its members and making sure they were well mannered and did not draw attention to themselves. Among other things, this meant that the Union should "warn the African students against visiting dubious night clubs and excessive drinking."[35] Women were not mentioned, but considering the comments about interracial couples made in the Union letter, their presence at these venues was likely implied. Education officials placed the onus for stopping race-based attacks solely on the

Union, and suggested that African students, not racist East Germans, were the ones who needed to change their behavior.

As the above examples suggest, GDR officials, like their imperial-era forebears, saw African sexuality as something that had to be controlled. Yet if African men became weak around German women, they were not held solely accountable. The blame for interracial sex was often assigned as much to German women as to African men, if not more. "Loose" German women and girls often appear at the center of discussions on African sexuality. For example, a woman complained to the KMU in late July 1967 that a Nigerian student had been bothering her granddaughter and her granddaughter's German boyfriend.[36] He often came uninvited to the granddaughter's flat. The KMU's response was terse and to the point. Her granddaughter had willingly entered into the relationship with the Nigerian student. According to him, she had even given him the key to her apartment. Now that the office of international student affairs was aware of the relationship, the representative who wrote to the grandmother told her that he had advised the student to reconsider his bond to her young granddaughter. After all, she already had three children of her own.[37]

The KMU implicitly rebuked the granddaughter for being a single woman with a sizeable family, and one who was sexually open enough to give a man continual access to her home. Nigerians were among the first Africans to study in East Germany, as there were Nigerian students in the country as early as 1951, when Nigeria was still a British colony.[38] Later, the GDR became very interested in creating ties with Nigeria, which had a solid political and economic association with the FRG.[39] In the post-Hallstein world of the mid 1970s, the KMU tried to conclude formal exchange agreements with Nigerian universities and compete with the FRG.[40] The idea of developing a lasting academic relationship with Nigeria also existed in the 1960s, while the doctrine was still in effect.[41] The grandmother wrote her letter to the KMU only a few weeks after the start of Nigeria's Biafran War at the beginning of July 1967. Before Biafra, the Soviet bloc had experienced difficulties gaining a foothold in Nigeria, which had rebuffed efforts of aid from the USSR and its partners. As Maxim Matusevich has argued, the Civil War in Nigeria provided the Soviets with an opportunity to support the Nigerian federal government when the West showed reluctance.[42] The GDR followed Soviet policy in the matter. In this context, it was important to proceed gingerly and not offend the Nigerian medical student in question, who was an honored guest. Meanwhile, the woman's granddaughter was dismissed as little better than a prostitute.

The apprehension surrounding African men and German women often fed into another fear, which KMU officials hinted at in their discussions of the Malian man and his East German wife: that Africans and Germans would have children together. The stereotype of the African male held in thrall to loose German women or girls was, indeed, complemented by the trope of the *Mischlingskind*. In the wake of the bar brawl in 1963 a local Leipziger wrote several scathing letters to the Dean of the KMU concerning German women and their relationships with African men. He made special reference to the "unfortunate children who will now become a burden on our social welfare system."[43] The man railed against what he perceived as the lowering of German women's moral values, as well as against the creation of children who would strain the GDR's social safety net, in language very reminiscent of both the imperial era and the Third Reich.

The majority of stories about the children of African men and German women that emerge from the University of Leipzig archives, however, make few direct references to race. They focus instead on absent African fathers and unpaid alimony. Of these stories, the most descriptive comes from a man who wrote the department of international student affairs at the KMU in 1973 to request information on a former Cameroonian student. The man's daughter met and had a relationship with the Cameroonian during Leipzig's June 1967 Agricultural Exhibition (Agra), and gave birth to a daughter the following March. While the man did refer to his granddaughter as a *Mischling-Tochter*, he seemed less concerned about her African heritage than he did about his own daughter's promiscuity. What upset him most was that at first, "she allegedly did not know the father's name." This meant that she could not ask the Cameroonian student for financial support. Five years later, she finally found a notebook with his name and address written inside, and this prompted her father to turn to the KMU. He hoped that if the former student were found, his granddaughter would not only receive alimony, but also finally have a father.[44]

This man's account displays some of the contradiction and ambivalence common to GDR narratives on African men and German women. He chastised his daughter for being loose, sleeping with, and getting pregnant by a man she barely knew. His image of her was not much different from the impression that the restaurant manager had of the German women who waited for African men at the bar, or that of a Leipzig landlady who complained about German girls participating in orgies with the Sudanese men who lived in her building.[45] Even so, he wanted to find his granddaughter's father, for money, to be sure, but also for more personal reasons. He gave no indication that he cared whether his granddaughter's father was African, only that he wanted her to know him.

Family acceptance of an African suitor did not always mean that the state would bless the relationship. In the early 1960s, a Togolese man fell in love with an East German law student. Her family warmed to him without reservations, and made him feel as though he belonged. They made plans to marry. Initially, the Togolese government, firmly allied with the West, refused to give him the necessary papers. Once the Togolese regime fell in 1963, the student went home and was able to get the required documents. By that time, he and his fiancée had a child together. Now, however, it was the GDR that stood in the way of the marriage. Local authorities would not issue a permit allowing them to marry when he returned to the country for a three-week visit in 1964. In 1967, he was living in Togo but planning yet another short trip to the GDR, and was still trying to get permission to marry. He wrote to Gerald Götting, at the time Vice President of the GDR's privy council, begging him to intercede in the matter.[46]

The records are silent on whether the couple ever married. The Togolese student also gave no reason for why he believed the local authorities in Aue, where his fiancée's family lived, rejected their application for marriage. On the face of it, the case may seem a simple one of small-town officials turning down the appeal of an interracial couple. Considering the highly ambivalent attitude toward African-German relations illustrated above, this may also well be so. However, this is an instance where we must tread carefully. In 1966, the African department of the GDR's Ministry of Foreign Affairs also recommended that another young women not marry her Togolese fiancé. The official who made the recommendation did so on the grounds that the GDR had neither political representation in Togo, nor any ties to the state.[47] Additionally, the Togolese student who could not receive permission to marry his fiancée from Aue had complained of the preferential treatment that students from Ghana, Guinea, and Mali received in a different context, while he was enrolled at the Free German Trade Union College in Bernau. He protested against their privileged status among the college staff, which contrasted sharply with the poor reception that greeted Togolese students at the school.[48] The SED viewed Ghana, Guinea, and Mali as friendly, socialist-leaning states, all of which ultimately allowed the GDR to establish trade missions.[49] Togo had no such political connections. With this evidence in mind, the decision may have been motivated as much by politics as questions of race.

Another case from 1972 highlights the difficulty of determining whether political consideration, racial discrimination, or a combination of both were responsible for official attitudes toward interracial relationships. In August of that year a Zairean attaché in Belgrade complained that the GDR was making it difficult for a Zairean student to leave East Germany with his wife. The attaché claimed that the GDR wanted proof that the student would have adequate means to support his wife in Zaire, including an apartment and a job, before they would be allowed to depart.[50] In what seems on the surface to be the polar opposite of the Zambian case, the attaché noted that, per a 1965 law, Zaireans were free to marry whomever they chose, and that no special permission from Zairean authorities was required.[51] Zaire, which is now the Democratic Republic of Congo, was by this point staunchly in the American camp. After Congolese independence in 1960, the West had feared that its first president, Patrice Lumumba, was getting too close to the Soviet Union. Once Lumumba was assassinated with Western help, the country had turned away from the USSR, and received American aid and military support through the end of the Cold War in 1990.[52]

These intriguing examples suggest that, while racism was still a serious barrier for interracial couples, their predicament must be understood within a wider political framework. Indeed, the GDR must be situated within an international context, and its geopolitical position addressed. Where an African came from may have been as important as the fact of his Africanness. Love between capitalists and communists could be taboo. Students from states like Togo and Zaire, who were rarities to begin with, given the lack of diplomatic connections between their nations and the GDR, may well have been discriminated against on racial bases. At the same time, their position as citizens of Western allies made them undesirable partners for political reasons, too.

Most accounts of absent African fathers are more banal. In 1982, the attorney for a woman in Leipzig wrote to the KMU asking for information on the income of a Tanzanian student, an agricultural engineer who had studied there from 1970 to 1975. He was the father of the woman's child, and she was presumably interested in alimony.[53] Likewise, in 1977 another Cameroonian man, who had studied medicine in Rostock during the 1960s and left for West Germany in 1971, was being sought in connection with a daughter he had fathered in 1966.[54] Moreover, in 1976 the ex-girlfriend of a Mozambican contacted the KMU because he had failed to send the latest alimony payment.[55]

These fragments represent a sampling of the various cases in which East German women petitioned the KMU to locate their husbands and help them get alimony. The stories of these absent African fathers can be compared with the reports on African-American men who formed relationships with West German women and then returned to the United States, leaving their girlfriends or wives and children behind.[56] However, we must be careful not to equate these two groups too closely. In the first place, while some of the racial stereotypes adhering to Africans and African Americans may have been similar, the two groups came from very different contexts and traveled to Germany with very different goals. The African Americans were mainly soldiers and occupiers, who were confronted with both American and German prejudices. Indeed, as Heide Fehrenbach and Maria Höhn have both argued, the American prejudice against blacks was stronger than the German, and African Americans were commonly forced to return to the United States after completing their tours of duty in the Federal Republic. They were compelled to leave because the United States military command frowned upon romantic relations between black GIs and white German women, and was eager to separate couples.[57]

The exact reasons why specific African men left their girlfriends and children in East Germany are often unclear. Since many Africans were sent to the GDR to study by their governments, they were expected to return and use their education to fulfill their duties to the state in fields such as tropical medicine or agriculture. Under such circumstances, they may have had little choice but to leave. Politics may have played a role in other situations, too. Cameroon, like Togo, did not have a political connection with the GDR, though there were also fathers from countries that did have ties, such as Tanzania. Visas to extend stays in the GDR seemed, furthermore, to have been difficult to acquire once exchange students completed their studies. The length of time that often elapsed between the birth of a child and search for absent fathers also indicates that some couples had broken up, and thereafter contact was lost. Finally, because the rates of single motherhood had been rising overall in the GDR since the 1960s, it is possible that the mothers of Afro-German children were considered unremarkable, and not in need of special governmental treatment or effort.[58]

Racial difference was not supposed to exist in the GDR, but the attitudes of GDR officials and people on the ground demonstrated that East Germans continued to make race-based assumptions about Africans. Class difference, too, allegedly disappeared under socialism. Yet the stories of relationships between African men and East German women indicate that the concept of morality was closely linked to that of class, and that the moral hierarchy suggested in discussions of interracial liaisons was perhaps standing in for a class hierarchy. The European belief that lower-class women were the only ones who would consort with African men was deep-rooted, stretching back to at least the nineteenth century and only gathering strength in the first half of the twentieth century. In the case of colonial Britain, Lucy Bland has shown that the press construed white women who had relationships with non-Western men as either poor or prostitutes; they were only with their lovers because of the monetary gain it would bring.[59]

The idea that poor whites were usually the only ones who would form bonds with black men was prevalent in Britain and its empire.[60] It also had a history in Germany, both before and after World War II. With rare exceptions, scholarship on interracial relationships in colonial Germany has tended to focus on connections between white men and black women in Africa itself.[61] With the influx of African American GIs in the FRG after the war, however, work such as Höhn's and Fehrenbach's has shifted focus to romances between white German women and black American soldiers. West German women who fraternized with African American GIs were sometimes depicted as economically disadvantaged. Höhn has shown that middle-class German men were disturbed by what they saw as lower-class women breaking sexual and racial taboos when they dated African-American men with disposable incomes. American wealth was leading them astray, and upsetting previously stable class hierarchies.[62] The "Veronikas" who dated the GIs were, moreover, described as prostitutes, only further reinforcing the sense that they were from the lower class.[63]

The idea that the women who went out with African men were lower class was also present in the GDR. It was, however, couched in terms of morality rather than economics. The women who had relations with Africans were described as "questionable" or "dubious," adjectives that would have been applied to women of blue-collar backgrounds in another time or place.[64] These women showed poor judgment in their actions when they flirted with Africans in bars or at parties, just as the working-class women across the border in the FRG did when they went out with the GIs.

Little is known about the actual class status of the East German women. The women's social standing is obscure, though the single mothers requesting alimony from long-absent partners likely needed it to support their families. But while the economic markers of class are unclear, moral markers are very evident. Weak morality may, moreover, have been correlated to more than the breaking of racial taboos. The state may have imagined, as McClellan has suggested, that the benefits of an interracial relationship were largely material.[65] Africans were able to traverse the border to the West, and in most cases return across it, whenever they liked.[66] Meanwhile, the GDR forbid its citizens travel outside the Eastern bloc. In theory, marriage to an African man could allow an East German woman to follow him outside the state. If she did so, she would be breaking Ulbricht's second moral commandment, which bid her to love and defend her fatherland.[67] Additionally, in departing for nonaligned or Western-affiliated countries women would enter the capitalist system, in itself a betrayal of the socialist GDR. In the FRG, clergy and politicians condemned the "Veronikas" for seeking out American GIs for the material comforts they could provide.[68] In the GDR, women may well have been chastised along similar lines.

Of course, examples of East German women leaving the GDR with their African partners are rare. Countries such as Zambia, or, for that matter,

Mali, which pressed the GDR to find a suitable training opportunity for a student married to an East German, since "as a tradesman, he will not be able to support a family with a European wife," were opposed to allowing the women to immigrate.[69] Obtaining permission to marry a foreigner was difficult, too, as McClellan notes.[70] And we have seen that the women who requested alimony had obviously neither married their spouses nor left the GDR. Still, GDR officials might well have viewed even the intent to abandon the state as moral treachery.

At the same time, the question of the offspring that might result from interracial relationships, whether or not the relationships ended in marriage, was sometimes handled very differently than it would have been in earlier eras, or even in the BRD. The case of the Nigerian student who helped facilitate abortions in the 1960s is illustrative. It encapsulates the confusion over the place of the ethnic other in the GDR, as well as the morality surrounding sexual and reproductive politics. The state punished the student with one year in prison, and immediate expulsion from the GDR after his release.

Upon delivering its sentence, the district court in Leipzig framed the crime that he and his two East German accomplices had committed in expressly moral terms. The verdict commented that, "(our) state and its institutions pay particular attention to the development of healthy families und happy people in secure material circumstances. The accused have behaved unscrupulously and with disdain for this humanistic goal ... and in addition to violating socialist law have crudely transgressed against the morality of our workers."[71] The court continued to address the illegal abortions as injurious to the GDR at its core. Drawing on the *Gesetz über den Mutter- und Kinderschutz und die Rechte der Frau* of 1950, the judgment against the student and his colleagues maintained that the abortions they enabled violated the sanctity of human life, and deprived the state of potential contributing citizens. It was an affirmation of the GDR's pronatal politics that McLellan and others have addressed; every individual was valuable, and every destruction of life therefore a crime.[72]

What the case further illuminates is the clear identification of mixed-race children as protected citizens of the East German state. This markedly differentiates it from discussions of cases involving abortion and interracial couples in the BRD. Fehrenbach has spoken to the issue of so-called eugenic abortions in postwar West Germany. She has shown that in the immediate postwar period of 1945–46, women who claimed rape by non-Western soldiers were likely to have their petitions for abortion approved.[73] This was true for both the Western and Soviet zones, as abortions on "moral" grounds were allowed in the latter.[74]

Donna Harsch has also demonstrated that "eugenic" abortions were permitted in the GDR in rare instances during the early 1950s. However, it is significant that these were not linked to racial considerations. She describes communist pronatalist policies as not unlike those of the Nazis, with the important distinction that race did not factor into decisions on whether a child was deemed fit for survival.[75] The Leipzig District Court certainly did not consider race when it punished the Nigerian student and his two East German associates for performing abortions on women pregnant with mixed-race children; they were prospective citizens, and their destruction was criminal. The incident of the "abortion ring" and its legal treatment thus further highlight GDR ambivalence toward race. The women who slept with African men were tramps, but their children were citizens. Marriage was allowed in some cases, but not in others. The GDR's conduct toward racial others was more inconsistent than authors such as McLellan have suggested, and likely reflected confusion among administrators and citizens over how and whether to integrate nonwhites into the GDR's body politic.

## Conclusion

In many ways, stereotypes of African men in the GDR were not starkly different from those of previous generations. What had changed was that in the Cold War the GDR preached a policy of socialist openness and tolerance, and claimed solidarity with the oppressed peoples of the world. Non-Westerners allegedly came to the country as equals, rather than subjects of a colonial state or hostile prisoners of war. The GDR had to compete with the FRG on any number of levels, and this meant accommodating Africans. While it does not involve German women, a case from the early 1970s is illustrative. In this instance, the director of international student affairs at the KMU had to negotiate an agreement that would allow the wives and families of Sudanese students to join them in the GDR, or risk upsetting an educational agreement with Sudan's government. The situation was especially critical, because "until now Sudanese students have only gone to imperial (i.e. western) nations, and never had difficulties (bringing their families)."[76] Since the GDR did not want to lose the students, or damage relations with Sudan, the director recommended that the women be permitted to come and study in the GDR, even though he worried about the precedent it might set in an environment where family apartments were scarce. Africans had power here: the GDR needed the Sudanese students, and had to honor their wishes, when in the past Africans might have been expelled from Germany, or worse. The GDR was also obliged to offer university placement to African women as well as men, when before 1945 there had been few African women in Germany at all.[77]

We must also remember that not all Africans were considered equal. Those from postindependence capitalist, or in some cases even nonaligned, nations were regarded with suspicion. While this likely did not make a major difference in daily life, apart from the freedom to travel across the border to the West, it influence which Africans the state allowed to participate in the East German polity. This differed from the situation in the FRG. As Höhn and Fehrenbach note, in West Germany, African Americans felt freer from racism than they did in the United States, but also encountered the redirection of prejudice from Jews to blacks under the influence of the American military.[78] My research demonstrates that discrimination in the GDR could be concretely attached to the role that African nations had in the broader, more complex arena of the Cold War and decolonization.

Contrary visions of the family also contributed to a difference in reception of interracial relationships in the East than in the West. Fehrenbach has shown that in West Germany, mothers of mixed-race children were commonly urged to give their offspring up. The belief was that they would not fit into German society, and would be better off being raised by "their own kind." Afro-German children were consequently sent to orphanages, or "repatriated" to the United States to live with adoptive African-American families.[79] Nothing similar happened in the East. Indeed, if we take the story of the Zairean student and his family as an example, the GDR sometimes actively tried to prevent Afro-German children from leaving the country. Moreover, the state definitely considered Afro-Germans to be citizens, as the trial on illegal abortion makes clear. This does not mean that Africans were not victims of prejudice in the East. Many of the stories above clearly illustrate that they were. Further, Peggy Piesche has demonstrated that Afro-German children in the GDR encountered frequent, everyday racism.[80] Nonetheless, there was never an active attempt to remove Afro-German children from East Germany. The doctrine of solidarity mandated their inclusion on an official level, if not in daily life.

The more open attitude toward single motherhood in the GDR may provide another explanation for the greater acceptance of interracial couples and their offspring. As mentioned above, and as Anne Salles and Dagmar Herzog have observed, by the end of communist rule in the East the ratio of children born to single mothers in the GDR was much higher than in the FRG.[81] The banality of single motherhood and the increasing openness toward sexuality in the 1970s and 1980s, which McLellan has noted, would have made the presence of interracial families less shocking in the East than in the West.[82]

The official fiction that race and racism had been expunged from the East still meant, however, that African students and their children occupied an ambivalent space in the GDR. The students were subject to a "moral" education in the GDR. This education was based on supposedly "primal" characteristics that had been assigned to Africans much earlier, in the colonial era. It contradicted state claims that race did not matter, as well as state efforts to include blacks in the body politic. At the same time, the mere presence of African students in East Germany as ambassadors of their countries who might lead the way to solidifying diplomatic relations was ultimately more critical than their moral character. African students were therefore both welcome for the political benefits they could bring to East Germany, and held at arm's length because of the persistent racism that often surfaced in debates over African male sexuality and the immorality of some East German women. African students were not driven out of the GDR; neither were their lovers or their children. But they were never fully integrated into the East German state either.

**Sara Pugach** is Associate Professor of History at California State University, Los Angeles, where she teaches classes on African and European history. She is the author of *Africa in Translation: A History of Colonial Linguistics in Germany and Beyond, 1814-1945* (University of Michigan Press, 2012), as well as of several articles and book chapters.

## Notes

1. Politisches Archiv des Auswärtigen Amts, Bestand: Ministerium für auswärtigen Angelegenheiten (hereafter known as PAAA-MfAA), C409, Studienplatz-Kontingent und Studienangelegenheiten sambischer Bürger in der DDR, letter from the Embassy of the GDR, Moscow, to the MfAA, 10 March 1967.
2. Katrina Hagen, "Internationalism in Cold War Germany" (Ph.D. diss., University of Washington, 2008), 352.
3. Toni Weis, "The Politics Machine: On the Concept of 'Solidarity' in East German Support for SWAPO," *Journal of Southern African Studies* 2 (June 2011): 351–67.
4. On the imperial context see Lora Wildenthal, *German Women for Empire, 1884-1945* (Durham, NC: Duke University Press, 2001), 186–88; Sara Pugach, *Africa in Translation: A History of Colonial Linguistics in Germany and Beyond, 1814-1945* (Ann Arbor: University of Michigan Press, 2012), 150–52.
5. Cynthia Miller-Idriss, *Blood and Culture: Youth, Right-Wing Extremism, and National Belonging in Contemporary Germany* (Durham: Duke University Press, 2009), 55.
6. Katherine Pence, "Showcasing Cold War Germany in Cairo: 1954 and 1957 Industrial Exhibitions and the Competition for Arab Partners," *Journal of Contemporary History* 47, no. 1 (2011): 69–95.

7. Hans-Jörg Bücking, *Entwicklungspolitische Zusammenarbeit in der Bundesrepublik Deutschland und der DDR* (Berlin: Duncker & Humblot, 1998), 98.

8. Young-Sun Hong, "'The Benefits of Health Must Spread Among All': International Solidarity, Health and Race in the East German Encounter with the Third World," in *Socialist Modern: East German Everyday Culture and Politics,* ed. Katherine Pence and Paul Betts (Ann Arbor: University of Michigan Press, 2008), 183–210.

9. PAAA-MfAA A14594, Einschätzung der politischen-ideologischen Arbeit mit afrikanischen Studenten in der DDR, Jan., März 1964, Report of Gottfried Lessing, 29 January 1964. This relatively early document addressed the need to step up the level of political and ideological education that African students received in the GDR. Later documents show that most Africans were required to participate in political and ideological lectures regardless of their field of study. For instance, in 1970, officials in the GDR foreign ministry were angered by the refusal of Malian students in Halle to attend these courses; the Malians claimed that their own government had forbidden them from doing so. See PAAA-MfAA C720/74, Helmut Plettner of the MfAA to the Handelsmission in Bamako, 3 April 1970.

10. Lutz Basse, "Das Ausländerstudium an Universitäten, Hoch- und Fachschulen der DDR," http://www.auslaender-in-der-ddr.com/home/studenten/situation-an-hoch-und-fachschulen/ (accessed 12 November 2014). Further, exchange students did not always welcome the chance to live with Germans; for instance, in 1976 Fräulein E., a Nigerian pharmacy student at the Ingenieurschule für Pharmazie in Leipzig wrote to the head of the school complaining that she was the only foreign student living among Germans, and wanted to live with other African students instead if possible. See University Archives, Leipzig (hereafter referred to as UAL) ZM 3931IIa, Schriftwechsel Studenten Nigeria, von 1974 bis 1981, letter of Fräulein E. to the *Ingenieurschule,* n.d., ca. 1976.

11. Damian Mac Con Uladh, "Studium bei Freunden? Ausländische Studierende in der DDR bis 1970," in *Ankunft, Alltag, Ausreise: Migration und interkulturelle Begegnung in der DDR-Gesellschaft,* ed. Christian Th. Müller and Patrice G. Poutrus (Cologne: Böhlau, 2003), 175–219, 83. Mac Con Uladh does remark that the conditions in the international student dorms were often poorer than those in dormitories housing German students.

12. Ginga Eichler, Personal Interview, 1 August 2014.

13. UAL StuA 114791, Bezirksgericht Leipzig, "Urteil im Namen des Volkes!", n.d., ca. 1965.

14. See, for instance, Gunther Franke, Horst Mutscher, and Albrecht Pfeiffer, *Das Institut für tropische Landwirtschaft der Karl-Marx-Universität Leipzig 1960 bis 1992* (Leipzig: Engelsdorfer Verlag, 2009), 17. The authors remark that one of the main goals of the institute was the education of students from tropical and subtropical nations, who would later serve their nations with the knowledge they had gleaned in the GDR.

15. Elizabeth Schmidt, *Cold War and Decolonization in Guinea, 1946-1958* (Athens: Ohio University Press, 2007), 172–74.

16. There are many examples of African students who left the GDR permanently, often for study or work in capitalist Europe; see for example PAAA-MfAA C 402, Vol. II,

letter of J.G. to Kenyan Education Minister Mbiyu Koinange, 14 September 1965, which claimed that many Kenyans had left the GDR for West Germany or England.

17. See Julia Roos, "Women's Rights, Nationalist Anxiety, and the 'Moral' Agenda in the Early Weimar Republic: Revisiting the 'Black Horror' Campaign against France's African Occupation Troops," *Central European History* 42, no. 03 (2009): 473–508; Tina Campt, *Other Germans: Black Germans and the Politics of Race, Gender, and Memory in the Third Reich* (Ann Arbor, MI: University of Michigan, 2004), 72ff; Eve Rosenhaft, "Blacks and Gypsies in Nazi Germany: The Limits of the 'Racial State'," *History Workshop Journal* 72, no. 1 (2011): 161–70.

18. UAL Pror. Stud. 17, Report, Dr. Moehle, Prorektor für Studienangelegenheiten, an die Regierung der DDR, Staatssekretariat für das Hoch- und Fachschulwesen, Sektor Ausland, Auslandsstudium, Betr.: Ausländische Studierende, 20 January 1959.

19. PAAA, MfAA, Ausbildung malinesischer Facharbeiter und Studenten in der DDR, 1961-1964, undated letter, approximately October 1963, from Heimleiter P., griechischen Internat "unbezwingbares Athen," Leipzig, to the MfAA, Berlin.

20. PAAA, MfAA A14452, Ausbildung malinesischer Facharbeiter und Studenten in der DDR, 1961-1964, Fritsch, MfAA Berlin, to Gross, Trade Mission in Bamako, 13 December 1963, u.a.

21. UAL Pror. Stud. 17, Report, Dr. Moehle, Prorektor für Studienangelegenheiten, to the Regierung der DDR, Staatssekretariat für das Hoch- und Fachschulwesen, Sektor Ausland, Auslandsstudium, Betr.: Ausländische Studierende, 20 January 1959.

22. UAL StuA 114791, "Urteil im Namen des Volkes!"; Der Bundesbeauftrage für die Unterlagen des Staatssicherheitsdienstes der ehemaligen Deutschen Demokratischen Republik, Ministerium für Staatssicherheit (hereafter referred to as BStU, MfS) AP 9161/80, Abschlußvermerk, III/C/301, Berlin, den 20.3.70.

23. UAL DHfK VWA 545, Sonderlehrgang 4 Frauen Guinea, 1966-1968, HA Ausländerstudium, Aktennotiz, 29 August 1967.

24. UAL DHfK VWA 545, Sonderlehrgang 4 Frauen Guinea, 1966-1968, HA Ausländerstudium, Aktennotiz, 3 March 1967.

25. Jennifer V. Evans, "The Moral State: Men, Mining, and Masculinity in the Early GDR," *German History* 23, no. 3 (2005): 355–70.

26. Eric D. Weitz, *Creating German Communism, 1890-1990: From Popular Protests to Socialist State* (Princeton: Princeton University Press, 1997), 372.

27. Josie McLellan, *Love in the Time of Communism: Intimacy and Sexuality in the GDR* (New York: Cambridge University Press, 2011), 14ff.

28. UAL Pror. Stud. 17, letter from the Restaurant- und Stellv. Objektleiter des HO-Objekts "Burgkeller" to die Volkspolizei, Abteilung Ausländerswesen, 12 April 1963.

29. Ibid. There was some implication in his report that Arabs may have occasionally caused issues, but much more rarely than Africans.

30. Ibid.

31. UAL ZM 3923b, Schriftwechsel Studenten Mali von 1963 bis 1985, Y.D., Generalsekretär of the Verband der Malinesischen Studenten und Praktikanten in der DDR, Sektion der JUSRDA, to Ernst-Joachim Gießmann, Staatssekretär für das Hoch- und Fachschulwesen der DDR, 17 December 1966.

32. UAL ZM 3923B, Schriftwechsel Studenten Mali von 1963 bis 1985, Dr. P. to Horst

Joachimi, Ministerrat der Deutschen Demokratischen Republik, Staatssekretariat für das Hoch- und Fachschulwesen, Abt. Ausländerstudium, 10 February 1967.

33. PAAA MfAA B1263/75Abt. Afrika, Sektion Gesamtafrikanische Fragen, Aufteilung des Studentenkontingents f. Afrikanischen Staaten, 1972-1973; Union afrikanischer Studenten in der DDR to Walter Ulbricht, "Besorgnisse der afrikanischen Studenten und Arbeiter in der DDR," February–March 1965.

34. Ibid.

35. PAAA MfAA B1263/75Abt. Afrika, Sektion Gesamtafrikanische Fragen, Aufteilung des Studentenkontingents f. Afrikanischen Staaten, 1972-1973 and earlier, report concerning "Information über die in Zusammenhang mit dem Brief der Union afrikanischer Studenten in der DDR festgelegten Maßnahmen vom 12. März 1965," 7 April 1965.

36. UAL ZM 3931/IIa, Schriftwechsel Studenten Nigeria, 1960-1968, letter from Mrs. L. to the KMU, 26 July 1967.

37. UAL ZM 3931/IIa, Schriftwechsel Studenten Nigeria, 1960–1968, 28 July 1967.

38. AE Ohiaeri, *Behind the Iron Curtain* (Enugu: Fourth Dimension Publishing, 1985), preface. Connections to Nigeria during the colonial era were made through Nigerian trade unions.

39. Gareth M. Winrow, *The Foreign Policy of the GDR in Africa* (New York: Cambridge University Press, 1990), 83.

40. UAL DIB 164, Report on establishing ties with African universities, c. 1975.

41. Indeed, it was a KMU historian, Walter Markov, who helped found Nigeria's University of Nsukka in the early 1960s. See Nick Hodgin and Caroline Pearce, *The GDR Remembered: Representations of the East German State since 1989* (Rochester: Camden House, 2011), 273.

42. Maxim Matusevich, *No Easy Row for a Russian Hoe: Ideology and Pragmatism in Nigerian-Soviet Relations, 1960-1991* (Trenton: Africa World Press, 2003), 105ff.

43. UAL Pror. Stud. 17, letter of Mr. W.B. to the Dean of the Universof Leipzig, n.d., ca. 1963.

44. UAL ZM 3314b, Schriftwechsel Studenten Kamerun, 1964 bis 1984, letter of Mr. S. to the Abt. Ausländerstudium, KMU, 12 March 1973.

45. UAL, ZM 3944/Ia, Schriftwechsel Studenten Sudan, 1965 bis 1974, Sandke, Oberleutnant der Volkspolizei-Kreisamt Leipzig, to the Karl-Marx-Universität, Direktorat Ausländerstudium, concerning "Information über die Verhaltensweise eines Studenten Ihrer Universität," 25 January 1974.

46. PAAA MfAA C327/70, Abt. Afrika, Sektion Mali, Beziehungen auf aussenpolitischen Gebiet sowie auf dem Gebiet des Hoch- und Fachschulwesens, der Volksbildung und des Sports zwischen der DDR und Togo, 1962-1968, J.D. to Gerald Götting, Lome, 23 March 1967.

47. PAAA MfAA, Abt. Afrika, Sektion Mali, Beziehungen auf aussenpolitischen Gebiet sowie auf dem Gebiet des Hoch- und Fachschulwesens, der Volksbildung und des Sports zwischen der DDR und Togo, 1962-1968, Mr. P of the Abteilung Afrika, Ministerium für Auswärtige Angelegenheiten, Berlin, to Ms. B., 3 August 1966.

48. Stiftung Archiv der Parteien und Massenorganisationen der DDR im Bundesarchiv (hereafter referred to as SAPMO), DY/34/24698, FDGB Bundesvorstand, Büro des Präsidiums, Protokollbüro, Sekretariatsbeschlüsse des Bundesvorstandes betr.

Gewerschaftshochschule, 1961-1963, "Denkschrift des Kollegen J.D., Togo, z. Zt. Student am Ausländerinstitut der Hochschule der Deutschen Gewerkschaften "Fritz Heckert," 5 June 1961.

49. Winrow, *The Foreign Policy of the GDR in Africa,* 41, 55.
50. PAAA MfAA B290.79, Studium von kongolesischen Studenten in der DDR und Bewerbungen, 1963-1972, letter from the Zairean Embassy in Belgrade to the Ministry of Foreign Affairs, 1 September 1972.
51. PAAA MfAA B290.79, Studium von kongolesischen Studenten in der DDR und Bewerbungen, 1963-1972, Proclamation of 9 August 1972, stating that the 1965 law gave Zaireans license to marry the partners of their choice.
52. Ch. Didier Gondola, *The History of Congo* (Westport: Greenwood Press, 2002), 127.
53. UAL ZM 3947a, Schriftwechsel Studenten Tansania, 1968-1985, letter from the Kriegsgericht Leipzig, Stadtbezirk West, to the Direktorat für Internationale Beziehungen, KMU, 10 February 1982.
54. UAL ZM 3914b, Schriftwechsel Studenten Kamerun, 1964 bis 1984, Studienrat Hass, Leiter des Referates Jugendhilfe, Rat der Stadt Rostock, to the Karl-Marx-Universität, 27 April 1977, and response of Dr. Jünger, KMU, to Hass, 9 May 1977.
55. UAL ZM 3926b, Schriftwechsel Studenten Mocambique, 1974 bis 1985, letter from Frau Z. to the Direktorat Internationale Beziehungen, Abt. Ausländerstudium, 18/10/76, and Bescheinigung that the student had returned to Mozambique, 30/11/76.
56. On this point see Heide Fehrenbach, *Race After Hitler: Black Occupation Children in Postwar Germany and America* (Princeton: Princeton University Press, 2005); Maria Höhn, *GIs and Fräuleins: The German-American Encounter in 1950s West Germany* (Chapel Hill: University of North Carolina Press, 2002).
57. Fehrenbach, *Race After Hitler,* 17ff; Höhn, *GIs and Fräuleins,* 85ff.
58. Anne Salles, "The Effects of Family Policy in the GDR on Nuptiality and Births outside Marriage," *Population* 61, no. 1–2 (January–April 2006): 141–51.
59. Lucy Bland, "White Women and Men of Colour: Miscegenation Fears in Britain after the Great War," *Gender & History* 17, no. 1 (2005): 29–61.
60. See for instance Will Jackson, "Bad Blood: Poverty, Psychopathy and the Politics of Transgression in Kenya Colony, 1939-59," *Journal of Imperial and Commonwealth History* 39, no. 1 (2011): 73–94, or Carina E. Ray, "'The White Wife Problem': Sex, Race and the Contested Politics of Repatriation to Interwar British West Africa," *Gender & History* 21, no. 3 (2009): 628–46.
61. Krista O'Donnell, "Home, Nation, Empire: Domestic Germanness and Colonial Citizenship," in *The Heimat Abroad: The Boundaries of Germanness,* ed. Krista O'Donnell, Renate Bridenthal, and Nancy Ruth Reagin (Ann Arbor: The University of Michigan Press, 2005), 40–58, among others, discusses the issue of the importation of German women to the colony of South West Africa, where fear of miscegenation between German men and native women was rife.
62. Höhn, *GIs and Fräuleins,* 172.
63. Ibid., 118–20.
64. UAL Pror. Stud. 17, Report, 20 January 1959; UAL ZM 3944/Ia, Schriftwechsel Studenten Sudan, 1965 bis 1974, Sandke, "Information über die Verhaltensweise eines Studenten Ihrer Universität," 25 January 1974.

65. McLellan, *Love in the Time of Communism*, 108.
66. This mobility did become a source of concern to some African governments. In 1964, Ghana asked the students who led the Ghanaian student association in the GDR to confiscate student passports and thereby prevent travel to West Berlin; see PAAA-MfAA A14594, Einschätzung der politischen-ideologischen Arbeit mit afrikanischen Studenten in der DDR, Jan., März 1964, Schwab, MfAA, to Prime Minister Willi Stoph, 16 March 1964. Meanwhile, in 1966 Mali tried to create a registry of all citizens studying overseas as a way to keep track of their movements; see PAAA MfAA A16972, Studium malinesischer Studenten an Hoch- und Fachschulen der DDR, 1964-1966, Rundschreiben 1174/MEN, Hinweise für die Kontrolle malinesischer Studenten im Ausland, 15 November 1966.
67. Walter Ulbricht, "Zur Geschichte der deutschen Arbeiterbewegung," in *Zur Geschichte der deutschen Arbeiterbewegung*, ed. Walter Ulbricht (Berlin: Dietz, 1964), 376–78.
68. Höhn, *GIs and Fräuleins*, 126ff.
69. PAAA MfAA A16972, Studium malinesischer Studenten an Hoch- und Fachschulen der DDR, 1964-1966, Schöche, Third Secretary to the Economic and Trade Mission of the GDR in Bamako to the Ministry for Foreign Affairs, Berlin, 23 September 1965.
70. McLellan, *Love in the Time of Communism*, 109–10.
71. UAL StuA 114791, "Urteil im Namen des Volkes!"
72. McLellan, *Love in the Time of Communism*, 6; Michael Schwartz, "Emanzipation zur sozialen Nutzlichkeit: Bedingungen und Grenzen von Frauenpolitik in der DDR," in *Sozialstaatlichkeit in der DDR: Sozialpolitische Entwicklungen im Spannungsfeld von Diktatur und Gesellschaft, 1945/49-1989*, ed. Dierk Hoffmann and Michael Schwartz (Munich: Oldenbourg, 2005), 47–88, 68.
73. Fehrenbach, *Race After Hitler*, 59ff.
74. Ibid., 211–12.
75. Donna Harsch, *Revenge of the Domestic: Women, the Family, and Communism in the German Democratic Republic* (Princeton: Princeton University Press, 2007), 152–53.
76. UAL ZM 3944/Ia, Schriftwechsel Studenten Sudan, 1965 bis 1974, letter from the Director of International Student Affairs, KMU, to the representative of the Minister for Higher Education in the GDR, 9 March 1971.
77. Among those few African women who did come to Germany prior to 1945, most were of upper class or even royal extraction. They include Princess Emily Ruete (see Emilie Ruete and Annegret Nippa, *Leben im Sultanspalast: Memoiren aus dem 19. Jahrhundert* (Frankfurt am Main: Athenäum, 1989)); Emily Engome Dayas (see Ralph A. Austen and Jonathan Derrick, *Middlemen of the Cameroons Rivers: The Duala and Their Hinterland, c.1600-c.1960* (New York: Cambridge University Press, 1999), 126); and Fatima Massaquoi Fahnbulleh (see Ayodeji Olukoju, *Culture and Customs of Liberia, Culture and Customs of Africa* (Westport: Greenwood Press, 2006), 104–05.
78. Höhn, *GIs and Fräuleins*; Fehrenbach, *Race After Hitler*.
79. *Race After Hitler*, 132ff.
80. Peggy Piesche, "Black and German? East German Adolescents Before 1989: A Retrospective View of a 'Non-Existent Issue" in the GDR," in *The Cultural After-Life*

*of East Germany: New Transnational Perspectives*, ed. Leslie Adelson (Washington, D.C.: AICGS Humanities 2002).

81. Salles, "The Effects of Family Policy in the GDR on Nuptiality and Births outside Marriage,"; Dagmar Herzog, *Sex after Fascism: Memory and Morality in Twentieth-century Germany* (Princeton: Princeton University Press, 2005), 215. Herzog states that one in three children were born out of wedlock in the GDR by the time the Wall fell; in the FRG, it was one in ten.

82. McLellan, *Love in the Time of Communism*, 94.

## Bibliography

Austen, Ralph A., and Jonathan Derrick. *Middlemen of the Cameroons Rivers: The Duala and Their Hinterland, c.1600–c.1960.* New York: Cambridge University Press, 1999.

Bland, Lucy. "White Women and Men of Colour: Miscegenation Fears in Britain after the Great War." *Gender & History* 17, no. 1 (2005): 29–61.

Bücking, Hans-Jörg. *Entwicklungspolitische Zusammenarbeit in der Bundesrepublik Deutschland und der DDR.* Berlin: Duncker & Humblot, 1998.

Campt, Tina. *Other Germans: Black Germans and the Politics of Race, Gender, and Memory in the Third Reich.* Ann Arbor: University of Michigan, 2004.

Evans, Jennifer V. "The Moral State: Men, Mining, and Masculinity in the Early GDR." *German History* 23, no. 3 (2005): 355–70.

Fehrenbach, Heide. *Race After Hitler: Black Occupation Children in Postwar Germany and America.* Princeton: Princeton University Press, 2005.

Franke, Gunther, Horst Mutscher, and Albrecht Pfeiffer. *Das Institut für tropische Landwirtschaft der Karl-Marx-Universität Leipzig 1960 bis 1992.* Leipzig: Engelsdorfer Verlag, 2009.

Gondola, Ch. Didier. *The History of Congo.* Westport: Greenwood Press, 2002.

Hagen, Katrina. "Internationalism in Cold War Germany." Ph.D. diss., University of Washington, 2008.

Harsch, Donna. *Revenge of the Domestic: Women, the Family, and Communism in the German Democratic Republic.* Princeton: Princeton University Press, 2007.

Herzog, Dagmar. *Sex after Fascism: Memory and Morality in Twentieth-century Germany.* Princeton: Princeton University Press, 2005.

Hodgin, Nick, and Caroline Pearce. *The GDR Remembered: Representations of the East German State since 1989.* Rochester: Camden House, 2011.

Höhn, Maria. *GIs and Fräuleins: The German-American Encounter in 1950s West Germany.* Chapel Hill: University of North Carolina Press, 2002.

Hong, Young-Sun. "'The Benefits of Health Must Spread Among All': International Solidarity, Health and Race in the East German Encounter with the Third World." In *Socialist Modern: East German Everyday Culture and Politics,* ed. Katherine Pence and Paul Betts, 183–210. Ann Arbor: University of Michigan Press, 2008.

Jackson, Will. "Bad Blood: Poverty, Psychopathy and the Politics of Transgression in Kenya Colony, 1939-59." *Journal of Imperial and Commonwealth History* 39, no. 1 (2011): 73–94.

Mac Con Uladh, Damian. "Studium bei Freunden? Ausländische Studierende in der DDR bis 1970." In *Ankunft, Alltag, Ausreise: Migration und interkulturelle Begegnung in der DDR-Gesellschaft,* ed. Christian Th. Müller and Patrice G. Poutrus, 175–220. Cologne: Böhlau, 2003.

Matusevich, Maxim. *No Easy Row for a Russian Hoe: Ideology and Pragmatism in Nigerian-Soviet Relations, 1960-1991.* Trenton: Africa World Press, 2003.

McLellan, Josie. *Love in the Time of Communism: Intimacy and Sexuality in the GDR.* New York: Cambridge University Press, 2011.

Miller-Idriss, Cynthia. *Blood and Culture: Youth, Right-Wing Extremism, and National Belonging in Contemporary Germany.* Durham: Duke University Press, 2009.

O'Donnell, Krista. "Home, Nation, Empire: Domestic Germanness and Colonial Citizenship." In *The Heimat Abroad: The Boundaries of Germanness,* ed. Krista O'Donnell, Renate Bridenthal, and Nancy Ruth Reagin, 40–58. Ann Arbor: The University of Michigan Press, 2005.

Ohiaeri, AE. *Behind the Iron Curtain.* Enugu: Fourth Dimension Publishing, 1985.

Olukoju, Ayodeji. *Culture and Customs of Liberia, Culture and Customs of Africa.* Westport: Greenwood Press, 2006.

Pence, Katherine. "Showcasing Cold War Germany in Cairo: 1954 and 1957 Industrial Exhibitions and the Competition for Arab Partners." *Journal of Contemporary History* 47, no. 1 (2011): 69–95.

Piesche, Peggy. "Black and German? East German Adolescents Before 1989: A Retrospective View of a 'Non-Existent Issue" in the GDR." In *The Cultural After-Life of East Germany: New Transnational Perspectives,* ed. Leslie Adelson. Washington, D.C.: AICGS Humanities 2002.

Pugach, Sara. *Africa in Translation: A History of Colonial Linguistics in Germany and Beyond, 1814-1945.* Ann Arbor: University of Michigan Press, 2012.

Ray, Carina E. "'The White Wife Problem': Sex, Race and the Contested Politics of Repatriation to Interwar British West Africa." *Gender & History* 21, no. 3 (2009): 628–46.

Roos, Julia. "Women's Rights, Nationalist Anxiety, and the 'Moral' Agenda in the Early Weimar Republic: Revisiting the 'Black Horror' Campaign against France's African Occupation Troops." *Central European History* 42, no. 03 (2009): 473–508.

Rosenhaft, Eve. "Blacks and Gypsies in Nazi Germany: The Limits of the 'Racial State'." *History Workshop Journal* 72, no. 1 (2011): 161–70.

Ruete, Emilie, and Annegret Nippa. *Leben im Sultanspalast: Memoiren aus dem 19. Jahrhundert.* Frankfurt am Main: Athenäum, 1989.

Salles, Anne. "The Effects of Family Policy in the GDR on Nuptiality and Births outside Marriage." *Population* 61, no. 1–2 (January–April 2006): 141–51.

Schmidt, Elizabeth. *Cold War and Decolonization in Guinea, 1946-1958.* Athens: Ohio University Press, 2007.

Schwartz, Michael. "Emanzipation zur sozialen Nutzlichkeit: Bedingungen und Grenzen von Frauenpolitik in der DDR." In *Sozialstaatlichkeit in der DDR: Sozialpolitische Entwicklungen im Spannungsfeld von Diktatur und Gesellschaft, 1945/49-1989,* ed. Dierk Hoffmann and Michael Schwartz, 47–88. Munich: Oldenbourg, 2005.

Ulbricht, Walter. "Zur Geschichte der deutschen Arbeiterbewegung." In *Zur Geschichte der deutschen Arbeiterbewegung,* ed. Walter Ulbricht, 376–78. Berlin: Dietz, 1964.

Weis, Toni. "The Politics Machine: On the Concept of 'Solidarity' in East German Support for SWAPO." *Journal of Southern African Studies* 2 (June 2011): 351–67.

Weitz, Eric D. *Creating German Communism, 1890-1990: From Popular Protests to Socialist State.* Princeton: Princeton University Press, 1997.

Wildenthal, Lora. *German Women for Empire, 1884-1945.* Durham: Duke University Press, 2001.

Winrow, Gareth M. *The Foreign Policy of the GDR in Africa.* New York: Cambridge University Press, 1990.

# Chapter 7

# Ambivalence and Desire in the East German "Free Angela Davis" Campaign

*Katrina Hagen*

In October 1970, communist and black movement activist Angela Davis was arrested for alleged involvement in the attempted prison escape of "Soledad Brother" George Jackson in California. Based on only a tenuous connection to the crime, Davis was tried for the capital crimes of conspiracy, murder, and kidnapping. She was ultimately acquitted in June 1972, but the imprisonment and trial of Angela Davis unleashed a worldwide storm of protest. While the U.S. government and law enforcement officials identified Davis as a threat to internal security, millions rallied to her cause. Five months after her arrest, the efforts of the National United Committee to Free Angela Davis (NUCFAD) resulted in the establishment of 200 activist groups throughout the country and 67 affiliates in the Americas, Africa, Europe, and Asia.[1] The international movement demanded her freedom and condemned the trial as a racist "frame up" in violation of her human rights.[2]

Throughout the course of Davis's imprisonment and trial from October 1970 to her acquittal in June 1972, a state-sponsored solidarity program made "Free Angela!" a rallying cry in East Germany. East Germans gathered "solidarity donations," signed petitions, and engaged in letter-writing campaigns. Worker and student groups collected signatures on banners and kerchiefs, which they sent to Davis in prison as symbolic tokens of encouragement. GDR mass organizations supported and facilitated such daily acts of solidarity. The Free German Youth, the youth wing of the ruling Socialist Unity Party (SED), organized rallies and promoted Davis's cause in youth publications, while launching an ambitious letter-writing campaign under the slogan, "One Million Roses for Angela," the goal of which was to send as many solidarity postcards to Davis in prison. Likewise, the Peace Council opened a major exhibit and information center in East Berlin, as well as smaller displays at factories throughout the country.[3] Youth clubs and "workers brigades" in various cities responded in kind by opening their own solidarity exhibits meant to educate and inspire support of Davis among GDR citizens. For example six thousand people were reported to have visited in the first eight days of one exhibition in the town of Wismar. These visitors signed letters of protest sent to Richard Nixon and wrote five thousand solidarity postcards mailed directly to Davis in prison.[4]

Recent scholarship has situated Angela Davis solidarity within a transatlantic civil rights movement connecting the two Germanys to the United States, as well as within the German-German Cold War. Martin Klimke and Maria Höhn have suggested that the East German "Free Angela" campaign was a spectacular example of a broader alliance dating to the 1950s with U.S. Civil Rights leaders and activists.[5] Such alliances underscored the East German support of what Michael Harrington dubbed the "Other America," which by the late 1960s and early 70s was identified especially with African Americans and other people of color.[6] An alliance with the "Other America" was one way of registering criticism of the U.S.-led capitalist-imperialist system, which included the FRG, while also signaling East German belonging among the progressive international forces in the communist bloc and Third World that would contribute to its final defeat. Sophie Lorenz suggests that the East German designation of Davis as "heroine of the Other America" can be understood by the persistent need for German-German differentiation in the context of growing diplomatic normalization in the early 1970s.[7] This process began with Willy Brandt's *Ostpolitik* and the demise of West Germany's Hallstein Doctrine, which aimed to block international diplomatic recognition of the GDR under the rationale that the FRG alone represented the German people.[8] Normalization culminated in the admission of both German states into the United Nations on equal footing in 1973. In the rhetoric of SED propaganda, a political alliance with Davis highlighted the fact that East Germany was the only anti-racist and anti-imperialist Germany even as a two-state model began to seem inevitable.

This essay follows current scholarship in showing that East German leaders saw in Angela Davis an opportunity to promote their ideological struggle with U.S.-led liberal capitalism and differentiate the GDR from the FRG. Davis's imprisonment and trial under threat of the death penalty epitomized the escalating racial violence in the United States that the East German leadership, as well as segments of the West German left, viewed as a domestic correlate to U.S. imperialism in Vietnam. To many Davis supporters on either side of the Cold War divide, imperialist violence at home and abroad indicated a movement toward fascism in the United States. Participation in the "Free Angela" campaign was thus one way to strike a blow against American proto-fascism while criticizing the West German–U.S. alliance and shoring up East Germany's anti-fascist credentials. Davis's membership in the Communist Party USA as well as her vocal critique of U.S. imperialism in Vietnam endeared her to the SED, catapulting her to the status not only as "heroine of the other America" but also as "communist superstar."[9] Her star quality and revolutionary glamour had the added benefit of making international solidarity and the GDR itself seem glamorous.[10]

This essay shows, however, that Davis's elevation to "heroine" of the "other America" and icon of state socialism involved selective interpretation and careful political scripting. East German leaders were concerned with Davis's connections to the New Left, in particular to her mentor Herbert Marcuse. Moreover, her particular brand of Marxism shared similarities with the Black Panthers' race-based model of national liberation that made them distinctly uneasy. This had in part to do with Marxist-Leninist theory, which rendered racism a "secondary contradiction," an element of the broader injustice of capitalist exploitation that would be resolved with the elimination of capitalism itself. Yet struggles in the GDR over Davis's politics did not only have to do with interpretive debates over Marxism-Leninism in the 1960s and 70s. While participation in the "Free Angela" campaign served the purpose of differentiating the GDR from the FRG at the level of Cold War rhetoric, uneasiness with Davis's racial politics in the GDR nonetheless resonated with related worries in West Germany. Commentators on either side of the Cold War divide shared a similar language when they branded radical black politics "racial extremism" and even "black racism." The Davis case thus reveals a common concern in the two Germanys in the 1970s over race-based claims for equality. Indeed, in East and West Germany, media emphasis on Davis's "star power," on her glamour and exotic difference as black woman, served to contain the threat posed by her revolutionary politics.

## Angela Davis, Anti-Fascism, and German Cold War Politics

While striking in its passion and scale, the "Free Angela" campaign was not a singular event but rather was part of a wider constellation of East German solidarity actions in the 1960s and 70s ranging from mass support of the North Vietnamese, to anti-apartheid agitation and the backing of late decolonizing states in southern Africa, to the campaign for release of political prisoners in Pinochet's Chile.[11] International solidarity was linked to Cold War considerations, and was among the most important East German foreign policy objectives until the 1970s.[12] The SED and mass organizations mobilized popular solidarity as an expression of Marxist-Leninist ideology, according to which proletarian internationalism structured the relationship between socialist states and the revolutionary working class in the rest of the world.[13] Taking its place alongside other socialist countries in lending ideological and material support to anti-colonial and anti-imperialist movements, and thus strengthening the international struggle against capitalism, marked an important step in the GDR's integration into socialist economic and political systems, while also signaling its successful postfascist rehabilitation.[14] International solidarity also played an important role in the East German approach to German-German Cold War relations. Both through diplomacy that concentrated largely on the Third World and a pronounced international propaganda campaign the GDR attempted to combat the Hallstein Doctrine by differentiating its record on racism and imperialism from the FRG's.

The "Free Angela" campaign fit within this broader solidarity agenda. The Davis case provided the opportunity for East German leaders to participate in the international human rights discourse pushed to the fore in the United Nations by Third World member states over the course of the 1960s.[15] Though Roland Burke has shown that many Third World member states denounced the human rights agenda by the early 1970s, calling for the sacrifice of rights in favor of development in their own domestic policies, the rhetoric remained strong within the United Nations, especially in the designation of "international years" and "decades" of action.[16] The General Assembly designated 1968 the International Year of Human Rights, 1971 the International Year for Action to Combat Racism and Racial Discrimination, and 1973 as the beginning of the Decade for Action to Combat Racism. In official statements to the UN in 1971 in response to the Year for Action to Combat Racism, the GDR showcased solidarity with Davis as evidence of its progressive and anti-racist domestic agenda, noting in particular the enthusiastic role played by "the younger generation of the GDR, which has been brought up in the spirit of peace and socialism." Such solidarity with Davis showed that "a social order and a system of government had been established in the GDR which ... precludes any resurgence of racism, racial discrimination and Nazism."[17] Pronouncements such as these were meant to demonstrate that the GDR was in step with progressive international developments, and thus worthy of recognition as a sovereign state.

The 1971 statement to the United Nations also made a veiled attempt to differentiate East from West Germany. Assertions that East German socialism, unlike West German liberal capitalism, "precluded" the possibility of a return of Nazi racism were central to the anti-fascist founding myth of the GDR and corresponding claims of a West German failure to overcome the past.[18] West Germany and the U.S.–West German alliance were always points of reference for the East German "Free Angela" campaign and political claims of successful anti-fascist rehabilitation more generally. At a rally on Davis's twenty-seventh birthday in January 1971, Werner Lamberz, of the Politburo and SED Central Committee, proclaimed that solidarity with Davis demonstrated that East Germany stood "on the correct side of the barricade that divides this world!"[19] The GDR placed the FRG among those states on the "wrong side" of the Cold War division of the world, in part because of its political-ideological ties to the United States.[20] Support of the United States not only meant endorsement of its imperialist aggression abroad—most notably in Vietnam—but also tacit approval of its domestic racial policies, which the GDR compared to the murderous racism of the Nazi state as well as to white minority and colonial regimes in Africa.[21] To GDR officials, state-sanctioned violence and a corrupt and racist legal system, which condoned police attacks on black activists such as Davis while extending leniency to perpetrators of "crimes against humanity" such as "My Lai Killer" Lieutenant Calley, were evidence that the United States was on the road to fascism.[22]

In declarations of support for Davis, East German authorities, activists, and the media condemned the "Gestapo tactics" and "racial terror" of the United States.[23] The fact that Davis faced the death penalty elicited implicit comparisons to Nazi genocide; her racist persecution could end in death in the "gas chamber." *Für Dich,* the illustrated women's magazine associated with the German Democratic Women's Federation (DFD), reported on 3 November 1970 that while the gas chambers of "Hitler's Germany had burst asunder" with the defeat of fascism in 1945, the threat of Davis's execution in California demonstrated that "the gas chamber-ideology of the Hitlerists had celebrated its resurrection on American soil."[24] This interpretation, which identified the state of California as "Hitlerists" and Davis's prosecution in terms of Nazi genocidal racism, demanded action by those who had destroyed Hitler's gas chambers in 1945. Not to act would be a failure to live up to the East German postwar responsibility to guard against a fascist resurgence.

This article that was meant to inspire support of the "Free Angela" campaign went further in its claims than most reportage. The East German press more often followed the official analysis that the situation in the United States remained proto-fascist. The SED explanation of Nazi fascism was based on Comintern definitions of the 1920s that adhered to Lenin's *Imperialism: The Highest Stage of Capitalism* (1916). As such, the SED viewed fascism as a product of the struggle for finance capital to advance its imperialist goals while combating the threat arising from the revolutionary workers movement.[25] In an article in the *Berliner Zeitung* published in February 1972, Dr. Rolf Heim, the head of the GDR Peace Council and member of the East German Committee for Human Rights, described the Davis trial in such terms. He claimed that it was "reminiscent in terrifying ways of similar criminal proceedings of class justice in the Weimar Republic," when the right-wing judicial system prosecuted communists, Social Democrats, and other defenders of the Republic, thus paving the way for the National Socialist seizure of power in 1933.[26]

Yet the official approach in East Germany identified the United States not as a fascist state as such, but rather one that resorted to "fascist methods" of political repression, thus making strategic alliances and protest still worthwhile. A radio story for the "Voice of the GDR" (*Stimme der DDR*) about the opening of the Peace Council's exhibition "Freedom for Angela" on 18 November 1971 offered a clarification in Davis's own words. Davis's education and experiences, the program suggested, had taught her that capitalism provided the conditions under which "fascism could flourish." Yet the announcer reminded that Davis followed a Marxist-Leninist stage theory of development. She had always maintained that the United States utilized "fascist methods," but was not yet ruled by a fascist government. It was thus still possible to work through "legal channels" to fight the "aggressive war" waged by the United States "through ever more frightening exterminatory violence (*Vernichtungsgewalt*)," and against the "colonial exploitation" that allowed "racial discrimination" to thrive. The announcer concluded that East German solidarity with Davis—the hero of the "other," the "true America"— and with the international working class as a whole, "must prevent fascist methods from becoming day-to-day fascism."[27]

Like their East German counterparts, many West Germans saw the Davis case as emblematic of dangerous developments in the United States. The headline "Fascism in America?" accompanied a November 1971 cover story on Davis in the liberal newsmagazine *Der Spiegel* that claimed it "absurd ... to compare the USA to Hitler," but nonetheless warned of fascist tendencies in United States.[28] In addition to an outpouring of support in letters and petitions, prominent leftist intellectuals and activists formed Angela Davis Solidarity Committees and staged a well-publicized conference in Frankfurt in July 1972, titled "On the Example of Angela Davis," that put forward a more incisive Marxian critique. Oskar Negt and Herbert Marcuse each pointed to the "criminalization of justice," evident in the racist targeting and police murder of African Americans, as a final step toward the development of fascism.[29]

FRG officials responded to citizen concerns that Davis's persecution was part of a movement toward fascism in the United States by citing confidence in the "200 year-old American democracy."[30] The West German government was indeed wary of openly criticizing the United States and worried that support of Davis could heighten homegrown protest against state policy on the radical left. The state turned away a number of international activists associated with the campaign, including Kathleen Cleaver.[31] In what the Marburg Angela Davis Committee described as a "night-and-fog action"—a term that recalled Nazi deportation of Jews to extermination camps—Munich immigration officials also arrested and threatened to deport Amadeo Richardson, an African-American student and anti–Vietnam War activist studying in Germany, because his politics reportedly "endangered" the "traditionally good relations between the [FRG] and the USA."[32] The protest over Richardson dovetailed with broader criticism on the radical student left that identified FRG association with the United States, and the targeting of political dissidents and student radicals as evidence of similar fascist tendencies in West Germany.[33]

## The "Free Angela" Campaign

While West Germany supported what socialist and leftist critics on both sides of the Cold War divide described as a proto-fascist U.S. government, the GDR allied with the "Other America." Not only a central target of the increasingly "Gestapo tactics" of the U.S.-led capitalist-imperialist system, the "Other America" also stood among the progressive international forces that would contribute to its final defeat. Yet this alliance was not without complications. As Klimke and Höhn have shown, the SED reserved the highest accolades for African-American activists with clear socialist leanings who viewed U.S. racism in relation to international class struggle, such as W.E.B. DuBois and Paul Robeson, who were celebrated as state guests when they visited the GDR in 1958 and 1960 respectively. By contrast, the SED met Dr. Martin Luther King, Jr.'s visit in 1964 with silence.[34] Unlike DuBois and Robeson, King supported the anti-communist politics that came to dominate the NAACP during the Cold War.[35]

Davis's membership in the CPUSA made her an appropriate symbol of the "Other America" in the GDR, yet some effort was required to interpret her politics as consonant with official SED interpretations of Marxist-Leninist praxis. In fact her connections to the New Left– and Third World–oriented Marxism that shaped much black revolutionary activism in the United States by the late 1960s rendered her a somewhat problematic symbol of mainstream socialist internationalism. GDR officials were particularly wary of Davis's association with the Black Panther Party (BPP) and her former professor and mentor Herbert Marcuse, whom she had known since her days at Brandeis as an undergraduate. Marcuse's attempt to move the working class from the center of Marxian analysis in favor of a focus on the revolutionary potential of African-American and Third World movements prompted much criticism from GDR policymakers and theorists, who identified him as a "petty bourgeois pseudo-left philosopher" whose popularity among the New Left rendered him among the most pernicious of Western Marxists.[36] While the SED did not denounce the Panthers openly, officials were suspicious of some aspects of their ideology. In one classified report, the Ministry of Foreign Affairs (MfAA) criticized the Panthers for failing to prioritize "universal class struggle against the imperialist system" while offering a "one-sided emphasis on the advancement of the Afro-American" instead. The MfAA claimed that such an approach could lead to "black racism."[37]

Such concerns echoed those by West German authorities who, like their East German counterparts, were threatened by political claims based on racial equality even while proclaiming official anti-racism to the international community. In a speech in honor of the UN International Year against Racism in March 1971, Chancellor Willy Brandt revealed the rather precarious position of the FRG when it came to U.S. race relations. In a carefully worded statement that avoided culpability in its use of passive voice, Brandt expressed concern that African-American GIs in West Germany "are encountering prejudice," similar to that experienced in the United States, where "freedom loving American citizens are suffering under racial tension." Nonetheless, he cited the anti-racism of the Basic Law and support of the UN Convention for the Elimination of All Forms of Racial Discrimination as evidence that "the FRG today belongs without doubt, to the countries of the world, where the right of human freedom is developed more than any place else." Brandt concluded by recognizing a special post-Nazi West German responsibility for vigilance against "any form of political extremism. Our nation and other nations have suffered from it. We have a special duty to be watchful."[38] While Brandt's statement was refreshing in that it addressed racism in Germany, it was far from open criticism of the U.S. record on racism or an alliance with the "other America."[39] By rejecting "any form of political extremism" Brandt elided right and left-wing "extremism." While such a formulation was typically used to conflate the two "Berlin dictatorships," in this context it also alluded to West German anxieties about political activity of African Americans on U.S. military bases, particularly Black Panthers, who protested the Vietnam War and advocated armed self-defense against the racist U.S. government. This was perceived as all the more dangerous given the existence of West German groups in solidarity with the Panthers and Third World revolutionaries. The most extreme of these were self-described "urban guerillas" such as the RAF, whose May 1972 bombing of the U.S. Headquarters in Heidelberg, like previous attacks, was a misguided attempt to bring global revolution to West Germany.[40] Brandt's statement was accompanied by reforms meant to improve the conditions of African-American GIs in Germany, and thus quell the protest.[41]

While Davis did not condone terrorism, her Marxist-Leninist critique of white supremacy, like that of the Panthers, was incompatible with liberal reformist approaches to racism, and her communism made her even more threatening in Cold War terms. A telegram from the FRG embassy in the United States identified Davis as "a militant activist of left-wing political extremism (*eine militante Aktivistin des politischen Linksextremismus*)."[42] Diplomatic correspondence during her trial dubbed Davis "a militant racial warrior and revolutionary (*eine militante Rassenkämpferin und Revolutionärin*)," and described her followers as "racial and worldview fanatics (*rassischen und weltanschaulischen Fanatikern*)."[43] Such descriptions not only evoked Nazism through references to "political extremists" and "race warriors," but also figured Davis and other African-American activists as the *source* rather than the *victims* of undemocratic tendencies—of "racial fanaticism"—in the United States, and, in light of recent developments, possibly also in West Germany.

Such destabilizing politics on the West German left would seem to be welcomed by the East German foreign policy establishment. Yet as the MfAA's worry about the Panthers' "black racism" suggests, a race- rather than class-based revolutionary analysis could provoke anxiety among white Germans on either side of the Wall. Moreover such an analysis was difficult to square with the East German party line. According to the MfAA, one of the Panthers' ideological shortfalls was the failure to develop a single revolutionary plan of action, instead drawing on "the eclectic combination of insights of classical Marxism-Leninism and the views of Mao, Che Guevara and Marcuse."[44] Rather than turning to the Soviet Union as a socialist example, the Panthers looked to anti-colonial revolutionary movements in Asia, Africa, and Latin America for their politics, and taking inspiration from the Maoist example, attempted to fit Marxist-Leninist theory to the position of African Americans.[45] Indeed, the Panthers were important in the dissemination of Third World–oriented Marxism-Leninism on the left.[46]

In the 1960s and early 1970s, Davis shared what the MfAA identified as this "eclectic" approach to revolutionary theory. After graduating from Brandeis in 1964, Davis spent three years studying German and European philosophy under prominent Western Marxists including Theodor Adorno, Jürgen Habermas, and Oskar Negt. She soon became active in the West German student movement, forming associations with radical students organized in the Socialist German Student League (SDS). Especially during its anti-authoritarian stage, lasting roughly from 1966 to 1968–69, the SDS found inspiration in theories such as Marcuse's, as well as those of Third World revolutionary intellectuals also calling for international rebellion, such as Fanon and Che Guevara. Indeed, radical West German students supported and saw themselves as working in solidarity with black liberation and anti-colonial activists.[47] During her stay in Frankfurt, Davis participated in SDS protest against the Vietnam War and U.S. neo-imperialism in the Third World more generally. In her autobiography, Davis explains, "it was my involvement in the demonstrative political activity led by German SDS which made me realize that I had to come home to wage the fight among my own people, black people."[48] Upon return to the United States in 1967, Davis became involved in the Los Angeles Black Panther Political Party (BPPP), which soon merged with the Student Nonviolent Coordinating Committee (SNCC). She later formed a brief association with Bobby Seale and Huey Newton's Oakland Black Panther Party.

Davis's association with the Panthers was short-lived, and she eventually reevaluated the "New Left" Marxism of the SDS, in particular its anti-communism.[49] Davis officially joined the CPUSA in 1968 in response to what she describes in her autobiography as a search for the strong political moorings that she found lacking in SNCC and the BPP (as well as her rejection of anti-communism and sexism within the movement).[50] In spite of her membership in the CPUSA, Davis's communism was less oriented toward the Soviet Union and the international working class than toward a revolutionary anti-racism and anti-imperialism that joined movements of the Third World and the United States. In fact, she entered the CPUSA through membership in the black collective, the Che-Lumumba Club, which posited a *race*-centered as opposed to a class-centered analysis of capitalist imperialism.[51]

Davis developed this aspect of her politics further through involvement in the Prisoner's Rights Movement, particularly in activism on behalf of the Soledad Brothers, a group of inmates at Soledad Prison who included George Jackson. Davis and others involved in the movement argued that the Soledad Brothers had been incarcerated as a result of actions directly related to the systemic racism and poverty of the so-called black ghetto and a proto-fascist criminal justice system. In Marcusean terms this was characteristic of the "preventive fascism" endemic to the United States, which aimed to thwart the very development of forces capable of revolutionary change.[52] Following an analysis that resonated with the Panthers' application of Fanon's colonial "lumpenproletariat" to urban African-American communities, Davis argued that this rendered the Soledad Brothers, and indeed all prisoners of color

**Figure 7.1.** Cover of Werner Lehmann's "Black Rose from Alabama" (1972)

who primarily came from the urban "lumpenproletariat," *political prisoners* rather than criminals.[53] Her participation in the campaign set in motion the chain of events that would eventually lead to Davis's 1970 arrest, when Jonathan Jackson used guns registered to Davis in an attempt to free his brother George Jackson, killing three prisoners as well as a judge in the process. Following an obscure California conspiracy law, Davis was charged with involvement in the crime, although she has always claimed to have had no part in Jonathan's plan.

While Davis's intellectual development and political commitments contradicted Soviet-oriented Marxism-Leninism, her membership in the Communist Party made her an attractive focus of solidarity with the "Other America" so long as her politics were interpreted "correctly." The East German "Free Angela" campaign and press accounts thus played up her association with the CPUSA, while downplaying her links to Marcuse and revolutionary black activism. Indeed, after meeting Davis in 1972, Klaus Steiniger, the jurist and journalist covering her trial for *Neues Deutschland,* reported that despite some ideological "holes" attributable to her association with Western Marxist Herbert Marcuse and the Panthers, she had "clearly grasped the significance of proletarian internationalism and the necessity of strong support of the socialist world system."[54] In a personal note to Steiniger, Davis pledged her reciprocal solidarity with the GDR. "Our fight against capitalist exploitation, racism and war," she explained, "requires a vigorous defense of the countries which have reached a stage of history where justice and equality prevails."[55] Her validation of the anti-racist self-presentation of the GDR, along with her commitment to socialism, no doubt spurred Steiniger's conclusion that defenders "of Angela Davis—the hero of the other America" were "the front line battalion of anti-fascism."[56]

## Ambivalences of Solidarity

In spite of Davis's support of the GDR, these "ideological holes" remained problematic. The East German media went to great pains to demonstrate that Davis indeed toed the appropriate socialist line. Indeed, the press deemphasized the revolutionary and racially subversive elements of Davis's politics in ways that resonated with news coverage in West Germany, where an emphasis on Davis's education and bourgeois upbringing combined with a focus on her appearance to contain her threat. Unlike other "leaders of the black militant movement," *Der Spiegel* reported, Davis was a "well traveled and educated" "bibliomaniac," who belonged to a black Girl Scout troop, took piano lessons, and earned high marks in school.[57] As in West Germany, journalists in East Germany recounted Davis's biography from her childhood spent in "bourgeois security" (*gutbürgerliche Geborgenheit*) to her entrance on the political scene in the 1960s and 70s. In the GDR, however, stories of Davis's piano lessons, participation in the Girl Scouts, and elite education served less to make her palatable to a middle-class white audience—although this could certainly have been one intentional or unintentional result—than to provide a backdrop for Davis's communist development.

A serialized political biography in *Für Dich* titled "Black Sister Angela," is a prime example of this approach. The twelve-part account by Helga Bobach described Davis's upbringing on "Dynamite Hill" in Birmingham, and her cultural and philosophical education, beginning with her first encounter with the *Communist Manifesto* through her formal training in Marxism and the German philosophical tradition under Marcuse at Brandeis and later at UC San Diego, as well as under Adorno in Frankfurt.[58] Bobach related Davis's life history as a didactic story of socialist development. While *Der Spiegel* offered an account of Davis's life in terms of bourgeois respectability that middle-class readers could relate to, Bobach was clear that Davis rejected the superficial comforts of such a life. Davis could have chosen a path leading to a happy life as an assistant professor at UCLA, or "a favorable marriage" that would have brought her back into the fold of the "black bourgeoisie."[59] Davis instead chose to follow her political convictions and a path that led her not to the safety of the library or to a suburban home, but rather to the dangers and uncertainty of the struggle for black and working class justice and eventually to the Communist Party.

Davis, moreover, chose the correct path to her ultimate entry into the Marxist-Leninist battle against capitalist imperialism. While active alongside the Black Panthers and in the black community (*Schwarze Gemeinde*), Bobach claimed Davis nonetheless resisted a strong ideological identification with the various political positions she encountered: "some want to return to African cultural traditions, and others are full of blind hatred for all whites." Bobach wrote that Davis—like two exceptional Black Panther leaders, Huey Newton and Bobby Seale—rejected the black cultural nationalism and "black racism" embraced by the majority of the black community.[60] Davis was convinced of the necessity of a unified movement that joined oppressed whites and blacks in a common struggle. Indeed, Davis understood that "it was imperative not only to free our own people, but also all of the oppressed of [the United States]"[61] Davis however, was "not lucky enough" to find a "better teacher" than Herbert Marcuse, whom Bobach described as "a seemingly 'radical Marxist' Professor, the idol of misguided youth." Marcuse taught "something he called 'Marxism,'" but which was actually "anarchistic heresy" that offered no challenge to U.S. liberal capitalism.[62] Fortunately,

according to Bobach, Davis soon surpassed Marcuse in her political understanding and made her way to the CPUSA.

In spite of attempts to spin Davis's politics correctly, Davis nonetheless
remained a potentially subversive figure. Bobach's account relied on a misleading and dishonest interpretation of Davis's influences and loyalties. Marcuse's teachings, as well as a black radical intellectual tradition that rejected
the ideology of universalist struggle, were central to Davis's intellectual and
political development. Moreover, Davis never, in fact, rejected Marcuse; she
left her studies at Frankfurt under Adorno in part because she wanted to
complete her doctoral degree under Marcuse's supervision, and even after
joining the CPUSA, she maintained a personal and intellectual relationship
with her former mentor.[63]

Media coverage of the Davis case simultaneously familiarized Davis,
both personally and politically, and exoticized her. Both tendencies worked
to counter the subversive potential of Davis's politics. While Davis's ties to
the New Left and black revolutionary politics made her a problematic "Hero
of the other America," her youth and dynamism, as well as her glamour
as a black woman, nonetheless gave her public appeal. The East German
media played up these qualities to shape Davis's image in ways that made
her an attractive figure for state-socialist mass consumption in spite of her
ideological shortcomings. Depictions of Davis in the East German popular
press resonated in some respects with West German liberal reportage. The
interest in Davis among the mainstream West German public was in part
a romanticized fascination with her as a radical black woman. Even serious
reportage construed Davis as somehow exotic, as exciting and transgressive
in both her aesthetics and her politics. As the November 1971 *Der Spiegel*
cover story illustrates, the West German media was preoccupied with Davis's
appearance and especially with her hair, which often served as not only a
symbol of Davis's "Black Power" but also as a marker of racial difference.
On the *Spiegel* cover, her prominent black afro appears in striking contrast
to a red background, dwarfing her features. In subsequent articles, she was
sensationally described as "the militant Madonna with an Afro-look,"[64] and
"the black woman with the 'bush hairdo' (*Buschfrisur*)."[65]

In West German press accounts such as these, depictions of her femininity and appearance acted at once to glamorize Davis and contain her
political challenge. With "her fist raised high in the Black-Power greeting,"
one *Der Spiegel* article described Davis as a "symbol of black resistance in
the USA."[66] However, commentators rarely failed to remind the reader that
while Davis may have been a "symbol figure" of a new black militancy, she
was also "a beautiful woman."[67] Writing in 1994 of similar representations
in the U.S. media, Davis criticized the emphasis placed on her early-70s aes-

thetic, rather than on the substance of her protest, and the interpretation of her afro as a *fashion* rather than a *political* statement.[68] Davis contended that such fascination with her "revolutionary glamour," acted both to depoliticize and to objectify her as a black woman. The West German fixation on Davis's "revolutionary glamour" and femininity can certainly be read in the same way. Emphasis on Davis's beauty and exoticized depictions of her appearance may have made Davis more palatable for a liberal audience who were drawn to her as an exciting figure of black resistance.

The East German solidarity apparatus and the popular media selectively embraced Davis's politics, while also emphasizing Davis's exoticism as a black woman. News stories and magazine features during her imprisonment and trial rarely failed to comment on her beauty. In the course of her political biography of Davis in *Für Dich,* Helga Bobach reported that one rarely met someone who combined "so much intelligence ... with such beauty." Bobach described her physical appearance in intimate and adoring detail: "her harmonious features, her gently curving mouth, her delicate yet powerful chin, and her eyes, the wise, dark eyes under her magnificent (*herrlich*) full hair."[69] Davis's appearance figured prominently in another notable example published shortly after her arrest that opened by fantasizing about Davis's first encounter with East Berliners at the May Day celebrations she attended in 1967 while still a student in Frankfurt. "The beautiful, dark-skinned woman," the article imagined, "captured the attention of the Berliners with her wide, curly hairstyle (*breiten, krausen Frisur*) in the, 'Afrika-Look.'"[70] On 20 January 1971—Davis's birthday—*Der Morgen* offered a similar estimation of the power of Davis's image and especially of her hair in the East German imagination. Over the months since Davis's arrest "her wise, sympathetic face has become familiar to all of us, as if we had known her for years." Indeed, the East German public had become acquainted with more than one "Angela," from the photos of the little girl in braids, to those of the young woman on the run with her hair smoothed tightly back into a bun, to the picture of her with a "great crown of curly hair" that had appeared on FBI wanted posters. It was this "Angela" that had become most dear to the GDR, "the protesting Angela Davis, who wears a wig (*Perücke*) [*sic?*] of frizzy black hair to show her pride in her colored (*farbige*) heritage."[71]

Accounts such as these reveal not only a reverence for Davis verging on hero worship, but also the power of her image. Such exoticized and, in the case of Bobach's suggestive portrayal in *Für Dich,* eroticized depictions of Davis emphasized her racial difference as a black woman. Davis's colorful and striking figure stood in marked contrast to the aging, bland bureaucrat-politicians who led the struggle for socialism in the Eastern bloc.[72] This combined with the intimate and physical language used to portray her in the media, to figure international solidarity at the level of affect and desire as well as political conviction. This portrayal of Davis functioned to strengthen bonds of solidarity and make the "Free Angela" campaign attractive to a wider East German population outside of the organizational and leadership circles.

The fact that Davis's politics were so difficult to categorize as either New or Old Left may have combined with her glamour and exotic racial difference to increase her mass appeal, especially among young people. Historians have shown that East German youth, like their West German counterparts, shared a fascination with Third World liberation in the late 1960s and 1970s. GDR adolescents and young adults were not only avid participants in the "Free Angela" campaign. Like their neighbors across the Wall, they also participated in large numbers in the anti–Vietnam War movement, which was particularly strong in the GDR.[73] Young people donated blood and collected money and books to send to their Vietnamese "brothers and sisters." They also joined "Friendship Brigades" that traveled to countries in Africa, Latin America, and Asia, where they participated in the building of socialism in the Third World.[74] All of these activities allowed East German youth to be part of the internationalist social and political culture identified with "1968" that had swept college campuses and sparked militant protest among young people around the globe.[75]

Some scholarship has argued that Third World solidarity had particular resonance for East German youth after the "Prague Spring," when the Warsaw Pact states invaded Czechoslovakia in August 1968 to quash the movement for political reform led by Alexander Dubček. The agitation for socialist reform in Prague and its military defeat indeed incited youth unrest and protest in the GDR that caused significant worry among authorities and teachers.[76] As Dorothee Wierling has argued, the Prague Spring provided a powerful symbol around which young people could organize, and through which they could express a range of grievances with a state that was increasingly "paranoid and controlling."[77] Although the 1968 invasion of Czechoslovakia marked a defeat of alternative visions of socialism within the Eastern bloc, such possibilities existed in non-European revolutionary politics. Indeed, Ulrich Mahlert suggests that youth who "were bitterly disappointed by the suppression of the Prague Spring transferred their hope to the liberation movements in the Third World."[78]

By contrast, Stephan Wolle has interpreted the greater visibility of Third World internationalism in the early 70s as part of Erich Honecker's "controlled opening." After Honecker replaced Walter Ulbricht in May 1971 as First Secretary of the SED, GDR authorities began to tolerate "revolutionary romance" that was until then proscribed. Border officials no longer confiscated Che Guevara posters and stickers from the West, and youth authorities relaxed policies on long hair and the wearing of revolutionary garb. At the same time young East Germans could now participate in spontaneous, nonparty demonstrations for the same causes as their West German counterparts, including protest against the Vietnam War and the imprisonment of Angela Davis.[79] Wolle suggests that this was superficial freedom at best, as it coexisted with continued social control and policing, as particularly evident in the case of the Tenth World Festival of Youth and Students 1973, at which Davis would be an honored guest. While the event brought GDR youth into seemingly open contact with young people from around the world, it followed intensive training of FDJ members in political protocol and a yearlong effort to preempt subversion through arrests and detention of those deemed politically or socially suspect, including the mentally ill.[80]

The "revolutionary romanticism" surrounding Davis and her official embrace by the party apparatus may have been part of this "controlled opening." Yet given the challenges that Davis's politics posed to East German interpretations of Marxism-Leninism, youth support of Davis required careful scripting. The popular magazine associated with the FDJ, *Junge Welt*, published an account of youth reception of the "Free Angela" campaign on 4 January 1971 that, when read against the grain, reveals Davis's subversive potential. The piece purported to be a letter to Davis from a young East German named Fritz Wengler. Wengler opened by praising Davis and the CPUSA for their "disciplined" contributions to the international struggle against imperialism. He expressed his desire and that of other young people in the GDR to follow Davis's example. Yet in light of Davis's own courage and willingness to risk her life for the cause, he remarked that "to many people here, the things that we identify as revolutionary seem small."[81] While Davis sacrificed her life, young people in the GDR demonstrated their socialist internationalism by earning good grades, going to work on time, following laws, conserving energy, and being honest and responsible.[82] In short, East German youth were "revolutionary" by simply being good socialist citizens.

Like the Davis biography published in *Für Dich*, the letter in *Junge Welt* offered a didactic story of proper socialist development, and in the process made clear what sort of "revolutionary" activity was permitted in the GDR. While Wengler ultimately argued against discontent, his letter nonetheless presented the East German socialist project of the early 1970s as mundane and even constricting. Indeed, the letter used the language of revolution as a call for conformity to state socialism. Rather than fight class war in the streets, East Germans were to do so by obeying authorities and by acting within the socialist architecture established after 1945. There was a great disconnect between Wengler's understanding of the meaning of "revolution" in East Germany and the types of revolutionary behavior that the GDR supported in the Third World and in the United States. By highlighting this disconnect, the letter suggested the subversive potential of solidarity with Davis and others who espoused a politics of confrontation and action rather than obedience and inaction—or what Wengler identified as "small" actions. This piece provided young East German readers with a lesson on the meaning of solidarity with Angela Davis. The letter indicated, however that "many people" in the GDR found a different meaning in Davis, namely, that socialist "revolution" in East Germany was trivial, boring, and even oppressive. The fact that the official magazine of the FDJ published such a letter, whether written by an actual East German youth named Fritz Wengler or by a staff writer, indicated that youth authorities in fact saw solidarity with Davis as potentially subversive for these reasons, and thus felt the need to manage the public interpretation of the solidarity campaign.

## Davis Visits the GDR

On 4 June 1972, Davis was acquitted of all charges in the state of California, and in September 1972, embarked on a journey to countries involved in the "Free Angela" campaign. West German activists invited Davis to stop in the FRG, much to the distress of the Foreign Office, which worried about the political damage that such a visit might have on its relations with the United States, as well as the potentially incendiary quality that her presence could have on the radical left and among African-American GIs on American military bases.[83] In the end this hand-wringing was for nothing, as Davis's tour focused not on the West but rather on socialist "brother countries" including the Soviet Union, Bulgaria, and Cuba, as well as Chile, currently ruled by Allende's Socialist Party. As she had promised Steiniger in the letter that she wrote in his trial notebook, Davis also included a stop in the GDR. Upon her arrival at Schönefeld Airport in East Berlin on 11 September 1972, Davis met a crowd of fifty thousand, mostly members of the Free German Youth (FDJ) and the Young Pioneers. *Neues Deutschland* reported that the crowd of young people "who had half a year ago been worried for Angela's life, her health," broke out into "thundering applause and chants" and waved banners reading *"Hoch Angela!"* (roughly "Cheers to Angela!").[84]

More than three thousand youth gathered the next day to celebrate Davis at a solidarity rally held at the historic East Berlin Friedrichstadt Palast. Young people presented Davis with baskets full of letters of greeting and warm wishes sent by children from all over the GDR. Members of the FDJ joined Davis on stage and shared what the solidarity campaign had meant to and taught them. *Neues Deutschland* reported that Angelike Holán, a philosophy student from Humboldt University, expressed "love for the Other America—hate for U.S. imperialism" in her speech. Holán exclaimed, "the future belongs to us, and you, Angela, are for us the representative of the future America, in which one day the red flags of the working class will wave."[85] Axel Marum, a high school student, recounted the part that he and his fellow students had played in the "Free Angela" campaign over the past two years: "at our school we could feel the international solidarity from the beginning. We sent you many greeting cards because we hoped that they would reassure you." Marum articulated a personal stake in the campaign in his description of his reaction to Davis's acquittal. "When I heard," he recalled, "it felt as if I had passed an exam. But to have you here with us is even better than we could have imagined." Indeed, he exclaimed, "your liberation shows how strong we all are together."[86] Davis returned Marum's expression of international solidarity by calling out "Friendship!" to the crowd.[87] This exchange highlights the connection felt by young people to Davis and her cause. Yet, that Marum would identify the feeling after "passing an exam" with a revolutionary victory only underscores the narrow limits of proper "revolutionary" behavior available to East German youth.

During her five-day stay in the GDR, workers, intellectuals, and party leaders joined schoolchildren in greeting Davis with enthusiasm. Davis met with employees of the Ernst Thälmann heavy machine works in Magdeburg, where workers issued greetings of solidarity and asked Davis for the honor of including her name in the Thälmann Brigade's book of honor.[88] Karl Marx University in Leipzig granted Davis an honorary doctorate in philosophy, acknowledging her as the most important defender of civil rights in the United States after Martin Luther King, Jr., and Paul Robeson (the two previous recipients of the award).[89] In a public demonstration of Davis's high regard in the GDR, former First Secretary of the SED Walter Ulbricht conferred upon her the "Great Star of National Friendship (*Völkerfreundschaft*)." Erich Honecker honored her personally in a public ceremony in which he presented her with a bouquet of roses and in "heartfelt words," recognized her "courageous actions and bravery." He declared Davis's release from prison to be "a victory of the world-wide solidarity movement against imperialist class justice."[90] In response to such honors, Davis thanked the GDR, in turn, for its tireless efforts during the "Free Angela" campaign and communicated her own feelings of gratitude and "heartfelt" sympathy for the East German socialist project. Such press portrayals and political speeches surrounding Davis's visit marked her freedom as yet more proof of the power of East German solidarity and anti-racism. At the same time, Davis's reciprocal support of the GDR, along with her frequent descriptions of East Germany as a "state free from racial prejudice,"[91] seemed to confirm that East Germany had overcome the burdens of the Nazi past successfully.

## Conclusion

While the GDR was by no means alone in the massive support of Davis offered by state-run organizations and citizens, the scope of East German support was notable enough to have been singled out by the American media and U.S. activists in the 1970s and also to be part of the memory of the international campaign. In June 1971, eight months into the two-year campaign, one NUCFAD representative reported to the *New York Times,* "We have received 100,000 pieces of mail from East Germany alone.... They're lying around in hundreds of mail bags unopened— because we don't have a big enough staff to do the work."[92] Shola Lynch's 2012 documentary about Davis's imprisonment and trial likewise highlights the outpouring of support from German youth in the course of the "One Million Roses for Angela Davis" campaign. Davis's sister Fania recalls "the Mailman arriving everyday with a huge sack of mail on his back, just addressed to Angela Davis, USA."[93] Indeed, the East German campaign was so successful that its output overwhelmed U.S. organizers at the time of the campaign and became an enduring symbol of the international support of Davis.

For the GDR, the "Free Angela" campaign served both domestic and foreign policy objectives. Support of Davis provided a means of differentiation from West Germany following the demise of the Hallstein Doctrine and in the context of increasing diplomatic normalization. In East Germany, open and enthusiastic support of the campaign buttressed claims of moral superiority over the West in a time when the world watched events in South Africa, in Vietnam, and in inner cities in the United States intently. An alliance with Davis and the "Other America" allowed East Germany to partake in the powerful rhetoric of anti-racism and human rights championed by the UN. It also demonstrated the GDR's continued commitment to anti-fascism—a commitment that East German authorities, and West German radical students and leftist critics, deemed lacking in the FRG.

Davis's broad popular appeal in the GDR not only served as a marker of the GDR's international legitimacy as the only anti-racist, anti-fascist German state; it also served to mobilize the East German public around international solidarity. People from all walks of life found something to celebrate and champion in Davis. Press accounts and campaign materials crafted Davis variously as familiar and exotic. Davis's "bourgeois respectability" made her an approachable "girl next door" turned comrade in the struggle, yet she was also a beautiful symbol of black power who elicited desire as well as loyalty. While Davis drew East German youth into the fold of socialist internationalism, she also represented a challenge to the status quo. The very qualities that may have allowed so many young people in particular to take up Davis's cause made her promotion not only to a hero of the "other America" but also an icon of international socialism a delicate operation. Indeed, the state-sponsored "Free Angela" campaign coexisted uneasily with Davis's particular version of Marxism-Leninism. The primacy of black and Third World peoples in Davis's political analysis, as well as her association with the New Left Marxism of figures such as Marcuse, defied East Germany's working-class and Soviet-oriented model of revolutionary change. East German officials echoed their West German counterparts when they expressed concerns over what they identified as "black racism" in the radical black internationalism espoused by both Davis and the Panthers.

In spite of official anti-racism on both sides of the Cold War divide, Davis's politics, and Third World–oriented Marxism more generally, clearly posed a challenge to white supremacy. This is evident not only in anxiety about "black racism" and "racial extremism" among foreign policy officials, but also in the more subtle racial and gender coding in the popular media in both East and West Germany. Exoticized depictions of Davis highlighted her racial difference and objectified her as a woman, thus neutralizing her political threat. At the same time, while the "Free Angela" campaign elicited heated debate about U.S. racism and the possible resurgence of fascism in the West, it largely yielded silence on the question of domestic racism in the two Germanys. Commentators failed to link the anti-racist message of the campaign to the pervasive discrimination against black Germans in each state. Black Germans, moreover, were not on the agenda during the International Year and Decade of Action to Combat Racism in either Germany. East German authorities had deemed the "racial problem" to have been solved in the GDR. Racism was incompatible with socialism; thus East Germany was by its very nature an anti-racist state. Scholars are just beginning to ask how the rhetoric of multicultural internationalism evident in the "Free Angela" campaign coexisted in East Germany with persistent associations of Germanness and "whiteness," and racism against black Germans, foreign workers, and students.[94] With this in mind, East German support of Davis could be seen as an outward and highly politicized expression of a state-mandated anti-racism that did not also imply an inward examination of East German society.[95]

**Katrina Hagen** holds a Ph.D. in history from University of Washington-Seattle. Her dissertation was titled *Internationalism in Cold War Germany.* She has published on Nazi legacies and German Cold War policies in the Congo.

# Notes

1. Bettina Aptheker, *The Morning Breaks: The Trial of Angela Davis*, 1st ed. (New York: International Publishers, 1975), 29. See statements of solidarity and support in Angela Y. Davis, ed., *If They Come in the Morning: Voices of Resistance* (New York: Third Press, 1971), 254–81.

2. Aptheker, *The Morning Breaks*, 29.

3. The Peace Council was the East German chapter of the World Peace Council, the organ of the international socialist peace movement that pursued world peace through anti-imperialism. On the Peace Council's activities surrounding anti–Vietnam War protest, see Günter Wernicke, "The World Peace Council and the Antiwar Movement in East Germany," in *America, the Vietnam War and the World*, ed. Andreas Daum, Lloyd C. Gardner, and Wilfried Mausbach (Washington, D.C.: Cambridge University Press, 2003), 299–319.

4. See *National Zeitung*, 9 January 1972; *Neues Deutschland*, 9 January 1972; *Berliner Zeitung*, 15 January 1972.

5. Maria Höhn and Martin Klimke, *A Breath of Freedom: The Civil Rights Struggle, African American GIs, and Germany* (New York: Palgrave Macmillan, 2010), 123–41.

6. Michael Harrington, *The Other America: Poverty in the United States* (New York: Macmillan, 1962) was an exposé of the living conditions of the American poor in part meant to counter faith in the U.S. free market economy expressed in John Kenneth Galbraith, *The Affluent Society* (Boston: Houghton Mifflin, 1958). *The Other America* was translated and published in the Soviet Union and the Eastern bloc in 1963. It was published in German translation in 1964 as *Das andere Amerika: Die Armut in den Vereinigten Staaten* (Munich: DTV, 1964). The book no doubt also came into East German circulation around this time. On Harrington's book see Maurice Isserman, *The Other American: The Life of Michael Harrington* (New York: Public Affairs, 2000), 176–78.

7. Sophie Lorenz, "'Heldin des anderen Amerikas'. Die DDR-Solidaritätsbewegung für Angela Davis, 1970–1973," *Zeithistorische Forschungen/Studies in Contemporary History, Online-Ausgabe* 10, no. 1 (2013). See also chapter 5 of my dissertation, "The 'Free Angela Davis' Campaign: Antiracism and the Other America," which views the Davis campaign in the context of the German-German Cold War. Katrina Hagen, "Internationalism in Cold War Germany" (Ph.D. diss., University of Washington, 2008).

8. On the Hallstein Doctrine see especially William Glenn Gray, *Germany's Cold War: The Global Campaign to Isolate East Germany, 1949-1969* (Chapel Hill: University of North Carolina Press, 2003).

9. Höhn and Klimke, *A Breath of Freedom*, 137.

10. Lorenz, "'Heldin des anderen Amerikas'," 14.

11. On GDR solidarity with Third World struggles see Günter Wernicke, "'Solidarität hilft siegen!' Zur Solidaritätsbewegung mit Vietnam in beiden deutschen Staaten," *Hefte zur DDR-Geschichte* no. 72 (2001); Hans-Georg Schleicher and Ilona Schleicher, *Special Flights: The GDR and Liberation Movements in Southern Africa* (Harare: SAPES Books, 1998); Ilona Schleicher, *Zwischen Herzenswunsch und politischem Kalkül: DDR-Solidarität mit dem Befreiungskampf im südlichen Afrika* (Berlin: Gesellschaftswissenschaftliches Forum, 1998); Brigitte Schulz, *Development Policy in*

*the Cold War Era: The Two Germanies and Sub-Saharan Africa, 1960-1985* (Münster: Lit, 1995).

12. Ingrid Muth, *Die DDR-Aussenpolitik 1949-1972: Inhalte, Strukturen, Mechanismen* (Berlin: Christopher Links, 2000), 20.

13. Ibid., 39. See also Schulz, *Development Policy in the Cold War Era.*

14. On the role of development projects and socialist visions of modernity in the GDR see Young-Sun Hong, "'The Benefits of Health Must Spread Among All': International Solidarity, Health and Race in the East German Encounter with the Third World," in *Socialist Modern: East German Everyday Culture and Politics,* ed. Katherine Pence and Paul Betts (Ann Arbor: University of Michigan Press, 2008).

15. On this point also see Lorenz, "'Heldin des anderen Amerikas'," 7.

16. Roland Burke, *Decolonization and the Evolution of International Human Rights* (Philadelphia: University of Pennsylvania Press, 2010). For a more optimistic view of these developments in the United Nations, see Paul Gordon Lauren, *Power and Prejudice: The Politics and Diplomacy of Racial Discrimination,* 2nd ed. (Boulder: Westview Press, 1996), 210–89.

17. "Report of the GDR Committee for the International Year for Action to Combat Racism and Racial Discrimination (December 1971)," in Alfred Babing, ed. *Against Racism, Apartheid and Colonialism: Documents Published by the GDR 1949-1977* (Berlin: Staatsverlag der Deutschen Demokratischen Republik, 1977). On the important role that anti-racism and international solidarity played in GDR education and youth policy see Mariane Krüger-Potratz, Annette Kaminsky, and Werner Winter, "Völkerfreundschaft und internationale Solidarität," in *Freundschaft!: Die Volksbildung der DDR in ausgewählten Kapiteln,* ed. Dankwart Kirchner (Berlin: BasisDruck, 1996); Jan-Peter Behrendt, *Zwischen proletarischem Internationalismus und Sicherheitsdenken: Afrikabilder in den Lehrplänen und Schulbüchern der DDR* (Hamburg: Helmut-Schmidt-Universität, 2004).

18. On the place of GDR anti-fascism in the German-German Cold War, see Mary Fulbrook, *German National Identity after the Holocaust* (Cambridge, U.K.: Polity Press, 2002); Jeffrey Herf, *Divided Memory: The Nazi Past in the Two Germanys* (Cambridge, MA: Harvard University Press, 1997).

19. Klaus Steiniger, *Free Angela Davis: Hero of the Other America* (Berlin: National Council for the National Front of the GDR, n.d. ca. 1972), 11.

20. On the place of anti-Americanism in GDR anti-fascism see Alan L. Nothnagle, *Building the East German Myth: Historical Mythology and Youth Propaganda in the German Democratic Republic, 1945-1989* (Ann Arbor: University of Michigan Press, 1999), 143–98.

21. On the intersection of debates over the Nazi past and decolonization in Africa, see Katrina Hagen, "Crimes against Humanity in the Congo: Nazi Legacies and the Cold War in Africa," in *Race, Ethnicity, and the Cold War: A Global Perspective,* ed. Philip E. Muehlenbeck (Nashville: Vanderbilt University Press, 2012).

22. Steiniger, *Free Angela Davis,* 74–78. On GDR self-identification as an anti-fascist and therefore anti-racist state see Alfred Babing, "Introduction," in Babing, *Against Racism, Apartheid and Colonialism,* 45–63, 50–53.

23. For summaries of the activity surrounding the "Free Angela" campaign in the GDR see "Report of the GDR Committee for the International Year for Action to Combat

Racism and Racial Discrimination," December 1971, in Babing, *Against Racism, Apartheid and Colonialism*, 201–7; Bundesvorstand des Demokratischen Frauenbundes Deutschlands, ed., *Geschichte des DFD* (Leipzig: Verlag für die Frau, 1989), 251–53.

24. "Der Heldin des Anderen Amerika," *Für Dich* 47 (3 November 1970), 8.

25. Ian Kershaw, *The Nazi Dictatorship: Problems and Perspectives of Interpretation*, 4th ed. (New York: Oxford University Press, 2000), 27. Kershaw notes that the Comintern definitions were finalized at the 1933 Communist International, and in the 1935 "Dimitrof definition," which defined fascism as: "the open terroristic dictatorship of the most reactionary, most chauvinistic, and most imperialist elements of finance capital," quoted in Kershaw, *The Nazi Dictatorship*, 12.

26. *Berliner Zeitung*, 22 February 1972.

27. "Stimme der DDR," Berliner Rundfunk, Berlin, 18 November 1971: Ausstellung "Freiheit für Angela Davis": BArch-SAPMO, DZ 9 DB.1830.

28. "Angeklagte Angela Davis: Faschismus in Amerika?" *Der Spiegel*, 26, no. 46 (8 November 1971), 137–46.

29. Both Marcuse and Negt speak of a "criminalization" of justice in numerous writings. For Negt's views, see for example, "Die Kriminalisierung der Justiz in den USA," in *Angela Davis Solidaritätskomitee, Am Beispiel Angela Davis* (Offenbach: Sozialistisches Büro-Verlag, 1971), 86–97. Marcuse also spoke and published widely on the Davis case: interview with Marcuse, "Dieser Terror is konterrevolutionär," *Konkret* 13 (15 June 1972); interview of Marcuse about Angela Davis, "Sie hat sich nicht verändert," *Der Spiegel* 26, no. 46 (8 November 1971): 148, 150; and "USA: Organisationsfrage und revolutionäres Subjekt. Fragen an Herbert Marcuse," *Kursbuch* 22 (December 1970): 45–60. This issue of *Kursbuch* as a whole engaged in the "fascism debate"; see especially the collection of U.S. press reports focusing heavily on the violence of the state apparatus toward African Americans, *Täglicher Faschismus: Evidenz auf Fünf Monaten*, 8–44.

30. See the following correspondence in which representatives of the Federal Government offer almost identical replies: Udo Preiser to Bundespräsident Heinemann (21 December 1971), and Office of the Bundespräsident reply to Udo Preiser (18 January 1972); Strunck, Vorsitzender der Deutschen Jungdemokraten, to Walter Scheel, Bundesminister des Äusseren (4 February 1972), Leiter des Ministerbüros reply to Strunck (22 February 1972): PA/AA, B 31, Ref. IA5, Bd. 414.

31. On Cleaver's attempt to enter the FRG see Wolfgang Kraushaar, ed. *Frankfurter Schule und Studentenbewegung. Von der Flaschenpost zum Molotowcocktail 1946-1995*, vol. 1 (Hamburg: Hamburger Edition, 1998), 501.

32. "Amadeo Richardson Heute in Marburg!" Leaflet from the Angela-Davis-Komitee Marburg, n.d. APO und Sozialbewegung Archiv, FU-Berlin. Bestandgruppe 19, "Internationalismus." Ordner: USA:BPP—Black Panther Party.

33. See Ingo Juchler, *Die Studentenbewegungen in den Vereinigten Staaten und der Bundesrepublik Deutschland der sechziger Jahre. Eine Untersuchung hinsichtlich ihrer Beeinflussung durch Befreiungsbewegungen und -theorien aus der Dritten Welt* (Berlin: Duncker & Humblot, 1996); Andrei S. Markovits and Philip S. Gorski, *The German Left: Red, Green and Beyond* (New York: Oxford University Press, 1993); Wilfred Mausbach, "Auschwitz and Vietnam: West German Protest Against America's War

During the 1960s," in *America, the Vietnam War and the World*, ed. Andreas Daum, Lloyd C. Gardner, and Wilfried Mausbach (Washington, D.C.: German Historical Institute, 2003).

34. Höhn and Klimke, *A Breath of Freedom*, 125–26, 129–31.

35. Ibid., 125.

36. Steiniger, *Free Angela Davis*, 21. The most developed example of this argument is in Herbert Marcuse, *One-Dimensional Man: Studies in the Ideology of Advanced Industrial Society* (Boston: Beacon Press, 1964).

37. Ministry of Foreign Affairs (MfAA), "Streng Vertraulich—Information: Über die Black Panther Party," Abt. USA/Kanada/Japan, Berlin, 17 March 1971: BArch-SAPMO: DY 30/J IV 2/2/3391.

38. Excerpts from Brandt's speech are included in the documentation to a meeting between FRG state officials and the U.S. Army-Europe regarding the problem of racism against African-American troops in West Germany: Chancellor Willy Brandt (21 March 1971), in "USAREUR/FRG Meeting on Equal Opportunity and Human Relations (2 December 1971)": PA/AA, B31, Ref. IA5, Bd. 323. For a discussion of governmental concern about charges of racism against African-American soldiers and fears that this would damage US-FRG relations, see the Foreign Office report to the Chancellor's Office and all state ministries, "Vorwurf der Diskriminierung farbiger Mitglieder der amerikanischen Streitkräfte seitens einiger Kreise der deutschen Bevölkerung" (Bonn, den 18. Oktober 1971): PA/AA, B31, Ref. IA5, Bd. 323.

39. Klimke and Höhn are somewhat more generous in their reading of Brandt. Höhn and Klimke, *A Breath of Freedom*, 168–69.

40. For a discussion of the RAF's political identification with the Black Panthers and Third World revolutionary movements see Juchler, *Die Studentenbewegungen in den Vereinigten Staaten und der Bundesrepublik Deutschland der sechziger Jahre*; Martin Klimke, "Black and Red Panthers," in Martin Klimke, *The Other Alliance: Student Protest in West Germany and the United States in the Global Sixties* (Princeton: Princeton University Press, 2009), 108–42; and Jeremy Varon, *Bringing the War Home: The Weather Underground, the Red Army Faction, and Revolutionary Violence in the Sixties and Seventies* (Berkeley: University of California Press, 2004).

41. Höhn and Klimke, *A Breath of Freedom*, 169–70.

42. Telegram to the AA from the FRG embassy, Washington (7 June 1972): PA/AA, B 31, Ref. IA5, Bd. 414. Such comparisons were in fact a common response in the FRG to black nationalist and revolutionary anti-racist politics, which in the 1960s and early 70s were often dubbed "black racism." For an analysis of such comparisons in the mid 1960s see David Braden Posner, "Afro-America in West German Perspective, 1945-1966" (Ph.D. diss., Yale University, 1997), 271–89. For similar designations of nationalist movements and revolutionary struggles for majority rule as "racial fanatics" and "black racists" in the context of African decolonization, see Hagen, "Crimes against Humanity in the Congo."

43. FRG General Consulate, San Francisco to the AA, "Strafverfahren gegen Angela Davis" (24 February 1972): PA/AA, B 31, Ref. IA5, Bd. 414.

44. Ministry of Foreign Affairs (MfAA), "Streng Vertraulich—Information: Über die Black Panther Party," Abt. USA/Kanada/Japan, Berlin, 17 March 1971: BArch-SAPMO: DY 30/J IV 2/2/3391.

45. Robin D.G. Kelley, *Freedom Dreams: The Black Radical Imagination* (Boston: Beacon Press, 2002), 94.

46. Nikhil Pal Singh, *Black is a Country: Race and the Unfinished Struggle for Democracy* (Cambridge: Harvard University Press, 2004).

47. On the Third World–oriented internationalism of the West German student movement see especially Quinn Slobodian, *Foreign Front: Third World Politics in Sixties West Germany* (Durham: Duke University Press, 2012); Werner Balsen and Karl Rössel, *Hoch die internationale Solidarität. Zur Geschichte der Dritte-Welt-Bewegung in der Bundesrepublik* (Cologne: Kölner Volksblatt Verlag, 1986); Sara Lennox, "Enzensberger, Kursbuch and 'Third Worldism': The Sixties' Construction of Latin America," in *"Neue Welt"/"Dritte Welt". Interkulturelle Beziehungen Deutschlands zu Lateinamerika und der Karibik*, ed. Sigrid Bauschinger and Susan L. Cocalis (Tübingen: Francke Verlag, 1994); Juchler, *Die Studentenbewegungen in den Vereinigten Staaten und der Bundesrepublik Deutschland der sechziger Jahre.*

48. Angela Y. Davis, "Prison Interviews," in *If They Come in the Morning*, 179.

49. For Davis's criticism of the anti-communism of the "European Left," by which she certainly refers to the West German SDS, see Davis, *If They Come in the Morning*, 162–63.

50. On Davis's break with the BPPP/SNCC, see ibid., 187–88. For an account of her relationship and break with the BPP, see ibid. 193–96.

51. Angela Y. Davis, "Prison Interviews," 180.

52. Angela Y. Davis, "Political Prisoners, Prisons and Black Liberation," in *If they Come in the Morning.*

53. For a summary of her position see ibid. On the Panthers' interpretation of Fanon see especially Nikhil Pal Singh, "The Black Panthers and the 'Undeveloped Country' of the Left," in *The Black Panther Party (Reconsidered)*, ed. Charles E. Jones (Baltimore: Black Classic Press, 1998), 68–70, 78; Singh, *Black is a Country,* 193–202.

54. "Information zu einigen Aspekten des USA-Aufenthalts des Genossen Dr. Klaus Steiniger (Reisegrund: Berichterstattung über den Davis-Prozeß. Zeitraum: 27.2-30.4.1972)," pg. 4: BArch-SAPMO: DY 30/ IV B 2/20/227.

55. Angela Davis to Klaus Steiniger, San Jose (26 April 1972): Barch-SAPMO: DY 30/ IV B 2/20/227.

56. Steiniger, *Free Angela Davis,* 87.

57. Mauz, "Angeklagte," 129, 105.

58. The series ran from September to November 1971: Helga Bobach, "Schwarze Schwester Angela. Eine Angela-Davis-Biographie," *Für Dich* 38–49 (September–November 1971).

59. Bobach, "Schwarze Schwester Angela," *Für Dich* 44, no. 5 (October 1971), 41.

60. Ibid., 28.

61. Davis, quoted in ibid.

62. Ibid., 27.

63. Cynthia A. Young, *Soul Power: Culture, Radicalism, and the Making of a U.S. Third World Left* (Durham, NC: Duke University Press, 2006), 192.

64. Gerhard Mauz, "Der letzte schöne Tag ihres Lebens?" *Der Spiegel,* 26, no. 25 (12 June 1972), 85-86, 85.

65. Gerhard Mauz, "Gaskammer geschlossen," *Der Spiegel*, 26, no. 10 (28 February 1972), 98.

66. Mauz, "Der letzte schöne Tag," 85.

67. Mauz "Angeklagte," 129.

68. Angela Y. Davis, "Afro Images: Politics, Fashion, and Nostalgia," in *The Angela Y. Davis Reader*, ed. Joy James (Malden: Blackwell, 1998).

69. Bobach, "Schwarze Schwester Angela," 30.

70. Victor Grossman, "Eine Frau aus Alabama," [title unclear], 47 (1970): BArch-SAPMO, DZ 9-246.

71. It is unclear why this reporter refers to Davis's natural hair as a wig. *Der Morgen*, 1 January 1971: BArch-SAPMO, DZ 9-246

72. Lorenz, "'Heldin des anderen Amerikas'." 14. See also Jon Raundalen, "A States-man's Welcome for FBI's Most Wanted" (paper presented at the "Crossovers: African Americans and Germany" conference, Münster, 22–26 March 2006).

73. On East German solidarity with Vietnam see especially, Wernicke, "'Solidarität hilft siegen!'"

74. Ulrich Mählert and Gerd-Rüdiger Stephan, *Blaue Hemden, rote Fahnen: die Ge-schichte der Freien Deutschen Jugend*, (Opladen: Leske + Budrich, 1996), 187–88; Uta G. Poiger, "Amerikanisierung oder Internationalisierung? Populär Kultur in bei-den deutschen Staaten," *Aus Politik und Zeitgeschichte*, no. B 45 (2003), 23.

75. On 1968 in East Germany see Timothy S. Brown, "'1968' East and West: Divided Germany as a Case Study in Transnational History," *American Historical Review*, no. 114 (February 2009): 69–96, and Timothy S. Brown, "East Germany," in *1968 in Europe: A History of Protest and Activism, 1956-1977*, ed. Martin Klimke and Joa-chim Scharloth (New York: Palgrave Macmillan, 2008). On 1968 in global perspec-tive more generally see Carole Fink, Philipp Gassert, and Detlef Junker, eds., *1968: The World Transformed* (Washington, D.C.: German Historical Institute, 1998).

76. On East German protest during and following the Prague Spring see Ulrich Mählert and Gerd-Rüdiger Stephan, *Blaue Hemden, rote Fahnen*, 177–80; Dorothee Wier-ling, "Youth as Internal Enemy: Conflicts in the Education of the 1960s Dictator-ship," in *Socialist Modern: East German Everyday Culture and Politics*, ed. Katherine Pence and Paul Betts (Ann Arbor: University of Michigan Press, 2008).

77. Ibid., 171.

78. Mählert and Stephan, *Blaue Hemden, rote Fahnen*, 187. Also quoted in Poiger, "Amerikanisierung oder Internationalisierung?," 23.

79. Stefan Wolle, *Der Traum von der Revolte. Die DDR 1968* (Berlin: Sonderausgabe für die Zentralen für politische Bildung in Deutschland, 2008), 232–43.

80. Ibid., 234–36; Höhn and Klimke, *A Breath of Freedom*, 138.

81. "Brief an Angela Davis," *Junge Welt*, 4 January 1971: BArch-SAPMO, DZ 9-246.

82. Ibid.

83. For the discussion of Davis's potential visit see, the Foreign Office debate over the issue, Ref. IA5, "Einreise der amerikanische Bürgerrechtskämpferin Angela Davis in die Bundesrepublik," 9 June 1972, Bonn, pg. 3: PA/AA, B82, Bd. 1136; AA, Ref IA5, "Einladung der amerikanischen Bürgerrechtskämpferin Angela Davis in die Bundesrepublik," Dr. Thomas, Bonn, 8 July 1972: PAAA/ B 31, Ref. IA5, Bd

414; and the discussion between the Foreign Office and the Ministry of the Interior, AA to the Federal Ministry of the Interior, "Einreise der amerikanischen Bürgerrechtskämpferin Angela Davis," Bonn 13 June 1972: PA/AA, B 31, Ref. IA5, Bd. 414.

84. "Die Jugend Berlins schloß Angela Davis freudig in die Arme," *ND*, Monday, 11 September 1972.
85. *Neues Deutschland*, 12 September 1972.
86. Ibid.
87. Ibid.
88. *Peace, Friendship, Solidarity: Angela Davis in the GDR* (Dresden: Verlag Zeit im Bild, n.d.), 15; "Wir wollen sie alle sehen," *ND*, 13 September 1972.
89. *Peace, Friendship, and Solidarity.*
90. "Erich Honecker empfing Genossin Angela Davis," *ND*, 12 September 1972.
91. Davis made such statements often during her five-day visit. See for example, "Erich Honecker empfing Genossin Angela Davis."
92. Sol Stern, "The Campaign to Free Angela Davis and Ruchell Magee," 27 June 1971, *New York Times Books*, http://www.nytimes.com/books/98/03/08/home/davis-campaign.html.
93. *Free Angela and All Political Prisoners*, directed by Shola Lynch, New York: Realside Productions, 2012.
94. On these questions see Jan C. Behrends, Thomas Lindenberger, and Patrice G. Poutrus, eds., *Fremde und Fremd-Sein in der DDR: zu historischen Ursachen der Fremdenfeindlichkeit in Ostdeutschland* (Berlin: Metropol, 2003); Bernd Bröskamp, ed. *Schwarz-weisse Zeiten: AusländerInnen in Ostdeutschland vor und nach der Wende: Erfahrungen der Vertragsarbeiter aus Mosambik* (Bremen: IZA, 1993); Peggy Piesche, "Black and German? East German Adolescents Before 1989: A Retrospective View of a 'Non-Existent Issue' in the GDR," in *The Cultural After-Life of East Germany: New Transnational Perspectives*, ed. Leslie Adelson (Washington, D.C.: AICGS Humanities 2002); Peggy Piesche, "Das Schwarze als Maske: Images der 'Fremden' in DEFA-Filmen," *iz3w*, no. 276 (2004); Uta Rüchel, '...auf Deutsch sozialistisch zu Denken...': *Mosambiker in der Schule der Freundschaft* (Magdeburg: Die Landesbeauftragte für die Unterlagen der Staatssicherheitsdienstes der ehemaligen DDR in Sachsen-Anhalt, 2001).
95. For a discussion of this phenomenon, see also Höhn and Klimke, *A Breath of Freedom*, 140–41.

# Bibliography

Angela Davis Solidaritätskomitee. *Am Beispiel Angela Davis*. Offenbach: Sozialistisches Büro-Verlag, 1971.

Aptheker, Bettina. *The Morning Breaks: The Trial of Angela Davis*. 1st ed. New York: International Publishers, 1975.

Babing, Alfred, ed. *Against Racism, Apartheid and Colonialism: Documents Published by the GDR 1949-1977*. Berlin: Staatsverlag der Deutschen Demokratischen Republik, 1977.

Balsen, Werner, and Karl Rössel. *Hoch die internationale Solidarität. Zur Geschichte der Dritte-Welt-Bewegung in der Bundesrepublik.* Cologne: Kölner Volksblatt Verlag, 1986.

Behrends, Jan C., Thomas Lindenberger, and Patrice G. Poutrus, eds. *Fremde und Fremd-Sein in der DDR: zu historischen Ursachen der Fremdenfeindlichkeit in Ostdeutschland.* Berlin: Metropol, 2003.

Behrendt, Jan-Peter. *Zwischen proletarischem Internationalismus und Sicherheitsdenken: Afrikabilder in den Lehrplänen und Schulbüchern der DDR.* Hamburg: Helmut-Schmidt-Universität, 2004.

Bröskamp, Bernd, ed. *Schwarz-weisse Zeiten: AusländerInnen in Ostdeutschland vor und nach der Wende: Erfahrungen der Vertragsarbeiter aus Mosambik.* Bremen: IZA, 1993.

Brown, Timothy S. "'1968' East and West: Divided Germany as a Case Study in Transnational History." *American Historical Review,* no. 114 (February 2009): 69–96.

———. "East Germany." In *1968 in Europe: A History of Protest and Activism, 1956-1977,* ed. Martin Klimke and Joachim Scharloth, 189–98. New York: Palgrave Macmillan, 2008.

Bundesvorstand des Demokratischen Frauenbundes Deutschlands, ed. *Geschichte des DFD.* Leipzig: Verlag für die Frau, 1989.

Burke, Roland. *Decolonization and the Evolution of International Human Rights.* Philadelphia: University of Pennsylvania Press, 2010.

Davis, Angela Y. "Afro Images: Politics, Fashion, and Nostalgia." In *The Angela Y. Davis Reader,* ed. Joy James, 273–78. Malden: Blackwell, 1998.

———, ed. *If They Come in the Morning: Voices of Resistance.* New York: Third Press, 1971.

Fink, Carole, Philipp Gassert, and Detlef Junker, eds. *1968: The World Transformed.* Washington, D.C.: German Historical Institute, 1998.

Fulbrook, Mary. *German National Identity after the Holocaust.* Cambridge, U.K.: Polity Press, 2002.

Galbraith, John Kenneth. *The Affluent Society.* Boston: Houghton Mifflin, 1958.

Gray, William Glenn. *Germany's Cold War: The Global Campaign to Isolate East Germany, 1949-1969.* Chapel Hill: University of North Carolina Press, 2003.

Hagen, Katrina. "Crimes against Humanity in the Congo: Nazi Legacies and the Cold War in Africa." In *Race, Ethnicity, and the Cold War: A Global Perspective,* ed. Philip E. Muehlenbeck. Nashville: Vanderbilt University Press, 2012.

———. "Internationalism in Cold War Germany." Ph.D. diss., University of Washington, 2008.

Harrington, Michael. *The Other America: Poverty in the United States.* New York: Macmillan, 1962.

Herf, Jeffrey. *Divided Memory: The Nazi Past in the Two Germanys.* Cambridge: Harvard University Press, 1997.

Höhn, Maria, and Martin Klimke. *A Breath of Freedom: The Civil Rights Struggle, African American GIs, and Germany.* New York: Palgrave Macmillan, 2010.

Hong, Young-Sun. "'The Benefits of Health Must Spread Among All': International Solidarity, Health and Race in the East German Encounter with the Third World." In *Socialist Modern: East German Everyday Culture and Politics,* ed. Katherine Pence and Paul Betts, 183–210. Ann Arbor: University of Michigan Press, 2008.

Isserman, Maurice. *The Other American: The Life of Michael Harrington*. New York: PublicAffairs, 2000.

Juchler, Ingo. *Die Studentenbewegungen in den Vereinigten Staaten und der Bundesrepublik Deutschland der sechziger Jahre. Eine Untersuchung hinsichtlich ihrer Beeinflussung durch Befreiungsbewegungen und -theorien aus der Dritten Welt*. Berlin: Duncker & Humblot, 1996.

Kelley, Robin D. G. *Freedom Dreams: The Black Radical Imagination*. Boston: Beacon Press, 2002.

Kershaw, Ian. *The Nazi Dictatorship: Problems and Perspectives of Interpretation*. 4th ed. New York: Oxford University Press, 2000.

Klimke, Martin. *The Other Alliance: Student Protest in West Germany and the United States in the Global Sixties*. Princeton: Princeton University Press, 2009.

Kraushaar, Wolfgang, ed. *Frankfurter Schule und Studentenbewegung. Von der Flaschenpost zum Molotowcocktail 1946-1995*. Vol. 1. Hamburg: Hamburger Edition, 1998.

Krüger-Potratz, Mariane, Annette Kaminsky, and Werner Winter. "Völkerfreundschaft und internationale Solidarität." In *Freundschaft!: Die Volksbildung der DDR in ausgewählten Kapiteln*, ed. Dankwart Kirchner, 171–259. Berlin: BasisDruck, 1996.

Lauren, Paul Gordon. *Power and Prejudice: The Politics and Diplomacy of Racial Discrimination*. 2nd ed. Boulder: Westview Press, 1996.

Lennox, Sara. "Enzensberger, Kursbuch and 'Third Worldism': The Sixties' Construction of Latin America." In *"Neue Welt"/"Dritte Welt". Interkulturelle Beziehungen Deutschlands zu Lateinamerika und der Karibik*, ed. Sigrid Bauschinger and Susan L. Cocalis. Tübingen: Francke Verlag, 1994.

Lorenz, Sophie. "'Heldin des anderen Amerikas'. Die DDR-Solidaritätsbewegung für Angela Davis, 1970–1973." *Zeithistorische Forschungen/Studies in Contemporary History*, Online-Ausgabe 10, no. 1 (2013).

Mählert, Ulrich, and Gerd-Rüdiger Stephan. *Blaue Hemden, rote Fahnen: die Geschichte der Freien Deutschen Jugend*. Edition Deutschland Archiv. Opladen: Leske + Budrich, 1996.

Marcuse, Herbert. *One-Dimensional Man: Studies in the Ideology of Advanced Industrial Society*. Boston: Beacon Press, 1964.

Markovits, Andrei S., and Philip S. Gorski. *The German Left: Red, Green and Beyond*. New York: Oxford University Press, 1993.

Mausbach, Wilfred. "Auschwitz and Vietnam: West German Protest Against America's War During the 1960s." In *America, the Vietnam War and the World*, ed. Andreas Daum, Lloyd C. Gardner, and Wilfried Mausbach. Washington, D.C.: German Historical Institute, 2003.

Muth, Ingrid. *Die DDR-Aussenpolitik 1949-1972: Inhalte, Strukturen, Mechanismen*. Berlin: Christopher Links, 2000.

Nothnagle, Alan L. *Building the East German Myth: Historical Mythology and Youth Propaganda in the German Democratic Republic, 1945-1989*. Ann Arbor: University of Michigan Press, 1999.

*Peace, Friendship, Solidarity: Angela Davis in the GDR*. Dresden: Verlag Zeit im Bild, n.d.

Piesche, Peggy. "Black and German? East German Adolescents Before 1989: A Retrospective View of a 'Non-Existent Issue' in the GDR." In *The Cultural After-Life of*

*East Germany: New Transnational Perspectives,* ed. Leslie Adelson. Washington, D.C.: AICGS Humanities 2002.

———. "Das Schwarze als Maske: Images der 'Fremden' in DEFA-Filmen." *iz3w,* no. 276 (2004): 39–41.

Poiger, Uta G. "Amerikanisierung oder Internationalisierung? Populär Kultur in beiden deutschen Staaten." *Aus Politik und Zeitgeschichte,* no. B 45 (2003): 17–24.

Posner, David Braden. "Afro-America in West German Perspective, 1945-1966." Ph.D. diss., Yale University, 1997.

Rüchel, Uta. *'…auf Deutsch sozialistisch zu Denken…': Mosambiker in der Schule der Freundschaft Magdeburg: Die Landesbeauftragte für die Unterlagen der Staatssicherheitsdienstes der ehemaligen DDR in Sachsen-Anhalt,* 2001.

Schleicher, Hans-Georg, and Ilona Schleicher. *Special Flights: The GDR and Liberation Movements in Southern Africa.* Harare: SAPES Books, 1998.

Schleicher, Ilona. *Zwischen Herzenswunsch und politischem Kalkül: DDR-Solidarität mit dem Befreiungskampf im südlichen Afrika.* Berlin: Gesellschaftswissenschaftliches Forum, 1998.

Schulz, Brigitte. *Development Policy in the Cold War Era: The Two Germanies and Sub-Saharan Africa, 1960-1985.* Münster: Lit, 1995.

Singh, Nikhil Pal. *Black is a Country: Race and the Unfinished Struggle for Democracy.* Cambridge: Harvard University Press, 2004.

———. "The Black Panthers and the 'Undeveloped Country' of the Left." In *The Black Panther Party (Reconsidered),* ed. Charles E. Jones, 57–105. Baltimore: Black Classic Press, 1998.

Slobodian, Quinn. *Foreign Front: Third World Politics in Sixties West Germany.* Durham: Duke University Press, 2012.

Steiniger, Klaus. *Free Angela Davis. Hero of the Other America.* Berlin: National Council for the National Front of the GDR, n.d. ca. 1972.

Varon, Jeremy. *Bringing the War Home: The Weather Underground, the Red Army Faction, and Revolutionary Violence in the Sixties and Seventies.* Berkeley: University of California Press, 2004.

Wernicke, Günter. "'Solidarität hilft siegen!' Zur Solidaritätsbewegung mit Vietnam in beiden deutschen Staaten." *Hefte zur DDR-Geschichte,* no. 72 (2001).

———. "The World Peace Council and the Antiwar Movement in East Germany." In *America, the Vietnam War and the World,* ed. Andreas Daum, Lloyd C. Gardner, and Wilfried Mausbach, 299–320. Washington, D.C.: Cambridge University Press, 2003.

Wierling, Dorothee. "Youth as Internal Enemy: Conflicts in the Education of the 1960s Dictatorship." In *Socialist Modern: East German Everyday Culture and Politics,* ed. Katherine Pence and Paul Betts, 157–82. Ann Arbor: University of Michigan Press, 2008.

Wolle, Stefan. *Der Traum von der Revolte. Die DDR 1968.* Berlin: Sonderausgabe für die Zentralen für politische Bildung in Deutschland, 2008.

Young, Cynthia A. *Soul Power: Culture, Radicalism, and the Making of a U.S. Third World Left.* Durham: Duke University Press, 2006.

Chapter 8

# True to the Politics of Frelimo?

Teaching Socialism at the
*Schule der Freundschaft*, 1981–90

*Jason Verber*

On 2 February 1981, construction began on the *Schule der Freundschaft* (School of Friendship) in Stassfurt, a small East German city just south of Magdeburg. Plans called for four residence halls, classrooms, a cafeteria, and sporting facilities. It was to be an unremarkable boarding school in almost every respect save one: in little more than a year's time, the *Schule der Freundschaft* would open its doors to a student body composed entirely of children from Mozambique, children who would be accompanied by a significant number of Mozambican teachers and other staff.[1] In Stassfurt these students would not only continue their education but also benefit from East German technical expertise, learning the skills necessary to help build a strong, independent economy in Mozambique and overcome the legacies of Portuguese colonial rule. Moreover, these young Mozambicans would have the opportunity to see socialism in practice in East Germany, returning home "prepared to live and to work as cognizant young citizens true to the ideas of socialism and the politics of Frelimo."[2] The GDR stood to benefit as well. The SED intended the project not only as a (genuine) expression of anti-imperialist solidarity with Frelimo—the Mozambican liberation movement turned ruling party—but also as a means to help cement close relations between the two states.

As an outcome of East German foreign policy in the developing world, the *Schule der Freundschaft* represented an important symbol, and a tangible expression of the GDR's commitment to otherwise abstract notions like "solidarity" and the "shared struggle against imperialism." Like other projects before it, the planning and construction of the school reflected both East Germany's ideological devotion to supporting class struggle around the world and its pragmatic efforts to win friends and allies. Aid and assistance of various kinds to liberation movements and fledgling states alike furthered the anti-imperialist cause but also had the potential to strengthen the GDR's position diplomatically. However, as an ongoing collaboration between Mozambique and the GDR, the *Schule der Freundschaft* exposed the limits of solidarity. The school's operations highlighted the difficulty of transforming the SED's vision of socialism into a reality as well as the party's interest in not just the quantity but also the quality of its socialist allies. The SED's "ideas of socialism" not only often failed to line up with the "politics of Frelimo," but they also imperfectly described the reality of "actually existing socialism" in the GDR. The *Schule der Freundschaft* threw the differences between these three brands of socialism into sharp relief.

The school represented a joint undertaking from the start. In theory, the roles that both states and their representatives would play were clearly defined, negotiated well in advance. In practice, however, such definitions broke down, especially as East German officials and administrators became increasingly concerned about the kind of socialist education and upbringing Mozambican students were receiving at the *Schule der Freundschaft*. Despite lofty aspirations, school officials discovered that sometimes "the ideas of socialism" and "the politics of Frelimo" were simply incompatible. The content of the curriculum was not a major concern. Much of this was copied verbatim from Mozambican and East German schools. Rather, East German officials at the school and in the government worried about the ways in which that curriculum was taught, as well as the kinds of relationships that developed among students and faculty at the *Schule der Freundschaft* and between Mozambicans and East Germans in Stassfurt. Concerns about teaching methodology reflected long-standing questions about Frelimo's ideological loyalties as well as the practical realities of building socialism in Mozambique. Similarly, student life outside the classroom seemed to many East German officials to reflect the survival of colonial and indigenous influences that ran counter to East German understandings of socialism. Perhaps most significantly, the issues surrounding how to deal with sex and violence threatened to undermine the socialist educational experience in Stassfurt.

The story of the *Schule der Freundschaft* is relatively well known, having received coverage in a variety of (mostly German-language) publications. In the field of education, the school has served as a lens through which to examine both Mozambican and East German educational policy.[3] It has provided fodder for scholars interested in race and postcolonialism, especially the period after the arrival of students from the former German colony of South West Africa (later known as Namibia).[4] The school is also a regular staple of analyses of East German foreign policy with regard to Mozambique in particular and East German relations with Africa as a whole.[5]

Despite such disparate fields of inquiry, however, certain patterns emerge in the scholarship on the *Schule der Freundschaft*. Perhaps the most important thread to run through much of this literature is the tendency to view the school in one of two ways: as an institution that communicated certain knowledge, ideas, and beliefs, or as a locus for encounters between Germans and non-Germans. The former approach is quite useful for understanding the school as an instrument of education and foreign policy alike, but it is entirely top-down. It privileges the information transmitted at the school via the curriculum or internationally via the symbolism of the school's very existence. The latter grants individuals a much more active role and acknowledges the unique opportunity for interaction that the school created, but it often reduces the role of the party and the state to one of reaction. This chapter combines elements of both approaches, but also upends them, examining the school as a means by which the East German regime came to learn more about not only the politics of Frelimo and socialism in Mozambique but also the reality of socialist solidarity in the GDR as a result of the interactions that took place at and around the *Schule der Freundschaft*.

The construction of the *Schule der Freundschaft* represented a novel turn in East German relations with the developing world in general and Mozambique in particular, but the idea for such a project did not appear out of thin air. Rather, it represented an extension of the foreign policy that the SED had pursued from the founding of the East German state onward. Central to both the rhetoric and content of this foreign policy was the notion of a shared struggle: the people of the GDR did not live simply in a socialist state, but fought on the forefront of a global struggle against imperialism. The Soviet Union's denunciation of any kind of "national path" to socialism beginning at the first meeting of the Cominform in September 1947 not only reserved a role for the Soviet Union in Eastern European political developments, but it also ensured a certain degree of internationalism.[6] Nikita Khrushchev's gestures toward peaceful coexistence in the late 1950s signaled a potential end to this global struggle, but the opportunities afforded by decolonization and the threat to the USSR's "claim to be the authoritative interpreter of Marxist thought" refocused Soviet efforts in the early 1960s, while the limits Khrushchev put on de-Stalinization helped ensure the rest of Eastern Europe would stay in line and follow suit.[7] Regardless of its origins, however, this belief in and commitment to a worldwide struggle drove the SED to reach out to not only socialist and communist parties around the world but to all manner of anti-capitalist and anti-imperialist organizations.

Building close relationships with the decolonizing and developing world was a key feature of East German foreign policy from the beginning. The West German government's claim that there was only one German state and its promise to view recognition of the GDR as an "unfriendly act" did little more than confirm the status quo in Europe, but in the rest of the world every newly independent state brought the GDR a new opportunity for diplomatic recognition.[8] In some cases, the regime's first goal was simply to make liberation movements and newly independent states aware of the existence of two German states. More often, however, efforts at establishing relations began with a detailed explanation of the myriad differences between the German Democratic Republic and the Federal Republic.

The SED maintained in the mid 1960s that "the *Auslandsinformation* [foreign information, i.e., propaganda abroad] of the GDR is an integral element of the foreign policy of our republic." Its objective was simple: "to strengthen the international position of our state and promote its international relations." Brochures and other publications made available in a variety of languages cast the GDR in the best light possible, and party officials organized film nights and discussions around the developing world in order to answer any questions people might have about either German state. According to the self-description of the SED, it was all part of an effort at the "systematic exposure and denunciation of the peace-endangering, revanchist, and neo-colonialist policies of the West German state."[9] Particularly in the decolonizing and postcolonial world, *Auslandsinformation* made special reference to the parallels between the East German struggle against fascism and militarism on the one hand, and the struggle of colonized peoples against imperialism on the other.[10] By painting themselves as comrades in arms, the SED hoped to win the sympathies and support of the developing world.

Rhetoric was not enough for the GDR, however; the East German regime also established its ideological bona fides to the developing world through concrete demonstrations of solidarity in the form of aid and assistance. By "putting their money where their mouths were," the SED intended to prove that the notion of a shared struggle was more than just idle talk and to put into practice their vision of socialist solidarity. Support also represented a practical response to West German foreign policy. Thanks in large part to the economic miracle, the Federal Republic quickly became one of the world's leading providers of development aid.[11] East German officials were quick to criticize West Germany's "so-called" aid. They argued it created dependency rather than promoting independence, and that it curtailed progressive and revolutionary forces.[12] Nevertheless, the GDR established a number of its own aid programs with funds to support organizations and states around the developing world in part to prevent the Federal Republic from buying the cooperation of newly independent states in the maintenance of the Hallstein Doctrine.[13]

Even after the Hallstein Doctrine, however, the East German government could not hope to compete with the Federal Republic in terms of financial aid. By 1969, West Germany had committed over DM 51 billion (approximately 26 billion Euros) to developing countries around the world, compared to only DM 530 million (roughly 271 million Euros) from the GDR—a significant portion of which the East German government never actually granted.[14] Although the GDR boasted the strongest economy in the Eastern bloc, the SED simply did not have the means to match the West German government deutsche mark for deutsche mark. Instead, the regime turned to shipments of finished goods manufactured in the GDR. In this way the SED sought to demonstrate solidarity and provide real assistance to liberation movements and fledgling states while also shoring up the East German economy. The GDR donated or sold at reduced prices everything from printing presses and typewriters to uniforms and motorcycles—anything that could be of use.[15]

The most valuable commodity the SED had to offer the developing world, however, was East German technical assistance. The GDR exported some knowledge directly to the developing world in the form of advisors and experts. Large numbers first arrived in Africa, for instance, in 1960, when the Politburo ordered the East German State Planning Commission to develop a program to dispatch East Germans with specialized skills and knowledge in fields like economics, foreign trade, agriculture, and mining.[16] They were joined in the mid 1960s by volunteers in the *Brigaden der Freundschaft* (Brigades of Friendship), the East German answer to the U.S. Peace Corps and the Federal Republic's unimaginatively named *Deutscher Entwicklungsdienst* (German Development Service).[17] In the years that followed, the SED sent increasing numbers of skilled workers and teachers to Africa and other parts of the developing world to share their skills and their knowledge.[18] At the same time, the SED brought large numbers of students and workers to the GDR to attend East German universities or receive technical training.

Formal plans to promote foreign study first coalesced in 1957, when the SED began to actively reach out to anti-imperialist states around the world and the State Secretary for Higher Education made one hundred places available to students from colonial and dependent territories, free of charge. These and other programs expanded rapidly, in large part as a result of their popularity around the world.[19] The number of foreign students grew from 1,800 in 1960 to 4,700 in 1970; by the fall of the Wall in 1989, between 64,000 and 78,400 foreigners had graduated from East German institutions of higher education.[20]

East German relations with Frelimo—and, after independence was achieved in 1975, the Mozambican state—followed the same pattern. The SED first began sending solidarity shipments to Frelimo—the *Frente de Libertação de Moçambique* (Front for the Liberation of Mozambique)—shortly after the organization's creation in 1962, when the Mozambican African

National Union, the National Democratic Union of Mozambique, and the National African Union of Independent Mozambique merged.[21] The regime's earliest commitment to help support Frelimo came in 1963 in the form of 20,000 East German marks (DDM)—little more than five thousand Euros—and by 1969 the independence movement had received upwards of 200,000 DDM (over 50,000 Euros), mostly in consumer goods. Given the organization's outlaw status prior to independence in June 1975, Frelimo received many of these goods in Tanzania, at their headquarters in Dar es Salaam and in camps elsewhere around the country.[22] The first of these shipments included typewriters, stencil machines, bicycles, motorcycles, collapsible boats, stretchers, compasses, medical equipment, medicines, textile goods, and shoes.[23] In addition to organizing these shipments, the Afro-Asian Solidarity Committee worked from the mid 1960s onward to secure training and education for Frelimo members, both in East Germany and in Frelimo camps in Africa.[24] Achim Kindler was the first East German to work alongside Frelimo as a teacher and advisor, arriving in Tanzania in 1967. Kindler and his successors not only educated children in Frelimo camps but also helped build the Frelimo education system from the ground up.[25]

In time, representatives from the FDGB, women's and youth groups joined East German educators in Africa. Frelimo delegations visited the GDR, including vacationing members of the Frelimo Central Committee. Exchange agreements between the SED and Frelimo also provided for the sharing of documentation and publications.[26] This flow of people and publications between East Germany and East Africa was a major part of SED propaganda efforts designed to "enhance and increase the influence and the connections of the GDR" by unveiling the Federal Republic's role in propping up Portuguese colonialism and demonstrating the GDR's commitment to the struggle against imperialism.[27] In the case of Frelimo and several other southern African organizations, the SED went so far as to provide support for that struggle "on a non-civilian level," sending Frelimo two and a half million East German marks (approximately 640,000 Euros) in weapons and ammunition in the last year of the war against Portugal alone.[28] Such military shipments, which began in 1967 and continued into the 1980s, were accompanied by training in the GDR with the East German army.[29] Taken in the aggregate, with military support included, East German aid to Frelimo and independent Mozambique between 1962 and 1989 totaled 148.2 million DDM (approximately 37.9 million Euros). This figure was easily the largest of any liberation organization or state in southern Africa.[30] Yet the difference between the SED's relationship with Frelimo and its relationships with other, similar organizations was not so much a matter of kind as one of degree.

It was perhaps the logical extension of a close relationship when Frelimo representatives proposed the construction of schools in the German Democratic Republic for children from Mozambique. Such a project would build upon the existing relationship between the two states on which the SED had worked so hard. Frelimo representatives were specific and persistent in their proposals. In early September 1980, the East German embassy in Maputo received a memorandum from the Mozambican Ministry for Education and Culture requesting the construction of schools in the GDR for a total of 2,000 Mozambican students, as well as vocational training for the same. The memorandum also requested assistance building technical schools for another 700 to 1,000 trainees in Mozambique.[31] The very next day, Central Committee Secretary for the Economy Günter Mittag wrote to East German Minister for Education Margot Honecker to inform her that a Mozambican delegation in Leipzig had made an identical request. Mozambican President Samora Machel himself repeated the request yet again several days later during his visit to the GDR.[32]

The construction of such schools for younger children was not unprecedented from the Mozambican side. Mozambique had experience sending children to Cuba, another socialist ally, and by 1981 over four thousand Mozambican children were studying there. Nor was Mozambique alone: by the mid 1980s, tens of thousands of international students were enrolled in schools in Cuba, many of them in primary and secondary schools on the Isle of Youth.[33] Mozambican officials made explicit reference to their experience working with the Cuban government in their appeals to the East German government, evidence that the proposed project could succeed.[34] Such references no doubt resonated with East German officials. Cuba represented not just another socialist state; it occupied a special place in the East German imagination in the 1960s and 1970s, serving as both a screen onto which East Germans could project their own revolutionary ideas and a point of comparison or source for inspiration.[35] Indeed, the Cuban model proved important throughout the planning stages of what eventually became the *Schule der Freundschaft*, providing solutions to potential problems. East German officials concerned about overcoming the language barrier, for example, looked to Cuba to see what was possible—not, however, at Portuguese-speaking Mozambican students studying in the Spanish-speaking country, but rather at the experience of Ethiopian primary school children there.[36]

The SED itself had recently taken similar, albeit much more limited steps in an endeavor designed to provide a safe environment for SWAPO children. At the request of SWAPO President Sam Nujoma, the SED converted a special SED school in the village of Bellin into a children's home for four- to six-year-olds from South West Africa/Namibia. Eighty children arrived on 18 December 1979—fewer than the 200 Nujoma had hoped, but a start. They arrived with a number of Namibian women who were charged with helping their East German colleagues to care for the children while at the same time training to become kindergarten teachers. This initial experiment was intended to last two years.[37]

A two-year experiment with eighty young children at an existing facility was one thing, but the construction and long-term operation of two new schools for thousands of school-age children was something entirely different. Despite Mozambican efforts, nothing could convince the East German Ministry for Education that the proposed scope of the project was feasible. Thus, already in the first week of internal discussion the East German regime arrived at a more limited counterproposal: one school with half as many students (one thousand rather than two thousand) who would receive the equivalent of fourth- through eighth-grade (rather than tenth-grade) instruction, as well as two years of vocational training.[38] Even at half the size, the project promised to be no small undertaking, involving multiple ministries in both the GDR and Mozambique as well as district officials in Magdeburg. Local government actually played a significant role in the project, overseeing construction and preparations for polytechnic instruction and job training. Local SED officials also assumed primary responsibility for public relations within the community, preparing pamphlets and otherwise spreading the word about the school and the guests that Stassfurt would soon welcome.[39] Cost estimates revealed the scope of the project, with initial projections for the construction of the school at just over 30 million East German marks, or approximately 7.67 million Euros.[40] A little more than half that figure was made available right away in 1981, when construction began.[41] On top of that sum came another eight million marks (2.05 million Euros) in projected operating costs for the first academic year, and at least six and a half million marks (1.66 million Euros) each year after that.[42]

Still, East German officials decided to move forward with the plan, recognizing it as an opportunity to strengthen ties with Frelimo and Mozambique. It was exactly the sort of project that took advantage of the GDR's academic and intellectual assets in a way that would directly benefit a fellow anti-imperialist state. The head of the SED's Department of Education, Dr. Lothar Oppermann, said the school would serve as "a living expression of the close bonds between the countries of socialism and those of the national liberation movement."[43] Although the struggle for political independence had been won, economic independence could only be achieved through the hard work of an educated workforce. The SED offered the school as one means to help dismantle the old colonial system, describing the school as one part of the GDR's "contribution to overcoming the difficult legacy of colonialism," and a "direct contribution to the emergence and advancement of socialism."[44] Such language situated the school firmly within the SED's ideological world view—indeed, it did so explicitly: "The tasks to be accomplished at this school are to be understood as one such combat mission [*Kampfaufgabe*] that fits into the worldwide struggle between the classes."[45] Although it was built in Stassfurt, the school occupied a special place on the "common front for peace and socialism."[46]

As a gesture of international solidarity, then, the *Schule der Freundschaft* fit neatly into the "ideas of socialism" propagated by the SED. However, the operation of the school from 1982 until its closure in 1990 reflected real concerns on the part of the SED about the "politics of Frelimo" in particular and the kind of socialism developing in newly independent states around the world in general. By the end of the 1970s, the SED harbored some doubts about the brand of socialism that Frelimo practiced. As the struggle for independence in Mozambique entered the late 1960s, Frelimo began to liberate rural territory from Portuguese rule and turn control of that land over to local peasants. It was during this time that the organization became increasingly Marxist in its outlook.[47]

Despite the promise of such homegrown socialism, however, some East German officials had a problem with the continued influence of capitalist states. Financial support flowing out of the United States, in particular, worried the SED, as did the large numbers of Mozambican students studying in capitalist countries.[48] Top Frelimo officials said all the right things throughout the 1970s, especially after Mozambique obtained its independence in 1975, but some officials in East Germany wondered about the remnants of colonial bourgeois culture and their influence on Mozambican development.[49] The SED was not alone—a member of the Soviet consular staff reflected similar concerns within the Communist Party of the Soviet Union when he described Mozambique as a "blank page" upon which the West still hoped to write.[50]

East German officials believed that the experience of coming to the GDR and living in a socialist country would be of immense help in promoting further development in Mozambique along socialist lines. They expected the GDR to make an impression, but also to prompt questions such as "Will we ever achieve a similar level of development in Mozambique?"[51] Students would not, however, have to look far for answers: "the example provided by the district of Magdeburg and the city of Stassfurt" would give students the "direct historical knowledge" they needed to see that socialism does not come "fully formed on a silver platter [*als etwas Fertiges auf den Tisch gelegt*]." Rather, it was the product of hard work, "as strong as one makes it himor herself."[52] Experiencing life under socialism firsthand, the SED believed, would be just as important as political lessons taught inside the classroom.

Indeed, one potential problem for East German officials was the lack of control they had over political education inside the classroom. The teaching staff at the *Schule der Freundschaft* was made up of both Mozambican and East German instructors. The total number of Mozambican staff the first year totaled twenty-three. Alongside them worked East German teachers, some 55 percent of them members of the SED, in excess of the 50 percent target East German officials had set for the school in light of its political importance.[53] The East German instructors taught everything from German language to natural sciences. They did not, however, teach politics. From the beginning, Frelimo officials had insisted that students learn certain subjects from Mozambican faculty, to which East German officials in the Ministry for Education and the SED had agreed. These subjects included Portuguese, geography, history, and political education.[54]

In theory, Mozambican control over these subjects made good sense: who better to bring to life the history of Mozambique and the story of Frelimo's struggle against colonial rule?[55] However, East German administrators and government officials began to have doubts early on about the political lessons that students at the *Schule der Freundschaft* were learning. Indeed, after only a few months in operation, the regime was already considering how to address the problem at the school. Vice-Minister for Education Werner Engst remarked in November 1982 that "we must be prepared to retrain the Mozambican teachers in the truest sense of the word, because they were trained to teach according to bourgeois methods and naturally also practice bourgeois methods. This retraining is necessary and we must consider how we can best accomplish it."[56] At first it was the way in which Mozambican teachers addressed specific issues that raised red flags: Minister for Education Margot Honecker noted that "one must check how one can best help the teachers to more clearly respond to the students' political questions." The division of Germany, in particular, was a topic Mozambican teachers could do a better job explaining.[57]

As the years went by, however, East German concerns extended beyond simple questions about content. The way that Mozambican instructors organized and ran their classrooms came under increasing scrutiny. Especially troubling were certain bourgeois tendencies and "'democratic' traits" like majority rule when selecting students for certain positions or making decisions about vacation travel. Children, it seemed, were receiving an "education towards independence/self-dependence [*Selbständigkeit*]" of the worst possible sort.[58] Such emphasis on the individual flew in the face of the entire East German approach in place at the school. As an internal document put it: "we operate from the well-known theoretical and methodological position that socialist character development cannot succeed without the collective and outside the collective."[59] Unfortunately, the individualistic pattern established in the school's classrooms spread to the dormitories as well, interfering with "the development of socialist personality characteristics" and "the formation of valuable societal motives" that East German administrators had intended for the children.[60]

Such developments were not merely problems unto themselves. According to school officials, they invariably gave rise to other, larger problems. One example of the knock-on effects that administrators at the *Schule der Freundschaft* returned to time and again was the sexual education of the Mozambican students, much of which occurred outside the classroom.[61] Sex had been an issue both sides addressed in negotiations before and during the school's construction. It had to be. Careful medical records at the school showed that, out of the first 900 children to arrive at the school, some 89 percent of the girls had reached puberty, and the boys were not far behind. Students had motive and opportunity, and interviews conducted with students two years later revealed many were indeed engaging in sporadic sexual activity, but that their physical development was far outstripping their knowledge. These conclusions were supported by the fact that six pregnancies had occurred in the first two years, a number only likely to increase as more of the children matured.[62] Indeed, in each of the years that followed, pregnancies at the school remained an issue, not only because the girls involved were often fifteen or sixteen years old, but also because the vast majority of these girls were sent back to Mozambique.[63] The problem, as *Schule der Freundschaft* director Claus Holzwirth described it, was that "the use of any remedy against pregnancy or for prophylactic purposes is essentially counter to the Frelimo party line." The only option for girls at the school was, he wrote, "politically motivated sexual abstinence."[64] Frelimo officials had insisted as much in February 1982 at a meeting between Mozambique's Minister of Health and the GDR's Director of the Institute for Infections and Tropical Diseases.[65] To Frelimo, leaving the *Schule der Freundschaft* early was "the lesser of two evils," a view that reflected the value Mozambican society placed on women's fertility and on motherhood.[66]

It became increasingly clear, however, that although this policy was in line with the "politics of Frelimo," it was incompatible with an East German version of socialism that increasingly embraced what the school's director himself referred to as new, revolutionary morals and lifestyles in the late 1970s and early 1980s.[67] For the regime this embrace of a new sexual morality was, as Josie McLellan puts it, "pragmatic rather than progressive," following rather than leading the East German populace "toward a sexually tolerant society."[68] And East Germans themselves were only willing to go so far. Homosexuality, for example, gained little public acceptance until the mid

1980s. Nonetheless, in the space created by Erich Honecker's 1971 appointment as first secretary of the SED, East Germany witnessed a sexual revolution.[69] The popularity of nudism, increased sexual activity among teenagers, higher divorce rates, and, of course, the legalization and ensuing frequency of abortion, all in the 1970s, testified to as much. Although the SED did not actively promote the sexual revolution, it did attempt to harness changing attitudes toward sex for its own ends. These included maintaining the place of women in the workforce while at the same time improving the birth rate, but also promoting East Germany's image at home and abroad.[70] The regime may have had no interest in leading a sexual revolution, but it had a very real interest in not appearing to stand in the way of one.

Whatever its limits, then, even a school administrator could see that an East German sexual revolution had occurred, an upheaval rationalized as spreading the progressive spirit of socialism beyond politics, the economy, and culture and into "the intimate sphere of people's lives."[71] The East German government had only legalized abortion in 1972, but by the early 1980s the lack of any legal grounds for an abortion under Mozambican law seemed almost backward.[72] Mozambican attitudes toward sex certainly seemed out of date. Director Holzwirth described them as "a legacy of colonialism and of traditional feudal society."[73] It was a legacy that Holzwirth hoped organized sexual education could help overcome, if the Mozambican government would simply allow it. In many ways, Holzwirth's proposed sexual curriculum mirrored the steps taken by the regime a decade earlier: improved access to contraceptives and abortions to keep Mozambican girls in school, but also comprehensive education about not just the biology of sex but the social framework in which it takes place, with an eye toward marriage and children one day.[74]

Yet in the eyes of school administrators and East German officials, the failure of Mozambican policies to effectively deal with the realities of students' extracurricular activities also undermined the school's mission to socialize these children. It was particularly destructive to the relationship between students and teachers.[75] Mozambican faculty, in cooperation with the school's branch of the Mozambican Youth Organization, established a system of observation and reporting to keep track of relationships between boys and girls at the school. These methods, which director Holzwirth described as "bordering on denunciations," inspired student distrust. This distrust manifested itself not only toward the Mozambican teachers, but toward East German instructors as well. It certainly did not help that many students assumed that female members of the Mozambican staff were themselves using contraceptives and, on occasion, having abortions.[76]

Even more concerning evidence of the school's failure to inspire students with the GDR's "real existing socialism" came in the form of violent encounters with East German youths. These highlighted not only how much remained to be accomplished at the school, but also the limits of solidarity within the general East German populace. These incidents became increasingly frequent as the initial cohort of fourteen- and fifteen-year-old Mozambicans matured into young adults. From the start, East German officials had encouraged interactions between the Mozambican students and the local populace in the hopes that these might foster a real sense of solidarity and contribute to the students' understanding of socialism in practice. While the vast majority of these interactions occurred without incident, over time they increasingly took place at local bars and discos where the mix of alcohol and hormones led to instances of violence. Isolated cases, though undesirable, might not have troubled school and party officials. However, the cases themselves suggested not simply the escalation of personal conflicts between individual students and GDR citizens, but rather an "us versus them" group mentality. For instance, on 11 October 1986 school officials heard news of a street brawl in the making. Some fifty Mozambican students jumped the school's fences, ready to face approximately eighty East German youths on foot and an additional thirty East German youths on mopeds.[77]

This was hardly an example of the cooperation and solidarity between the GDR and Mozambique that the *Schule der Freundschaft* was meant to embody. Rather, it was a case of the kind of violence that emerged around East Germany's growing skinhead community in the early 1980s. Imported from Britain via West Germany, at first the phenomenon revolved not so much around neo-Nazism as around football. Violence, however, was a hallmark from the beginning, and foreigners were frequent victims. Mark Fenemore argues that the treatment afforded foreigners by the East German regime caused them to be "seen as 'symbols of socialist domination' rather than people with whom one could develop genuine relationships of solidarity or friendship." This created an "association between foreigners and puppets of the state" that made non-Germans like the students from Mozambique easy targets for venting frustration with the regime.[78]

Indeed, this incident and others like it belied the notion that East Germans and Mozambicans were fighting on the same side as they worked to overcome the legacies of colonialism. Such incidents also suggested that the GDR may not have fully overcome its own past. One well-documented case from May 1987 illustrates the problem particularly effectively. It began when eleven Mozambican trainees were refused entrance to a disco on the grounds that the building had already reached its capacity. Unhappy and unafraid to show it, the Mozambicans and East Germans outside the disco traded insults. The East German youths' choice of words was revealing. One called the Mozambicans "black pigs," and another told them that "back in the *Führer*'s day you would have been skinned, slowly killed, and then burned."[79] Fighting broke out, and only stopped when other East German trainees intervened. Several of the East Germans involved sought out the Mozambicans again a few days later, but the police were called in to prevent further violence.[80] The damage, however, was already done. These and other incidents exposed the limits of not only the *Schule der Freundschaft*'s ability to instill socialist values but also the East German population's success in realizing those values itself.

## Conclusion

The *Schule der Freundschaft* represented an extended encounter between not two but *three* brands of socialism: the one developing in Mozambique, the ideal model aspired to by the SED, and the reality on the ground in East Germany. All three mattered a great deal to the East German regime. The ideologically pure brand of socialism that the SED espoused at home and abroad not only reflected the party's ambitions for the future but also played an important role in establishing the GDR as a potential ally for fledgling states in the developing world. Despite the party's lock on political power, of course, there were limits to the SED's ability to implement that vision in East Germany.[81] Such limitations did not, however, prevent the SED from also pursuing a kind of "mission to socialize" in other parts of the world. Efforts to ensure other states developed socialism along lines similar to the GDR foundered not only on the SED's very real lack of direct influence, but also on the SED's unwillingness to use the indirect influence its aid and assistance programs afforded it lest it endanger its hard-won diplomatic relationships.

The *Schule der Freundschaft* is an ideal case in point. On the one hand, the idea for the school reflected both the idealism of the SED and its pragmatic efforts to build and maintain relationships around the world. On the other hand, the school was meant to help promote a certain kind of socialist development in Mozambique (and, to a lesser extent, a certain kind of international solidarity in East Germany). Once the school was running, however, it also exposed the regime to the kind of socialist development that was actually taking place, at home and in Mozambique. On issue after issue the SED took the measure of Frelimo and found the organization wanting in some way, yet for the sake of "solidarity" the party never directly challenged the "politics of Frelimo" in defense of the "ideas of socialism." By the 1980s, such confrontation—at home as much as abroad—posed too great a risk for a regime content merely to maintain the status quo.

Jason Verber teaches World History at Western Governors University. He received his Ph.D. in History from the University of Iowa.

## Notes

1. A smaller number of children and adults from South West Africa/Namibia also later came to the school as part of an agreement between the GDR and the South West Africa People's Organization. See "Protokoll Nr. 14 der Sitzung des Sekretariats des ZK vom 8. Februar 1984," 8 February 1984, Stiftung Archiv der Parteien und Massenorganisationen der DDR im Bundesarchiv, Berlin (SAPMO-BArch) DY/30/J IV 2/3A/4044, 1–8; L Oppermann et al., "Vorlage für das Sekretariat des ZK. Betreff: Sicherung der Weiterführung der Betreuung, Bildung und Erziehung von Kindern der SWAPO in der DDR," 27 January 1984, SAPMO-BArch DY/30/J IV 2/3A/4045, 10–13.

2. "Photo Album 1983-1984," n.d. 1984, Bundesarchiv, Berlin (BArch) DR 2/29460.

3. Mathias Tullner, "Das Experiment 'Schule der Freundschaft' im Kontext der mosambikanischen Bildungspolitik," in *Freundschaftsbande und Beziehungskisten: Die Afrikapolitik der DDR und der BRD gegenüber Mosambik,* ed. Hans-Joachim Döring and Uta Rüchel (Frankfurt am Main: Brandes & Apsel Verlag, 2005); Annette Scheunpflug and Jürgen Krause, *Die Schule der Freundschaft: ein Bildungsexperiment in der DDR* (Hamburg: Universität der Bundeswehr Hamburg, 2000); Annette Scheunpflug and Lutz R. Reuter, "Die Schule der Freundschaft in der DDR—Transkulturalität, Vermittlung und Aneignung," in *Transkulturalität und Pädagogik: interdisziplinäre Annäherungen an ein kulturwissenschaftliches Konzept und seine pädagogische Relevanz,* ed. Michael Göhlich (Weinheim: Juventa, 2006).

4. Tanja R. Müller, "'Memories of Paradise'—Legacies of Socialist Education in Mozambique," *African Affairs* 109, no. 436 (2010); see also Stefanie-Lahya Aukongo, *Kalungas Kind: Wie die DDR mein Leben rettete,* 2nd ed. (Reinbek bei Hamburg: Rowohlt, 2009).

5. Katrin Lohrmann and Daniel Paasch, "Die 'Schule der Freundschaft' in Staßfurt: Zwischen Politik und Solidarität," in *Freundschaftsbande und Beziehungskisten: Die Afrikapolitik der DDR und der BRD gegenüber Mosambik,* ed. Hans-Joachim Döring and Uta Rüchel (Frankfurt am Main: Brandes & Apsel Verlag, 2005); Helmut Matthes, "Zwischen Erwartungen und Wirklichkeit," in *Wir haben Spuren hinterlassen!: die DDR in Mosambik,* ed. Matthias Voß (Münster: Lit Verlag, 2005); Matthias Voß, ed. *Wir haben Spuren hinterlassen!: die DDR in Mosambik* (Münster: Lit Verlag, 2005); Ulrich Van der Heyden, Ilona Schleicher, and Hans-Georg Schleicher, eds., *Die DDR und Afrika,* 2 vols. (Münster: Lit, 1993); Hans-Joachim Döring, *Es geht um unsere Existenz: die Politik der DDR gegenüber der Dritten Welt am Beispiel von Mosambik und Äthiopien* (Berlin: Links, 1999).

6. Ted Hopf, *Reconstructing the Cold War: The Early Years, 1945—1958* (New York: Oxford University Press, 2012), 84.

7. Jeremy Friedman, "Soviet Policy in the Developing World and the Chinese Challenge in the 1960s," *Cold War History* 10, no. 2 (May 2010), 251.

8. On the Hallstein Doctrine and West German efforts to isolate East Germany, see Rüdiger Marco Booz, *"Hallsteinzeit." Deutsche Außenpolitik 1955-1972* (Bonn: Bouvier Verlag, 1995); Werner Killian, *Die Hallstein-Doktrin: der diplomatische Krieg zwischen der BRD und der DDR 1955-1973* (Berlin: Duncker und Humblot, 2001); William Glenn Gray, *Germany's Cold War: The Global Campaign to Isolate East Germany, 1949-1969* (Chapel Hill: University of North Carolina Press, 2003).

9. "Die Entwicklung der Auslandsinformation der DDR seit dem VI. Parteitag der SED," n.d. 1965, 2, SAPMO-BArch DY/30/IV A 2/21/7.

10. Such strategies remained important even into the 1980s. See Afro-Asiatisches Solidaritätskomitee in der Deutschen Demokratischen Republik, "Tagung der Afro-Asiatischen Solidaritätskomitees der DDR am 10.12.1965. Referat," 10 December 1965, 5–8, SAPMO-BArch DY/30/IV A 2/20/113; Hartmut Schilling, "Beitrag auf der Internationalen Konferenz zur Unterstützung der Völker der portugiesischen Kolonien, Südafrikas, Südwestafrikas und Zimbabwes (Khartoum, Sudan, 18.-20. Januar 1969)," 13 January 1969, 2, SAPMO-BArch DY/30/IV A 2/20/796; Abteilung Internationale Verbindungen, *Bericht der Delegation der DDR zur Internationalen Konferenz der Solidarität mit dem Kampf der afrikanischen und arabischen Völker gegen Imperialismus und Reaktion vom 14. bis 17. 9. 1978 in Addis Abeba/Äthopien* (Berlin: 1978.9.22, n.d.), 1, SAPMO-BArch DY/30/J IV 2/2A/2179, Fiche 2, 102–22; "Stenografische Niederschrift des Gesprächs des Generalsekretärs des Zentralkomitees der SED und Vorsitzenden des Staatsrates der DDR, Genossen Erich Honecker, mit einer Delegation der afrikanischen Frontstaaten am Dienstag, dem 21. April 1987 im Amtssitz des Staatsrates," 1987, 19, SAPMO-BArch DY/30/J IV 2/2A/3012, Fiche 1, 24–44.

11. Pressure from the United States also played a key role. See Hubert Zimmerman, "'… They Have Got to Put Something in the Family Pot.' The Burden Sharing Problem in German American Relations 1960-1967," *German History* 14, no. 3 (1996): 325–46; Heide-Irene Schmidt, "Pushed to the Front: The Foreign Assistance Policy of the Federal Republic of Germany, 1958-1971," *Contemporary European History* 12, no. 4 (2003): 473–507.

12. ADN, "'Entwicklungshilfe'—Teil des Bonner Neokolonialismus. ADN-Interview mit dem Stellvertreter des Ministers für Auswärtige Angelegenheiten der DDR Dr. Wolfgang Kiesewetter," *Neues Deutschland*, 8 April 1967, FES ZASS II DW 4-12e; Abteilung Agitation/Propaganda, "Beschluß des Politbüros zur massenpolitischen Arbeit vom 27.9.1960. Disposition zum Thema: 'Der Neokolonialismus, ein Wesenszug des wiedererstandenen deutschen Imperialismus' (Einige Materialhinweise)," 28 October 1960, 16, SAPMO-BArch DY/30/IV 2/20/53, Fiche 2, 109–21.

13. See for example Walter Ulbricht, "Protokoll Nr. 38/56 der ausserordentlichen Sitzung des Sekretariats des ZK am 9.11.1956," 9 November 1956, DY/30/J IV 2/3/536, 1-5; "Betr.: Vorlage für das Sekretariat," 20 January 1960, SAPMO-BArch DY/30/IV 2/20/55, Fiche 1, 14.

14. Gareth M. Winrow, *The Foreign Policy of the GDR in Africa* (New York: Cambridge University Press, 1990), 43.

15. "Anlage Nr. 3 zum Protokoll Nr. 7 vom 10.2.1959," 10 February 1959, SAPMO-BArch DY/30/J IV 2/2 631, 12–13; Ministerium für Auswärtige Angelegenheiten,

"Vorlage an das Politbüro. Betrifft: Entwicklung der Beziehungen der DDR zu den afrikanischen Staaten," 17 February 1960, 3, SAPMO-Barch DY/30/J IV 2/2 682, 27–38; Walter Ulbricht, "Protokoll Nr. 2/61 der Sitzung des Sekretariats des ZK vom 11. Januar 1961," 11 January 1961, 3, SAPMO-Barch DY/30/J IV 2/3/719, 1–8; "Protokoll Nr. 19/61 der Sitzung des Sekretariats des ZK vom 2. Mai 1961," 2 May 1961, 7, SAPMO-Barch DY/30/J IV 2/3 A/776, 1–10; Barry Ibrahima to Willy Stoph, "Anlage Nr. 8 zum Protokoll Nr. 9 von 2.4.63: Brief an Willi Stoph," 11 February 1963, SAPMO-Barch DY/30/J IV 2/2 873, Fiche 2, 128–32; Abteilung Afrika, "Handmaterial über die Tanganyika African National Union (TANU) Tanganyikas," 15 March 1967, 1, SAPMO-Barch DY/30/IV A 2/20/954.

16. Ministerium für Auswärtige Angelegenheiten, "Vorlage an das Politbüro. Betrifft: Entwicklung der Beziehungen der DDR zu den afrikanischen Staaten," 4.

17. EO Schwab to Arno Goede, "Bildung und Entsendung von 'Brigaden der Freundschaft'," Hausmitteilung, 5 July 1963, SAPMO-BArch DY/30/IV A 2/16/146; "Vorlage über die Bildung von 'Brigaden der Freundschaft'," 1963, SAPMO-BArch DY/30/IV A 2/20/2, 107–23.

18. For instance, in the 1980s a number of East German teachers went to SWAPO camps to teach children there. "Protokoll Nr. 11," 18 May 1981, 1, SAPMO-Barch DY/30/J IV 2/3A/3630, 1–9; "Protokoll Nr. 34," 3 July 1981, 6, SAPMO-Barch DY/30/J IV 2/3A/3655, 1–9; "Protokoll Nr. 92," 4 August 1982, SAPMO-Barch DY/30/J IV 2/3A/3826, 1–4; "Protokoll Nr. 102," 14 December 1981, 3, SAP-MO-Barch DY/30/J IV 2/3A/3727, 1–5; "Protokoll Nr. 107," 14 September 1984, 2, SAPMO-Barch DY/30/J IV 2/3A/4142, 1–7.

19. "Betr.: Erweiterung des Ausländerstudiums in der Deutschen Demokratischen Republik," 9 September 1957, SAPMO-Barch DY/30/IV 2/20/1, Fiche 3, 235–37; Kulturabteilung, "Fakten über die kulturellen Beziehungen zu Afrika im Jahre 1961," 31 January 1962, SAPMO-Barch DY/30/IV 2/20/53, Fiche 3, 226–30.

20. The figures are from Damian Mac Con Uladh, "Guests of the Socialist Nation? Foreign Students and Workers in the GDR, 1949-1990" (Ph.D. diss., University College London, 2005), 40.

21. "Entwurf: Arbeitsplan des Afro-Asiatischen Solidaritätskomitees der DDR für das Jahr 1964," n.d 1964, SAPMO-Barch DY/30/IV A 2/20/112; Abteilung Afrika, "Übersicht über die Reaktion schwarz-afrikanischer Staaten zu den Hilfsmaßnahmen der W.V.-Staaten gegenüber der CSSR Stand 23.8.1968, 16.00 Uhr, ergänzt Monat 8.00 Uhr," 26 August 1968, DY/30/IV A 2/20/795.

22. Döring, Es geht um unsere Existenz, 143; see also Henning von Löwis of Menar, "Das Engagement der DDR im Portugiesischen Afrika," Deutschland-Archiv 10, no. 1 (1977): 37–38.

23. "Einschätzung der Arbeit und der Beziehungen des Solidaritätskomitees," 2 October 1963, 4, DY/30/IV A 2/20/112; Frelimo received such shipments right up until independence. See, for example, Solidaritätskomitee der DDR, Abteilung Internationale Verbindungen, "Vorlage für das Sekretariat des ZK der SED. Betrifft: Übergabe von Solidaritätssendungen an die SWAPO in Dar es Salaam und die FRELIMO in Loucernco Marques sowie an die Regierung Madagaskars und die AKFM in Tananarive (2 Sondermaschinen der Interflug)," 1975, SAPMO-Barch DY/30/J IV 2/3A/2766, 56–58.

24. "Entwurf: Arbeitsplan des Afro-Asiatischen Solidaritätskomitees der DDR für das Jahr 1964," 8.
25. Matthias Voß, "Um de nós—einer von uns! Gespräch mit Achim Kindler, der als Lehrer im Auftrag des Solidaritätskomitees der DDR als erster DDR-Bürger bei der FRELIMO arbeitete," in *Wir haben Spuren hinterlassen!: die DDR in Mosambik—Erlebnisse, Erfahrungen und Erkenntnisse aus drei Jahrzehnten,* ed. Matthias Voß (Münster: Lit, 2005), 40.
26. "Vereinbarung zwischen dem Zentralkomitee der Sozialistischen Einheitspartei Deutschlands und dem Zentralkomitee der Volksbrefreiungsfront von Mocambique über Zusammenarbeit in den Jahren 1972 und 1973," 20 April 1972, 2, DY/30/IV 2/2.035/146, Fiche 1, 1–2.
27. "Anlage Nr. 8 zum Protokoll Nr. 16 vom 19. 5. 1964," 19 May 1964, 1, DY/30/J IV 2/2 931, Fiche 2, 110–15; see also Walter Ulbricht, "Protokoll Nr. 16/64 der Sitzung des Politbüros des Zentralkomitees am Dienstag, dem 19. Mai 1964, im Sitzungssaal des Politbüros," 19 May 1964, DY/30/J IV 2/2 931, Fiche 1, 1–9; "Entwurf: Arbeitsplan des Afro-Asiatischen Solidaritätskomitees der DDR für das Jahr 1964."
28. Abteilung Internationale Verbindungen, "Vorlage für das Politbüro des ZK. Betr.: Unterstützung der Befreiungsfront von Mocambique (FRELIMO) auf nichtzivilem Gebiet," 1 October 1974, SAPMO-Barch DY/30/J IV 2/2A/1827, Fiche 1, 1–2; "Protokoll Nr. 44/74 der Sitzung des Politbüros des Zentralkomitees am 22. Oktober 1974," 22 October 1974, 74, SAPMO-Barch DY/30/J IV 2/2A/1826, 4–12.
29. See Klaus Storkmann, *Geheime Solidarität: Militärbeziehungen und Militärhilfen der DDR in die "Dritte Welt"* (Berlin: Christoph Links, 2012).
30. Döring, *Es geht um unsere Existenz,* 209.
31. Huettner to Werner Engst, Willerding, and Schalk, Telegram, 4 September 1980, BArch DR 2/50686, vol. 2.
32. Günter Mittag to Margot Honecker, 5 September 1980, BArch DR 2/50686, vol. 2.
33. Jorge I. Domínguez, *To Make a World Safe for Revolution: Cuba's Foreign Policy* (Cambridge: Harvard University Press, 1989), 171–73; Jane McManus, *Cuba's Island of Dreams: Voices from the Isle of Pines and Youth* (Gainesville: University Press of Florida, 2000).
34. Emil Beck, "Einrichtung einer Schule für mocambiquanische Schüler in der DDR," 15 October 1980, 2, BArch DR 2/50686, vol. 1.
35. See Jennifer Ruth Hosek, *Sun, Sex and Socialism: Cuba in the German Imaginary* (Toronto: University of Toronto Press, 2011), chaps. 2 and 4.
36. Geerhardt, "Direktive für eine Studiendelgation des Ministerium für Volksbildung in die Republik Kuba," 13 February 1981, BArch DR 2/50619, vol. 2; "Bericht über den Aufenthalt einer Studiendelegation des Ministeriums für Volksbildung in der Republik Kuba," 1981, BArch DR 2/50616, vol. 1; Yusuf A. Nzibo, "Cuban Technical Assistance to Eastern Africa," *Transafrican Journal of History* 12 (1983): 75–99; JR Hough, "Educational Development in Ethiopia," *Compare: A Journal of Comparative and International Education* 17, no. 2 (1987): 157–66; Soviet examples, by contrast, were of almost no help; Soviet officials liked the idea of the school, but had no experience at that level, choosing to focus instead on secondary schools and universities. Bollmann, "Vermerk über ein Gespräch in der Botschaft der UdSSR am 13.7.1981," 13 July 1981, BArch DR 2/50686, vol. 1.

37. Abteilung Volksbildung, "Vorlage für das Sekretariat des ZK der SED. Betr.: Errichtung eines Kinderheimes für namibische Vorschulkinder in der DDR," 12 September 1979, SAPMO-BArch DY/30/J IV 2/3A/3366, 64–71; "Information zum Stand der Realisierung der Beschlüsse des Sekretariats des ZK zur Weiterführung der Arbeit des SWAPO-Kinderheims Bellin," n.d 1982, SAPMO-BArch DY/30/5756.

38. Werner Engst to Margot Honecker, 8 September 1980, BArch DR 2/50686, vol. 2; "Standpunkt zum Ersuchen des Ministeriums für Erziehung und Kultur der Volksrepublik Mocambique zur Schaffung von Spezialschulen in der DDR für mocambiquanische Schüler," 8 September 1980, BArch DR 2/50686, vol. 2; Beck, "Einrichtung einer Schule für mocambiquanische Schüler in der DDR."

39. "Entwurf. Vorlage Politbüro," 5 December 1980, BArch DR/2/13990; Rat des Bezirkes Magdeburg—Bezirksplankommission, "Ergebnisse und Vorschläge zur Ausbildung, Betreuung und Unterbringung von Jugendlichen aus der VR Mocambique in Staßfurt," 20 November 1980, BArch DR/2/13990. Reprints of these materials remained in circulation for years; see "Eine Schule der Freundschaft entsteht in Staßfurt," 1987, BArch DR 2/50619, vol. 1.

40. Figures calculated based on the internal exchange rate of two East German marks to one West German mark in the GDR during this period and the standard exchange rate between the Euro and the Deutschmark. See Jonathan R. Zatlin, *The Currency of Socialism: Money and Political Culture in East Germany* (New York: Cambridge University Press, 2007), 75, footnote 34.

41. "Entwurf. Vorlage Politbüro," 2.

42. "Überschlägliche Berechnung des jährlichen Finanzbedarfs für das Objekt zur Beschulung, Betreuung und Ausbildung mocambiquanischer Schüler in Staßfurt," 14 January 1981, BArch DR 2/11231, vol. 2.

43. Abteilung Volksbildung, "Information. Betriff: Zur Arbeit der Grundorganisation der SED in der 'Schule der Solidarität' (Objekt Mocambique)," 2 September 1982, 1–2, SAPMO-BArch DY/30/5756.

44. "Eine Schule der Freundschaft entsteht in Staßfurt," 2; Abteilung Volksbildung, "Information. Betriff: Zur Arbeit der Grundorganisation der SED in der 'Schule der Solidarität' (Objekt Mocambique)," 2.

45. Abteilung Volksbildung, "Information. Betriff: Zur Arbeit der Grundorganisation der SED in der 'Schule der Solidarität' (Objekt Mocambique)," 2.

46. Ibid., 4.

47. Merle L. Bowen, *The State against the Peasantry: Rural Struggles in Colonial and Postcolonial Mozambique* (Charlottesville: University Press of Virginia, 2000), 49–53.

48. J Cruz Pinto, "Einige Angaben über die nationalistischen Organisationen der Kolonien unter port. Herrschaft," 6 November 1967, 3, SAPMO-BArch DY/30/IV A 2/20/114.

49. Paul Markowski, "Information für das Sekretariat des ZK. Nr. 41/76. Betrifft: Zu aktuellen politischen und ideologischen Problemen in der Tätigkeit der Befreiungsfront von Mocambique (FRELIMO)," 6 May 1976, 3, SAPMO-BArch DY/30/IV B 2/20/69.

50. Bollmann, "Vermerk über ein Gespräch in der Botschaft der UdSSR am 13.7.1981," 2.

51. Werner Engst, "Aktennotiz über diskutierte Probleme anläßlich des Besuches der Genossin Honecker an der Schule der Freundschaft (25.6.1983)," 27 1983, 5, BArch DR 2/11233.

52. Ibid.

53. Lothar Opperman to Kurt Hager, 14 April 1982, SAPMO-BArch DY/30/5756; "Mündliche Information 'Schule der Freundschaft'," 15 September 1981, 4, BArch DR 2/50619, vol. 1.

54. Ministerium für Erziehung und Kultur, Volksrepublik Mocambique, "Übersetzung. Memorandum. Zu prüfende Gesichtspunkte der Zusammenarbeit zwischen der Volksrepublik Mocambique und der Deutschen Demokratischen Republik," 28 August 1980, BArch DR 2/50686, vol. 2; Rat des Bezirkes Magdeburg—Bezirksplankommission, "Ergebnisse und Vorschläge zur Ausbildung, Betreuung und Unterbringung von Jugendlichen aus der VR Mocambique in Staßfurt," 1.

55. This was, in condensed form, the contents of fifth- and sixth-grade history for the school's students. The next two classes covered world history from the slave trade to the present. At each grade level instruction in history was meant to serve as a cornerstone of students' political upbringing in Marxism-Leninism. See, for example: Ministerrat der Deutschen Demokratischen Republik Ministerium für Volksbildung, *Schule der Freundschaft Rahmenlehrplan Geschichte Klassen 7 und 8* (Berlin: Volk und Wissen Volkseigener Verlag, 1983), 5.

56. Werner Engst, "Niederschrift aus der Diskussion zur Information über die Schule der Freundschaft in der MDB am 9.11.1982," 10 November 1982, 3, BArch DR 2/11232.

57. Engst, "Aktennotiz über diskutierte Probleme anläßlich des Besuches der Genossin Honecker an der Schule der Freundschaft (25.6.1983)," 5.

58. Claus Holzwirth to Bezirksschulrat, 30 May 1985, 1–2, BArch DR 2/50618, vol. 1.

59. "Zur Aufgabenstellung, zu Inhalten und Ergebnissen der Erziehungsarbeit im Internatsbereich," 27 May 1983, 2, BArch DR 2/50616 vol. 2.

60. Ibid.

61. Holzwirth to Bezirksschulrat, 30 May 1985.

62. G Patz and Minister für Gesundheitswesen, 2 November 1984, 1–2, BArch DR 2/50618, vol. 1.

63. Abortions could be performed in certain cases, but only with approval from officials back in Mozambique, approval that become more difficult to obtain as time passed. See Rat des Bezirkes Magdeburg, Abt. Volksbildung, "Übersicht über aktuelle Fragen an der Schule der Freundschaft," 9 July 1984; Bittner to Patz, 1 October 1984, BArch DR 2/50618, vol. 1; "Vermerk über die Gespräch mit dem Botschafter der VR Mocambique in der DDR, Genosse Julio Goncalo Braga, am 12.11.1984 in der Botschaft der VR Mocambique," 12 November 1984, BArch DR 2/50618, vol. 1; Hönel to Engst, 14 January 1985, BArch DR 2/50618, vol. 1; S Bollmann to Margot Honecker, "Rückführung der VRM-Jugendlichen der 'Schule der Freundschaft'," 21 April 1987.

64. Holzwirth to Bezirksschulrat, 30 May 1985, 3.

65. Elisabeth Sequeira, Rocha, and HG Kupferschmidt, "Protokoll. Abschrift über die geplante Durchführung der medizinischen Voruntersuchungen der mocambiqua-

nischen Schüler, Lehrer und Erzieher, die für einen mehrjährigen Aufenthalt in der DDR vorgesehen wird.," 2 February 1982, 2, BArch DR 2/50618, vol. 1.

66. Holzwirth to Bezirksschulrat, 30 May 1985, 3.

67. Claus Holzwirth, "Konzeptionelle Festlegungen und Maßnahmen zur Sexualerziehung," 13 November 1984, 1, BArch DR 2/11231, vol. 1.

68. Josie McLellan, *Love in the Time of Communism: Intimacy and Sexuality in the GDR* (New York: Cambridge University Press, 2011), 208.

69. Ibid., 12.

70. Ibid., 208.

71. Holzwirth, "Konzeptionelle Festlegungen und Maßnahmen zur Sexualerziehung," 1.

72. "Vermerk über die Gespräch mit dem Botschafter der VR Mocambique in der DDR, Genosse Julio Goncalo Braga, am 12.11.1984 in der Botschaft der VR Mocambique," 3; Donna Harsch, "Society, the State and Abortion in East Germany, 1950-1972," *American Historical Review* 102, no. 1 (1997): 53–84.

73. Holzwirth, "Konzeptionelle Festlegungen und Maßnahmen zur Sexualerziehung," 2.

74. Ibid.

75. Such was the case to an even greater extent when sexual relations occurred between teachers and students. See Claus Holzwirth, "Meldung über ein besonderes Vorkommnis Nr. 4/84," 24 February 1984.

76. Holzwirth to Bezirksschulrat, 30 May 1985, 3.

77. Hönel to Margot Honecker, "Der amtierende Direktor der Schule der Freundschaft in Staßfurt, Gen. Peter Koch, meldet am 15.10.1986, 15.20 Uhr folgendes Vorkommnis, verbunden mit einer Information zur Lage (IN-Telegramm an stellv. Min., Gen. Engst)," 16 October 1986, 1–2, BArch DR 2/50617.

78. Mark Fenemore, *Sex, Thugs and Rock 'n' Roll: Teenage Rebels in Cold-War East Germany* (New York: Berghahn Books, 2007), 229.

79. J Scheidig to Werner Engst, "Gen. STM Engs zur Information," 20 May 1987, 1, BArch DR 2/50617.

80. Ibid.

81. See Mary Fulbrook, *Anatomy of a Dictatorship: Inside the GDR, 1949-1989* (New York: Oxford University Press, 1995); Eric D. Weitz, *Creating German Communism, 1890-1990: From Popular Protests to Socialist State* (Princeton: Princeton University Press, 1997); Catherine Epstein, *The Last Revolutionaries: German Communists and Their Century* (Cambridge: Harvard University Press, 2003).

# Bibliography

Aukongo, Stefanie-Lahya. *Kalungas Kind: Wie die DDR mein Leben rettete.* 2nd ed. Reinbek bei Hamburg: Rowohlt, 2009.

Booz, Rüdiger Marco. *"Hallsteinzeit." Deutsche Außenpolitik 1955-1972.* Bonn: Bouvier Verlag, 1995.

Bowen, Merle L. *The State against the Peasantry: Rural Struggles in Colonial and Postcolonial Mozambique.* Charlottesville: University Press of Virginia, 2000.

Domínguez, Jorge I. *To Make a World Safe for Revolution: Cuba's Foreign Policy.* Cambridge: Harvard University Press, 1989.

Döring, Hans-Joachim. *Es geht um unsere Existenz: die Politik der DDR gegenüber der Dritten Welt am Beispiel von Mosambik und Äthiopien.* Berlin: Links, 1999.

Epstein, Catherine. *The Last Revolutionaries: German Communists and Their Century.* Cambridge: Harvard University Press, 2003.

Fenemore, Mark. *Sex, Thugs and Rock 'n' Roll: Teenage Rebels in Cold-War East Germany.* New York: Berghahn Books, 2007.

Friedman, Jeremy. "Soviet Policy in the Developing World and the Chinese Challenge in the 1960s." *Cold War History* 10, no. 2 (May 2010): 247–72.

Fulbrook, Mary. *Anatomy of a Dictatorship: Inside the GDR, 1949-1989.* New York: Oxford University Press, 1995.

Gray, William Glenn. *Germany's Cold War: The Global Campaign to Isolate East Germany, 1949-1969.* Chapel Hill: University of North Carolina Press, 2003.

Harsch, Donna. "Society, the State and Abortion in East Germany, 1950-1972." *American Historical Review* 102, no. 1 (1997): 53–84.

Hopf, Ted. *Reconstructing the Cold War: The Early Years, 1945–1958.* New York: Oxford University Press, 2012.

Hosek, Jennifer Ruth. *Sun, Sex and Socialism: Cuba in the German Imaginary.* Toronto: University of Toronto Press, 2011.

Hough, JR. "Educational Development in Ethiopia." *Compare: A Journal of Comparative and International Education* 17, no. 2 (1987/01/01 1987): 157–66.

Killian, Werner. *Die Hallstein-Doktrin: der diplomatische Krieg zwischen der BRD und der DDR 1955-1973.* Berlin: Duncker und Humblot, 2001.

Lohrmann, Katrin, and Daniel Paasch. "Die 'Schule der Freundschaft' in Staßfurt: Zwischen Politik und Solidarität." In *Freundschaftsbande und Beziehungskisten: Die Afrikapolitik der DDR und der BRD gegenüber Mosambik,* ed. Hans-Joachim Döring and Uta Rüchel, 91–99. Frankfurt am Main: Brandes & Apsel Verlag, 2005.

Mac Con Uladh, Damian. "Guests of the Socialist Nation? Foreign Students and Workers in the GDR, 1949-1990." Ph.D. diss., University College London, 2005.

Matthes, Helmut. "Zwischen Erwartungen und Wirklichkeit." In *Wir haben Spuren hinterlassen!: die DDR in Mosambik,* ed. Matthias Voss, 12–33. Münster: Lit Verlag, 2005.

McLellan, Josie. *Love in the Time of Communism: Intimacy and Sexuality in the GDR.* New York: Cambridge University Press, 2011.

McManus, Jane. *Cuba's Island of Dreams: Voices from the Isle of Pines and Youth.* Gainesville: University Press of Florida, 2000.

Müller, Tanja R. "'Memories of Paradise'—Legacies of Socialist Education in Mozambique." *African Affairs* 109, no. 436 (2010): 451–70.

Nzibo, Yusuf A. "Cuban Technical Assistance to Eastern Africa." *Transafrican Journal of History* 12 (1983): 75–99.

Scheunpflug, Annette, and Jürgen Krause. *Die Schule der Freundschaft: ein Bildungsexperiment in der DDR.* Hamburg: Universität der Bundeswehr Hamburg, 2000.

Scheunpflug, Annette, and Lutz R. Reuter. "Die Schule der Freundschaft in der DDR—Transkulturalität, Vermittlung und Aneignung." In *Transkulturalität und Pädagogik: interdisziplinäre Annäherungen an ein kulturwissenschaftliches Konzept und seine pädagogische Relevanz,* ed. Michael Göhlich, 169–84. Weinheim: Juventa, 2006.

Schmidt, Heide-Irene. "Pushed to the Front: The Foreign Assistance Policy of the Federal Republic of Germany, 1958-1971." *Contemporary European History* 12, no. 4 (2003): 473–507.

Storkmann, Klaus. *Geheime Solidarität: Militärbeziehungen und Militärhilfen der DDR in die "Dritte Welt"*. Berlin: Christoph Links, 2012.

Tullner, Mathias. "Das Experiment 'Schule der Freundschaft' im Kontext der mosambikanischen Bildungspolitik." In *Freundschaftsbande und Beziehungskisten: Die Afrikapolitik der DDR und der BRD gegenüber Mosambik,* ed. Hans-Joachim Döring and Uta Rüchel, 100–109. Frankfurt am Main: Brandes & Apsel Verlag, 2005.

Van der Heyden, Ulrich, Ilona Schleicher, and Hans-Georg Schleicher, eds. *Die DDR und Afrika.* 2 vols. Münster: Lit, 1993.

Voß, Matthias, ed. *Wir haben Spuren hinterlassen!: die DDR in Mosambik—Erlebnisse, Erfahrungen und Erkenntnisse aus drei Jahrzehnten.* Münster: Lit Verlag, 2005.

Weitz, Eric D. *Creating German Communism, 1890-1990: From Popular Protests to Socialist State.* Princeton, NJ: Princeton University Press, 1997.

Winrow, Gareth M. *The Foreign Policy of the GDR in Africa.* New York: Cambridge University Press, 1990.

Zatlin, Jonathan R. *The Currency of Socialism: Money and Political Culture in East Germany.* New York: Cambridge University Press, 2007.

Zimmerman, Hubert. "'...They Have Got to Put Something in the Family Pot!' The Burden Sharing Problem in German American Relations 1960-1967." *German History* 14, no. 3 (1996): 325–46.

# PART IV

# Socialist Mirrors

# "The Black Façade of the Universities of German Revisionism"

Soldiers of the Struggle against Revisionism
Maoyuan Hongqi
(The Red Flag of the Shanghai University of International Trade)
Nr. 6/1968.

*Editor's note:* The following article appeared in the midst of the Chinese Cultural Revolution in a publication of the Red Guards in Shanghai. The author's familiarity with East German universities suggests that he or she may have spent time in the GDR. Chinese students and instructors were regular visitors on East German campuses since the early 1950s. After the Sino-Soviet split, their number decreased but did not disappear. Chinese students and instructors often made trouble for the authorities by propagating a more radical, Maoist brand of socialism, particularly among their fellow foreign students. The lineaments of the Chinese critique of East German "revisionism" are visible in this piece, including accusations of institutional hierarchy, ideological impurity, and the alleged distance of the SED from the working class. Many Chinese students were called back to participate in the Cultural Revolution in early 1967. The author may have been one of these returnees.

• • •

"Revisionism is a bourgeois ideology. The revisionists blur the difference between socialism and capitalism, between the dictatorship of the proletariat and the dictatorship of the bourgeoisie. In reality, what they represent is in no way a socialist, rather a capitalist idea."—Mao Zedong

The ruling clique of German revisionism has betrayed the dictatorship of the proletariat. It follows Soviet revisionism, carries out a revisionist line and has transformed the socialist GDR into a bourgeois and fascist dictatorship state. In order to consolidate its reactionary rule and restore capitalism, the ruling clique of German revisionism has built up the universities of the GDR as huge camps to train the successors of the bourgeoisie.

The universities of the old Germany were prime examples of the implementation of the Anglo-American education system. After the establishment of the GDR, the German revisionist clique dabbed some Soviet revisionist paint on the Anglo-American foundations of the education system, thus turning the German universities into a gigantic mish-mash of American, English, and Soviet education systems.

Bourgeois professors and specialists practice dictatorship in the universities of German revisionism. The highest organ of state power in the universities is the Senate, composed almost entirely of professors. The Senate elects the Rector, the Faculty Council elects the deans of the faculties. Elections occur every five years. The SED still hangs up the sign of Marxism and the Communist Party but, in reality it has long turned into a club-like people's party. In the universities, it follows behind the Senate and the Rector and has no right to decide about the big issues of the schools. Its activities are limited solely to corrupting a number of people for entry into the party, cashing party contributions, and leading the collection of regular reports on goings-on. The party is stuffed with bourgeois intellectuals at the rank of Ph.D. and professor. These people enjoy the highest honors in the party, have the most to say and control the leading positions in the universities at all levels. Bourgeois intellectuals dominate the universities and have a strict ranking system.

The situation in the institutes, the basic units of the universities, is such that only a professor may be entrusted with the function of institute director. An institute may have only one professor. If this professor does not die or is not transferred, nobody else can be named professor, regardless of how high their academic level is. The absolute authority of the institute director is maintained in this way. These professors enjoy privileges and have the power to sit high above everyone, doing as they please.

All decision-making power in the institutions is in the hands of the professors, including scheduling, course content, enrollments, examinations, promotion to the next year of study, distribution of graduates, retention or departure of employees, support of aspirants, selection of research topics, conclusion of contracts with other institutions, and delegation of employees for business trips or overseas training.

Power relations in the institutes are formed like pagodas and have a feudal coloring. Professors—doctors—assistants—laboratory assistants—material provisioners—cleaning staff—instrument cleaners. In reality, the relationships are as follows: the professors direct and determine, the doctors and assistants spin intrigues ... the cleaning staff and instrument cleaners are people of a truly low standing.

The professor and the doctors claim the scientific accomplishments of the institute as their own and make them redound to their prestige and advantage. The awkward theory of the so-called "division of labor" is used widely to maintain and consolidate this system of exploitation. The intellectual work of the professors and doctors is claimed to be "valuable." It would be a "waste" to make them work in the laboratories and clean the instruments themselves. This is the lowest defamation of workers.

The revisionist German governing clique has established diverse systems of regulations to strengthen and consolidate the basis of their rule. To preserve the interests of the privileged classes with high salaries, they raise the social status of the bourgeois intelligentsia, lifting some of the so-called scholars, celebrities, doctors and professors up to the heavens. Celebrations and gatherings are held to mark the sixtieth and seventieth birthdays of every professor. The Central Committee of the party of the German revisionists, including Ulbricht himself, sends telegrams of congratulations. They receive generous bonuses and medals on every holiday. Ordinary workers and laborers at the universities share no part of this. On May Day every year, all the universities designate the most "progressive" individuals, and the strange thing is that among those photos hanging under the honor roll, one finds absolutely none of the workers who labored diligently throughout the year. This is a great insult to the magnificent holiday of the world proletariat. In order to train so-called top cadres (Spitzenkader), the German revisionist clique has adopted unaltered the whole academic system built up by the old Germany. As soon as a professor, associate professor, Ph.D., etc., has gained a position, he is surrounded by a halo, so that the young people are enticed to strive for "prestige and advantage" and the attainment of an academic degree and a high salary as the sole goal of struggle.

The salary gap between the bourgeois intellectuals and ordinary workers in the German revisionist universities is shocking. The average fixed income of a professor is 5,000 marks, and those of some well-known professors can reach 15,000 to 20,000 marks. A cleaner's wage, by contrast, amounts to 200 marks at the most, meaning a difference of the nth degree. In addition to high salaries, the professors and specialists have diverse additional income: fees for books and articles, for the training of aspirants, for participating in examinations, for scientific reports, etc.; there is money for everything. The real income, therefore, is much higher. Furthermore, these high wage-earning classes also enjoy various privileges. The legally-fixed annual leave of professors is a week more than normal workers and employees. Some famous professors have the right to permanent vacation. They can take leave whenever they want and for as long as they want. They even have privileges in their pensions. When professors retire, their pensions are thousands of marks. When a professor dies, their family receives 300 marks a month. By contrast, average workers only receive 170 marks in retirement income. When a worker dies, his dependents receive only 60 marks of support monthly. As a porter stated aptly: "These people (the higher income classes) that are rich anyway, get so much in their retirement, and we, who have no savings as it is, can get neither full nor happy on our pensions!"

The high wage-earning class turns the institutes they run into their own independent kingdoms, and use the institute employees as their slaves. Thus, for example, the Director of the Microbiological Institute in Jena claims for himself all the wine planted by the institute. Each year during the wine harvest, his subordinates have to spend a number of days pressing wine for him. A professor in Freiberg has one of the workers wash his private car. They even treat the secretaries like servants; they have to make them coffee and wash their dishes.

The high wage-earning class leads an extremely luxurious life. The above-mentioned director of the Microbiological Institute does not know how to spend his money, so he keeps dogs for pleasure. He has five dogs and sits with them every day at the table feeding them sausages and milk. It is not surprising that his subordinate employees say: "His dogs attend a banquet every day, and we have only our daily dry bread to eat."

Old men and women, some over 80 years old, still have to do arduous physical labor, e.g., an 83-year-old worker in the cafeteria of the University of Leipzig, who has one foot in the grave and still cleans up, washes dishes, and continues to be exploited and oppressed by the bloodsuckers of the high wage-earning class.

It is not only the material living standards of the working people that are low. They are oppressed even more politically, with no right to express their opinion in matters of state. It's called a "workers' and farmers' state," but the great majority who sit in the highest organ of government—the Volkskammer—are professors, scholars, and traitors to the interests of the working class and the working people.

To safeguard their own grandeur, professors build a wall around themselves and intimidate their assistants; each is his own king. A worker is worth less than a dog in their eyes. The following incident took place at the University of Chemistry in Merseburg. An assistant put a piece of sodium in a retort, and a senior laboratory assistant, over fifty years old, who did not know better, washed it out with water. An explosion led to their immediate death. A Chinese student wanted to bring a wreath to express his grief for the old woman. But the institute prevented the Chinese student from doing so, saying, "An old woman died, no need to get too upset. There's an up side, we'll save on her pension later." In a revisionist State that already restored capitalism, you can see how the bourgeoisie exploits and oppresses the worker and peasant masses to the point of death.

To train a broad, educated class as the social foundation for revisionism, the leading clique of German revisionism induces young students to turn away from politics, instills them with the ideology of seeking prestige and advantage, propagates the primacy of money, and poisons the youth.

In their universities, one hears neither of proletarian revolution nor sees a proletarian solution. No political-ideological work is carried out among the young students. Because they are following the course of creating a "party of the entire people" and an "association of the whole people," most students only have to fill out a form to become a member of the youth organization. There is no form of political activity inside the youth organization. The permanent activity of the organization consists of organizing dance and film events, excursions, etc.

As a result of this revisionist poisoning, the youth have no wide-ranging ideals. They admit openly that the goal of their studies is to earn more money in the future and to be able to climb to the top with relative speed. It is difficult for the sons and daughters of the poorest working and farming families to enroll in university at age eighteen. After completion of compulsory education, as a rule, they become apprentices in factories or attend various trade schools and work on a special technology to lighten the burden of the family on the one hand, and because there are no ways of getting out of it, on the other. In this way, the doors of the university are only really opened specially for the sons and daughters of the high wage-earning classes, in order for these classes to train their own successors.

After entering the university, the students' learning process is stimulated by promoting the pursuit of prestige and advantage. Thus, for example, the size of one's scholarship depends on one's grades. Students with good grades get the largest scholarship. In addition, the best students are selected annually from the university and across the whole country. The very best students in the whole country can receive a monthly stipend of 500 marks. This corresponds to twice the wage of an ordinary worker. Moreover, there are constant competitions in universities, such as mathematics competitions and foreign language competitions. The winners receive material rewards to stimulate the interests of students for learning these subjects.

To degenerate the younger generation and lead them to decadence, the German revisionist clique of leaders has given the green light to Western "yellow culture." Already, English and American blue films along with jazz lead the cultural world of leisure at the universities. The youth have degenerate morals, and the number of crimes committed is innumerable. Some older workers say: "The behavior of this generation of youth is a disgrace for the Germans." To anesthetize the youth further and loosen their ties to reality, the ruling clique of German revisionism has thrown the doors of the churches wide open. It is not only old people who go to church, but also the youth, and no small number of the youth organization's members go to pray and listen to music. Especially at Christmas, people crowd into the churches.

The German revisionists boast that there is a so-called "connection to productive labor'" in their schools. But how does it work in reality? The state and the universities have the students go to the factories and work for wages to compensate for the serious labor shortage in the country. The vast majority of students are arrogant. The students want to work intellectually but not physically, usually they design something or finish off a blueprint. Only very few participate in physical labor with the workers, much less become connected to them.

Under these diverse influences, many German students care nothing for politics and have grown distant from class struggle. They fear war above all, do not distinguish between the kinds of wars, and protest against all of them. The revisionist education system operated by the leading clique of German revisionism poisons even more of the German youth than those that suffer under it. Yet the rays of the great ideology of Mao Zedong have already awoken the progressive German youth and shine the way forward. A fire can grow from a spark. The day of the downfall and collapse of the kingdom of German revisionism and all its evil spirits is announcing itself already.

[Archival Source: Winzer to Ulbricht, Stoph, Honecker, Hager, Axen. 7 Nov 1968 Bundesarchiv NY 4182 1222]

# Chapter 9

# The Uses of Disorientation
## Socialist Cosmopolitanism in an Unfinished DEFA-China Documentary

*Quinn Slobodian*

The 1950s were officially a decade of "socialist brotherhood" between East Germany and the People's Republic of China. Both founded in October 1949, the two nations celebrated their symmetrical status at the easternmost and westernmost points of the socialist "peace camp" in regular public pageantry and rituals of shared identity.[1] They also developed a major economic relationship. By 1959, the GDR followed only the Soviet Union in its volume of trade with China.[2] Film was a major medium for communicating and, ideally, building solidarity between the two socialist populations. Chinese films were screened regularly at official events, in theaters and in factories, and East German films were shown across China. The East German film studio *Deutsche Film-Aktiengesellschaft* (DEFA) made fourteen documentary films about China between 1954 and 1960, ranging from ten-minute newsreel segments to hour-long features.[3] Film was the primary way that the solidarity between the two countries was made visible.

The following chapter introduces East Berlin as a center of transnational film production in the 1950s and the central coordinating role of the Dutch director Joris Ivens. It describes the production of two major collaborative films by DEFA in the mid 1950s as well as its first feature documentary about China. The second half of the chapter concentrates on the final, unfinished film in the sequence of collaboration between China and East Germany. Preparations for the feature-length documentary with the working title *Yo I—Friendship* began in 1957 and were abandoned finally in 1961, when the Sino-Soviet split transformed the relationship of East Germany and China from warm partnership to cool, and even hostile, distance. The Chinese–East German collaboration began in a moment of relative political openness in both East Germany and the PRC and ended when the political conditions for collaboration evaporated abruptly.

**Figure 9.1.** Poster for German-Chinese Friendship Month, July 1951.

On the East German side, *Yo I* was led by Dutch director Joop Huisken and German screenwriter Alex Wedding, the pen name of children's book author Grete Weiskopf, who had a long personal relationship with China. Wedding and Huisken were striving toward a breakthrough in socialist film aesthetics in their work with Chinese filmmakers. In what would have been a transcendence of the conventions of socialist multilateralism, in which countries were portrayed on film in relative isolation from one another, Wedding and the Chinese screenwriters sought to depict the human and material entanglement of the two republics. The film's unrealized treatments show a vision for *Yo I* that included Chinese people in East Germany and East Germans in China. Though anxieties of comparison ran throughout the production, the treatment suggested at key points what could be called the uses of disorientation in producing a sense of socialist cosmopolitanism that rose above individual national contexts into a shared transnational space. Looking at the unrealized project of *Yo I* indicates a path not taken in the culture of socialist internationalism and provides insight into the frictions encountered in efforts of collaboration across the socialist bloc between countries with radically different histories.

## Transnational Filmmaking in East Berlin

East Berlin's suburban Babelsberg studio was a hub of transnational film production in the mid 1950s. The period was an ambivalent one for East German film. On the one hand, DEFA was brought under tighter political control after 1953 when film projects were required to pass through layers of party approval and conform to the dictates of the Five Year Plan.[4] On the other hand, the use of film as a tool of cultural diplomacy facilitated multiple coproductions with socialist as well as nonsocialist partners.[5] DEFA produced four major films with French companies alone in the period from 1956 to 1960.[6] The primary axis of collaboration was Ivens, recognized as one of the world's premier documentarians, who relocated to East Berlin in 1953 after making a film with Soviet partners for DEFA about the World Festival of Youth and Students held there in 1951.[7] Ivens had made his name in the 1930s with the film, *The Spanish Earth* (1937), shot in Republican strongholds during the Spanish Civil War, with a narration written and read by Ernest Hemingway.[8] He followed this with a film shot in China, *The 400 Million* (1939) and another, *Indonesia Calling* (1947), about Indonesian resistance to Dutch colonialism.

Ivens led the production of the two biggest projects of transnational documentary filmmaking at DEFA at mid decade: *Song of the Rivers* (*Lied der Ströme*, 1954) and *The Compass Rose* (*Die Windrose*, 1957). Both were assembled out of segments shot by a range of directors worldwide alongside archival footage. The films expressed the conventions of socialist realism in the 1950s, blending the genres of documentary and fiction freely.[9] Some segments, such as those of Italian director Gillo Pontecorvo and Brazilian director Alberto Cavalcanti in *The Compass Rose* tended toward intimate neorealism, while the Soviet and Chinese contributions were characterized by broad theatrical gestures and dramatic staged tableaus. While some pieces, such as the French segment of *The Compass Rose* were entirely fictional with performances by professional actors, others incorporated lay actors and more naturalistic settings. Ivens accepted this blurring of genres at the time, distancing himself from what he called "purists" who opposed all staging or scripting as unacceptable deviations from the documentary form.[10] In the logic of the "type" in socialist realism, the function of the documentarian was to convey both visible reality and its deeper political truth.[11] In the words of an East German review of a Soviet film about China, the goal "was not to show only the fact, but, at the same time, its direction, its content."[12] Embellishment, scripting, and staging reflected fidelity rather than disloyalty to social reality.

In their production, *Song of the Rivers* and *The Compass Rose* were representative of a mode that could be called socialist multilateralism. In contrast to the socialist cosmopolitanism described later in this chapter, socialist multilateralism was a means of representing the world without disrupting the primacy of the nation-state container. The films were mosaics, depicting national contexts as discrete entities rather than attempting to portray an entangled reality. Collaboration was used to portray struggles happening simultaneously and in parallel, untroubled by extensive border-crossing. The mixture of national populations happened only at international congresses, where the participants became a single proverbial body in moments of assembly.

*Song of the Rivers* was constructed around such a gathering in the World Federation of Trade Unions conference in Vienna in 1953. Ivens embellished the footage of the congress with montages of scenes from along the world's major rivers, including the Yangzi, the Volga, the Mississippi, the Amazon, the Nile, and the Ganges. The production team was star-studded, including a score by Dmitri Shostakovich, lyrics by Bertolt Brecht, a cover drawing by Pablo Picasso, and a vocal performance by Paul Robeson.[13] Involving collaboration from eighteen countries, the film remained nonetheless, as Hans Schoots asserts, "a product of centralist thinking … that reduced workers to extras in a single global movement."[14] The choreography of the crowd scenes emphasized the single-minded will of the masses: "everyone smiles, everyone agrees, everyone clasps hands, everyone claps in unison, everyone rises to their feet when leaders orate, again and again."[15] The impression conveyed was of a diverse world united under the elevated leadership of socialist elites.

The East German press was euphoric about *Song of the Rivers*. Calling it one of East Germany's "most interesting and moving films," the official newspaper *Neues Deutschland* reported that audiences interrupted the screenings with "minutes of applause" in Moscow, Vienna, Paris, Brussels, and London.[16] Appearing in the immediate wake of Stalin's death in a time of intense German-German competition, when hatred for the imperialist enemy was encouraged openly, the film was offered as a validation of the binary communist world view.[17] An East German reviewer of the film wrote that "One sees, for example, Chinese building a dam and Negroes engaged in coolie labor, one sees moving cranes in the Soviet Union in a factory, and people laboring in the Amazon with primitive tools. Both are images of labor, yet they are a world apart: on one side is labor as drudgery and curse, as ugliness and arduousness; on the other, it is a creative process of beauty and liberation. One sees the brutal bludgeoning of struggling workers protesting in the Western world and one sees the peaceful demonstrations of liberated men in Moscow."[18] *Song of the Rivers* sought to cement the claim of the Soviet bloc as the standard-bearer of the international working class at a time when this was under challenge, most proximately, through the failed East German workers' uprising in 1953. This struggle was captured in the subject of the film, the Soviet-led WFTU, which sought supremacy in international labor movement over the U.S.-led International Confederation of Free Trade Unions (ICFTU), founded five years earlier.

*Song of the Rivers* was a primary vector for the message of geopolitical rivalry, translated into eighteen languages and seen reportedly by 250 million people, including 40 million in China.[19] Despite the glowing reviews, the popular reception in the GDR was far more modest. Though designated as of "the highest priority" by the East German trade unions, screenings were still less than one-fifth full.[20] Indeed, *Song of the Rivers* became a case study in the difficulties of compelling workers to consume officially produced films.

In spite of the tepid domestic response, *Song of the Rivers* was followed by another large international production, *The Compass Rose*, commissioned formally by the Women's International Democratic Federation. *The Compass Rose* comprised five episodes from working women's lives in Brazil, Italy, France, the Soviet Union, and China. The only segment directed by a woman was by Wu Kuo Ying, the director of the Documentary Film Studio in Beijing, whose segment portrayed the challenges (and eventual successes) of a young woman facing patriarchal structures after being elected as a political representative in her village.[21] In 1954, the directors, including Wu and an assistant, traveled to Berlin to work on the film.[22] The coproduction included many well-known figures of the communist-leaning left, including Brazilian author Jorge Amado, French actor Yves Montand, and the Italian team that would go on to make *The Battle of Algiers* (1966), Pontecorvo and Franco Solinas. The Italian segment was among the most difficult to make and Pontecorvo and Solinas eventually shot their short film about a wildcat factory occupation by female workers without legal authorization.[23]

Ivens and the production team faced challenges of censorship in both films. American authorities prohibited the distribution of *Song of the Rivers* outright, and British and French censors removed segments from it.[24] French censors rejected the first version of the French segment of *The Compass Rose* and Ivens instructed Pontecorvo to downplay the political message in his segment to emphasize the "human side" in hopes of avoiding future censorship.[25] DEFA responded more creatively in other cases. When the authorities prevented *Song of the Rivers* from entering England for the London premiere, they sent a copy on a narrower film format that did not require official approval.[26] Elsewhere, they used censorship as a way of drawing attention to the incursion of state power into the space of socialist truth-telling. In France, they let black film roll in the space where scenes had been cut. At the Paris premiere of *Song of the Rivers,* DEFA producer Hans Wegner recounts, there was a "whole stretch of black film after the panning shot to the Statue of Liberty in New York. This way, the observers knew very clearly that certain things were being said about America that the censors did not like." Left to the imagination of what was largely a sympathetic audience, the blank space could be filled by whatever particular grievance the individual observer might harbor against the United States. The technique seemed to work. Wegner told Huisken that he knew the "opposite" of the censor's intentions had been achieved when there was thunderous applause after the blank stretch showed for the third time.[27]

Even without the excisions of censors, it was challenging to convey unified films out of footage from disparate sources. The raw material for *The Compass Rose* was five segments in five languages. DEFA's solution was to leave the diegetic sound unaltered but add a voiceover written by Walter Scheer summarizing the dialogue throughout. According to Wegner, the goal was "to preserve the entire atmosphere of each individual episode."[28] The voice of Helene Weigel, who introduced the film on camera and spoke throughout, provided a through-line and also arguably domesticated the global reach of the film through the narration of a unifying German actor. Appearing in an easy chair in a cozily furnished room in the film's opening sequence, Weigel's appearance gave a storybook effect to the film's world-spanning material. The image of the compass rose itself, an artifact evoking the Age of Exploration, cast the film as an adventure tale as much as a social documentation.

*Song of the Rivers* and *The Compass Rose,* the two "world films" produced by Ivens at DEFA, were exemplary instances of transnational collaboration.

Wittingly or not, they also reproduced a vision of the globe comparable to the World Youth Festivals of the postwar period, or indeed the World's Fairs of the nineteenth century. Nations were represented serially and as equivalent units but in relative isolation from one another. Rather than attempting to portray transnational entanglement, the films showed the world as a mosaic with each nation as an individual tile. The DEFA censors approved of the national emplotment in *The Compass Rose*. The official judgment on the film decreed that "without forgetting the overall context, the authors of the individual episodes have designed their episodes to show the situation of women in their respective countries that are representative of the current most pressing problems in the political and social state of their countries."[29] The films followed the conventions of socialist internationalism by depicting, in Toni Weis's pithy phrase, "solidarity between peoples" rather than the "solidarity between people."[30]

## A Socialist Magic Carpet Ride

The major East German–Chinese coproductions of the 1950s emerged directly out of Ivens's films. Huisken and Robert Ménégoz, the codirectors of the sixty-eight-minute color documentary *China—Country Between Yesterday and Tomorrow* (1956) both assisted Ivens on *The Song of the Rivers* and Huisken was asked to assist Wu in China on her contribution for *The Compass Rose*.[31] By 1954, Huisken and his French codirector, Ménégoz, had begun filming in China. The finished film was consistent with the mode of socialist multilateralism, and provided an exoticized depiction of the PRC as an allegory of socialist national development.[32]

Huisken had worked with Ivens since the beginning of his career in the 1920s. The title of his first film, *Friends of the Soviet Union* (1933), reflected his political sympathies.[33] During the Nazi occupation, Huisken was drafted to work at the nationalized Berlin film studio, *Universum Film Aktiengesellschaft* (UFA), where he remained until the end of the war.[34] Huisken's acquaintances from the underground resistance persuaded him to stay and help build DEFA at the conclusion of the war where he became one of the few members of the documentary team with filmmaking experience.[35] He was one of the studio's most prolific producers, completing ten films before 1956 and twenty-five more before his death in East Berlin in 1979.[36]

Ménégoz had a similarly leftist history. According to the biography supplied to DEFA, he fought as a partisan during the war and began making films about popular struggle and workers in the early 1950s. French censors banned two of his early films, including one about the activism of dockworkers and another recounting the Paris Commune of 1871. Before beginning work with Ivens in 1954, he shot a series of documentary films in Sub-Saharan Africa.[37] Ménégoz represented the French film production company PROCINEX on the China documentary, which had also helped produce *The Compass Rose,* and would distribute the East German–made films in France.[38]

Both the aesthetics and the content of *China* were relatively tame and conformed to the conventions of the era. The film alternated between three staged and scripted storylines: a tinker traveling through industrial construction sites, a female farmer on her wedding day, and a female engineer traveling from the city to the countryside to complete a dam. Both the promotional material and the voiceover, written by author Bodo Uhse, emphasized the picturesque. Scenes throughout the film invoked traditional Chinese screen paintings. Shots of hills reflected in water were, according to the voiceover, "as in the pictures of the old masters, as in the poems from a hundred, a thousand years, earlier."[39] Repeating the material almost verbatim, the film's promotional flyer promised the "experience [of] China in the blaze of color of its landscape, its mountains, its rivers, lakes and islands, as in pictures of the old masters, as in poems written thousands of years ago."[40] Celebrating the exoticizing effect of the film, an East German reviewer raved that it was "as if a fairy tale magic carpet had carried us thousands of kilometers away for one and a half hours."[41]

Though the film was a coproduction, with Chinese camera assistants and the imprimatur of the Chinese Ministry of Culture, the position of the voiceover, and by extension, the viewer, was that of the outsider.[42] Over shots of banners and signs with Chinese characters, the narrator asked "who knows what the mysterious characters around us are saying?" The obvious answer would be a person who read Chinese. But this perspective was not the one taken by the filmmakers. Even as a sense of disorientation was produced through confrontation with the illegible, the disorientation was tamed by linking it to conventions of traditional art and the voyeuristic mode of tourism. The consistent default to an exoticizing gaze was balanced by a flat assertion of equivalence. A reviewer wrote perfunctorily: "with everything new and unknown that captures our gaze, we notice one thing: How similar the workers in the whole world are. How familiar these Chinese faces are to us after only a few minutes. The film says we are brothers."[43] Despite moments of insight into everyday life in the PRC, the film remained a travelogue framed by the rhetoric of socialist universalism.

The effect of the film was largely a product of Uhse's script. The author's investment in China reveals something about the function of the Asian socialist republic for East German intellectuals in the 1950s. Uhse, born in

1904, was part of a cohort of communist authors and artists, many politicized by the Spanish Civil War, who spent the war years in exile and returned to the GDR after 1945. At the turn of the 1950s, erstwhile émigrés to the West became targets of intense suspicion and fabricated accusations of "Zionism," "cosmopolitanism," and espionage.[44] The wave of persecution across the socialist Eastern European bloc culminated in the show trials of Rudolf Slansky and many others in Czechoslovakia in late 1952, and only Stalin's death prevented such trials in the GDR itself.[45] Shaken by these events (even if not openly critical of them), many former émigré intellectuals appeared to turn to China in the spirit of escapism, seeking an alternate projection screen for their visions of socialism. Along with Uhse, authors Stephan Hermlin and Anna Seghers traveled to and published work about China in the 1950s.[46] This group, which would be known as the "friends of China," would preserve and reproduce an image of the country like that presented by Uhse in the 1957 documentary: both in and out of the time of the socialist West.

## Entangled Biographies of People and Things

Another member of this former émigré group, Alex Wedding, would help create a filmic vision of the Chinese–East German relationship that transcended the exotic and sought to portray the transnational biographies of people and things. Wedding was the pen name of Grete Weiskopf. Born in Salzburg in 1905, Weiskopf (née Bernheim) joined the German Communist Party in 1925 and married Czech author Franz Carl Weiskopf in 1928. She and her husband knew Uhse in their first station of exile in Paris before the couple left for the United States and Uhse departed for Mexico. Upon returning to Prague in 1949, Wedding's husband was promptly sent to Beijing as the Czechoslovak ambassador, where they stayed until their relocation to Berlin and reunification with Uhse and others in 1953.[47] There is evidence of Wedding's revulsion at the Stalinist show trials in the draft of an obituary for Uhse she wrote in 1963. In a line removed by the East German editors, she describes the author looking "bad" and "agitated" in 1953, which she called the "year of the unholy Slansky trial."[48] Wedding's complaint about the omission was met with the sanguine response that "we have to edit out lines in every submission" and there had not been time to contact her.[49]

The trauma of the purges in the early 1950s may have deepened Wedding's identification with China, to which she dedicated her creative work in that decade. Unlike the previous DEFA filmmakers who had produced China films, Wedding's perspective on China was based on extended personal experience. She was one of very few residents of East Germany who had met the Chinese leadership, including Mao and Zhou Enlai, with whose wife she was in correspondence.[50] She wrote three children's books based on her time in China, remained in contact with German émigré photographer Eva Siao in China, and gave talks about China around East Germany in the early 1950s.[51] China was not a geography mediated only through images, narratives, or short visits but one that she had lived firsthand for several years.

Wedding's treatment for *Yo I* reflected the naturalness of her own transnational life course. She sought scenarios that drove the point home that German reality was not only inextricable from China but unimaginable in isolation from it. Using the language of recent historiographical debates, one could say that her goal was to depict signs of transnational entanglement, rather than simply comparison.[52] The program was to discover objects, scenes, or individuals that did not stand in for one or the other nation, but for the interaction between the two, and the interweaving of national lives. Her Chinese counterparts joined her in this effort intermittently but there were also major disagreements about how much fiction was admissible in the genre of documentary. The debates between the German and Chinese filmmakers illustrate vividly the frictions encountered in constructing cultures of socialist internationalism.

Wedding and Huisken began their collaboration at a propitious moment. The second half of the 1950s was a key moment for filmmaking in both the GDR and the PRC. While socialist realism had been the official policy for East German film since 1952, structures of state oversight in the film sector loosened in the course of the so-called Thaw after Nikita Khrushchev's speech at the Twentieth Congress of the Soviet Communist Party in 1956.[53] Control over scripts devolved from the Ministry of Culture to DEFA in 1957 and so-called "Artistic Working Groups" (*Künstlerische Arbeitsgruppe*) within the studio granted filmmakers newfound autonomy.[54] An easing of conditions took place in China slightly earlier. The Chinese Communist Party launched the Hundred Flowers campaign in the summer of 1956, giving intellectuals and artists unprecedented latitude in cultural production as part of an effort to rejuvenate the party structure.[55] Lasting from summer of 1956 until late summer of 1957, the campaign created new possibilities for dissent and departure from the mode of socialist realism. Filmmakers took the opportunity to make work that drew on a diverse range of aesthetic modes, while writers launched wide-ranging critiques in film journals and newspapers.[56]

The moments of openness in East Germany and China overlapped briefly but were also tragically out of sync. The period of artistic freedom expanded in the GDR just as it ended in China. Beginning in the fall of 1957, Chinese artists, writers, and filmmakers that had been experimenting suffered reprisals in the form of lost jobs, imprisonment, and even execution in the "anti-rightist campaigns."[57] Huisken and Wedding began their film in the precise window of openness created by the Hundred Flowers Campaign. What they experienced as a sudden coldness and ideological rigidity from their Chinese counterparts in late 1957 may well have been the symptom of a wild swing from liberation to repression about which they knew either nothing, or very little, as outsiders. When DEFA tightened political control again in the summer of 1958, the East German window of opportunity closed too.[58]

Preparations for *Yo I* began in summer of 1957 when Huisken was in Beijing.[59] The first exchanges with their Chinese counterparts (who remain unfortunately unnamed in archival records) established that the film would be examined closely for its ideological message. The first East German draft proposed following a shipment of East German trucks to China as a theme but the Chinese rejected this as inappropriate for a coproduction. They preferred a theme of cooperation between the two countries.[60] Wedding wrote her treatment with this in mind. Her narrative arc still followed an East German shipment, organized around the real-life plans for a ten-thousand-ton freighter voyage from Warnow to Canton, but was built around instances of reciprocal border-crossing, with Chinese objects, individuals, and ideas entering Germany as frequently as the other way around.[61]

One of Wedding's focuses was on the movement of commodities. This tactic echoed the consumerist visions of the era's other DEFA films in emphasizing material prosperity or, as she put it, the way that "the life of the people of the German Democratic Republic has grown richer since its friendship with the People's Republic of China."[62] She used commodities as material links between the nations. One proposed sequence featured a close-up of a pineapple at a village festival in China fading into an image of a pineapple on a can. In the "very lively sequence" that follows, "we now see factories for preserves, cigarette factories, textile factories but, above all, the finished products of these factories. Canned preserves, cigarette packs, colorful kerchiefs, etc. pass in sequence across the image. We see the same products on the stand of the PRC at the Leipzig Fair."[63] The Leipzig Trade Fair was an important point of interaction and economic exchange between the GDR and China, beginning with the opulent Chinese stand in 1951, which featured glass cases of agricultural products in vials, snaking displays of lacquerware and cloisonné and draped trains of textile alongside the industrial products of electrical wires, gauges, and rubber tires.[64] Wedding also brought Chinese products out of the trade fair and into everyday life, envisioning a scene where "we see a German child eating Chinese mandarins, a woman buying Chinese silk in the state-run department store, a display with cans of Chinese meat on Stalin Boulevard, a worker tears open a pack of

Chinese cigarettes and smokes."[65] Solidarity is expressed here in terms of an expanded field of shared consumption. The proposed scenes brought home the fact that everyday life had traces of China strewn within it, in places easily overlooked.

Wedding also sought scenes that conveyed cultural and personal border-crossing. She shared the news with Huisken at one point that there was an exhibition at East Berlin's Academy of the Arts of Chinese painters who also painted scenes of Germany. She enthused that they would be perfect for the film.[66] Other scenes in the treatment expressed her transnational vision. One scene worth quoting at length comes after she notes the fact that the author Lu Xun had brought the artistic work of Käthe Kollwitz to the attention of Chinese artists in the 1920s, and Guo Morou had translated Goethe's *Faust*. The scene cuts to a room in a student dormitory:

> A young German student runs busily to and fro. He's preparing for the lecture. He sets books upright, puts them in his bag, getting dressed as he goes. A gramophone plays a Chinese song all the while. He tries to sing along with some of the Chinese words. Someone calls him. It is time to go. He sticks his head out of the door and a Chinese student is waiting for him in the corridor, addressing him in German. They leave the building together. We see them in the courtyard of Peking University. They meet other German and Chinese students, streaming toward the main building. The students take their places in the auditorium and the professor begins the lecture. The students take notes intently. The German students write Chinese… Slowly, Chinese sounds turn into German as the image fades to the lecture hall of the University of Leipzig. Chinese students are sitting here between German students and take notes intently as well. They write in German.[67]

Wedding's scene disrupts the viewer's expectations brilliantly. On seeing a German student, a German or Chinese viewer would expect a German location. The Chinese song would give the viewer pause, and hearing the German attempt a few Chinese words further pause. Seeing the Chinese student would seem to relocate the scene in China, until he speaks German. The transition to Germany and the sight of a Chinese student writing in German would further toy with the see-sawing expectations one could expect from socialist viewers unused to seeing national citizens other than statesmen outside of their national containers.

The presence of a Chinese student in Germany and a German student in China was not entirely fantastical in 1957. The number of Chinese university students in East Germany had nearly doubled in the year that Wedding wrote her treatment, raising the total from 127 to 202, and adding up to one-fifth of the total number of foreign students.[68] Conversely, there were fifty-one German students in China by 1957.[69] Yet the scene represents something more than reportage. With clear roots in Wedding's own experience as an expatriate in China, one could argue that it seeks to illustrate the possibility of a socialist cosmopolitanism, where origin, language, and place of residence have become delinked in an aspirational dynamic of supranational communication.

The notion of cosmopolitanism had explicitly negative connotations in state socialism. The Stalinist purges of the early 1950s used the charge to indict supposed deviants from the party line, including Jews and émigrés who (like Wedding) had gone west rather than east during the Second World War.[70] As several of the contributions to this volume demonstrate, the East German state policed interpersonal interactions intensely even as it propounded international solidarity as one of its core principles.[71] In the face of the official opposition to the scrambling of national identities, Wedding's treatment was bold in its effort to dissolve constrained categories of ethnicity, language, and geography.

There was a history of robust transnational traffic between the countries. Chinese students and political activists worked closely with the German Communist Party (KPD) in Berlin of the 1920s and early 1930s.[72] Future CCP leaders, including Zhou Enlai, Deng Xiaoping, and Zhu De spent time in Germany in this period.[73] The official representative of the Comintern in Yenan with Mao and the beginnings of the Red Army was Otto Braun, alias Li Teh, who lived until his death in the GDR.[74] Yet until Wedding's proposal, it was not such individual connections that were the subject of the culture of fraternal solidarity—likely as the very fact of transnational trajectories often led to later purges. Rather, it was a ritualized vocabulary of official receptions between political leaders and a depiction of the republics living in parallel but without touching.

Wedding's Chinese counterparts also adopted the theme of entanglement in their treatment, adopting some of her elements while revising others. Like her, they included scenes of Germans and Chinese working side by side in factories. The relationship, they wrote, is "as intimate as brothers. The German brothers impart their technical knowledge to the Chinese student workers patiently and unreservedly."[75] In one instance, their proposal for a possible introductory scene went even further than Wedding's model of entanglement, using techniques of photomontage to produce the effect of simultaneity reminiscent of the 1920s Soviet documentaries of Dziga Vertov. They suggested an opening segment in which one saw a "train traveling quickly on the mainland of two countries of which the cities, rural districts, mines, construction sites, rivers, mountain ranges, etc. are all in sight at the same time. On the train there are newspapermen and foreign students."[76] In this filmic vision of a shared socialist modernity, China and East Germany have not only become intertwined but indistinguishable with both possessing features of the advanced nation, seen from the window of the quintessential industrial product of the train. The identity of the landscape is literally blurred. On the rails of socialist modernity, China becomes East Germany becomes China.

The Chinese included a scene similar to Wedding's dormitory but with a subtle, and telling, difference. The student in their version was Chinese, and in his dormitory at a German university, he listens to the radio to hear "Chinese music begin to pervade the air. It leads him to think of his homeland, envisioning what great changes are taking place every day in his own country."[77] Rather than the German student who seeks immersion (and perhaps escape) in the Chinese melody and, by extension, the Chinese project of building socialism, the Chinese student uses music to perform a silent act of patriotic attentiveness and symbolic return. The adaptation is significant given the history of Chinese education migration. Chinese students had been drawn to travel abroad for education in metropolitan capitals in Europe and Japan for a century. The treatment suggested that China itself had reclaimed the primacy of focus after the revolution. One might depart, but only to return. The flows from one country to the other in the treatments for *Yo I* could imply a dissolution of national identity but they could also be used to reinforce it.

## Metaphor and Misrecognition

Problems began to plague the German-Chinese collaboration in late 1957. On their second trip to China in December, Wedding noted a "mistrust of foreigners" and observed that the political "development was very strongly nationalistic."[78] By this time, the anti-rightist campaign was well underway in China and those involved in cultural branches may have been careful to govern their speech. From the German perspective, the project seemed to founder on distrust of foreigners and disagreements over the blending of fiction and documentary. Yet Huisken and Wedding's own ignorance about Chinese social realities may have borne equal blame in the faltering cooperation.

The first point of friction came when Wedding and Huisken suggested that a "young exemplary weaver" named Ismena Nötzold travel from the GDR to Shanghai to meet with a young Chinese female weaver and "allow

Ismena and, with her, the film's viewers too, to experience how a female Chinese worker lives in the new China," including the transformation of gender relations, labor practices, and forms of child-rearing. The first question from their Chinese colleagues was "whether Ismena was delegated." When Huisken and Wedding answered that she was not, they were told that she could not come to the PRC because "if she was not delegated and came to China anyway, this did not correspond to the principles of socialist realism." In another case, the DEFA team suggested showing "typical people of the New China, people that transform their country and thereby reach a higher level of development themselves. We wanted to show a worker who was a farmer until only recently. Our Chinese colleagues responded that such workers probably existed. But a worker who used to be a farmer is a worker now. And it does not correspond to the principles of socialist realism to show him as a farmer, because then he would have to play the farmer."[79] To Wedding and Huisken, it seemed that the Chinese were pushing back against the socialist realist principle of "the type." It was not sufficient for Nötzold to actually be a textile worker. Her role in the film would have to be validated by democratic principle in action. It was not sufficient for a worker to have been a farmer; he needed to *still* be a farmer to appear on film in this role.

Looking at the transaction from the Chinese perspective, however, it becomes plausible that the misunderstanding was founded equally in East German ignorance. The two-year period before the Chinese-German exchange had been one of massive reorganization in agriculture. In 1955, Mao broke with his previous policy by announcing that thoroughgoing agricultural collectivization would no longer have to wait until industrialization had been achieved.[80] Beyond boosting production, encouraging agricultural development would also be a means of preventing overly rapid urbanization and urban underemployment, a problem that China had faced in the early 1950s.[81] The process of creating cooperatives was ongoing as Huisken and Wedding met the Chinese filmmakers, making it an inopportune time to promote the transition from farmer to industrial worker as the paradigm of progress. Furthermore, the East German filmmakers seemed to forget that the single most distinctive trait of Maoism was its valorization of the peasantry itself as a vanguard class. In the Chinese context, it would not be necessary to show individuals moving "to a higher level of development" by transitioning from workers to farmers to illustrate the victories of socialism. The farmer and the worker shared the same status.

What seemed like an obstinate fidelity to verisimilitude on the part of the Chinese may have actually been resistance to the proposed content. The Germans themselves had rejected scenes based on their own conceptions of real existing socialism. They objected, for example, to a proposed scene of

German Pioneers taking a Chinese student to a store in East Germany to buy gifts and another of a German worker (implausibly) picking up a Chinese student in his car for a drive.[82] In another case, the Chinese vetoed the concluding image of the film, which was to show the exchange of a ship's model by East German Young Pioneers for a small tiger from the Chinese Pioneers. Huisken and Wedding argued that "there are tigers in China. But in Germany, there are only tigers in zoos. And small tigers are especially well-loved by film audiences." The Chinese struck down this proposal, asking "if Chinese Pioneers had ever given a small tiger to German Pioneers. When we responded in the negative, it was explained that such a gift also does not respond to the principles of socialist realism."[83] While the objection may have been based on the tenets of realism, it could have also stemmed from displeasure with the roles implied by the transaction: East Germany as maritime industrial power and China as exotic wildlife sanctuary.

Frustrated, Wedding and Huisken insisted that "the development of documentary film in recent years has shown that overall developments can be most convincingly shown through the destinies of individual people who are, in the end, part of the masses."[84] The filmmakers went to great lengths to defend their model of metaphor in film. They argued that "documentary film is about condensed truth. As in literature, characteristic qualities of many people are abstracted, selected and made concrete in individual figures."[85] Unmoved, the Chinese rebutted that Huisken and Wedding wanted "to create situations in film…that in real life would never occur" which, in their opinion, "stood in contradiction to the principle of the documentary film as such."[86]

Not long after this fruitless exchange, Wedding recounts that the Chinese sent word to Berlin that they wanted Huisken removed from the job.[87] She wrote that DEFA managing director Günther Klein fired him verbally, "refusing to put it in writing because he did not want to take responsibility" for the decision.[88] After Wedding quit in solidarity with Huisken, the film project continued with a new team, the optimistic new working title *A New Song, A Better Song* (*Ein neues Lied, ein besseres Lied*) and production costs that had run over 700,000 Marks by 1960.[89] The film project was canceled a year later as East Germany followed the Soviet Union into a phase of open antagonism with the PRC in the course of the Sino-Soviet split.[90]

## Conclusion

The lack of a written record makes it difficult to speculate about the exact reasons for Huisken's firing but the frictions in the film project are suggestively symptomatic of the larger misunderstandings between China and the Soviet Bloc that led to the split. China had been expanding its ties to the African and Asian nations since the Bandung Conference in 1955. Already in 1954, Zhou had introduced the "five principles of peaceful coexistence" with Indian leader Jawaharlal Nehru and Burmese leader U Nu.[91] Yet when Khrushchev spoke of "peaceful coexistence" in 1957, he meant coexistence with the United States and other "Western imperialist powers," an implication that CCP leadership never entertained.

The inability of the Soviet Union and other Eastern European countries to comprehend the particularity of the position of the decolonizing and recently postcolonial world was a major factor in the Chinese alienation from the Soviet Union in the late 1950s and early 1960s. By 1960 at the latest, Mao became convinced that Khrushchev was pursuing détente at the expense of support for China and other Asian and African nations.[92] The failure of the East German filmmakers to understand the potential humiliation involved in seeing tigers as China's primary export, and agricultural labor as an occupation only to be transcended, would have surely resonated with these simmering resentments.[93] Both the Sino-Soviet split and the failure of *Yo I* were also stories about the inability to bridge the gap of historical experience between the industrialized North and the global South.

*Yo I* foundered on mutual misrecognitions in the midst of a political climate turning toward internal repression in both countries. Yet in their unrealized script, Wedding and her Chinese colleagues depicted an interweaving of everyday lives across borders, attempting something that none of the DEFA "world" documentaries had succeeded in doing (or tried to do) before. As a failed project of socialist cosmopolitanism, *Yo I* left a lasting vision of the uses of disorientation in creating a political self-understanding beyond the nation.

**Quinn Slobodian** is associate professor of history at Wellesley College and author of *Foreign Front: Third World Politics in Sixties West Germany* (Duke, 2012).

## Notes

1. David Tompkins, "The East is Red? Images of China in East Germany and Poland through the Sino-Soviet Split," *Zeitschrift für Ostmitteleuropa-Forschung* 62, no. 3 (2013): 396–99.
2. Beda Erlinghagen, *Von "wildgewordenem Kleinbürgertum" und "Weltherrschaftsplänen": die Volksrepublik China im Spiegel der DDR-Presse (1966-1976)* (Cologne: Papy-Rossa, 2009), 35.

3. For a treatment of these films see Quinn Slobodian, "'Wir sind Brüder, sagt der Film': China im Dokumentarfilm der DDR und das Scheitern der politischen Metapher der Brüderlichkeit," in *Das Imaginäre des Kalten Krieges. Beiträge zu einer Wissens- und Kulturgeschichte des Ost-West-Konfliktes in Europa*, ed. Sibylle Marti and David Eugster (Essen: Klartext, 2015); see also Qinna Shen, "A Question of Ideology and Realpolitik: DEFA's Cold War Documentaries on China," in *Beyond Alterity: German Encounters with Modern East Asia,* ed. Qinna Shen and Martin Rosenstock (New York: Berghahn Books, 2014).

4. Thomas Heimann, "Von Stahl und Menschen. 1953 bis 1960," in *Schwarzweiss und Farbe: DEFA-Dokumentarfilme 1946-92,* ed. Günter Jordan and Ralf Schenk (Berlin: Filmmuseum Potsdam & Jovis, 1996), 50; Sebastian Heiduschke, *East German Cinema: DEFA and Film History* (New York: Palgrave Macmillan, 2013), 11–12.

5. Heimann, "Von Stahl und Menschen. 1953 bis 1960," 54.

6. Marc Silberman, "Learning from the Enemy: DEFA-French Co-Productions of the 1950s," *Film History* 18, no. 1 (2006): 21.

7. Hans Schoots, *Joris Ivens: Living Dangerously* (Amsterdam: Amsterdam University Press, 2000), 237, 242.

8. The voiceover was read originally by Orson Welles but later redubbed. Ibid., 129.

9. Heimann, "Von Stahl und Menschen. 1953 bis 1960," 70.

10. Günter Agde, "Die doppelte Werkstatt. Joris Ivens, die frühe DDR und die DEFA," in *DEFA international: grenzüberschreitende Filmbeziehungen vor und nach dem Mauerbau,* ed. Michael Wedel, et al. (Wiesbaden: Springer, 2013), 211–12.

11. See Leonid Heller, "A World of Prettiness: Socialist Realism and its Aesthetic Categories," in *Socialist Realism without Shores,* ed. Thomas Lahusen and EA Dobrenko (Durham: Duke University Press, 1997), 51–75.

12. Hermann Müller, "So einen Farbfilm sah ich noch nie," *Neues Deutschland,* 28 January 1951.

13. Schoots, *Joris Ivens,* 244–45.

14. Ibid., 244.

15. David Caute, *The Dancer Defects: The Struggle for Cultural Supremacy during the Cold War* (New York: Oxford University Press, 2003), 268.

16. KJW, "Vom Schicksal eines Dokumentar-Films," *Neues Deutschland,* 10 August 1955.

17. Christoph Classen, "Emotionale Vergemeinschaftung? Krieg und Politik im Radio der frühen DDR," in *Die Massen bewegen: Medien und Emotionen in der Moderne,* ed. Frank Bösch and Manuel Borutta (Frankfurt am Main: Campus, 2006), 344.

18. n.d. "Lied der Ströme," *Sonntag,* 12 September 1954.

19. Schoots, *Joris Ivens,* 245.

20. Annette Schuhmann, *Kulturarbeit im sozialistischen Betrieb: gewerkschaftliche Erziehungspraxis in der SBZ/DDR 1946 bis 1970* (Cologne: Böhlau, 2006), 267, 271–72.

21. Wegner to Kurze, Ministerium für Maschinenbau. 23 March 1955. BArch, DR 118/1767.

22. Schulz, DEFA to Hotel Johannishof. 28 July 1954. BArch, DR 118/1767; Schulz, DEFA to Hotel Newa. 27 July 1954. BArch, DR 118/1767.

23. Ivens to IDFF. 19 December 1955. BArch, DR 118/1767.

24. Charles Musser, "Utopian Visions in Cold War Documentary: Joris Ivens, Paul Robeson and Song of the Rivers (1954)," *CiNéMAS* 12, no. 3 (2002): 114; Tony

Shaw, *British Cinema and the Cold War: The State, Propaganda and Consensus* (New York: IB Tauris, 2001), 190.

25. Antoine [Maestrati] to Wegner. 7 February 1956. BArch, DR 118, 1768; Ivens to Pontecorvo. 19 April 1955. BArch, DR 118, 1768.

26. Wegner to Huisken. 29 January 1955. FP, N077, 3.3.

27. Ibid.

28. Wegner to Huisken, 23 May 1955. FP, N077, 3.3.

29. Schneider. DEFA. Beurteilung des Films "Die Windrose," 4 January 1957. BArch, DR 118/1767.

30. Toni Weis, "The Politics Machine: On the Concept of 'Solidarity' in East German Support for SWAPO," *Journal of Southern African Studies* 2 (June 2011), 366.

31. Wegner to Huisken, 23 May 1955. FP, N077, 3.

32. For a longer discussion of this film see Slobodian, "'Wir sind Brüder, sagt der Film'."

33. Günter Jordan and Ralf Schenk, eds., *Schwarzweiss und Farbe: DEFA-Dokumentarfilme 1946-92*, 1. Aufl. ed. (Berlin: Filmmuseum Potsdam & Jovis, 1996), 407.

34. Hans-Joachim Funk, "Die Dinge gingen sehr viel unkompliziertere vor sich," in *Alltag des Dokumentarfilms. Erinnerungen an die Jahre des Anfangs, 1946-1950*, ed. Günter Jordan (Berlin: Verband der Film- und Fernsehschaffenden der DDR, 1987), 84.

35. Joop Huisken, "Wir sind gestartet, um vorwärtszukommen," in *Alltag des Dokumentarfilms. Erinnerungen an die Jahre des Anfangs, 1946-1950*, ed. Günter Jordan (Berlin: Verband der Film- und Fernsehschaffenden der DDR, 1987), 75; Eva Fritzsche, "Wir haben alle voneinander gelernt," in *Alltag des Dokumentarfilms. Erinnerungen an die Jahre des Anfangs, 1946-1950*, ed. Günter Jordan (Berlin: Verband der Film- und Fernsehschaffenden der DDR, 1987), 78.

36. Jordan and Schenk, eds., *Schwarzweiss und Farbe: DEFA-Dokumentarfilme 1946-92*, 407.

37. "Robert Menegoz-Genestal," BArch, DR 118, 1768.

38. A. Maestrati, Procinex to Wegner. 6 June 1956. BArch, DR 118, 1768; Silberman, "Learning from the Enemy."

39. Abschrift. Titelliste. "China—Land zwischen gestern und morgen" 29 January 1957. FP, JH/N077.

40. Reproduced in Forster, "'Vorwärts rollt das Rad...'," 8.

41. Wolfgang Joho, "Bilddichtung der Wirklichkeit," *Sonntag*, 31 March 1957.

42. Abschrift. Titelliste. "China—Land zwischen gestern und morgen" 29 January 1957. FP, JH/N077.

43. G. Sch. "Land zwischen gestern und morgen," *Tribüne*, 28 March 1957.

44. Josie McLellan, *Antifascism and Memory in East Germany: Remembering the International Brigades, 1945-1989* (New York: Oxford University Press, 2004), 59.

45. Tony Judt, *Postwar: A History of Europe since 1945* (New York: Penguin, 2005), 185.

46. Stephan Hermlin, *Ferne Nähe* (Berlin: Aufbau, 1954); Bodo Uhse, *Tagebuch aus China* (Berlin: Aufbau-Verlag, 1956). On the attitude of this group in the 1950s see McLellan, *Antifascism and Memory in East Germany*, 62, 68, 191; see also Weijia Li, *China und China-Erfahrung in Leben und Werk von Anna Seghers* (New York: Peter Lang, 2010); Tompkins, "The East is Red?," 410.

47. Zlata Fuss Phillips, *German Children's and Youth Literature in Exile, 1933-1950* (Munich: Saur, 2001), 256.

48. Grete Weiskopf, "Erinnerung und Abschied [an Bodo Uhse]," [Draft]. Akademie der Künste Archive, Berlin (hereafter AdK), Alex Wedding Papers (hereafter AW), NR 31.

49. Redaktion *Sonntag* to G. Weiskopf. 9 July 1963. AdK, AW, NR 31.

50. Teng Ying Chao (Madame Zhou Enlai) to Wedding. 2 March 1952. AdK, AW, NR 787.

51. Wedding to Siao. 24 February 1954. AdK, AW, NR 649.

52. See Michael Werner and Bénédicte Zimmermann, "Beyond Comparison: Histoire Croisé and the Challenge of Reflexivity." *History and Theory* 45, no. 1 (2006): 30–50.

53. Daniela Berghahn, *Hollywood behind the Wall: The Cinema of East Germany* (Manchester: Manchester University Press, 2005), 36; Jessica CE Gienow-Hecht, "Culture and the Cold War in Europe," in *The Cambridge History of the Cold War*, ed. Melvyn P. Leffler and Odd Arne Westad (New York: Cambridge University Press, 2010), 417.

54. Berghahn, *Hollywood behind the Wall*, 26.

55. Maurice Meisner, *Mao's China and After*, 3rd ed. (New York: Free Press, 1999), 166–68.

56. Yingchi Chu, *Chinese Documentaries: From Dogma to Polyphony* (New York: Routledge, 2007), 60; Yomi Braester, "A Genealogy of Cinephilia in the Maoist Period," in *The Oxford Handbook of Chinese Cinemas*, ed. Carlos Rojas and Eileen Cheng-Yin-Chow (New York: Oxford University Press, 2013), 100–109.

57. Chu, *Chinese Documentaries: From Dogma to Polyphony*, 60. The Hundred Flowers campaign officially came to an end in June 1957. On the anti-rightist campaign that followed see Meisner, *Mao's China and After*, 180–84.

58. Heiduschke, *East German Cinema*, 13.

59. Wedding, n.t., n.d. [likely journal entries] AdK, AW, NR 365.

60. Huisken. Bericht über meine Reise nach China im Juni und Juli 1957. Filmarchiv Potsdam (hereafter FP), Joop Huisken Papers (hereafter JH), N077.

61. Aktennotiz. Betr. Ko-Produktion mit China. 18 Jun 1957. FP, JH, N077, 3.3. A short film was ultimately completed about this trip. *Von Wismar nach Shanghai* (dir. Rudolf Schemmel, 1958).

62. Untitled treatment. [Alex Wedding], FP, JH, N077. On the use of consumerist tropes see Slobodian, "'Wir sind Brüder, sagt der Film': China im Dokumentarfilm der DDR und das Scheitern der politischen Metapher der Brüderlichkeit."

63. Konzeption für einen abendfüllenden deutsch-chinesischen Gemeinschaftsfilm. n.a. n.d. FP, JH/N077.

64. On the use of the Leipzig Trade Fair as a site of cultural diplomacy see Katherine Pence, "Showcasing Cold War Germany in Cairo: 1954 and 1957 Industrial Exhibitions and the Competition for Arab Partners," *Journal of Contemporary History* 47, no. 1 (2011): 83. For images see "China Exhibition Hall in Leipzig, 1951" http://hahn.zenfolio.com/p1067231941 (accessed 26 July 2013).

65. Untitled treatment. [Alex Wedding], FP, JH, N077.

66. Wedding to Huisken. n.d. FP, JH, N077.

67. Untitled treatment. [Alex Wedding], FP, JH, N077.

68. The numbers are for the 1956–57 academic year. Entwurf. Beschluß des Ministerrats über die Erweiterung des Ausländerstudiums in der DDR. 21 Feb 1956.

SAPMO-BArch DY 30/IV 2/9.04/638; Staatsekretäriat für Hochschulwesen, Unterabteilung Ausländerstudium, Entwurf, 1957. SAPMO-BArch DY 30/IV 2/9.04/638. The numbers in the Soviet Union were much larger. Eight thousand Chinese students traveled to the Soviet Union to study between 1948 and 1963. Elizabeth McGuire, "Between Revolutions: Chinese Students in Soviet Institutes, 1948-1966," in *China Learns from the Soviet Union, 1949-present*, ed. Thomas P. Bernstein and Hua-Yu Li (Lanham: Lexington Books, 2010), 361.

69. Joachim Krüger, "Das erste Jahrzehnt der Beziehungen," in *Beiträge zur Geschichte der Beziehungen der DDR und der VR China: Erinnerungen und Untersuchungen,* ed. Joachim Krüger (Münster: Lit, 2002), 102.

70. On the charge of cosmopolitanism in the Stalinist show trials from 1948 to 1953 see Judt, *Postwar,* 182–93

71. Weis, "The Politics Machine," 366.

72. Gregor Benton, *Chinese Migrants and Internationalism: Forgotten Histories, 1917-1945* (New York: Routledge, 2007), 30–35.

73. Ibid., 30–36.

74. Otto Braun, *Chinesische Aufzeichnungen (1932-1939)* (Berlin: Dietz, 1973).

75. "Draft Scenario for the Film to be jointly produced by China and GDR" n.d. n.a. [by Chinese partners] FP JH, N077.

76. Ibid.

77. Ibid.

78. Wedding, n.t., n.d. AdK, AW, NR 365.

79. Hauptverwaltung Film. Ministerium für Kultur. Bericht des Gen. Joop Huisken und der Gen. Alex Wedding über die Zusammenarbeit mit den Genossen vom Pekinger Dokumentarfilmstudio an unserer Co-Produktion. 24 Jul 1958. FP JH, N077.

80. Maurice Meisner, *Mao's China and After,* 139–40.

81. Ibid., 131.

82. [Wedding and Huisken] Response to their script. n.d. AdK, AW, NR 100/4.

83. [Wedding and Huisken] Response to their script. 16 Jan n.d. AdK, AW, NR 100/4.

84. Ibid.

85. Ibid.

86. Hauptverwaltung Film. Ministerium für Kultur. Bericht des Gen. Joop Huisken und der Gen. Alex Wedding über die Zusammenarbeit mit den Genossen vom Pekinger Dokumentarfilmstudio an unserer Co-Produktion. 24 July 1958. FP JH, N077.

87. Hand-notes. n.d. n.t. AdK, AW, NR 365.

88. If true, this would explain the absence of documentation in the DEFA files at the Federal Archive.

89. Klein to Wendt. Ministerium für Kultur. 19 June 1959. BArch, DR 118, 1870; Alfred Fritzsche. Beschluß-Protokoll. 2 Nov 1959. BA, DR, 118, 1870. With the title taken from Heinrich Heine's anti-nationalist poem, *Germany: A Winter's Tale* from 1843, it is interesting to speculate about whether DEFA directors intended a subtle critique of either the PRC—or the GDR itself—with this choice of title. Oley, Produktionsleiter. Kalkulation auf der Grundlage des Vertrages vom 2 Nov 1957 und dem gemeinsamen Beschlussprotokoll vom 5 Mai 1960 für die Gemeinschaftsproduktion "China-DDR." 6 May 1960. BArch, DR 118, 1870. The average DEFA

feature film cost 1.5 million Ostmarks, making this already an expensive venture. Silberman, "Learning from the Enemy," 25.

90. See Beda Erlinghagen, "Anfänge und Hintergründe des Konflikts zwischen der DDR und der Volksrepublik China. Kritische Anmerkungen zu einer ungeklärten Frage," *Beiträge zur Geschichte der Arbeiterbewegung* 49, no. 3 (2007): 111–46.

91. Chen Jian, "China, The Third World and the Cold War," in *The Cold War in the Third World,* ed. Robert J. McMahon (New York: Oxford University Press, 2013), 89.

92. The first salvo of the Sino-Soviet split came in the form of the so-called "Lenin Polemics" published in CCP newspaper in April 1960 and was followed by open confrontation at Party Congresses in June. Lorenz M Lüthi, *The Sino-Soviet Split: Cold War in the Communist World* (Princeton: Princeton University Press, 2008), 163, 174.

93. Radchenko argues that the asymmetry of the alliance between China and the Soviet Union was at the core of their quarrel. Being dictated to by the far inferior power of East Germany may have been even more galling to the Chinese sense of stature. Sergey Radchenko, *Two Suns in the Heavens: The Sino-Soviet Struggle for Supremacy, 1962-1967* (Washington, D.C.: Woodrow Wilson Center, 2009), 9.

# Bibliography

Agde, Günter. "Die doppelte Werkstatt. Joris Ivens, die frühe DDR und die DEFA." In *DEFA international: grenzüberschreitende Filmbeziehungen vor und nach dem Mauerbau,* ed. Michael Wedel, Barton Byg, Andy Räder, Skyler Arndt-Briggs, and Evan Torner, 203–16. Wiesbaden: Springer, 2013.

Benton, Gregor. *Chinese Migrants and Internationalism: Forgotten Histories, 1917-1945.* New York: Routledge, 2007.

Berghahn, Daniela. *Hollywood behind the Wall: The Cinema of East Germany.* Manchester: Manchester University Press, 2005.

Braun, Otto. *Chinesische Aufzeichnungen (1932-1939).* Berlin: Dietz, 1973.

Caute, David. *The Dancer Defects: The Struggle for Cultural Supremacy during the Cold War.* New York: Oxford University Press, 2003.

Classen, Christoph. "Emotionale Vergemeinschaftung? Krieg und Politik im Radio der frühen DDR." In *Die Massen bewegen: Medien und Emotionen in der Moderne,* ed. Frank Bösch and Manuel Borutta, 344–68. Frankfurt am Main: Campus, 2006.

Erlinghagen, Beda. "Anfänge und Hintergründe des Konflikts zwischen der DDR und der Volksrepublik China. Kritische Anmerkungen zu einer ungeklärten Frage." *Beiträge zur Geschichte der Arbeiterbewegung* 49, no. 3 (2007): 111–46.

———. *Von "wildgewordenem Kleinbürgertum" und "Weltherrschaftsplänen": die Volksrepublik China im Spiegel der DDR-Presse (1966-1976).* Cologne: PapyRossa, 2009.

Fritzsche, Eva. "Wir haben alle voneinander gelernt." In *Alltag des Dokumentarfilms. Erinnerungen an die Jahre des Anfangs, 1946-1950,* ed. Günter Jordan, 76–81. Berlin: Verband der Film- und Fernsehschaffenden der DDR, 1987.

Funk, Hans-Joachim. "Die Dinge gingen sehr viel unkompliziertere vor sich." In *Alltag des Dokumentarfilms. Erinnerungen an die Jahre des Anfangs, 1946-1950,* ed. Günter Jordan, 82–95. Berlin: Verband der Film- und Fernsehschaffenden der DDR, 1987.

Gienow-Hecht, Jessica CE. "Culture and the Cold War in Europe." In *The Cambridge History of the Cold War,* ed. Melvyn P. Leffler and Odd Arne Westad, 398–419. New York: Cambridge University Press, 2010.

Heiduschke, Sebastian. *East German Cinema: DEFA and Film History.* New York: Palgrave Macmillan, 2013.

Heimann, Thomas. "Von Stahl und Menschen. 1953 bis 1960." In *Schwarzweiss und Farbe: DEFA-Dokumentarfilme 1946-92,* ed. Günter Jordan and Ralf Schenk, 49–91. Berlin: Filmmuseum Potsdam & Jovis, 1996.

Heller, Leonid. "A World of Prettiness: Socialist Realism and its Aesthetic Categories." In *Socialist Realism without Shores,* ed. Thomas Lahusen and EA Dobrenko, 51–75. Durham: Duke University Press, 1997.

Hermlin, Stephan. *Ferne Nähe.* Berlin: Aufbau, 1954.

Huisken, Joop. "Wir sind gestartet, um vorwärtszukommen." In *Alltag des Dokumentarfilms. Erinnerungen an die Jahre des Anfangs, 1946-1950,* ed. Günter Jordan, 72–75. Berlin: Verband der Film- und Fernsehschaffenden der DDR, 1987.

Jian, Chen. "China, The Third World and the Cold War." In *The Cold War in the Third World,* ed. Robert J. McMahon, 85–100. New York: Oxford University Press, 2013.

Jordan, Günter, and Ralf Schenk, eds. *Schwarzweiss und Farbe: DEFA-Dokumentarfilme 1946-92.* 1. Aufl. ed. Berlin: Filmmuseum Potsdam & Jovis, 1996.

Judt, Tony. *Postwar: A History of Europe since 1945.* New York: Penguin, 2005.

Krüger, Joachim. "Das erste Jahrzehnt der Beziehungen." In *Beiträge zur Geschichte der Beziehungen der DDR und der VR China: Erinnerungen und Untersuchungen,* ed. Joachim Krüger, 65–111. Münster: Lit, 2002.

Li, Weijia. *China und China-Erfahrung in Leben und Werk von Anna Seghers.* New York: Peter Lang, 2010.

McLellan, Josie. *Antifascism and Memory in East Germany: Remembering the International Brigades, 1945-1989.* New York: Oxford University Press, 2004.

Meisner, Maurice. *Mao's China and After.* 3rd ed. New York: Free Press, 1999.

Musser, Charles. "Utopian Visions in Cold War Documentary: Joris Ivens, Paul Robeson and Song of the Rivers (1954)." *CiNéMAS* 12, no. 3 (2002): 109–53.

Radchenko, Sergey. *Two Suns in the Heavens: The Sino-Soviet Struggle for Supremacy, 1962-1967.* Washington, D.C.: Woodrow Wilson Center, 2009.

Schoots, Hans. *Joris Ivens: Living Dangerously.* Amsterdam: Amsterdam University Press, 2000.

Schuhmann, Annette. *Kulturarbeit im sozialistischen Betrieb: gewerkschaftliche Erziehungspraxis in der SBZ/DDR 1946 bis 1970.* Cologne: Böhlau, 2006.

Shaw, Tony. *British Cinema and the Cold War: The State, Propaganda and Consensus.* New York: IB Tauris, 2001.

Shen, Qinna. "A Question of Ideology and Realpolitik: DEFA's Cold War Documentaries on China," in *Beyond Alterity: German Encounters with Modern East Asia,* ed. Qinna Shen and Martin Rosenstock, 94–114. New York: Berghahn Books, 2014.

Silberman, Marc. "Learning from the Enemy: DEFA-French Co-Productions of the 1950s." *Film History* 18, no. 1 (2006): 21–45.

Slobodian, Quinn. "'Wir sind Brüder, sagt der Film': China im Dokumentarfilm der DDR und das Scheitern der politischen Metapher der Brüderlichkeit." In *Das Imaginäre des Kalten Krieges. Beiträge zu einer Wissens- und Kulturgeschichte des*

*Ost-West-Konfliktes in Europa.* ed. Sibylle Marti and David Eugster, 45-68. Essen: Klartext, 2015.

Tompkins, David. "The East is Red? Images of China in East Germany and Poland through the Sino-Soviet Split." *Zeitschrift für Ostmitteleuropa-Forschung* 62, no. 3 (2013): 393–424.

Uhse, Bodo. *Tagebuch aus China.* Berlin: Aufbau-Verlag, 1956.

Weis, Toni. "The Politics Machine: On the Concept of 'Solidarity' in East German Support for SWAPO." *Journal of Southern African Studies* 2 (June 2011): 351–67.

# Chapter 10

# Imposed Dialogues

## Joerg Foth and Tran Vu's GDR-Vietnamese Coproduction, *Dschungelzeit* (1988)

*Evan Torner and Victoria Rizo Lenshyn*

What were the limits of East German international solidarity with the Global South? In the last several decades, scholars of political history and international relations have answered this question through their respective disciplines.[1] Thomas Barnett argues, for example, that state-level East German interaction with the Global South was motivated by compensation for the state's inferiority vis-à-vis West Germany and the Soviet Union, and ultimately failed to provide peace or long-term economic development for all countries involved.[2] Brigitte Schulz sees the GDR adopting a paternalistic attitude toward nonwhite guest-workers from Angola or Vietnam in the GDR, while currying favor exclusively with Old Left political elites in recently formed postcolonial states.[3] Young-Sun Hong finds the East German encounter with the Global South reflecting white European assumptions about the Global South and already coopted by the rubrics provided by said assumptions. As she puts it, development aid "was often used by both blocs to cement alliances with third world countries, and political leaders often discussed such aid in militarized terms."[4] The confrontations between socialism's utopian "solidarity" promise and Cold War realities have been well documented and thoroughly dissected, albeit through a model of cultural transmission that presumes Global North interests acting on the global South and not vice versa.[5] Yet the artifacts produced by these often awkward encounters between the GDR and the rest of the world have only begun to be seriously explored as moments of intercultural exchange and transnational friction.

This chapter explores an encounter in film production between the East German DEFA studios[6] and the Vietnamese Feature Film studios that sheds light on larger issues of artistic and structural dialogue between the two socialist states. Serving in the capacity of international relations, film is a medium that both crosses and erects borders between nation-states. State-organized film industries produce films as industrial instruments of culture used to placate certain stakeholders, from whom revenue is harvested for more films. The German Democratic Republic (GDR) and the Democratic Republic of Vietnam (DRV) initiated a film exchange as part of these mutual efforts, as is clear from the 1957 contract that protected the financial interests of both countries, including the percentage of revenues owed (Article 9), forms of payment and payment deadlines (Article 10), the limits of the rightsholders in coproduction (Article 11), statistical reports of screenings, ticket sales, and box-office revenues (Article 14), and the financial responsibility of lost or damaged material (Article 15).[7]

While past studies of East German cinema have focused on its ideological processing of GDR domestic issues, recent work has resituated the thousands of archived DEFA films in terms of their relationship to the international sphere during the Cold War.[8] This article further restructures the conversation by emphasizing the parity between the actors and networks at stake in the film without erasing the disparities that emerged from actual praxis. In doing so, we hope to assist the project advanced by Saër Maty Bâ and Will Higbee, among others, who wish to rethink "a binary or Eurocentric approach to cinema ... in order to propose new methodologies that will lead to an alternative 'un-centered' version of knowledge that gives credit to multiple viewpoints in order to arrive at original and innovative ways of studying film history, theory and practice in a globalized context."[9] As German film historians, we can deploy seemingly marginal films to interrogate the boundaries of Germany and the philosophies and attitudes one might attribute to it. The GDR was a nation that, despite its myth of solidarity, had trouble accounting for difference. Our analysis below seeks a precise articulation of what that trouble looked like.

The subject of the following chapter is the 1988 East German–Vietnamese coproduced feature *Dschungelzeit* (*Ngon Thap Ha Noi / Time in the Jungle*, dirs. Joerg Foth and Tran Vu), a little-known box-office flop that adapted the true history of Germans who abandoned the French Foreign Legion for the Viet Minh resistance in the late 1940s.[10] The storyline begins when Armin (Hans-Uwe Bauer), a defector from Hitler's army during World War II who had joined the Legion in Vietnam, meets up with Vietnamese intellectual and resistance fighter Hai (Bui Bai Binh), who helps him escape from the Legion to the Viet Minh resistance stronghold in the mountains. There, they run a printing press used to produce informational texts about the Vietnamese colonial struggle that would convince other Germans to defect. They eventually attract a group of former Nazi German legionnaires who help the Viet Minh build a resistance camp in the jungle. This camp is only put to short-term use, however, as the French forces push into the mountains, and the foundation of the GDR in 1949 tempts some of the left-leaning German exiles to return home to their now-socialist home country.

The intense cultural dialogue that takes place in the narrative of *Dschungelzeit* also mirrors that which surrounded the film during its six fraught years of development. On the one hand, it was one of the first coproductions between the Socialist Republic of Vietnam and a Central European power. As such, it was carefully conceived in terms of structural parity, with two directors, two producers, an equal number of screenwriters, and even two main actors. The contract itself indicates good intentions from both nations in a spirit of communist internationalism: "Both sides will strive to settle the eventual disputes that emerge from the realization of this contract through mutual negotiations and in the name of friendship between the two states and countries."[11] On the other hand, the film's outcome expressed what transnational collaboration could not produce: a coherent, successful film that would reach its intended audiences in East Germany and Vietnam respectively. Conflicts and contradictions at the political, production, and aesthetic levels emerged due to structural impositions of state socialism and outright cultural differences that the film attempted to reconcile.

The case of *Dschungelzeit* reveals how international solidarity became a negotiated space. Parity in transnational collaboration faded quickly to disparity, and the perceived solid structure of each nation was rendered permeable. At a time when many scholars are interrogating that strange object we call a "nation," this truly interstitial film—a film more or less disowned by both its production partners after its release—inadvertently opened up an authentic intercultural dialogue, with all the productive alienation and reorientation that such a dialogue entails.[12]

## Solidarity and the Transnational

Some clarification of terms is in order, especially with regard to "solidarity" and "transnationalism." The International Solidarity Movement itself was used as a means of generating popular support for global South countries such as Cuba, Chile, and Vietnam in their struggles against U.S. interference. But GDR politicians also employed the discourse of solidarity regularly to justify any number of economic and political engagements with the Global South, from arms deals to musical tours to shipments of factory components. Such solidarity was always approached as a catch-all ideal that justified both state-level pragmatics and ground-level participation, despite wildly varying agendas and outcomes. Films of the 1970s and 1980s thoroughly problematized this discrepancy between the ideal of solidarity and the disillusionment surrounding its implementation, especially when it came to actual interpersonal relations between people from the global South and the East German general population.[13]

By "international solidarity" in a theoretical sense, we mean the socio-economic and political support of countries with socialist sympathies against capitalist countries, which formed a vital component of GDR foreign and domestic policy.[14] The term "transnationalism" has also become muddled since the term was introduced as a counter-research category to "globalization" in the 1980s and 1990s.[15] Transnational objects or relations mediate any given nation through asymmetrical interaction with other nations. The perspective proposes that the "nation" itself is both a merely contingent constellation of actors and interests, but also a key component in what Randall Halle describes as an "affiliative and ideational network" that legitimates, enables, and/or hinders the movement of goods, people, and ideas across its perceived territories.[16] The transnational interaction at the core of *Dschungelzeit*, for example, involves both the film's historical and fictional conceits: a late 1940s alliance between exiled Germans and the Viet Minh against the French, serving the founding myths of both the GDR and DRV; and the nuances of the coproduction itself, with negotiations between specific film teams and cultural diplomats that parallel GDR-Vietnam relations in the 1980s. These cross-border flows of individuals and objects reveal different registers of cultural interpretation. They are the subjects of a transnational film history.

Yet since the establishment of transnational methodologies in film studies in the last decade, finer-grained tools have been required to delineate different modes of cinematic transnationalism.[17] Mette Hjort's taxonomy of *transnationalisms,* which is leveled at the problem of academics' "tendency to use the term 'transnational' as a largely self-evident qualifier requiring only minimal conceptual clarification," provides us with a rubric to evaluate the products at hand more rigorously.[18] Within Hjort's classification, GDR film coproductions such as *Dschungelzeit* would be considered exemplary forms of an affinitive, milieu-building, and opportunistic cinematic transnationalism. They are "affinitive" in that both socialist GDR and Vietnam perceived their vested national interests as similar, "milieu-building" in that part of the coproduction's purpose was to develop Vietnamese film infrastructure for the future benefit of both coproducing countries, and "opportunistic" in terms of the production's apparent de facto function, namely, to provide each country's cultural officials legitimacy to go abroad to meetings and vacation spots.[19]

Thus, a nuanced portrait of this coproduction emerges when one reconsiders how the discourse of solidarity was used within the GDR. In light of our research, "solidarity" becomes a demystified idea that exists at the intersection of a variety of cultural practices. Solidarity masks different instrumental purposes, while also motivating political idealists to seek space beyond mere instrumentality. Transnationalism as a theoretical framework unseats the notion of the nation by seeing how nations interact with one each other, intertwining together as goods, people, and products are displaced and moved across borders. But we can also unseat the concept of "transnationalism" by further exploring what power relations that might entail. International coproductions such as *Dschungelzeit* were intended to discipline the DEFA directors of the 1980s, but also permitted genuine spaces of intercultural collaboration to exist. The Socialist Republic of Vietnam's film infrastructure, however, required the influx of foreign capital such as that of the GDR during a time when the shift to the market economy endangered its well-established leftist film culture. One must take the perceived needs and interests of both nations in a transnational relationship into account, while also recognizing that the "nation" is a shifting construct in the minds of those supposedly acting on its behalf.

## GDR—Vietnam

The East German–Vietnamese coproduction must be set within the context of the recent history of interaction between the countries. The National Socialist German government took proxy control of French Indochina in 1940 through its Japanese allies. In the First Indochina War (1946–54), ethnic Germans fought for both the French in the Foreign Legion and for the Viet Minh as defectors from the Legion.[20] By the mid 1950s, both East Germany and Indochina were in periods of nation-building as minor players in the world socialist camp, navigating between the influence of Moscow and Beijing. The Second Indochina War, known to Americans as the Vietnam War and to the Vietnamese as the American War, launched the resistance of the National Liberation Front and the People's Army of Vietnam into the central discourse of the global Left during the 1960s and 70s, challenging not only capitalist expansionism from Washington, D.C., but also the Soviet revolutionary model from Moscow.[21] By the 1980s, the period of the coproduction, the Socialist Republic of Vietnam had fulfilled East Germany's fantasy of fighting off the chief capitalist aggressor, the United States of America. This victory gave Vietnam, as with North Korea and Cuba before it, significant symbolic capital in the GDR and the rest of the Eastern bloc. Though both the GDR and Vietnam were perceived as somewhat marginal in the global economy, the GDR's status as a wealthier, industrial country allowed it to draw upon the Vietnamese as contract laborers in the GDR.[22] In turn, the GDR invested in the rebuilding of Vietnamese cities such as Vinh (see Schwenkel's contribution in this volume).[23] By the end of the twentieth century, both Germany and Vietnam would become what Claire Sutherland calls "soldered states"—nations formerly cut in two along capitalist/communist lines that are still in the process of finding a shared national identity.[24]

The symbolic importance of Vietnam within the socialist bloc meant that *Dschungelzeit* was not the first East German film treating the topos of Vietnam. Previous works, including *Geschwader Fledermaus* (1958, dir. Erich Engel), *Flucht aus der Hölle* (1960, TV series), a number of Heynowski & Scheumann documentaries during the American Vietnam War, and the unfilmed scripts *Schicksal in Vietnam* (1964) and *Wer den Tiger reitet...* (1966), confirm the connection between Vietnam and postcolonial warfare within the GDR media imaginary.[25] *Geschwader Fledermaus* was shot almost entirely on DEFA sets and concerns conscientious Americans helping to sabotage their own war effort during the First Indochina War.[26] *Schicksal in Vietnam* was, in fact, the first failed attempt at a coproduction between the GDR and Vietnam. The script was about a Nazi soldier fleeing from Hitler's army and entering the French Foreign Legion, and it was submitted to Hanoi by 1964. The GDR received no reply from Vietnam for two years, however, leading DEFA screenwriters to develop and submit *Wer den Tiger reitet...*, a Vietnamese-centered tale about French colonial resistance.[27] The second script draft of *Tiger* was finally rejected three years later in 1969, after the American Vietnam War inspired filmmakers such as Walter Heynowski and Gerhard Scheumann to make documentaries rather than feature films on the topic.[28]

The script for the film that would become *Dschungelzeit* pitched a slightly different angle than the scenarios of war depicted above. Written by Peter and Leonja Wuss, and developed with Vietnamese writer Banh Bao, it was based primarily on the biographies of German defector legionnaires Erwin Borchers and Kaspar Schmalenbach. The initial draft, called "Der Turm von Hanoi," invoking the biblical gravitas of the Tower of Babel, was to be a story about "both realistic and idealistic relations of success and failure within the processes of the world."[29] It was to be a film about cultural difference and socialist unity, as well as the quieter solidarities found between the French Foreign Legionnaires and Viet Minh as they reconciled their respective social and national identities in the late 1940s.

Yet the initial 1983 agreement between the DEFA delegation and the Vietnamese to make the film proved far more ambitious than the modest picture they might have intended. The Wuss team and their Vietnamese partners insisted on absolute parity in the coproduction, requiring the doubling of film personnel and the elevation of the film to the status of a national-diplomatic object to justify its substantial costs. What followed was six years of inertia in production, as both East Germans and Vietnamese became mired in a complex intercultural exchange. Simply put: national and consumer interests frequently superseded those of film production.

*Dschungelzeit*'s director, Joerg Foth, notes that the film received lavish financial investment from the studios as a high-profile international coproduction despite little progress being made on the actual filmmaking:

> Every DEFA shoot abroad was not only an occasion for tourism, but also shopping. ... Each member of the DEFA team received 43 Ostmarks [East German currency] daily for expenses while abroad, whereas 30 per day was the usual sum... And vice versa, our international film partners also loved to travel for free and/or on the studio's tab, and to spend their expense accounts on souvenirs. I had never seen it as excessive as it was with *Dschungelzeit,* nor will I ever again. From 1984 to 1987, I became increasingly certain that the whole film project was just an excuse to travel back and forth as much as possible. The Vietnamese way of doing business was an art of negotiation that was absolutely suited for delaying the first day of shooting until the cows came home.[30]

Based on Foth's embittered account, the facilitation of real economic exchange on mutual trips between the two countries took precedence over progress toward the goals of filmmaking. Given the primarily financial nature of the initial film agreements in 1957, this comes as no surprise. In addition, the DEFA delegations found themselves overfunded but underprepared to deal with the unfamiliar logistics of the actual Vietnamese locations.[31]

Young DEFA director Foth was hired in 1984 as the implementer of Wuss and Bao's script, and he assumed the duty (against his colleagues' advice) out of "feelings of solidarity" for the Vietnamese.[32] Foth was to codirect with older director Tran Vu, who came of age during the revolutionary period of the film and whose interests in the coproduction also allegedly stemmed from his own personal experiences of solidarity with defectors from the French Foreign Legion during the American War. As he recalled: "I was very close to the theme of parole for German defectors, because I too actually met people like that back then. Our victory in the struggle for liberation had many objective reasons behind it, not the least of which was genuine human solidarity. We had a clear and very severe concept of the enemy, but any defectors—be they Africans, Germans or Frenchmen—were welcomed as friends and treated with spontaneous levels of deep sympathy."[33] Vu took on the film as part of a series of long-term collaborations with author Bao, who had also experienced firsthand the French occupation of Vietnam and the work of defectors such as Armin.[34] Yet Vu found DEFA's filmmaking impersonally "industrial," while actor Carl Heinz Choynski remarked how, in Vietnam, "totally basic things were simply not readily available, such as there being no guarantee that everyone would reliably get sufficiently drinkable water."[35] A film projected to begin shooting with equal numbers of German and Vietnamese crew in 1984 saw its first clapboard finally fall on 24 March 1987 with about four dozen Germans commanding hundreds of Vietnamese extras and six actual staff members. Idealism faded to pragmatism as typical global North–global South relations—of financier and service provider, of leaders and followers—took hold.

## Frictional Aesthetics in *Dschungelzeit* (1988)

The film's transnational aesthetic reflects the two historical moments of German/Vietnamese encounter upon which the film touches: the French Indochina War in 1949 and the 1980s of the coproduction. While both directors insisted the film was a true collaboration made in the interests of solidarity, the process that each described illustrates how this film was, in fact, a negotiation of artistic styles, cultural traditions, and politics. To borrow a concept from Anna Tsing, the encounter between the culturally specific bodies and objects through a set of global circumstances also leads to a kind of "friction" that stands not only as obstacle, but also as a creative energy where new intercultural dialogues take place.[36] As imposed as these dialogues are—whether during the late 1940s setting of the film or the late 1980s socialist solidarity context of its making—they question the assumptions each country had about itself, its own power of authority, and its relationship to the other.

An overview of some of the film's major themes helps illustrate the point. Armin and the other defectors all exist in the mountain stronghold as displaced Germans, who are soon confronted with the limits of their ability to live among the villagers and aid the Viet Minh. These limits appear both internally and externally motivated on both sides. First, there is the increasingly evident misguided idealism of solidarity. This is clear in the way that Hai and his associates attempt to employ European individuals, European philosophy, and modern technology for Vietnam's liberation effort, and how those Europeans, embodied in the complicated post–World War II expatriate German soldier, seek purpose and meaning inside Vietnam's liberation struggle. Second, mutual distrust prohibits the realization of such ideals, as is clear in the village prohibition against Europeans carrying weapons to help defend the village against attack. Third, cultural misunderstandings ensue, evident most clearly in personal relationships (both romantic and platonic), as well as the Germans' desire for material comforts. Each narrative conflict appears to reinforce the respective national and cultural identities of each country, especially as they are located in a war emerging from a violent European–Southeast Asian colonial encounter. Even as these misunderstandings appear to reinforce stable national and cultural identities, however, the film also plays with them and critically engages with the idea of the nation-state through the combination of narrative techniques such as location, actions, and objects, bringing the different cultures and temporalities into dialogue.

## International Socialist Solidarity

As an international coproduction motivated by the international socialist solidarity movement, the uneven process of crossing and erecting borders resulted in a transnational production that engages with not only the misguided idealism of the film's conception, but also the stability of the nation that is inherent in such a movement. The narrative is set in Vietnam, which permits Germany, as a political and cultural entity contained by borders, to remain an unstable idea throughout, assembled fragmentarily through objects, bodies, images, and text. The tropical landscape locates the Vietnamese and their struggle geographically, highlighting the breach of Vietnam's territorial and political borders. Yet the setting does not limit the film's interrogation of a homogeneous Vietnamese nation-state either, as is clear when Armin and Hai travel together from the city into the mountainous liberated zone of Viet Bac—territory in the hands of the Viet Minh outside the center of French colonial power in Hanoi where political and military powers could be called into question.

For the Vietnamese, Armin and Hai's relocation to the mountains recalls Claire Sutherland's discussion of mountainous landscapes as a site where national myths were both built and undermined. Mountains marked Vietnam's "division into rival regions" in the seventeenth century, and colonial divisions in the twentieth century, reinforcing cultural difference, stereotypes, and varying allegiances within Vietnam's populace. Yet mountains are also allegedly important for unification purposes. For example, Sutherland describes the Truong Son range as the "backbone" of the country where Ho Chi Minh's trail was used to "liberate the South and to unify the country."[37] In *Dschungelzeit,* intellectuals such as Hai are influenced by Western thought, and they travel to the peasants to unify the nation against colonial aggression. Hai and his associates bring not only European thought but Europeans themselves, to help the cause.[38] This combination is what Sutherland has described as the Viet Minh's strategic combination of nationalism and internationalism, that is, the notion that through international socialist solidarity, the Vietnamese could find a forum for asserting their own self-determination and protecting Vietnamese traditions.[39]

The combination of nationalism and internationalism is projected onto the protagonist Armin, the "stateless" German, who appears at the center of the question of belonging. Interestingly enough, the printing apparatus that Armin is given to run also has German origins, and Armin's identity in the Viet Minh stronghold soon becomes tied to the German machine. When Hai brings him to the village, he introduces him as "Armin, originally from the country [Heimat] of the printing press." Here, he uses the word Heimat, this ideal and abstract notion of homeland that inherently suggests a sense of belonging. With Armin's exile after defection—first from Hitler's army, then from the French Foreign Legion—the suggestion of belonging evoked by the Heimat concept is striking, both for Armin and the bulky, metallic European printing apparatus. Here, the displaced machine extends to the displaced German, both located outside German national borders while simultaneously reminding us of them. Hoang explains that Armin's work in Vietnam will correspond to his talents as a printer, not a fighter: "If you don't want to go back, we would have work for you. You're a talented printer, right? ... Let the fight on the front be our problem. We're convinced of our victory. Every legionnaire who stops shooting us, who defects, who leaves Vietnam, is helping us." The printing press is reminiscent of Benedict Anderson asserting the primacy of the printed word in the sense of belonging to a singular—albeit imagined—national community.[40] In this moment, however, Armin uses the tool to aid the liberation of the Vietnamese nation rather than the reconstruction of the German one, which he has already rejected.

The different elements come together here. The "stateless" Armin assumes a role tied to the machine, a symbiosis that locates the transnational encounter between people and object for a cause beyond the nation, whether Vietnam or Germany. The object of pursuit is a more basic right at the heart of the international socialist ideal: liberation from the false consciousness imposed by imperialist (or capitalist) aggression that hinders collective access to basic human needs such as resources, personal development, and self-determination. These more universal ideals converge in the displaced Armin and his printing machine, locating the efforts of international solidarity through him. Still addressing Germans in the German language, the printing apparatus allows stateless Germans to communicate across borders in solidarity with the Viet Minh efforts to liberate Vietnam from colonial and imperial aggression, much the way the film apparatus does for a 1980s East German audience under the ideal of international socialist solidarity.

German print, however, is not only produced in the Viet Minh mountainous stronghold by Armin's printing press. Periodicals from East Germany imploring defectors to return "home" and help the newly liberated socialist East Germany's nation-building cause also move across Vietnam's borders and land in the mountains where the defectors are staying. Such correspondence actually undercuts the idealism of solidarity first suggested by Armin's position in the village and his enthusiasm to contribute to Vietnam's anti-colonial struggle. The announcement that Armin and his fellow Germans receive from this "new" Germany offers amnesty to all defectors: "Don't fight against a friend of the German people. Come home, return to Germany, where an honorable and meaningful life awaits you."

## Inability to Trust

By the 1950s, it was not only the GDR calling the defectors home. The Vietnamese were sending them home, a gesture that communicated their distrust of the Europeans' motives in northern Vietnam and their desire for self-determination and self-liberation without European intervention.[41] Though Europeans were welcomed into the ranks of the resistance in the 1940s, by as early as 1950, Chinese advisers had displaced the Europeans amid the ranks of the Viet Minh resistance. Armin's role with the printing press assures the transience of their stay, which corresponds with the historical dilemma Heinz Schütte follows in his biographical study of the legionnaires Erwin Borchers, Rudy Schröder and Ernst Frey. The film preserves a bit of the historical ambivalence that remained from the real history of German defectors in Vietnam.

The skepticism and distrust of the legionnaires was directed at Germany. This was a subtle critique that could be read for the postwar period of the film's setting, or the late 1980s context of its production. Armin's response to Hoang's initial suggestion that Armin go "home" to Germany was met with disbelief. Armin immediately rejects Comrade Hoang's suggestion of "a new Germany, a democratic one" with the declaration: "Never again Germany [*nie wieder Deutschland*]." Yet temporalities are blurred in these exchanges, with the film suggesting that audiences contemplate the skepticism toward the success of this "new" socialist Germany. For example, the announcement from East Germany is preceded by images of artifacts of this "new" Germany, such as the first East German stamp series from 1950, including one with the picture of a competitive skier leaning toward the lower left corner as he moves down the mountain, which, as filmmaker Jörg Foth pointed out, replaced the Nazi stamp from the 1936 Winter Olympics with the "visual replication" of a forward-leaning soldier.[42]

The suggestion of aesthetic continuities from Nazi Germany to postwar East Germany portrayed the inherent distrust that defectors felt toward the idea of a German homeland in 1949. But it might also mount a retrospective critique in the 1980s of East Germany's failure to separate its political moral compass entirely from the GDR's historical and current enemies—Nazi Germany and West Germany. This point is reinforced when Armin is tasked with opening a sack of intercepted German post, the contents of which initiate feelings of abandonment and displacement. Setting aside a letter, Armin says: "Here, a loathsome guy from Frankfurt is writing to his loathsome cousin in the Legion about how much he admires him." It is unclear if the letter is from Frankfurt am Main in West Germany or Frankfurt an der Oder in East Germany, an ambiguity that Foth indicates was written deliberately into the conception of the film, again pointing out that some of the moral lines between East and West Germany remained blurred. Ultimately, the defectors were not desired in their adopted homeland and were themselves skeptical about their "real" one, leaving the impression that any solidarity between German exiles and the Vietnamese rebels might be seen as instrumental at best. The bittersweet departure of the Germans from Vietnam back to Germany resonates in a film made thirty-five years later.

When the Germans finally leave the mountains and end their time with the Viet Minh, they must cross a bridge with paratroopers on the other side. As the troops start across the bridge, the camera zooms in to reveal that the paratroopers have the same faces as the defectors. The lack of European actors forced the Germans to pose as Frenchmen. Nevertheless, the soldiers open fire and the Germans in the bush retaliate, killing all the men on the bridge. In a violent juxtaposition, the images of murder cut to a sequence of serene close-ups of bright, tropical flowers, accompanied by the startling sounds of gunfire. The scene that Foth and Vu created resulted, on the one hand, from the imbalance of German-Vietnamese actors on set. On the other hand, it extended the narrative well beyond the circumstances of the nation-state and the international conflict to a modernist, psychological message. Foth reflected on a quote from Heiner Müller when discussing this scene: "The moment of truth—when in the mirror / the image of your enemy appears."[43] This self-reflexive scene first presents binaries such as good/bad, death/life, and man/nature; however, with the ugly sound of gunfire overlaying the images of flowers, it becomes clear that the human condition lies in the poise *between* these dualities, such that the men must overcome the binaries in themselves. The only undeniable "evil" in the film can be found in the common enemy: the French colonizers, the fascist imperialists, and—as the end shot reveals focusing on a gun that Hai hands to Armin—the American enemy backing the whole operation against the Viet Minh, as suggested by the gun label Ithaca Gun Co., Inc., from Ithaca, New York.

## Cultural Misunderstandings

In *Dschungelzeit,* moments of personal turmoil on the German side are experienced alongside the Vietnamese struggle. Often these struggles appear to run parallel rather than intersecting with each other, thanks to the friction of several cultural-historical disconnections. Since the film was dubbed in Vietnamese for Vietnamese audiences and in German for German audiences, for example, it is already difficult to trace the successes and failures of the cultural encounter at the level of language. There is one exception: Van's performance of the second act of the traditional Buddhist opera, *The Goddess of Thi Kinh,* which remains in Vietnamese in the German version of the film. Her performance, which tells the story of an injustice committed against the protagonist Thi Kinh, is visually interrupted with close-ups of Armin's hands opening the intercepted German mail that is marked with European handwriting and German stamps. The sequence shows a clear breakdown in the characters' abilities to put aside their differences. They are not presented as a unit, with the camera focusing instead on each face in turn, as they look off-camera and sneak stolen glances at each other, always avoiding eye contact. While Van's performance of Thi Kinh tells a story of "endurance and renunciation" as key to finding "liberation from prejudice," Armin's simultaneous task with the German mail reinforces his cynicism gained in exile and defeat.[44] Armin has found the contents of the German post far more affecting than this opera performance, which he, like German audiences watching the film, undoubtedly does not understand due to the lack of subtitles or voiceover, and most likely experiences as a merely colorful and exotic cultural moment. However, it is clear that Hai and Lien, who sit next to him, are fully absorbed by the message of injustice and perseverance in Van's performance of Thi Kinh.

In this sequence, dialogue, like the faces, is directed off camera until Armin finally decides to distract himself from his own despondency by turning his attention to Hai's parallel story of abandonment: "You're thinking of your wife," he says, to which Hai turns to him looking surprised and responds, "I love her very much." Unfortunately for Hai, his wife had grown tired of waiting for him to return home and moved to the center of enemy territory: France. This scene introduces another part of the narrative that is perhaps the film's most notable preservation of Vietnamese tradition: the unrequited love story. Van's performance of Thi Kinh suggests this to Vietnamese-speaking audiences, and it is only hinted at for German-speaking audiences by Lien's rather cynical comment of what they are watching: a performance about "how one is seduced," clearly identifying with the disappointed party in an unrequited love story. In the second act of Van's performance, the protagonist Thi Kinh, whose husband and love of her life falsely accused her of trying to murder him in act one, seeks social and familial rehabilitation by disguising herself as a male monk who joins a temple, where he/she meets a village woman whose unrequited love of him/her leads to more false accusations of a sexual affair and resultant (but impossible) pregnancy.

If love seems hopeless among the Vietnamese at this time of political upheaval, as Hai's failed marriage and Lien's unrequited love of Hai indicate, any of the possible relationships between German defectors and the village women also fail by the end of the movie. The defector Gecko offers a drunken proposal to one of the women, and insists on staying in Vietnam in order to marry. Though she flirts with him, the language barriers are too much of an obstacle for the relationship to gain any meaning beyond physical attraction. The young woman, Van, flirts shyly with Armin and fills in as caretaker when he is injured, but when Armin turns to "go home," she moves on with her village and their budding relationship is stopped short. According to the filmmaker Tran Vu, love narratives were a point of contention between the two directors.[45] The GDR team wanted to include a love relationship that corresponded with Borchers's actual long-term relationship with a Vietnamese woman, while Tran Vu and his team found the idea impossible. Yet the opportunity for defectors to stay in Vietnam after 1954 for marriage, ideology or otherwise, was the exception and not the rule.[46]

As the film's action is set at the start of the Cold War, and its time of production marks what came to be its end, this national extension to Southeast Asia in the name of solidarity begs reflection for the two political periods it represents. Hong has argued that "with the progress of decolonization, the Cold War was increasingly fought by the two German states within a global arena."[47] In the film, the German defectors' positions in Vietnam are precarious at best. They may only help by writing agitation literature until the village press is eventually destroyed. They are asked to aid in the anti-colonial cause by leaving the country and going "home"—a nonexistent place for the defectors, which we see with Armin's disbelief in the idea of a democratic Germany that Hoang insists on: "Home? There is no 'home' anymore. ... A democracy? Where does it come from, this country?" For Armin, Germany does not enjoy the right to start over; it has ties to its past that cannot be severed. Thus, he has cut his own ties to the idea of a German homeland. Armin and the other Germans build a "new" home there in the mountains, despite the warnings about their unstable position with the Viet Minh in northern Vietnam. The resultant structure, however, indicates their failure to adjust to their adopted home as well, and it suggests that they, too, have not severed all ties with their German past. Using natural materials from the jungle, they build a two-story European-style house with many of the comforts of home, such as running water. Unfortunately, the architectural structure is a clear target for enemy planes, virtually announcing that there is a Viet Minh stronghold in the village that is hiding defectors from the French Foreign Legion.

The construction of the makeshift home, rather than signifying permanence, is meaningful in its transience, and indicates a clear turning point for the Viet Minh and the Germans, which is foreshadowed by Van's solo of the revolutionary song, "Epic of the Lo River." The song was written by Vietnamese musician and Viet Minh resistance fighter Van Cao two years earlier (1947) in the aftermath of the French bombings of Viet Minh headquarters along the Lo River. It is briefly recontextualized during Van's performance, which is accompanied by the out-of-tune European instruments played by the German legionnaires at the housewarming celebration of their new home. For Vietnamese audiences, however, the song was undoubtedly viewed as a harbinger of the French bombing of the hamlet shortly after Van's performance, effectively forcing the villagers and their German comrades out of the mountains to futures unknown.

Despite the confusion and uncertainty after the bombing, the film does suggest how this moment of ruin might be read. Though the film credits list the song simply as "Vietnamese Folk Music," the historic events that surround Van Cao's composition, however devastating, were ultimately a victory for the Viet Minh. Moreover, the songwriter was as interesting as the song. Van Cao composed the national anthem of the Socialist Republic of Vietnam in 1944, "Marching Song," which Vietnamese audiences likely would have recognized immediately. One author describes the influence of Van Cao's anthem as transcending geography, class, and social station: "All the patriotic Vietnamese, from the national defending soldiers to the women operating in the jungles of the Northern Vietnam, the mothers in the Southern Vietnam's resistance area, the political prisoners on Con Dao (Poulo Condor) Island, on Phu Quoc Island, in Tong Nha (the Saigon regime's Police Headquarters), in Phu Loi prison, all sang the song, urging them to keep firm their fighting spirit, braving their lives in the fight against the enemy."[48] The patriotic and militaristic message of the implied anthem, of soldiers marching forward to fight the good fight for the nation, is an association made when the group marches out of the mountains to fight the war on the front. Moreover, for the German-speaking audiences who would lack the linguistic skills and cultural references, the German defectors' slow exploration of the rubble of their new home after the French bombs is interrupted with footage of rubble landscapes from Germany after World War II. This editing provides a visual reminder of the patriotic message of the East German national anthem, written by Hanns Eisler in 1949, the same year our protagonist leaves the Vietnamese mountains and "goes home": "From the ruins risen newly, to the future turned, we stand. Let us serve your good weal truly, Germany, our fatherland." Though the futures of the displaced Germans as they march out of the mountains with the villagers is unclear, the film suggests their return to the new Germany against this backdrop of a parallel history with the Vietnamese, which includes the occupation of imperial/fascist forces, the destruction of cities and infrastructure by foreign armies, and the rebuilding that takes place afterward under socialist leadership.

## Conclusion

*Dschungelzeit* reflects on the history of two nation-states' experience of war, initiating an intercultural dialogue about the limits of international solidarity. Despite both directors' motivations to make a film out of solidarity, the process of their collaboration drew attention to what those limitations were, and they also found their way into the film narrative: misguided idealism steeped in the asymmetrical power relations embedded in the ideology of solidarity; the enduring mutual distrust on each side; and the ongoing cultural misunderstandings that became evident in the limits of interpersonal relationships and language. By the same token, the film's long period of production itself constituted a kind of genuine, sustained economic and national exchange, followed by an end product that reproduced the very process of sticky cultural negotiation in its aesthetic, narrative, and intertextual dimensions. The conversation in both the production process and the film itself developed from "we" (the white GDR) know what "they" (nonwhite populaces) want, to discovering that "we" do not know and need to actually talk to "them." *Dschungelzeit*'s transnational soul-searching finds its purpose here after all, even if the film never found the audiences to appreciate it.

**Evan Torner** is an Assistant Professor of German Studies at the University of Cincinnati, having received his Ph.D. at the University of Massachusetts Amherst in 2013 and having spent 2013–14 at Grinnell College as an Andrew W. Mellon Postdoctoral Fellow. He has published on East Germany, critical race theory, science fiction, transnational genre cinema, and game studies. His projects underway include the *Handbook of East German Cinema: The DEFA Legacy* with Henning Wrage (Walter De Gruyter, 2017), a monograph based on his dissertation entitled *Solidarity? Race in East German Cinema* and the monograph *A Century and Beyond: Critical Readings of German Science-Fiction Cinema.*

**Victoria Rizo Lenshyn** is a PhD candidate in German and Scandinavian Studies at the University of Massachusetts Amherst, where she also received graduate certificates in Women, Gender and Sexuality Studies and in Film Studies. Her dissertation, *Bridging Contradictions: Socialist Actresses and Star Culture in the GDR,* examines the political and cultural meaning of celebrity, in particular that of female stars, in former East Germany as a contested concept under socialism. Her publications examine the national and international dimensions of DEFA films and actors, including a forthcoming co-edited volume on the international connections between GDR cinema and other national film industries and markets during the global Cold War.

# Notes

1. Noteworthy studies not immediately discussed below include Katrina Hagen, "Internationalism in Cold War Germany" (Ph.D. diss., University of Washington, 2008); Hans Siegfried Lamm and Siegfried Kupper, *DDR und Dritte Welt* (Munich: R. Oldenbourg Verlag, 1976); Harald Möller, *DDR und Dritte Welt* (Berlin: Köster, 2004); Achim Reichardt, *Nie Vergessen—Solidarität üben!* (Berlin: Kai Homilius, 2006); Arlene Teraoka, *East, West and Others: The Third World in Postwar German Literature* (Lincoln: University of Nebraska Press, 1996). See also Quinn Slobodian's essay on race and racism in this volume.
2. Thomas PM Barnett, *Romanian and East German Policies in the Third World: Comparing the Strategies of Ceaușescu and Honecker* (Westport: Praeger, 1992), 95.
3. Brigitte Schulz, *Development Policy in the Cold War Era: The Two Germanies and Sub-Saharan Africa, 1960-1985* (Münster: Lit, 1995), 74, 187.
4. Young-Sun Hong, "'The Benefits of Health Must Spread Among All': International Solidarity, Health and Race in the East German Encounter with the Third World," in *Socialist Modern: East German Everyday Culture and Politics,* ed. Katherine Pence and Paul Betts (Ann Arbor: University of Michigan Press, 2008), 193.
5. Hong's work constitutes a notable exception to this model, as can be also seen in her article for this edited volume. Jennifer Ruth Hosek, *Sun, Sex and Socialism: Cuba in the German Imaginary* (Toronto: University of Toronto Press, 2011) is another noteworthy transnational study that somewhat levels the playing field with regard to the North-South cultural exchange, namely, in the case of East Germany and Cuba.
6. DEFA stands for "Deutsche Film-Aktiengesellschaft"—literally "German Film Company."

7. Heinrich Sperker and Le Vien, "Vertreter des Vertrags zwischen dem VEB DEFA Außenhandel Berlin und dem Staatlichen Filmunternehmen der Demokratischen Republik Vietnam" (Hanoi: 17 May 1957). Archival documentation made available by Juliane Haase at the DEFA Stiftung in Berlin.

8. See, for example, the essays collected in Michael Wedel et al., eds., *DEFA international: grenzüberschreitende Filmbeziehungen vor und nach dem Mauerbau* (Wiesbaden: Springer, 2013).

9. Saer Maty Ba and Will Higbee, *De-Westernizing Film Studies* (New York: Routledge, 2012), 13. Another laudable collection of essays that accomplishes this is Natasa Durovicova and Kathleen E. Newman, *World Cinemas, Transnational Perspectives,* AFI Film Readers (New York: Routledge, 2010).

10. Heinz Schütte, *Zwischen den Fronten: Deutsche und österreichische Überläufer zum Viet Minh* (Berlin: Logos, 2006).

11. See the contract, "*Turm von Hanoi*: Vertrag zwischen dem Spielfilmstudio Vietnams und dem VEB DEFA-Studio für Spielfilme" (Hanoi: 3 October 1986), 11.

12. See Dieter Wolf, "Das andere Gesicht des Krieges. Dieter Wolf im Gespräch mit Tran Vu, Ko-Regisseur der ersten Koproduktion DDR-SRV: 'Dschungelzeit,'" *Film und Fernsehen* 4 (1988): 44–49; Evan Torner, "Apocalypse Hanoi: An Interview with Joerg Foth about *Dschungelzeit* (1988)," *Guy in the Black Hat* (blog), last modified 22 September 2011, http://guyintheblackhat.wordpress.com/2011/09/22/apocalypse-hanoi-an-interview-with-joerg-foth-about-dschungelzeit-1988/ (accessed 15 October 2012).

13. See, for example, depictions of the alienation felt by Chilean exiles living in the GDR in films such as *Verzeihung, sehen Sie Fussball?* (1983, dir. Gunther Scholz), *Isabel auf der Treppe* (1984, dir. Hannelore Unterberg), and *Blonder Tango* (1985, dir. Lothar Warneke); or the disheartenment at the idea that regular East German (financial) donations to the Vietnamese casualties of the American War in Vietnam were meaningful, as seen in *Die Taube auf dem Dach* (1973, dir. Iris Gusner). Such themes in the feature films were in contrast to propaganda films like *400cm³* (1966, dirs. Walter Heynowski & Gerhard Scheumann), which showed East Germans dutifully entering a blood bank to donate blood to the injured Vietnamese.

14. Möller, *DDR und Dritte Welt*, 9; Barnett, *Romanian and East German Policies in the Third World*, 5; Schulz, *Development Policy in the Cold War Era*, 23.

15. See Nina Glick Schiller, Linda G. Basch, and Cristina Szanton Blanc, *Towards a Transnational Perspective on Migration: Race, Class, Ethnicity, and Nationalism Reconsidered* (New York, NY: New York Academy of Sciences, 1992); Arjun Appadurai, *Modernity at Large: Cultural Dimensions of Globalization* (Minneapolis: University of Minnesota Press, 1996), 48–65. See also Young-Sun Hong, "The Challenge of Transnational History," *H-German FORUM* (19 January 2006), http://h-net.msu.edu/cgi-bin/logbrowse.pl?trx=vx&list=h-german&month=0601&week=c&msg=Ug5gaQJIb0mI99%2B4nOj7Ww&user=&pw= (accessed 19 January 2009).

16. Randall Halle, *German Film after Germany: Toward a Transnational Aesthetic* (Urbana: University of Illinois Press, 2008), 28.

17. For what many consider to be the field's seminal article, see Tim Bergfelder, "National, Transnational or Supranational Cinema? Rethinking European Film Studies,"

*Media, Culture & Society* 27, no. 3 (2005): 315–31. See also Elizabeth Ezra and Terry Rowden, eds., *Transnational Cinema: The Film Reader* (New York: Routledge, 2006).

18. Mette Hjort, "On the Plurality of Cinematic Transnationalism," in *World Cinemas, Transnational Perspectives*, ed. Natasa Durovicova and Kathleen E. Newman (New York: Routledge, 2010), 13.

19. This cynical evaluation and self-reflection of the actual coproduction "activity" is evident in an interview Evan Torner conducted with *Dschungelzeit* director Joerg Foth on 5 October 2010 (see footnote 12). It also constitutes a kind of "third rail" of film scholarship, that the right to film is associated with the right to travel—given comparisons with academia—although it is a topic to be found in Hosek, *Sun, Sex and Socialism*.

20. Schütte, *Zwischen den Fronten*, 24–26.

21. Odd Arne Westad, *The Global Cold War: Third World Interventions and the Makings of Our Times* (New York: Cambridge University Press, 2007), 158–206.

22. For more on the history of Vietnamese laborers in the GDR, see Karin Weiss and Mike Dennis, eds., *Erfolg in der Nische?: die Vietnamesen in der DDR und in Ostdeutschland* (Münster: Lit, 2005). See also Marianne Krüger-Potratz, Georg Hansen, and Dirk Jasper, *Anderssein gab es nicht: Ausländer und Minderheiten in der DDR* (New York: Waxmann, 1991); and Eva Kolinsky, "Meanings of Migration in East Germany and the West German Model," in *United and Divided: Germany since 1990*, ed. Mike Dennis and Eva Kolinsky (New York: Berghahn Books, 2004), 145–75.

23. Christina Schwenkel, "Post/Socialist Affect: Ruination and Reconstruction of the Nation in Urban Vietnam," *Cultural Anthropology* 28, no. 2 (2013): 252–77.

24. Claire Sutherland, *Soldered States: Nation-Building in Germany and Vietnam* (Manchester: Manchester University Press, 2010).

25. On the level of media exchange, Vietnam had been a limited market for French-dubbed DEFA films since the late 1950s. The contract signed in Hanoi dated 17 May 1957 and one in East Berlin dated 9 February 1960 specify how these DEFA films were to circulate in Vietnam, though the complete list of circulating titles is not currently available.

26. While it appears peculiar that the GDR would portray American resistance in a postcolonial war, several DEFA productions in the 1950s were preoccupied with American workers victimized by and struggling against domination by their capitalist masters. Two examples are *Lied der Ströme* (1954, dir. Joris Ivens) and *Hotelboy Ed Martin* (1955, dir. Karl-Heinz Bieber).

27. Dieter Wolf, *Gruppe Babelsberg: unsere nichtgedrehten Filme* (Berlin: Das Neue Berlin, 2000), 176–77.

28. Key documentaries on Vietnam by Heynowski and Scheumann include, but are not limited to: *400 cm³* (1967), *Piloten im Pyjama* (1968), *100* (1971), *Remington Cal. 12* (1972), *Vietnam 1-4* (1976–77), *Am Wassergraben* (1978), and *Ein Vietnamflüchtling* (1979). For more on Studio H&S and their work, see Rüdiger Steinmetz, "Heynoski & Scheumann: The GDR's Leading Documentary Film Team," *Historical Journal of Film, Radio and Television* 24, no. 3 (2004): 365–79; see also Nora

M. Alter, *Projecting History: German Nonfiction Cinema, 1967-2000* (Ann Arbor: University of Michigan Press, 2002), 13–42.

29. Joerg Foth, *Regiekonzeption: Turm von Hanoi* (Berlin: 27 October 1984).

30. Joerg Foth, excerpted and translated from Evan Torner's email exchange with the director (4 January 2014).

31. Based on private discussions with the director Foth and producer Hans-Erich Busch conducted by Evan Torner in November 2011.

32. See Torner, "Apocalypse Hanoi," 2010. Solidarity initiatives were commonplace in the GDR and, as Young-Sun Hong's and Christina Schwenkel's entries in this volume demonstrate, genuine empathy toward populations perceived as oppressed *did* emerge, especially among the younger GDR generations. Foth's affect could be seen as a product of the times in which he lived.

33. Wolf, "Das andere Gesicht des Krieges," 47.

34. Ibid.

35. Carl Heinz Choynski, *Det is nich allet Kunst!: ein Schauspielerleben* (Berlin: Das Neue Berlin, 2011), doi:9783360021205, 173.

36. Anna Lowenhaupt Tsing, *Friction: An Ethnography of Global Connection* (Princeton: Princeton University Press, 2005).

37. Sutherland, *Soldered States: Nation-Building in Germany and Vietnam*, 38.

38. Hai in this fashion rubs against the grain of historical resistance leaders such as Ho Chi Minh, Pol Pot, and Yeng Sari, who may have spent some time in France, but primarily studied in China, underscoring long-term suspicion toward Western and Central Europe in the Viet Minh movement. Nevertheless, according to Foth, artifacts of European affinity remained behind. For example, Vu himself was never without his blue plastic Air France handbag.

39. Sutherland, *Soldered States: Nation-Building in Germany and Vietnam*, 42–43, 66–71.

40. Benedict R. O'G Anderson, *Imagined Communities* (London: Verso, 1983).

41. Schütte, *Zwischen den Fronten: Deutsche und österreichische Überläufer zum Viet Minh*, 202, 266–69.

42. E-mail conversation among Jörg Foth, Evan Torner, and Victoria Lenshyn. 8 October 2012.

43. Torner, "Apocalypse Hanoi," 2010. There are also affinities with Ho Chi Minh's aphorism that "Good and evil are not inborn traits." This was also a popular sentiment at the time, illustrated by the Pogo strip with the quote: "We have met the enemy and he is us." The flower images echo the flower's role as an international symbol against the American invasion in Vietnam, with the most famous example being the Flower Power march against the Pentagon on 21 October 1967.

44. Tai Thu Nguyen, *History of Buddhism in Vietnam* (Washington, D.C.: Council for Research in Values & Philosophy, 2009), 180.

45. Wolf, "Das andere Gesicht des Krieges," 47–48.

46. Erwin Borchers, for example, married a Vietnamese woman and stayed until 1966. Schütte, *Zwischen den Fronten: Deutsche und österreichische Überläufer zum Viet Minh*, 278.

47. Hong, "'The Benefits of Health Must Spread Among All'," 184.

48. Ngo Ngoc Ngu Long quoted in Dale A. Olsen, *Popular Music of Vietnam: The Politics of Remembering, the Economics of Forgetting* (New York: Routledge, 2008), 133.

# Bibliography

Alter, Nora M. *Projecting History: German Nonfiction Cinema, 1967-2000.* Ann Arbor: University of Michigan Press, 2002.

Anderson, Benedict R. O'G. *Imagined Communities.* London: Verso, 1983.

Appadurai, Arjun. *Modernity at Large: Cultural Dimensions of Globalization.* Minneapolis: University of Minnesota Press, 1996.

Ba, Saer Maty, and Will Higbee. *De-Westernizing Film Studies.* New York: Routledge, 2012.

Barnett, Thomas PM. *Romanian and East German Policies in the Third World: Comparing the Strategies of Ceauşescu and Honecker.* Westport: Praeger, 1992.

Bergfelder, Tim. "National, Transnational or Supranational Cinema? Rethinking European Film Studies." *Media, Culture & Society* 27, no. 3 (2005): 315–31.

Choynski, Carl Heinz. *Det is nich allet Kunst!: ein Schauspielerleben.* Berlin: Das Neue Berlin, 2011. doi:9783360021205.

Durovicova, Natasa, and Kathleen E. Newman. *World Cinemas, Transnational Perspectives.* AFI Film Readers. New York: Routledge, 2010.

Ezra, Elizabeth, and Terry Rowden, eds. *Transnational Cinema: The Film Reader.* New York: Routledge, 2006.

Hagen, Katrina. "Internationalism in Cold War Germany." Ph.D. diss., University of Washington, 2008.

Halle, Randall. *German Film after Germany: Toward a Transnational Aesthetic.* Urbana: University of Illinois Press, 2008.

Hjort, Mette. "On the Plurality of Cinematic Transnationalism." In *World Cinemas, Transnational Perspectives,* ed. Natasa Durovicova and Kathleen E. Newman, 12–33. New York: Routledge, 2010.

Hong, Young-Sun. "'The Benefits of Health Must Spread Among All': International Solidarity, Health and Race in the East German Encounter with the Third World." In *Socialist Modern: East German Everyday Culture and Politics,* ed. Katherine Pence and Paul Betts, 183–210. Ann Arbor: University of Michigan Press, 2008.

Hosek, Jennifer Ruth. *Sun, Sex and Socialism: Cuba in the German Imaginary.* Toronto: University of Toronto Press, 2011.

Kolinsky, Eva. "Meanings of Migration in East Germany and the West German Model." In *United and Divided: Germany since 1990,* ed. Mike Dennis and Eva Kolinsky, 145–75. New York: Berghahn Books, 2004.

Krüger-Potratz, Marianne, Georg Hansen, and Dirk Jasper. *Anderssein gab es nicht: Ausländer und Minderheiten in der DDR.* New York: Waxmann, 1991.

Lamm, Hans Siegfried, and Siegfried Kupper. *DDR und Dritte Welt.* Munich: R. Oldenbourg Verlag, 1976.

Möller, Harald. *DDR und Dritte Welt.* Berlin: Köster, 2004.

Nguyen, Tai Thu. *History of Buddhism in Vietnam.* Washington, D.C.: Council for Research in Values & Philosophy, 2009.

Olsen, Dale A. *Popular Music of Vietnam: The Politics of Remembering, the Economics of Forgetting.* New York: Routledge, 2008.

Reichardt, Achim. *Nie Vergessen – Solidarität üben!* Berlin: Kai Homilius, 2006.

Schiller, Nina Glick, Linda G. Basch, and Cristina Szanton Blanc. *Towards a Transna-*

*tional Perspective on Migration: Race, Class, Ethnicity, and Nationalism Reconsidered.* New York: New York Academy of Sciences, 1992.

Schulz, Brigitte. *Development Policy in the Cold War Era: The Two Germanies and Sub-Saharan Africa, 1960–1985.* Münster: Lit, 1995.

Schütte, Heinz. *Zwischen den Fronten: Deutsche und österreichische Überläufer zum Viet Minh.* Berlin: Logos, 2006.

Schwenkel, Christina. "Post/Socialist Affect: Ruination and Reconstruction of the Nation in Urban Vietnam." *Cultural Anthropology* 28, no. 2 (2013): 252–77.

Steinmetz, Rüdiger. "Heynoski & Scheumann: The GDR's Leading Documentary Film Team." *Historical Journal of Film, Radio and Television* 24, no. 3 (2004): 365–79.

Sutherland, Claire. *Soldered States: Nation-Building in Germany and Vietnam.* Manchester: Manchester University Press, 2010.

Teraoka, Arlene. *East, West and Others: The Third World in Postwar German Literature.* Lincoln: University of Nebraska Press, 1996.

Tsing, Anna Lowenhaupt. *Friction: An Ethnography of Global Connection.* Princeton: Princeton University Press, 2005.

Wedel, Michael, Barton Byg, Andy Räder, Skyler Arndt-Briggs, and Evan Torner, eds. *DEFA international: grenzüberschreitende Filmbeziehungen vor und nach dem Mauerbau.* Wiesbaden: Springer, 2013.

Weiss, Karin, and Mike Dennis, eds. *Erfolg in der Nische?: die Vietnamesen in der DDR und in Ostdeutschland.* Münster: Lit, 2005.

Westad, Odd Arne. *The Global Cold War: Third World Interventions and the Makings of Our Times.* New York: Cambridge University Press, 2007.

Wolf, Dieter. *Gruppe Babelsberg: unsere nichtgedrehten Filme.* Berlin: Das Neue Berlin, 2000.

# PART V

# Internationalist Remains

# Chapter 11

# Affective Solidarities and East German Reconstruction of Postwar Vietnam

*Christina Schwenkel*

The year 2010 saw a large number of commemorative activities in Vietnam, including the millennial anniversary of the founding of the capital city of Hanoi. It also marked the *Year of Germany in Vietnam,* celebrating thirty-five years of diplomatic relations between the two countries. Advertisements and promotional materials announced more than fifty events over twelve months in Hanoi and Ho Chi Minh City focusing on the arts, the environment, and urban living. Both German President Horst Köhler and Vietnamese President Nguyễn Minh Triết enthusiastically supported the collaborative project and its broader vision of productive exchanges in culture, technology, and education with the aim to foster closer economic cooperation through expanded trade and foreign investment.

The observance of the thirty-five-year milestone received broad coverage in the Vietnamese press, with entire periodicals, such as the *Vietnam Business Forum,* devoted to exploring the "broad and warm ties" that bound the two countries since 23 September 1975. The date, however, made for an awkward political dilemma given that it expunged a lengthier history of diplomacy between Vietnam and the German Democratic Republic (GDR) dating back to 1950. Privileging the Bundesrepublik as the starting point of bilateral relations with the Socialist Republic of Vietnam served to sideline the morally questionable role that West Germany had played in the U.S. "war of aggression," as it was called in Hanoi, with its political and financial support of the United States and the Republic of (South) Vietnam. More important for this chapter is the erasure of forty years of East German diplomatic history and, in turn, the affects and sensibilities that formed through diverse forms of "solidarity assistance" during and after the war with the United States that laid the foundation for the "warmth" experienced between the two countries today.

Strategic forgetfulness to advance foreign policy is a common practice of governance. Not without ambivalence, states frequently choose to tactically disremember certain pasts and shelve lingering animosities in order to rebuild relations, even in the absence of formal redress and reparations. Such gestures of rapprochement may not be entirely voluntary. One need only consider the coercive nature of diplomacy and the asymmetrical relations of power that govern international affairs. The political and economic ties that subsequently develop may also prove mutually advantageous. Germany, for example, remains Vietnam's principal trading partner in the European Union, with bilateral trade reaching USD 7.42 billion in 2013.[1] The United States, on the other hand, holds the position of Vietnam's second largest trading partner, only after China—yet another country with which strategic forgetting of past transgressions has also become a geopolitical and economic necessity.[2]

The erasure of GDR diplomatic history in Vietnam risks discounting the extent to which contemporary development initiatives and their capitalist achievements have foundations in the socialist past. Some of Vietnam's major exports to Germany today, including coffee and cashew nuts, are the lasting product of mutual assistance programs of the 1980s designed to alleviate scarcities and bring economic and infrastructural benefits to both socialist countries.[3] Whether these programs were a success or failure is not my concern here. Rather, I am interested in, first, the impact that these forms of assistance had on individual lives both in Vietnam and Germany today, from practitioners who worked on-site to beneficiaries of aid; and second, how the material and technological legacies of "solidarity" continue to be experienced and remembered by people today. President Triết himself recognized this pivotal past when he met with Egon Krenz, the former General Secretary of the SED, in September 2010, an event that was not included in the official program of the *Deutschland Jahr in Vietnam* but was nonetheless covered in the Vietnamese press.[4] The performative enactment of socialist formalities, including the use of a fraternal discourse to express sentiments of unity and enduring camaraderie, reaffirmed the instrumental role of the GDR in Vietnam's "struggle for national independence," as Triết articulated to Krenz. This differed remarkably from the forward-looking economic rationality voiced by Köhler and Triết that underpinned the thirty-five-year anniversary festivities. Through his proxemic interactions, press photographs conveyed the differing affective connections of Triết, positioned between a meaningful socialist past (with Krenz) and a promising capitalist future (with Köhler). The lingering double handshake between Krenz and Triết, whose close corporeal proximity and fixed eye contact suggested familiarity and mutual respect, contrasted starkly with the reserved, one-hand shake between Köhler and Triết, whose forward-leaning stance to offset bodily distance conveyed a more cautious and formal relationship.

It is the lingering sentiment of solidarity (*tình đoàn kết*) expressed in the meeting between Krenz and Triết that I examine in this chapter. I use the term "sentiment" to move beyond state rhetoric and official policy to get at the meaningful, lived experiences of internationalism and the cross-cultural collaborations that transpired to give between East German and Vietnamese citizens shape to what I am calling "affective solidarities." I use the plural to highlight the multiplicity of meanings and associations that overlapped, diverged, and at times bumped up against one another. Theorizations of solidarity have typically focused on the realm of political rationality and the ability of solidarity discourses to foment political agency, galvanize loyalties, and transform geopolitical practices.[5] Here I am concerned with more affective domains of sentiment, and the role they have played in making and sustaining strongly felt dispositions of human connectedness in the post–Cold War era. A focus on affectivity does not reduce the concept of solidarity to an essentialist belief in a global humanity with shared interests and sympathies that unconditionally unite all of humankind.[6] It does, however, maintain that solidarity can be more than a mere "politics machine" productive of political subjectivities and state ideologies alone.[7] As Alexei Yurchak reminds us, "for many, 'socialism' as a system of human values and as an everyday reality of 'normal life' (*normal'naia zhizn'*) was not necessarily equivalent to 'the state' or 'ideology'; indeed, living socialism … often meant something quite different from the official interpretations provided by state rhetoric."[8]

My intention is not to glorify or idealize the notion of solidarity (or "living socialism" for that matter), or to accept it uncritically as an unproblematic given. Yet I do seek to move the discussion beyond the conventional belief that solidarity must be something inauthentic, naïve, manipulated, and imposed from above. As an anthropologist, I am interested in the diverse and, at times, conflicting articulations of solidarity expressed by people who were responsible for putting socialist policy into action. By shifting the lens to affect, I go beyond official ideology and atomized feelings to get at the intersubjective attachments and bonds that formed between people through in-field practices of "anti-imperialist solidarity" that continue to resonate and form the basis of human relationships today. When contextualized within the history of a war that incited mass global protest, the desire to act internationally in support of a "fraternal" (*brüderlich*) socialist country signified as much an ethical as a political stance against imperialism and war. In contrast to West German anti-war activists who were unable to put their politics into direct action given their location in a country aligned with forces bent on subverting the revolution, for East Germans who worked in Vietnam (and they numbered in the hundreds), solidarity was more than distanced, sympathetic identification with the struggles of Third World Others.[9] As the object of acts of solidarity, the Vietnamese population did not remain wholly abstract and unknowable as Weis argues in the case of GDR support of SWAPO.[10] Nor did they exist merely as tokens of racial otherness, though clearly imaginaries of the heroic Other underpinned and motivated the dynamics of their work. Rather, because of the urgent need for total urban reconstruction, specialists were assigned to travel to and live in Vietnam for extended periods of time (from one to two years, and sometimes more) during and immediately after the war, allowing for their humanist ethics and political values to coalesce in the collective work of rebuilding a devastated city.

As this volume makes clear, the GDR had an extensive history of advocating support for, and practicing solidarity with, the revolutions that were unfolding across the socialist Third World after the end of the Second World War. Indeed, Honecker's call for "Solidarität mit Vietnam—jetzt erst recht!" (Solidarity with Vietnam—now more than ever!) captured the postracial idealism *of fraternal equality* that informed proletarian internationalism of the time. In this chapter, I am interested in the translation of official state discourses of *Solidarität,* such as that expressed by Honecker, into meaningful social practice that gave shape to new communities of sentiment among citizens of the GDR and Vietnam. And yet, in no way did affective solidarity transcend racial and gendered difference as the socialist state promoted; rather, otherness was fundamentally reaffirmed through the global inequalities that structured the very need for and ability to carry out such work. Images conveyed through the East German press of fellow citizens helping their noble brothers in Vietnam proved a powerful discursive and ideological force that suggested the GDR's material and technological capabilities to bring about change in an underdeveloped and subjugated socialist country.

## "Solidarität hilft siegen": Victory through Solidarity

Historically, anti-colonial and anti-imperial resistance movements have been far more effective at fomenting sentiments of international solidarity that transcend national borders than the class-based concept of proletarian internationalism. As Eric J. Hobsbawm has argued, the international labor movement faced particular difficulties in galvanizing a strong sense of shared proletarian identity and transborder solidarity due to dissimilar labor interests and work environments, despite Marx and Engels's assertions to the contrary.[11] Today, few question the idea that workers around the world experience capitalist oppression in vastly different ways owing to geopolitical inequalities and the racialization and gendering of laboring bodies. While the moral teachings of working-class internationalism strove to educate the masses about the racial and gender equality of all peoples, in practice, such lessons proved difficult to realize, as Slobodian argues about state anti-racism

**Figure 11.1.** Poster of GDR solidarity, War Remnants Museum, Ho Chi Minh City, 2006

policies in this volume's introduction. Yet moral discourses of shared humanity did shape and inspire a dynamic ethos of anti-imperialist solidarity for anti-war activists who identified with the subjugated masses of Third World Others. As Hannah Arendt has argued, the principle of solidarity suggests the formation of nonhierarchical communities of common interest that incite and guide political action.[12] During the war in Vietnam, this ethical and ideological position allowed for a stronger sense of shared identification to emerge among the population of anti-war activists that centered on a common and concrete enemy—imperialism—rather than a more abstracted proletarian identity that was difficult to articulate across industrialized (worker-driven) and agricultural (peasant-based) economies.

This is most clearly articulated in the example of the war in Vietnam, when local Vietnamese experiences with U.S. military violence were taken up as global socialist concerns across the communist bloc. In East Germany, racialized representations of the Vietnamese people as gentle and innocent kin in need of help—often expressed through the image of the child—fueled empathic sentiments, as they did around the world (e.g., through the image of the burned body of Phan Thị Kim Phúc).[13] Solidarity campaigns in East Germany, through voluntary and coerced mechanisms, garnered extensive humanitarian and other aid to Vietnam, the most abundant of any European socialist country.[14] This socialist *assistance,* as it was called to differentiate such support from capitalist *aid* (1994), extended back to 1950 after diplomatic ties were first established with the Democratic Republic of Vietnam (DRV) at the height of its revolution and war of resistance against French colonialism.[15] In these early years, the GDR offered technical and financial support to aid the process of building a postcolonial nation-state under the leadership of Hồ Chí Minh, including the construction of a printing house, the training of Vietnamese secret service and police by the Ministry of State Security, and the production of Vietnamese currency in East Germany (see Schaefer's contribution in this volume). Instrumental military assistance, as per an agreement with the Ministry of National Defense in 1956, also materialized in the form of weapons, training, and equipment—support that continued through the war with the United States.[16] On the humanitarian front, the renovation of the colonial Yersin Hospital in Hanoi led to the technologically advanced *Bệnh viện Hữu nghị Việt Nam—CHDC Đức* (Vietnam-Democratic Republic of Germany Friendship Hospital) in 1958, which to this day remains one of Vietnam's largest and most respected centers for orthopedic surgery.[17] In the pursuit of national and international self-interest, this scope of assistance emboldened the GDR government to make even stronger moral and political claims to its self-ascribed role as benevolent and generous benefactor to subjugated Third World countries.

As war with the United States escalated in the 1960s, the official solidarity movement called upon citizens to show their strong support for *das sozialistische Bruderland*. The use of socialist kinship terminology in political discourse and the media emerged as an effective rhetorical device to evoke the affective ties formed in the collective struggle against imperialism coupled with the social and economic obligations that accompanied the bonds of socialist siblinghood. Under the motto *Solidarität hilft siegen* (Solidarity brings victory), the East German government depicted itself as playing an active and pivotal role on the global stage in the united front supporting Vietnam's anti-colonial struggle. East Germans of all ages, some passionately, others begrudgingly, responded to calls for *Solidaritätsaktionen* to support the "just struggle" of the "heroic Vietnamese" through their encouraged participation in anti-war demonstrations, the crafting of children's protest letters sent to the White House, blood drives, food donations, fundraisers, information sessions, and solidarity work with visiting Vietnamese delegations, among other social and political activities intended to secure a steady flow of donations.[18]

The GDR press represented such forms of political mobilization as the public's commitment to, and embodiment of, a socialist ethos of humanitarian internationalism to demonstrate the nation's resolute adherence to its political and moral principles to the world, especially the capitalist West. In Vietnam, on the other hand, the besieged socialist state viewed the material, financial, and technological support provided by the GDR as pivotal in the war against the United States. Even today, Vietnamese citizens remember such assistance as having made critical contributions to the war effort, both materially and psychologically. Such support continues to be recognized and commemorated in Vietnam at museum and other public exhibitions, but it also suggests in controversial ways (in Vietnam), a greater *international* role in achieving independence that complicates the image of a poor but resilient people single-handedly standing up against a stronger and better equipped enemy.

After U.S. air strikes ended in early January 1973, the focus of the GDR's support shifted to national reconstruction. A decade of extensive air strikes had left most of northern Vietnam's industry and infrastructure in ruins. In a display of international socialist solidarity, communist countries from Cuba to North Korea pledged to assist Vietnam in its economic recovery. A bilateral agreement between the GDR and the DRV signed on 9 January 1973 charted a plan for mutual assistance that stipulated an increase in material aid and further cooperation in the fields of science and technology in exchange for market access to much needed Vietnamese-produced food and manufactured goods.[19] While the GDR provided technical and medical assistance in the form of diesel engines, electronics, medical equipment,

**Figure 11.2.** "The GDR Supported Vietnam" exhibit, War Remnants Museum, Ho Chi Minh City, 2006

industrial machinery, and construction materials, the DRV exported to East Germany agricultural foods and products from its craft and textile industry. Over and above government aid, individual citizens and mass organizations collected more than 30 million Marks of solidarity donations, referred to as

*Solidaritätsspenden,* to help fund educational and humanitarian projects that included restoration of the Friendship Hospital in Hanoi and the construction of training centers for craft and trade workers.[20]

With its emphasis on sustaining the "spirit of socialist internationalism" (*Geist des sozialistischen Internationalismus*), the media stepped up efforts to thwart compassion fatigue and maintain popular support for the strengthening of aid in a moment when the war appeared to be ending in Vietnam's favor. By February 1973, the amount of assistance extended to the DRV, as reported in the press, amounted to more than 1.5 billion GDR Marks, including a total of 56 million GDR Marks as charitable donations.[21] Not unlike the case of North Korea, the GDR emerged as one of the largest providers of postwar international aid to Vietnam, second only to the Soviet Union.[22] Similarly, much of this aid was channeled into urban areas ravaged by U.S. *Luftterror,* or what the Vietnamese called the "war of destruction" carried out by American *Luftpiraten* or "air pirates" (*giặc lái*).[23]

East Germany's extensive experience with urban reconstruction of postwar industrial cities, both nationally (e.g., Dresden) and internationally (e.g., Hamhùng, North Korea) was well known in the DRV and prompted Hanoi to approach Berlin for assistance with rebuilding Vinh City, one of the country's most devastated urban areas, located in the impoverished province of Nghệ An. During the war, massive carpet-bombing between 1964 and 1973 took a heavy toll on the city, leaving it uninhabitable with few intact structures and no remaining industry. Reporting from Hanoi, the GDR war correspondent Hellmut Kapfenberger described the provincial capital as having been "virtually wiped out" (*nahezu ausradiert wurde*).[24] In interviews, GDR technicians likewise referred to the emptied city as a moonscape, while Vietnamese locals, who had evacuated to mountainous areas, described returning to a flattened landscape littered with smoking ruins and bomb craters. On 19 May 1973, Prime Minister Phạm Văn Đồng sent a letter to the Chairman of the Council of Ministers in the GDR requesting assistance with the city's reconstruction. Perhaps seeing an opportunity to boost its international image through urban renewal of yet another international city,[25] the GDR government swiftly agreed to take on what would become the largest and most successful urban reconstruction project in Vietnam. One month later, on 20 June, Chairman Willi Stoph confirmed with Hanoi that the Central Committee of the SED and the GDR government, "in an expression of solidarity and fraternal bonding with the Vietnamese people" would provide the necessary financial and material assistance to support the redesign and reconstruction of Vinh.[26]

Bilateral and global ambitions motivated this new stage of cooperation between the GDR and the DRV. Berlin's missive to Hanoi affirmed that such assistance would foster closer fraternal ties between the people and the parties of both countries, while continuing to strengthen and build international socialism. Four months later, on 22 October 1973, representatives of the DRV and the GDR signed the agreement in Berlin. The seven-year project (initially through 1978, later extended to 1980) would involve more than two hundred East German experts and thousands of Vietnamese workers and specialists.[27] Notably, it was the only major international project in the DRV at the time that required the long-term residency of large groups of foreigners. As such, although relations between nationals and nonnationals were closely monitored and certain interactions forbidden (such as sexual relations and visits to Vietnamese homes), everyday contact did take place, mostly but not only at the work site. Friendships formed, and are still maintained today owing to new forms of social media and the ease of international travel. To adhere to the claim of "no contact" between East Germans and others as found in much of the literature would be to deny historical agency and the lived experiences of internationalism. It also risks reproducing the very discourse of isolation that attention to socialist global connectivities has disrupted.[28] Including the voices and the stories of people involved in these transnational projects, as I do below, presents a very different story that unsettles easy assumptions that policy and politics define the parameters of human experience.

Officials in Hanoi applauded the bilateral agreement to rebuild Vinh, as did local authorities in Nghệ An. In a public speech in Berlin days before its ratification, Communist Party Secretary Nguyễn Duy Trinh declared to the East German population, "Your solidarity is true internationalism."[29] On the one hand, the interpretation of solidarity voiced here in a context of international diplomacy linked the material and spatial properties of the built environment—the rebuilt industrial city—to an authenticated political allegiance. On the other hand, for the practitioners on the ground whose job it was to embody and perform internationalism through the labor of reconstruction, solidarity came to take on other, acutely personal meaning. It is to these experiential dimensions and their emotional sensibilities that I now turn.

## Urban Reconstruction and Affective Attachments in Vinh

During the Cold War, the circulation of architectural knowledge and urban planning practices among fraternal socialist countries, particularly between the East bloc and Third World, served to reify particular visions of urban futurity rooted in ideologies of industrial productivity and egalitarian modes of living. For East Germany, the circulation of capital, material resources, scientific technologies, and technical expertise was central to its assistance to wartime and postwar Vietnam and put into practice an ethos of anti-imperialist solidarity endorsed by the state and anti-war activists. East Germany's paramount project, entitled "Assistance in the Construction and Design of Vinh City" [*Hilfe beim Aufbau und bei der Projektierung der Stadt Vinh*], aimed to transform the devastated and impoverished provincial capital. From a postwar landscape dotted with ruins and makeshift shelters would emerge a modern industrial city with new and rebuilt factories, wide boulevards, city parks, schools and daycares, a stadium, trade center, cinema, central market, and high-rise block housing. Similar to other model socialist cities around the world, Vinh was to become a municipal center for civilizing and transforming rural workers into industrious, urban citizens.[30] Not unlike GDR projects in Tanzania and North Korea (see also Young-Sun Hong's contribution to this volume), this would be accomplished through the construction and allocation of high-rise public housing—a first in Vinh City—meant to evince socialist prosperity through advanced technological infrastructure and modern standards of living.

The *Wohnkomplex* or microdistrict of Quang Trung became the largest and most ambitious urban project to showcase East German scientific and technical ingenuity. Designed to be a self-contained residential area with apartment blocks and on-site public goods and services, the *Wohnkomplex* was a modality of urban planning and social-spatial engineering that traveled to Vinh via East German experts and Vietnamese architects who had studied in Moscow or Weimar.[31] Like other mass housing projects, Quang Trung required a large swath of land—in this case thirty hectares in the city center—on which to build thirty-six five-story blocks that could house more than fifteen thousand "priority" residents (cadres and workers with revolutionary credentials or exceptional job performance) in need of permanent housing. Owing to the country's demolished infrastructure, all manufacturing equipment and essential construction materials, from cranes down to screws and nails, had to be donated by East German enterprises and then transported by sea from Rostock to Vietnam. The almost magical and sudden appearance of mechanized technology across the city—bulldozers, lorries, industrial and truck-mounted cranes (FH 1600s, MB88s, ADK 70s…), cars, hoists, excavators, stone crushers, pumps, pipes, and steel—seemed to reaffirm the economic and techno-scientific superiority of East Germany and the backwardness of Vietnamese society. The presence of such material abundance, as well as strong and able-bodied men amid extreme destitution and devastation reinforced among the local population an optimistic belief in socialism as the best path to urban development, well-being, and plentitude.[32]

For the East German practitioners I interviewed, the reconstruction work they carried out in Vietnam represented an important formative period of their lives that they continue to remember fondly today.[33] Representing a broad range of expertise, groups of up to forty specialists traveled to Vietnam on one- or two-year renewable contracts that came with substantial perks (such as additional income paid by the Vietnamese government).[34] Several stayed more than one term, and more than a dozen have returned to revisit the city and their Vietnamese colleagues since reunification. The majority of experts were men, with the exception of a small number of women, mainly cooks and administrators, who accompanied their husbands. Although they lived and ate separately from local residents (with German foodstuffs imported each quarter), the experts worked closely with Vietnamese specialists and brigades of skilled workers, and at times engaging in sporting events after hours. Vladislav Todorov has referred to the intimacy of such everyday, routine relations, which fostered a meaningful sense of "collective comradeship," as "technological togetherness."[35] I use the term affective solidarity to get at the shared sensibilities and emotional affinities that transpired over time, and were often considered to transcend racial, national, gender, and even linguistic barriers. Tensions regarding conflicting work ethics and "different understandings of time," according to one GDR expert, surfaced in the workplace owing to the constant pressure to build quickly and efficiently. Yet the planners and engineers I interviewed recalled work relations as typically amicable and mutually supportive. Several considered themselves active participants in the struggle against U.S. imperialism. Their expressions of empathy toward the Vietnamese, coupled with a strong belief in their equality as fellow human beings resonated with official doctrines of anti-racism at the time and were fundamental to their understanding of solidarity as informed by deeply moral, humanitarian, and political commitments.

As a central conflict zone, Vinh had been heavily mined and bombed for years before the experts arrived. The specter of danger, especially of unexploded ordnance (UXO), had an ominous presence during their stay (and still does today in some areas) and influenced their mobility and labor. Reconstruction inevitably became high-risk work for all involved, however disproportionately, as GDR specialists were not involved in UXO removal. And yet, carried out collectively in construction zones scattered with warning signs, the shared exposure to hazards served to strengthen the sentimental alliances among both groups, according to Vietnamese and East German respondents. For example, residents of Quang Trung housing often commented to me that East German specialists, unlike other nationals, refused to abandon their work site in the face of mounting threats, from the peril of war to the devastating flood of 1978 when other foreign specialists chose to evacuate to Hanoi. Not only did GDR experts refuse to leave, residents recollected, but they also joined in the efforts to fortify the dyke and prevent rising floodwaters from further engulfing the city. In their view, this showed a genuine commitment to solidarity work.

Both groups remembered the period of reconstruction as a time of hardship and scarcity, reinforcing a sense of shared vulnerability, even if the parameters of experience differed markedly. East German workers were considerably better off and could always leave if medically or otherwise necessary (and some did). One man died by electrocution on his last day of work. This was a story frequently recalled by his compatriots and Vietnamese housing residents, who remembered the untimely "sacrifice" (*hy sinh*) and its exact location in the complex. In the early years of the project, while the war continued in the South, experts also had to contend with shortages and tactical difficulties from the demolition of urban infrastructure—for example, a lack of power, potable water, and standing bridges—though these obstructions and their potential health repercussions (as illness did figure into their memories) paled in comparison to the daily suffering endured by the local population. The GDR experts recognized, rather uncomfortably, the vast disparities between the two groups despite the narrative of postracial unity and shared socialist prosperity. While the Vietnamese went hungry, beholden to a failed ration system, the East Germans were comparatively well fed. And yet, in conversations, both Vietnamese and East Germans recalled the redistribution of material wealth under prohibitive conditions, such as covertly passing out chocolate, cigarettes, meat, and beer to Vietnamese co-workers and children away from the eyes of local police. Such acts of care and their material effects reaffirmed in memory the sentimental bonds of solidarity for each side.

In their attempt to overcome racial and social difference, East German experts did not dwell on the inequalities that set them apart from the Vietnamese. Instead they emphasized the work of reconstruction as *coproduction* within a cohesive moral community. Their understanding of solidarity, in other words, was rooted in the affective *process* rather than material *product* (the built environment) as seen with the Vietnamese delegation in Berlin earlier in the chapter. Experts emphasized mutuality, interdependence, embeddedness, and semblance. Ideas were shared, codeveloped, and negotiated. Joint work and action informed the urban planning and implementation process (though labor was highly differentiated, for example, women were involved in bricklaying and construction under German and Vietnamese male supervision). Structural inequality, however, threatened to undermine this narrative aspiration.

The emphasis on balanced contributions at times shifted to claims about the full empowerment of the Vietnamese team in an effort to distinguish socialist solidarity work from liberal development projects. In the word of one chief architect: "Urban planning was completely in the hands of the Vietnamese. They had the ultimate say in the plans. We were only there to support and advise them."[36] Toni Weis has argued that the discursive construction (and performance) of solidarity in the GDR placed it in radical opposition to Western notions of development, considered a "capitalist smokescreen" for the continuation of neo-colonial rule rather then a means to procure independence.[37] As a discursive apparatus and applied practice, GDR solidarity was tethered less to a distanced politics of pity as identified in liberal humanitarianism than to a posture of proximate sympathy and a common will to act.[38] Indeed, the French etymological roots of solidarity point to a mutuality of commitment rather than "suffering at a distance."[39] Yet, similarities may offset the differences given that both "solidarity" and "development" worked to facilitate military expansion and secure new market transactions, though in dissimilar ways and to radically different ends. Moreover, despite the emphasis on social equality and supranational alliances, *Hilfe*, the official term adopted in GDR project documents (help, or *giúp đỡ* in Vietnamese), suggested an uneven and hierarchical power relationship also found in development practices: there existed a benefactor who bequeathed and a beneficiary who received.

GDR experts tended to distance themselves from the intimations of paternalism embodied in the term *Hilfe* in order to set themselves apart morally and politically from so-called neocolonial projects. The ideological positioning that underpinned and informed the work of reconstruction was captured in a three-part series on Vinh entitled "Solidarität in Aktion," published in the periodical *Die Brücke* in 1981. Dieter Stöhr, head of operations at Eisenberg Transport Engineering who worked in Vinh from 1979 to 1980, wrote the op-ed pieces at a moment when the project was coming to an end, but had yet to be completed. In Stöhr's narrative, it was through the beneficence of the GDR state (materialized in the labor of the specialists) and an evolving productive partnership, that their Vietnamese counterparts had become increasingly self-reliant in rebuilding their city and transforming it into a prosperous center of culture and industry: "The Vietnamese people saw this kind of solidarity as essential. No paternalism in the form of colonial domination, just genuine assistance that guaranteed the autonomous development of their country."[40] Stöhr thus portrayed the project of reconstruction in purely benevolent, but nonetheless enabling, terms. Beholden to an aim of national autonomy and self-sufficiency, the anti-paternalism of solidarity resonated ironically with liberal (and neoliberal) ideals of self-reliance and self-care. Because of its purely altruistic aim, Stöhr went on to claim, GDR assistance was highly regarded and celebrated in Vietnam.

Stöhr's assessment was not entirely off the mark. East German support was—and still is—regarded highly in Vinh, but not for its material and technical achievements alone. In 2010–11, I spent nine months in the housing blocks conducting ethnographic research on postsocialist redevelopment of the *Wohnkomplex*. On a daily basis, I interacted and spoke with the original recipients of apartments, the "priority" residents who make up more than 60 percent of the housing population today. This included a number of architects who codesigned the original blueprints, electrical engineers who built the power lines, female bricklayers who laid the foundation for the blocks, and so forth. While GDR understandings of solidarity had been closely tied to a vision of *collaborative* practices, for the Vietnamese, solidarity assumed a deeper meaning in relation to the steadfast *commitment* of the experts to fulfill their obligations to the city. Residents expressed being moved emotionally (*cảm động*) by the willingness of the technicians to leave behind their families and the material comforts of home to travel to war-torn Vietnam and *stay*. They were the only group of foreigners, I was frequently told, to do so (the other exception, some would raise, being the Cubans farther south). Their achievements were also contrasted with failed socialist projects in other urban areas that never came to fruition for reasons that often lay beyond the control of the allied country. This had no effect, however, on their affective attachments: in the thinking of much of the older population in Vinh, the East Germans had come and fulfilled their promise to rebuild the city.

After its construction, Quang Trung housing, with its staggered rows of five-story buildings, came to stand as a unifying symbol of the pride of the city, though there were complaints that its "foreign" style did not fit with local cultural practices of dwelling.[41] One woman explained the symbolic meaning of the high-rises to her in a celebratory narrative of modernity that was common among older residents. After the war, there was little left in the city but rubble and ruin until the East Germans came and helped to construct "beautiful and modern" buildings with "spacious, bright, and well-ventilated" flats. There were kitchens, bathrooms, and indoor plumbing. These were a first for most tenants who were used to living with rudimentary, shared facilities. In socialist internationalist terms, Quang Trung had been a solidarity gift bestowed upon the Vietnamese by their socialist kin (*anh em*) in the GDR. Residents pointed to the letters "VĐ" (Việt Đức; Vietnam-Germany) above each building entrance as a material reminder of the meaningful sentiments (*tình cảm*) and bonds of friendship (*hữu nghị*) that the gift of reconstruction had sealed historically between the two countries.

The affective ties that formed over the course of the seven-year project are still felt strongly today by the war-era generations of residents and

**Figure 11.3.** Vietnam-Germany (Việt Đức), Block A5

continue to animate their recollections of reconstruction. Casual conversations and interviews produced entertaining stories of GDR experts cycling around the city in European summer clothing, of receiving candies on the streets as young children playing outside their homes, of the professional and yet joking relationships that transpired at the workplace, and of the teasing interactions with female workers. In the teleological understanding of socialist progress as moving through distinct stages of material and technological development, Vietnamese residents rationalized the hierarchical division of labor between East German engineers and Vietnamese laborers, and the large gap between the GDR's relative wealth and Vietnam's entrenched poverty, as a reflection of the natural order of things. In contrast to Vietnam, which had been held back economically by a history of colonial exploitation and imperial aggression, the GDR was considered more advanced technologically, its standard of living higher, and its society "more civilized" (*văn minh hơn*). For the hundreds of Vinh City residents who had worked or studied in the GDR, East Germany had been a "paradise" (*thiên đường*) compared with their own impoverished conditions.[42] And while the new façade of their city conveyed an image of socialist modernity and postwar recovery, infrastructure breakdown from a lack of maintenance kept residents from enjoying socialism's promise of betterment. Even the admired fountain that Stöhr had designed and built as a space of leisure and a symbol of prosperity stopped flowing for a lack of water soon after the experts departed.

## Transmission of Affect: Sustaining Sentiments of Solidarity Back Home

By the end of 1980, GDR state funds had run out and reconstruction was brought to a halt before Areas D and E in the Quang Trung *Wohnkomplex* could be completed. A faltering economy back home, as well as mounting difficulties securing goods through patronage networks of donation and distribution, led to an official decision not to further extend the agreement. In interviews, East German technicians expressed that the difficult task of rebuilding an annihilated city lacking in infrastructure jointly with the Vietnamese had been tremendously challenging and yet deeply rewarding. For them, the Vietnamese were a group of individuals who were more than abstract targets of technical assistance, but nonetheless exemplified a glorified image of Third World peasants up against a modern imperial power.

During their terms of contract, these technicians often projected their political passions and attachments both internally toward the immediate work at hand in Vietnam, and also externally, back home in letters to family members and reports to the media. The GDR government recognized the strategic importance of conveying these intimate experiences to the East German public to showcase the success and productivity of the GDR's policies of international socialism in action abroad. Print media became particularly useful in encouraging and reaffirming a sympathetic public in the GDR in hopes of sustaining active support for Vietnam. It was through eyewitness accounts from the experts published in the local and national press that East Germans learned about, and could follow the progress of, the reconstruction efforts taking place in Nghệ An. The series of articles in *Die Brücke* was just one example of how the media interpellated the readership as active international participants, channeling political agency and desires—or compulsions—to help into progressive solidarity activities at home. As Stöhr related in his first article in 1981, it was through such mediated coverage in East Germany that the name of *Vinh* emerged as a metonym for "solidarity with Vietnam."[43]

News coverage in the early years of reconstruction had the task of rationalizing and justifying socialist intervention in Vietnam. On 28 January 1974, one year to the day that the ceasefire in Vietnam had gone into effect (an anniversary noted in the GDR press), the *Freiheit Halle* newspaper printed an exclusive interview with Dr. Karl-Heinz Schlesier, one of the project's chief urban planners. Born in 1932, Schlesier had served as deputy chief architect of the team of urban planners that had rebuilt Dessau (1958–64) and then as chief architect on the construction of Halle-Neustadt from 1964 to 1973. In 1973, he traveled to Vietnam as part of the first delegation of urban planners to tour and assess the condition of Nghệ An, and he subsequently served as Deputy Head of the GDR Working Group of Vinh (*Arbeitsgruppe der DDR Vinh*) until 1975 when he was called back to East Germany to participate in Honecker's *Wohnungsbauprogramm (Mass Housing Program)*. In my interviews with him, Schlesier emphasized both the political and humanitarian concerns that motivated his work in Vietnam. The war against the United States had weighed heavily on him he told me. He had grown up during the Second World War and identified strongly with pacifism and anti-militarism. Like many in the GDR at the time, he had also aligned himself with the anti-colonial revolutions unfolding in the Third World, and especially the struggle against American imperialism in Vietnam. The reports of abuse, torture, and death appalled him, he recalled. He viewed his participation in Vinh's reconstruction as a way to contribute directly to Vietnam's struggle—which he described in moral terms as a small and impoverished country up against a brutal and powerful imperial enemy—as well as to its victory.[44]

The dialogue with Schlesier in the *Freiheit Halle* marked the start of a series of articles on Vinh over the next six months. The individual pieces introduced the readership to the history and culture of Nghệ An, to its mass destruction, and to the early phases of the city's reconstruction (a linear narrative also repeated in *Die Brücke,* which focused on the last phase of the project rather than its first). In the January 1974 discussion, Schlesier shared his first impressions of Vinh: a ravaged city with hopeful, spirited people—reifying an image of the heroic population as poor and yet happy, victimized and yet invincible. Indeed one of the accompanying photos in the article showed a Vietnamese woman as she paused from the arduous labor of filling bomb craters to smile for the camera. Through persuasive descriptions and images, Schlesier's words were intended to elicit powerful sentiments of compassion and, more importantly, an enduring sense of responsibility toward the Vietnamese even after the end of the air war. "Vinh is totally destroyed, but not dead," he commented to the journalist. "It lives and is more alive than ever," he asserted, drawing on the romantic trope of the indestructible spirit of a noble peasant nation.[45] But its residents also faced tremendous challenges including a critical lack of education and health facilities for children, he added, leading up to the article's objective. Here text and image served to hail readers as much-needed participants in the effort to rebuild Vinh—international solidarity workers from afar. Schlesier beckoned to his fellow citizens, appealing to their sympathies, to help the residents of Vinh, and especially their children, to overcome insurmountable difficulties through additional solidarity donations. Such moral and political appeals proved effective at mobilizing another round of support: a few months later, on 1 June, and again on 6 June, the *Freiheit Halle* reported on the construction of a teaching college in Vinh funded by individual (including student) contributions to Halle's mass organizations. The *Geist* of international solidarity as coproduction—even at a distance—appeared to have been campaigned successfully if not affectively, as evident in the article's bold headline: "Wir bauen mit an der Hochschule für Vinh!" (Together we build a college for Vinh!).[46] As Gerd Horten has documented, this moment in the early to mid 1970s marked the high point of solidarity between a period of resistance to official campaigns in the early years of war and the waning of its emotive appeal after reunification and the defeat of the United States, despite GDR state efforts to maintain its momentum.[47]

## Conclusion: Remembering and Forgetting the GDR in Vietnam

During the Cold War, socialist assistance was key to building strong diplomatic relations between the then-called Second and Third Worlds. Aid was explicitly political and ideological, as it is inclined to be between countries; there was nothing uniquely socialist there. One goal of governmental aid is to strengthen state alliances and reaffirm political friendships. Likewise, the acceptance of diplomatic gifts in the form of capital, commodities, technology, or even human resources (technicians, trainees, workers, etc.), serves to lock two countries in a dense web of mutual obligation and reciprocity. Circulations of aid can likewise reveal competing spheres of interest seeking greater political influence, as Armstrong shows transpired between the Soviet Union and China in their rival support of North Korea, and then again in Vietnam, which emerged as the new battleground for struggles over power and aid.[48] And yet for the practitioners who carried out these projects, as I have shown above, socialist assistance also enabled a more humanist ethics of solidarity to be put into practice, an ethics that was deeply political, optimistic, and future-oriented. Unlike humanitarianism today, solidarity work did not maintain a semblance of neutrality.[49] The overt goal, on the contrary, was to overthrow imperialism and establish a new society founded on a set of values that many GDR experts genuinely believed in (such as justice and equality). As such, in the case of urban reconstruction in Vinh, solidarity was less a means to express support for a political *system* than it was to support a political *cause* and *solution*.

And yet, there was much more to the practice of international solidarity during the war in Vietnam, not least because of the manifold understandings of what solidarity stood for and meant. While, for governments, the economic and material obligations were of key diplomatic importance, for the people engaged in the work of solidarity, the human dimensions—the sentiments and attachments that developed around ideas of cooperation (for the East Germans) and commitment (for the Vietnamese)—were just as significant and motivating. Such affects, and the people who voiced them, are often left out in analyses that privilege the political and ideological, denying historical agency and the possibility of human bonding. While recognizing that affect is itself deeply political and may be used by the state to harness political passions for nation-building, a focus on affective solidarities allows for narrative stories and recollections of the *lived* experiences of international solidarity to emerge, even as these experiences were highly differentiated, if not at times laden with contradiction.[50] Memories of the attachments formed under the banner of solidarity should not simply be dismissed as nostalgic yearnings for a socialist past when relationships were considered more authentic. Cross-cultural tensions surfaced intermittently in the process of reconstruction. Yet framed as overwhelmingly positive, these narratives also point to the meaningful values attached to solidarity's productive work—to the labor and materiality of urban reconstruction—that continue to shape lives and subjectivities today.

Returning to the thirty-fifth anniversary and the *Year of Germany in Vietnam,* what might it mean for the reunified Germany to acknowledge this material history in its foreign policy relations with the Socialist Republic of Vietnam today? Might the story of Vinh (with beneficiaries rather than victims) pose a threat to its growing influence in the region given its own questionable role in the war? In a recent book, the East German war correspondent Hellmut Kapfenberger claims, rather uncritically, that contrary to the West, East Germans have few regrets or shame when it comes to their actions during the war.[51] Whether accurate or not, much effort has been made to remove this past from the political and material landscape. For the Vietnamese state, the unspoken rules of diplomacy have changed considerably with new packages of aid and prospects of foreign investment. Perhaps it is not surprising, then, that many projects supported by German official development assistance (ODA) have focused on the city of Vinh, including support for the demolition of the decaying blocks in Quang Trung. It may be that Vietnam—if not Vinh—has emerged as a new battleground of German memory politics. Yet the GDR might have the advantage here, at least in Nghệ An, far from the national capital of Hanoi. Memories of solidarity remain strong and influential, not least because of the moral subjectivities and transnational connectivities that formed: from Vietnamese students and workers in East Germany who continue to hold onto their cosmopolitan identities to East German experts who retain their high status and respect in Nghệ An. These social bonds and relationships will be more difficult to expunge, even as they exist in uneasy tension with the tacit demands of a new political economic order built upon a now-discredited past.

**Christina Schwenkel** is associate professor of anthropology at the University of California Riverside and author of *The American War in Contemporary Vietnam: Transnational Remembrance and Representation*. She has conducted historical and ethnographic research in Vietnam and Germany on transnational coproductions of postwar memory. Her recent work "Imaging Humanity: Socialist Film and Transnational Memories of the War in Vietnam" examines East German and Cuban documentaries of the bombing of northern Vietnam. She is currently writing a book about socialist urban design and postwar reconstruction of Vinh City with the material and technical assistance of East Germany.

## Notes

1. "Beziehungen zwischen Vietnam und Deutschland." Auswärtiges Amt, March 2014. http://www.auswaertiges-amt.de/DE/Aussenpolitik/Laender/Laenderinfos/Vietnam/Bilateral_node.html.
2. Christina Schwenkel, *The American War in Contemporary Vietnam: Transnational Remembrance and Representation* (Bloomington: Indiana University Press, 2009).
3. See Bernd Schaefer's contribution to this volume and Nguyễn Thanh Đức, *Quân Hệ Thương Mại Và Đầu Tư Việt Nam—CHLB Đức [Trade and Investment Relations between Vietnam and the Federal Republic of Germany]* (Hanoi: Khoa Học Xã Hội, 2005).
4. See, for example, "Việt Nam luôn ghi nhớ sự ủng hộ của CHDC Đức [Vietnam will always remember the support of the Democratic Republic of Germany]." Lao Động [Labor], 15 September 2010, http://laodong.com.vn/Doi-ngoai/Viet-Nam-luon-ghi-nho-su-ung-ho-cua-CHDC-Duc/15796.bld.
5. David Featherstone, *Solidarity: Hidden Histories and Geographies of Internationalism* (New York: Zed Books, 2012), 16. A significant exception is Herbert Marcuse. For his distinction between "solidarity of sentiment" and "solidarity of interests" see Quinn Slobodian, *Foreign Front: Third World Politics in Sixties West Germany* (Durham: Duke University Press, 2012), 97–98.
6. For example, as espoused by International Human Solidarity Day on 20 December, underwritten by the United Nations as a day to "celebrate our unity in diversity." http://www.un.org/en/events/humansolidarityday/.

7. Cf. Toni Weis, "The Politics Machine: On the Concept of 'Solidarity' in East German Support for SWAPO," *Journal of Southern African Studies* 2 (June 2011): 367.

8. Alexei Yurchak, *Everything Was Forever, Until It Was No More: The Last Soviet Generation*, In-Formation Series (Princeton: Princeton University Press, 2006), 8.

9. Slobodian, *Foreign Front*, 99. Günter Wernicke, "'Solidarität Hilft Siegen!' Zur Solidaritätsbewegung Mit Vietnam in Beiden Deutschen Staaten," *Hefte zur DDR-Geschichte*, no. 72 (2001).

10. Weis, "The Politics Machine: On the Concept of 'Solidarity' in East German Support for SWAPO," 361.

11. Hobsbawm quotes an address delivered by Engels at the Federation of Nations in London in 1945 where Engels declared "the proletarians in all countries have one in the same interest, one in the same enemy, and one in the same struggle." Eric J. Hobsbawm, "Working Class Internationalism," in *Internationalism in the Labor Movement, 1830-1940*, ed. Frits van Holthoon and Marcel van der Linden (Leiden: EJ Brill, 1988), 8.

12. Hannah Arendt, *On Revolution* (New York: Penguin Books, 2006).

13. Christina Schwenkel, "Imaging Humanity: Socialist Film and Transnational Memories of the War in Vietnam," in *Transnational Memory: Circulation, Articulation, Scales*, ed. Chiara De Cesari and Ann Rigney (Boston: De Gruyter, 2014).

14. Gerd Horten, "Sailing in the Shadow of the Vietnam War: The GDR Government and the 'Vietnam Bonus' of the Early 1970s," *German Studies Review* 36, no. 3 (October 2013): 567; Wernicke, "'Solidarität Hilft Siegen!'," 44–45.

15. Jude Howell, "The End of an Era: The Rise and Fall of G.D.R. Aid," *The Journal of Modern African Studies* 32, no. 2 (1994).

16. Vietnam National Archives III, Văn Phòng Chính Phủ 1957–1995, File 7409.

17. In 1991, the name of the hospital was changed to the "Vietnam-Germany Hospital" [*Bệnh viện Việt Nam—Đức*], thus expunging the history of GDR humanitarian support from the urban landscape. Note the term "friendship" [*hữu nghị*] from socialist terminology has been removed in this instance, as well as in the diplomatic exchange between Triết and Köhler for the thirty-fifth anniversary celebration, though it was notably used at the Triết–Krenz reunion.

18. Vietnam National Archives III, Văn Phòng Chính Phủ 1957–1995, File 7409; Bundesarchiv, Berlin, File DY24 8760; Hoover Archives, Stanford University.

19. Vietnam National Archives III, Văn Phòng Chính Phủ 1957–1995, File 7409.

20. "Solidarität mit dem Volk Vietnams in der DDR tief verwurzelt." *Neues Deutschland*, 11 January 1973; see also Horten, "Sailing in the Shadow of the Vietnam War," 570–71.

21. "Werkstätten für Vietnam," *Neue Zeit*, 20 February 1973. The Vietnamese government reported the amount of GDR support during the American War years of 1965 to 1973 as 270 million Rubles, of which 150.3 million Rubles constituted "free" (non-repayable) aid. Vietnam National Archives III, Văn Phòng Phủ Thủ Tướng 1954–1985, File 9132.

22. Vietnam National Archives III, Văn Phòng Phủ Thủ Tướng 1954–1985, File 5578. Charles K. Armstrong, "'Fraternal Socialism': The International Reconstruction of North Korea, 1953–62," *Cold War History* 5, no. 2 (2005).

23. On the role of U.S. *Luftpiraten* in East German documentary films, see Nora M. Alter, "Excessive Pre/Requisites: Vietnam through the East German Lens," *Cultural Critique*, no. 35 (Winter 1996–97). Schwenkel, "Imaging Humanity."

24. "Neues Kapitel in der Chronik der Stadt Vinh," *Neues Deutschland*, 12 August 1973.

25. On Hamhùng, North Korea, see Hong in this volume and Rüdiger Frank, *Die DDR Und Nordkorea: Der Wiederaufbau Der Stadt Hamhung Von 1954–1962* (Aachen: Shaker Verlag, 1996). On Zanzibar and Tanzania, see Garth A. Myers, *Verandahs of Power: Colonialism and Space in Urban Africa* (Syracuse: Syracuse University Press, 2003), chap. 6.

26. Vietnam National Archives III, Văn Phòng Phủ Thủ Tướng 1954–1985, File 4409.

27. The architects Otto Knauer and Hans Grotewohl—son of GDR President Otto Grotewohl—who designed and directed the reconstruction of Hamhùng, and Dr. Karl-Heinz Schlesier, one of the chief architects in the construction of Halle-Neustadt, headed the *Arbeitsgruppe* (work unit) in Vinh.

28. Christina Schwenkel, "Rethinking Asian Mobilities: Socialist Migration and Post-Socialist Repatriation of Vietnamese Contract Workers in East Germany," *Critical Asian Studies* 46, no. 2 (2014); Anne E. Gorsuch and Diane Koenker, eds., *The Socialist Sixties: Crossing Borders in the Second World* (Bloomington: Indiana University Press, 2013).

29. "Eure Solidarität das ist wahrer Internationalismus." *Neues Deutschland*, 21 October 1973.

30. See Lewis H. Siegelbaum, "Modernity Unbound: The New Soviet City of Sixties," in *The Socialist Sixties: Crossing Borders in the Second World*, ed. Anne E. Gorsuch and Diane Koenker (Bloomington: Indiana University Press, 2013).

31. However, note that these were brick, not prefabricated housing or *Plattenbauten*. Christina Schwenkel, "Post/Socialist Affect: Ruination and Reconstruction of the Nation in Urban Vietnam," *Cultural Anthropology* 28, no. 2 (2013). On the Soviet-influenced microdistricts—or microrayons—in East German urban planning see Greg Castillo, "Promoting Socialist Cities and Citizens: East Germany's National Building Program," in *Selling Modernity: Advertising in Twentieth-Century Germany*, ed. Pamela E. Swett, S. Jonathan Wiesen, and Jonathan R. Zatlin (Durham: Duke University Press, 2007).

32. The Vietnamese government drew a clear line, however, between aspirations for *national* development and *individual* consumption. It took great cautions to limit Vietnamese access to East German lifestyles and consumer practices that were considered "bourgeois socialist" so as not to create a desire for goods that the postwar state could not provide. Martin Grossheim, "'Revisionism' in the Democratic Republic of Vietnam: New Evidence from the East German Archives," *Cold War History* 5, no. 4 (2005): 451–77.

33. Interviews were carried out in Germany in 2006, 2008, 2011, and 2012. Fieldwork in Vinh City was carried out in 2006 and 2009, and again in 2010–11, during which I lived in the *Wohnkomplex* of Quang Trung.

34. For example, one architect continued to receive his monthly income in the GDR of 600 East German Marks, in addition to 1,000 Deutsch Marks paid by the Vietnamese government, which he could use to purchase goods from the GENEX catalog at home or convert to Vietnamese *đồng* at a set rate of 1.66 DM to one Vietnamese

*đồng* for the purchase of local and imported goods, such as cigarettes or beer (at 1 *đồng* per bottle).

35. Vladislav Todorov, *Red Square, Black Square: Organon for Revolutionary Imagination* (Albany: State University of New York Press, 1995), 48.
36. Interview, 21 August 2012, Berlin.
37. Weis, "The Politics Machine: On the Concept of 'Solidarity' in East German Support for SWAPO," 357.
38. Arendt, *On Revolution.*
39. Luc Boltanski, *Distant Suffering: Morality, Media, and Politics* (New York: Cambridge University Press, 1999).
40. Dieter Stöhr, "Solidarität in Aktion," *Die Brücke,* no. 8 (1981).
41. Myers also uses the term of pride to describe how urban residents in Zanzibar felt about the Michenzani housing complex, built by the GDR. Myers, *Verandahs of Power.* Christina Schwenkel, "Traveling Architecture: East German Urban Designs Abroad," *International Journal for History, Culture and Modernity* 2, no. 2 (2014): 155–74.
42. Schwenkel, "Rethinking Asian Mobilities," 248. On the trope of paradise in recollections of Mozambicans who studied in East Germany see Tanja R. Müller, "'Memories of Paradise'—Legacies of Socialist Education in Mozambique," *African Affairs* 109, no. 436 (2010): 451–70.
43. Stöhr, "Solidarität in Aktion."
44. Interviews with Dr. Schlesier took place in Berlin, twice at the "Viet Haus" at his request, in 2006, 2008, 2011, and 2012.
45. "Zerstörtes Vinh ist voller Leben," *Freiheit Halle,* 28 January 1974; Further reports from Schlesier on the status of the project in Vinh can be found in the 17 May and 28 June editions.
46. "Wir bauen mit an der Hochschule für Vinh," *Freiheit Halle,* 6 June 1974.
47. Horten, "Sailing in the Shadow of the Vietnam War," 568–71.
48. Armstrong, "'Fraternal Socialism'."
49. See Didier Fassin, *Humanitarian Reason: A Moral History of the Present Times* (Berkeley: University of California Press, 2012).
50. Schwenkel, "Post/Socialist Affect."
51. Hellmut Kapfenberger, *Berlin—Bonn—Saigon—Hanoi: Zur Geschichte Der Deutsch-Vietnamesischen Beziehungen* (Berlin: Verlag Wiljo Heinen, 2013).

## Bibliography

Alter, Nora M. "Excessive Pre/Requisites: Vietnam through the East German Lens." *Cultural Critique,* no. 35 (Winter 1996–97): 39–79.

Arendt, Hannah. *On Revolution.* New York: Penguin Books, 2006.

Armstrong, Charles K. "'Fraternal Socialism': The International Reconstruction of North Korea, 1953-62." *Cold War History* 5, no. 2 (2005): 161–87.

Boltanski, Luc. *Distant Suffering: Morality, Media, and Politics.* New York: Cambridge University Press, 1999.

Castillo, Greg. "Promoting Socialist Cities and Citizens: East Germany's National Building Program." In *Selling Modernity: Advertising in Twentieth-Century Germany,* ed.

Pamela E. Swett, S. Jonathan Wiesen, and Jonathan R. Zatlin, 287–306. Durham: Duke University Press, 2007.

Fassin, Didier. *Humanitarian Reason: A Moral History of the Present Times*. Berkeley: University of California Press, 2012.

Featherstone, David. *Solidarity: Hidden Histories and Geographies of Internationalism*. New York: Zed Books, 2012.

Frank, Rüdiger. *Die DDR Und Nordkorea: Der Wiederaufbau Der Stadt Hamhung Von 1954-1962*. Aachen: Shaker Verlag, 1996.

Gorsuch, Anne E., and Diane Koenker, eds. *The Socialist Sixties: Crossing Borders in the Second World*. Bloomington: Indiana University Press, 2013.

Grossheim, Martin. "'Revisionism' in the Democratic Republic of Vietnam: New Evidence from the East German Archives." *Cold War History* 5, no. 4 (2005): 451–77.

Hobsbawm, Eric J. "Working Class Internationalism." In *Internationalism in the Labor Movement, 1830-1940*, ed. Frits van Holthoon and Marcel van der Linden, 1–16. Leiden: EJ Brill, 1988.

Horten, Gerd. "Sailing in the Shadow of the Vietnam War: The GDR Government and the 'Vietnam Bonus' of the Early 1970s." *German Studies Review* 36, no. 3 (October 2013): 557–78.

Howell, Jude. "The End of an Era: The Rise and Fall of G.D.R. Aid." *The Journal of Modern African Studies* 32, no. 2 (1994): 305–28.

Kapfenberger, Hellmut. *Berlin—Bonn—Saigon—Hanoi: Zur Geschichte Der Deutsch-Vietnamesischen Beziehungen*. Berlin: Verlag Wiljo Heinen, 2013.

Müller, Tanja R. "'Memories of Paradise'—Legacies of Socialist Education in Mozambique." *African Affairs* 109, no. 436 (2010): 451–70.

Myers, Garth A. *Verandahs of Power: Colonialism and Space in Urban Africa*. Syracuse: Syracuse University Press, 2003.

Nguyễn Thanh Đức. *Quân Hệ Thương Mại Và Đầu Tư Việt Nam – CHLB Đức [Trade and Investment Relations between Vietnam and the Federal Republic of Germany]*. Hanoi: Khoa Học Xã Hội, 2005.

Schwenkel, Christina. *The American War in Contemporary Vietnam: Transnational Remembrance and Representation*. Bloomington: Indiana University Press, 2009.

———. "Imaging Humanity: Socialist Film and Transnational Memories of the War in Vietnam." In *Transnational Memory: Circulation, Articulation, Scales*, ed. Chiara De Cesari and Ann Rigney, 219–44. Boston: De Gruyter, 2014.

———. "Post/Socialist Affect: Ruination and Reconstruction of the Nation in Urban Vietnam." *Cultural Anthropology* 28, no. 2 (2013): 252–77.

———. "Rethinking Asian Mobilities: Socialist Migration and Post-Socialist Repatriation of Vietnamese Contract Workers in East Germany." *Critical Asian Studies* 46, no. 2 (2014): 235–58.

———. "Traveling Architecture: East German Urban Designs Abroad." *International Journal for History, Culture and Modernity* 2, no. 2 (2014): 155–74.

Siegelbaum, Lewis H. "Modernity Unbound: The New Soviet City of Sixties." In *The Socialist Sixties: Crossing Borders in the Second World*, ed. Anne E. Gorsuch and Diane Koenker, 66–83. Bloomington: Indiana University Press, 2013.

Slobodian, Quinn. *Foreign Front: Third World Politics in Sixties West Germany*. Durham: Duke University Press, 2012.

Todorov, Vladislav. *Red Square, Black Square: Organon for Revolutionary Imagination.* Albany: State University of New York Press, 1995.

Weis, Toni. "The Politics Machine: On the Concept of 'Solidarity' in East German Support for SWAPO." *Journal of Southern African Studies* 2 (June 2011): 351–67.

Wernicke, Günter. "'Solidarität Hilft Siegen!' Zur Solidaritätsbewegung Mit Vietnam in Beiden Deutschen Staaten." *Hefte zur DDR-Geschichte* no. 72 (2001).

Yurchak, Alexei. *Everything Was Forever, Until It Was No More: The Last Soviet Generation.* In-Formation Series. Princeton: Princeton University Press, 2006.

Chapter 12

# La Idea de Carlos Marx
## Tracing Germany in the Cuban Imaginary

*A Collaborative Essay by*
*Victor Fowler Calzada and Jennifer Ruth Hosek*

**Jennifer Ruth Hosek**: *Good Bye, Lenin!* (Becker, 2003) took Havana by cultural storm as the featured contribution in the *Muestra Alemana,* the German film series at the Havana Film Festival in 2003.[1] The cinema where it screened was sorely inadequate. Crowds lined up in front of the 23 y 12 theater many hours before the 9 P.M. start, vying for the approximately 250 seats left to the general public after the VIPs were accommodated. The crush into the theater was so great that it broke a thick glass theater door.[2] The crowd did not disperse after the screening began; festival personnel added a late night showing to accommodate some of the disgruntled hopefuls who remained outside throughout the projection. The film was screened a third time at *Cine Chaplin* theater located conveniently adjacent to ICIAC (*Instituto Cubano de Arte e Industria Cinematográficos* [The Cuban Institute of Cinematographic Art and Industry]), which holds over one thousand seats and is known for having the best viewing conditions in Cuba. Afterward, it was projected all day—five showings—in the FNLC (*Fundación del Nuevo Cine Latinoamericano* [Foundation of New Latin American Cinema]), at the firm request of the Foundation's president and one of its founders, the Nobel Prize–winning Colombian author Gabriel García Marquez. During this period, several thousand people saw the film.

Although the Festival and ICAIC made efforts to meet the demand for public showings, it remained less than satisfied. The subsequent *Semana de Cine Alemán* (German film week) was held at *Cine Chaplin* and *Good Bye, Lenin!* was not projected twice as the other films were, but three times on Sunday afternoon and evening, convenient for many Cuban viewers. The programmer of ICAIC, Tony Mason, was in complete support of this run organized by the German Embassy/Goethe Institute. At the same time, despite its popularity the comedy was not shown on television, which suggests that other sectors of the government were less amenable to its dissemination than the film institute, with its reputation for comparative openness. This situation notwithstanding, *Good Bye, Lenin!* became a well-circulated part of the unofficial movie dissemination scene in Havana and was also treated in university classrooms, particularly in German-language courses. It is tempting to believe unconfirmed accounts that government officials were asked to at least one private screening followed by a strategic discussion about Cuban national and international policies.

I did not see *Good Bye, Lenin!* in Havana, but Cuban colleagues told me about the splash that it made. Such discussions got me thinking about tendencies in reading transnationally. By transnational readings I mean those that account for a variety of extranational influences including flows such as movements of people and ideas and structural instantiations such as governmental and corporate policies. German Studies and Comparative Literature after 1945 are products of convictions about the benefits of transnational readings. After the Second World War, European and U.S. politicians and intellectuals cared about studying Europe as one of many hot spots of area studies. The uninterrupted tradition of transatlantic scholarship expresses a desire for understanding and communication between North America and Europe for a plethora of reasons including cultural lessons and geopolitical strategy. In this penchant for transatlantic exchange, U.S. Germanic and German Studies have long been de facto methodologically transnational. With the possible exception of work on German colonialism in Africa, the look South has been less frequent. For instance, Germany's ties to Latin America and the Caribbean remain understudied despite occasional recognition of the close affiliations between socialist East Germany (German Democratic Republic, GDR) and revolutionary Cuba.

By weaving together the nonhomogenized voices of a Cuban poet with ties to Germany and a German Studies professor with ties to Cuba, this piece seeks to express the camaraderie of political color between these two COMECON satellite nations as part of a much larger tapestry. My (Hosek's) investigative weft shows why Cubans care about German film in general and about three newer films whose reception I write about here: *Good Bye, Lenin!, Das Leben der Anderen (The Lives of Others,* dir. von Donnersmarck, 2006), and *Barbara* (dir. Petzold, 2012). Cuban public intellectual Victor Fowler's essayistic warp demonstrates that this Cuban reception is part of long-term, wide-reaching connections with Germany in its varied historical permutations. Our hope is that our interlacing offers a viable generic form for more such collaborative work, in which one of the challenges is speaking with, or, as the Algerian feminist writer Assia Djebar writes, speaking "very close to," without speaking for.[3] Victor and I further hope that our investigation suggests how increased South-North focus could globalize transnational inquiries outside of postcolonial studies that currently focus on the opposition of East and West.[4] Significant in their own right, Southern perspectives on the North are variously instructive. For instance, this contribution highlights Cuban identifications with and aversions to the GDR and its subsequent filmic representations and, in this manner, amplifies knowledge about "peaceful coexistence" and its aftermath, particularly in the lived experiences of global socialism.

•  •  •

Cuban academics and journalists have written no significant treatments of *Good Bye, Lenin!, Das Leben der Anderen,* or *Barbara.* The dearth of scholarship has several likely causes. Publication in Cuba is limited sometimes by politics and generally by material constraints. Partisanship influenced the official reception of these films. Materially speaking, physical resources such as computers, printing presses, and paper are scarce, as is the labor power necessary for production. Most professors are so burdened by teaching and other responsibilities that they find it difficult to write. Most are not paid to research, a situation historically common in poorer countries and increasingly common in richer ones as well. Moreover, contemporary German film is a specialized field such that other topics take precedence in print media. In Northwestern contexts such as the United States or Germany, a lack of published work on texts implies that they did not resonate with the intellectual community; in the global South, silence does not indicate indifference.

The lack of such traditional sources necessitated a research method appropriate to the circumstances. In order to map Cuban readings of these three movies, I employed strategies more common in journalism and ethnography than in cultural or film studies. I interviewed audience members in Cuba in discussions that included film screenings at the request of my interlocutors. I gathered data during frequent visits to Cuba from 2005 to 2014, speaking with small groups of various ages and political identifications, most of whom have or will obtain university degrees and who work in the cultural or educational sectors. For each film, I communicated with approximately fifty people, and about 30 percent of each group of fifty spoke with me about all of the films. Using an open interview method, I prompted my interlocutors to tell me what themes they saw. In the ensuing discussions, my questions aimed to encourage speakers to expand on their comments. Finally, particularly in the case of *Barbara,* I asked directly what parallels these viewers might see between the diegetic reality—the fictional world of the film—and their own. As the contributions of Victor Fowler in this essay make clear, the responses are part of a long-standing and expansive German-Cuban discourse and imaginary.

**Victor Fowler Calzada:** *The Cuban intellectual tradition is marked by the German. From very early on and until his death in 1862, the Cuban writer, teacher, and philosopher José de la Luz y Caballero was one of the Cuban intellectuals most clearly influenced by German culture; he was totally fluent in the language, a translator, and his aphorisms are one of the greatest Cuban testimonies of love to German culture. He defined Germany as "this second motherland mine" and yet, he felt obliged to write in an open debate in the press: "No one could have gathered the abundant harvest of Germany better than I, and I have even been granted importance for introducing the idealism of that nation, which I idolize, to my country; yet, I have consciously considered, in spite of having taken on my shoulders the work of studying German idealism, that knowledge of it could damage rather than benefit our land."⁵ Luz y Caballero's meaning is not clear. Was the author speaking about himself, asserting his patriotism after some type of accusation? Or, was he warning about some terrible menace in the epistemology of German idealism, a thought structure that tempted a prohibited rethinking: slaves and slavery in Cuba. Luz y Caballero was speaking about German idealism and, more than this, about the inner substance of the Enlightenment: "Don't allow yourselves to be deceived by the beauty of words" ("Nemo vos decipiat in sublimitate sermonum," a phrase of Saint Paul's). In a country whose prosperity was based on slave labor, Luz y Caballero touched a heartbreaking limit, as in that space, one could enjoy such foreign theory and complain about Spaniard colonial rule, but only as an exercise detached from implementation, an unfinished work of philosophy, an aesthetic pleasure for the mind.*

*Close to the end of the century, José Martí, the greatest Cuban politician and poet of his time, placed Germany at the center of his political thinking from a very different point of view. While Luz y Caballero was worried about the possible damages of German idealism in a slave society, Martí was organizing the last of the wars against Spanish rule, making alliances, uniting sectors of Cuban society who wanted freedom. In his thought, Revolution is solely a means to obtain freedom from colonial submission and not a matter of class confrontation. Contrast Martí's ideal to the rage and resentment of the German workers in U.S. factories, anarchists or socialists fighting in the battle of labor against capital. Maybe this explains the enigmatic final line of this strophe from Martí's poem to his friend Enrique Estrázulas:*

> *And thus I live, and I don't know:-*
> *Devoured by burning illness;*
> *Always confronted with a vision!*
> *Always with the German at my feet!⁶*

*More than a hundred years later, we remain unprepared to feel the anguish of the beginnings of "geopolitics" from the perspective of the nations that were to be swallowed.*

*In Trinidad, a colonial city in Cuba's heartland, my great-grandfather, a Negro man, declared himself an admirer of Kaiser Wilhelm II and hung a shocking picture of his hero on a wall in my family house. My mom remembers the story as part of the family folklore that visitors in days when the memory of World War I were still fresh didn't understand at all; some were offended. Cultural sensibility is replete with secrets and when something uncanny happens in front of our eyes, maybe we are unveiling one of them.*

*I'm trying to see what my great-grandfather saw. Maybe he was not referring directly to the Kaiser (my mom remembers the picture of an old military man, adorned with medals, with a striking posture and big moustache), but expressing his frustration against history and traditions: Spanish colonialism, slavery and violent racism against blacks, the United States' modernity, and the domination of Cuban life by Cuban upper classes and politicians. The Kaiser, the rule of law, the War, contained the promise of a paradoxical New Order in which my great-grandfather may perhaps have found an even less secure and prosperous place. Who knows? Nobody asked him, but it is not a coincidence that in the next decade Cuba was one of the Latin American countries in which a fascist political party was founded and granted legitimacy. I recently discovered a chat forum in which someone writes that Hitler mused about trying to settle Germans in Cuba. And one of the versions of the somber witticism of the destiny of Hitler's cranium relates that when Russians found and identified Hitler's burned body, they severed the head and put it into a Habanero cigar box.*

• • •

**Hosek:** Such intellectual histories nourish cultural and political ties between Germany and Cuba. Reinhold Begas's emblematic 1883 statue of Alexander von Humboldt in front of Berlin's Humboldt Universität names the Prussian geographer "the second discoverer of Cuba" on its plinth and the well-known *Casa Humboldt* in Havana where Humboldt lived and worked are physical traces of these connections that feature particularly in the oeuvre of the East German *Deutsche Film-Aktiengesellschaft* (German Film Corporation—DEFA). Humboldt's stay in Latin America is depicted in Rainer Simon's *Die Besteigung des Chimborazo* (*The Ascent of Chimborazo*, 1989), and, as I have explored elsewhere, revolutionary Cuba features in documentaries and fictions, including the DEFA coproductions.[7] Collaboration between the GDR and Cuba included increasingly robust flows of workers, students, tourists, and experts as well as commodity and cultural exchange. For instance, while revolutionary Cuba's cement and beer industries developed with German support, GDR workers enjoyed island beaches as employment perks, and all could partake of cane sugar, rum, oranges, and Caribbean socialist ideas.

• • •

**Fowler**: *After the triumph of the Revolution, thousands of Cubans visited the GDR to study, work, or for other reasons (my father was one). They returned deeply impressed by—maybe it sounds cliché—characteristics like hard work, order, discipline, seriousness, and rigor. Alongside this, they carried memories of liberal sexual behavior and a society with an abundance of consumer goods. The opposite of life in Cuban society. The book* Abenteuer DDR. Kubaner und Kubanerinnen im deutschen Sozialismus *[I came back like another person. Cubans in the GDR] relates the experiences of a group that studied and worked in East Germany between 1961 and 1989. The foreword presents its content as a sort of raw material "... a contribution towards closing the existing holes in the genre of memoirs from the students, the apprentices and employees hired in the GDR."⁸ Although eleven interviews cannot speak for the 300,000 Cubans who visited East Germany, it is enough to open a window onto cultural differences: nudity and order, collisions and collusions, influences and questions.*

*For someone of my generation, Germany was mainly the GDR and the GDR was the country of the future. The testimony of René Caparrós Aguiar, one of the interviewees, not only shows that the assumed future was kept hidden, but also that the opportunity to see could be a terrible mental burden:*

> *In the GDR everything was planned, foreseen and regulated, which didn't correspond to our mentality. In the GDR the possibility of improvising didn't exist, it was not possible to put into practice something not planned previously; it didn't matter if it was something logical or necessary. This was very difficult for a revolutionary accustomed to fighting against any type of stagnant structure. My stay in the GDR was like a visit to the future of my country. ... But the people that surround me, who don't know that future, cannot accept it, since they don't have an idea of what the result can be. Many things that were absolutely normal in Germany were considered a chimera here [in Cuba]. Therefore, every time that I opened my mouth to give my opinion on some problem, people [in Cuba] saw me as a snob or as a false Messiah.⁹*

*Another testimony, from the historian Sonia Moro, parts the curtain upon an insignificant episode that reveals an incredible phantom of ideological control, part of the colossal battle for hearts and minds that marked the epoch. She studied in East Germany in the sixties, a time when young people, including Cubans, liked to dance the Twist; but, in her words, "the Cuban Embassy said: 'You should dance to Cuban music.'"¹⁰ They speak from incompatible points of view: the young student and the diplomat, pleasure and ideology, the culture of the "New Man" fostered by socialist systems and the "decadent" cultural practices of capitalism.*

*And yet, the economist Carlos M. Menéndez summarizes the prevailing feel-*
*ings among the Cubans who studied or worked in East Germany: "They enlarged*
*my vision of the world. The discipline, the order, the organization, all this helped*
*me very much, even more than the study of economics."*[11]

• • •

**Hosek:** Victor's commentary here emphasizes GDR-Cuban ties in part because the U.S.-led embargo indeed curtailed mainstream FRG-Cuban relations. At the same time, it should be remembered that the Iron Curtain was
porous and that transnational relations between both GDR and Cuban citizens and West German and Cuban citizens exceeded official politics. Cubans
in East Germany engaged with West Germans and with West German media. West German leftists regularly visited and reported about Cuba. As part
of their multifaceted official relationship with Cuba, the GDR organized
*Kulturtage der DDR* (GDR cultural days), which included film screenings,
as well as additional film weeks. Cuban intellectuals particularly appreciated
West Germany's New German Cinema. Fringe film festivals in West Germany such as Oberhausen and the world-renowned Leipzig festival in the
GDR favored Cuban documentaries, where many, such as those of Santiago
Alvarez, won prizes. Cuban filmmakers studied and worked at the *Hochschule für Film und Fernsehen* (Film and Television University) in Potsdam
and GDR filmmakers visited Cuba in many capacities.

The dissolution of the Soviet Union influenced the Cuban-German relationship significantly.[12] As international cooperation between the GDR and
Cuba ended in 1990, *Cathedra Humboldt* was founded. Linked to the *Uni-
versidad de La Habana* (University of Havana), it aimed to sustain cultural
exchange. When the Goethe Institute entered Cuba via the German embassy
in the early 1990s, the Cathedra narrowed its focus to language teaching. It
now teaches German to all interested students and organizes a yearly meeting of the *Deutschlehrerverband,* the national organization of Cuban teachers
of the language. The Goethe Institute supports this event financially and
provides it with teaching material as it increasingly takes the formal lead in
the propagation of German culture in Cuba.

Since the early 1990s, the primary official vehicles for dissemination of
German films to Cuban audiences have been the annual *Festival Internacio-
nal del Nuevo Cine Latinoamericano de La Habana* (Havana International
Festival of New Latin American Cinema; commonly, Havana Film Festival)
in December and the annual *Semana de Cine Alemán* in June. With the support of the Goethe Institute, the cultural section of the German Embassy has
contributed the selection of German films at the Havana Film Festival (the
*Muestra Alemana*) since 1995. The embassy does the primary organizing for

these screenings, with funding from the central Goethe Institute in Munich. The Goethe Institute purchases the rights for three viewings, meaning that the film festival is at liberty to screen any film more than once. For instance, in 2013, Jan Ole Gerster's *Oh Boy* (2012) was shown several times because of its popularity. The December Muestra focuses on German films less than two years old. The June film weeks generally present three of the December films again and add an additional three to four films less than several years old. One or two German films a year at the festival may be presented independently of the Goethe umbrella, e.g., Michael Haneke's *Das Weiße Band* (2009). Generally these works are donated by the individual distributor, producer, or director.

The dissemination of German films in Cuba is similar to that of other nations. Film weeks financed by a particular embassy or cultural institution such as the *Alliance Française* or *Instituto Cervantes* are common. *Alliance Française* has a strong presence in Havana and its large film festival in April is quite popular. Spain and Italy frequently organize contemporary and retrospective film weeks, as do Norway, Denmark, and Finland.

The central and regional Goethe Institutes play the largest role in choosing films for these events. Every year, Goethe employees are trained by the central Goethe Institute and they attend the *Berlinale* and the *Internationalen Hofer Filmtage* (Hof International Film Festival) to select ten to fifteen films for which the rights are purchased. Regional institutes choose films for their events from these offerings, sometimes with the advice of the central Goethe Institute. Occasionally they purchase the films from German distributors, but in this case, the local office bears the costs. This system means that local offices can select representative films that may have particular local interest. In the case of the Havana Film Festival, as a final step, the Havana Goethe Institute presents their choices to the Festival organizers for authorization before they are taken into the Muestra Alemana portion of the program. ICAIC collaborates on the German Film Week. Historically, the German choices are never overruled.[13]

Festival programmers schedule works largely according to projected demand. Havana is known for its palatial, centrally located cinema houses that were built in the heydays of cinema as public spectacle from the 1920s to the 1950s, when Havana was popular with international high rollers including Hollywood stars. The largest cinemas screen films with more popular appeal, such as action features and those with Spanish-language soundtracks. During the first years of the Muestra Alemana, German films were traditionally shown in the six hundred-seat 23 y 12 cinema named for its location a half a block from the intersection of 23rd Avenue and 12th Street. This main intersection also houses ICAIC and the building from which Castro publicly announced the Revolution's socialist character. It was in the course of this speech too that the new government's official photographer Alberto Korda snapped the iconic image of Che Guevara that circulated in West Berlin, West Germany, and globally, facilitated by Korda's liberation of copyright and left-leaning editor Giangiacomo Feltrinelli's dissemination.[14] As the Muestra Alemana became more popular, the screenings were moved to the centrally located Theatre Acapulco, with over a thousand seats.

According to Alberto Ramos Ruiz, programmer of the Havana Film Festival, the large and faithful audience for German film considers it "prestigious cinema, with solid plots, interesting themes and remarkable performances."[15] As would be expected in other parts of the globe as well, most Cuban aficionados of foreign film would respond to the label intellectuals: academics, artists, members of the film industry, students, and professionals with a significant amount of formal education. Decades of strong public education and affordable access to a broad range of cultural events in urban areas have yielded larger interested publics than in many other countries in Latin America. An overlapping public for German culture and film includes those who have spent time in or otherwise had dealings with the Germanys. The attention to German film in Cuba thus builds on the history of interaction with the GDR. Moreover, similarities between these two countries gained immediacy with the GDR's dramatic, symbolic dismantling in 1989 and subsequent filmic depictions of GDR state socialism and its aftermath.

• • •

**Fowler:** *I was there for the broadcasting on public TV of the famous Pink Floyd concert to honor the fall of Berlin Wall; but the concert took place in 1990 and I was watching ten years after. Perhaps my testimony means nothing because I was only a solitary man enjoying wonderful rock music in his room at the artist colony Villa Waldberta on Starnberg Lake in Bavaria. The striking detail in this scene is that the sole viewer is crying, simply allowing the tears to roll. The concert audience is jumping, clapping their hands, waving in a gigantic dream of solidarity, possibility and future; a group of them at the Brandenburg Gate, overtaking the symbol: the Wall. A world has finished, forever.*

*Years before, a German friend, a university professor, came to Havana. One night as we drank beer, she began to remember. My recollections are nothing, sabes, but she was one of the witnesses; very close to the Brandenburg Gate, in a café with some colleagues, when something unusual diverted their attention: small groups, mainly young people, passing and looking in. "I couldn't forget their eyes," she said.*

*I have thought many times about such sights: re-constructing the moment, trying to understand what happened two or three blocks away from the Wall.*

*The image of people, hundreds, walking and gazing like zombies, is something horrible and touching at the same time; newcomers stand at the window displays, the people of the Trabant discovering Mercedes Benz. They were like babies who entered the world for the first time and their eyes are mine, the eyes of my generation, of my country.*

*"What did you do?" I asked my friend.*

*"We invited them to drink beer and we celebrated together until very late," she said, "but you know, even when I arrived home I didn't believe it. I needed to hear the morning news to understand that the world had changed."*

• • •

**Hosek:** The reception of *Good Bye Lenin!* was foreshadowed by the reception of Margarethe von Trotta's *Das Versprechen* (*The Promise*, 1994) in Cuba in 1997, which demonstrated how the international publicity given to the festival could allow for moments of vocal public critique. Festival Director Iván Giroud enthusiastically agreed to a screening in full awareness of its critical perspective on the Berlin Wall. *Das Versprechen* was shown during the presentation of the film awards and yet the most important critics preferred to attend the 23 y 12 theater. An audience member related to me, that, in contrast to the vocal responses usual in Cuban cinemas, the mostly Cuban public was very quiet during most of the film, if to avoid any infraction that might justify halting the projection. However, at the denouement, this public silence was spontaneously broken when the protagonist Barbara walks grimly across the border through the revelers, explaining to a reporter that, *"Ein Vogel der 30 Jahre im Käfig gelebt hat, hat das Fliegen verlernt"* ("A bird that has lived in a cage for 30 years has forgotten how to fly"). In response, the audience suddenly rose to their feet and burst into loud applause, while one young Cuban even jumped onto the stage in front of the projection screen clapping and cheering. That year, Von Trotta was the Goethe Institute guest at the Festival, but was not at the screening. Afterward, the departing audience was questioned by many international reporters waiting outside the cinema. And, members of this same public also spoke loudly to Cuban television producer Luciano Castillo outside the cinema, shouting that *Das Versprechen* should be broadcast on the small screen. The police were present, but did not intervene, perhaps because of the international festival context.

The reception of *Good Bye Lenin!* six years later would be just as dramatic and involve more viewers. The multiplicity of Cuban-German connections, coupled with the film's subject matter, comedic genre, and international popularity, set it up to generate excitement in the Caribbean nation. Globally speaking, *Good Bye, Lenin!* is and probably will remain *the* mainstream feature film on unification.[16] The narrative revolves around a teenager, Alex, who attempts to hide the fact of the fall of the Wall from his mother, Christiane Kerner. With the more or less enthusiastic support of his sister, Ariane, her West German boyfriend, Rainer, his West Berlin colleague, Denis, and his Russian girlfriend, Laura, Alex recreates the GDR within the domestic space of the apartment of his family, to which he and Adriane return his invalid mother after her heart attack. The plot develops around the machinations they undertake to hide the truth from Christiane and Alex's eventual acceptance of the new Germany.

One of the works on this topic taught most frequently in North American German Studies classrooms, *Good Bye Lenin!* is seen as accessible because it employs youthful protagonists, humor, and family drama rather than sociological analysis. For their part, Cuban viewers cared about the film for three main reasons: its particular engagement with the dissolution of the German Democratic Republic; the fact that Cubans were affected at least as intensely by the fall of the Iron Curtain as Germans themselves;[17] and the fact that islanders with many ties abroad in Miami and elsewhere identified with migration from East Germany to West.

While Becker's film is widely seen as a comedy, its humor amuses Westerners more than Easterners. In my assessment based on personal discussions and experience, Eastern German audiences frequently left screenings of the film rather solemnly. As my research here shows, Cubans also tended toward reading *Good Bye, Lenin!* earnestly. Reporting for the international federation of film critics, Jan Schulz-Ojala suggests that, for Cuban viewers, the film is "like a mirror of many things to happen in Cuba too."[18] My interviews highlighted the ways in which Cuban viewers took the message of failed socialist utopia seriously, as if wanting to put Marxism's head on straight in preparation for the simulated newscast that Alex creates for his mother to explain the passage of citizens across the newly open border.

Most of the comments of my interviewers moved between Alex's familial story and the societal story of the *Wende*. Many Cubans commented on the function of lies both within the family and within the larger society. According to many of their readings, dissimulation between the characters is what kept the GDR functioning, what kept Alex's recreation of the GDR going, and what kept and keeps the family together. They pointed out that Christiane's lie to her children about their father's departure and her opportunist practices in relation to the state stabilized both the GDR and the family. Alex's lie to Christiane about the circumstances that instigated her heart attack and about the contemporary political events maintains her as a mother and as a symbol of the ossified GDR structure. Many Cuban viewers found that the deception in *Good Bye, Lenin!* expresses familial love and the desire for familial unity. They also noted that lies were organized along generational divisions and simultaneously divided the generations from each other. This generational, societal perspective is seldom articulated by Western critics, although many consider the story in domestic terms.[19] Linking public and private, Cubans saw a society in which generational relations are marked by the lie and shaped by political circumstances, and this can draw families apart.

My interlocutors also read the family as divided by economic forces. Female commentators, in particular, remarked on the responsibility of the father who had migrated, who had done too little in their eyes to maintain contact with his family in the GDR. They noted the difference in living standards between Alex's father and his family in the GDR and were surprised that his father seemingly did not send funds to this family along with his letters. Several audience members made specific parallels with Cuba, a nation in which many men migrate and in which their connection to their family back home often changes radically over time. Many Cuban viewers read the story as a coming-of-age film in which the modern-day hero Alex creates his own "protective wall" to shield himself from the new world. They were particularly struck by what they saw as Alex's desire to protect himself from the new "borderless" society of limitless choice.

Many Northwestern critics have noted the depiction of consumer behavior in the movie. I contend that the film shows—and Western viewers read—such consumption ironically. This irony forecloses some ways of understanding consumer culture in the work, notably the particular relevance of choice.[20] That *Good Bye, Lenin!* is so very much about choice first became clear by attending to Cuban reception. Citizens of a society that officially continues to value production over consumption, these viewers repeatedly characterized the filmic world as a world of consumer choice. For them, such choice is evidenced in the plethora of media genres and information suggested by the accessibility of pornography and satellite dishes. Moreover, they read this situation politically. It is cause for concern that, once given options, Easterners chose pornography and sports over the alternatives that decentralized production offers, such as local independent filmmaking and international news and information. This Cuban perspective on the definition and significance of choice newly illuminates the filmic project. Martin Blum points out that consumer choice is political, yet his analysis focuses on the choices that exist within the larger FRG. For him, consumption of remakes of GDR goods resists the larger FRG's political system.[21] Yet, such resistance does not produce alternatives. The Cuban vantage points clarify that the politics of consumer choice can mean that only certain choices are available, while other choices are de facto foreclosed in a market-driven economy.

More importantly, perhaps, for many Cubans, the lack of political choice within a landscape of consumer choice is both political and dangerous.

• • •

**Fowler**: *In 2002, in Berlin, the night of 1 May, very late, a big riot was broadcast and I saw the charge of the police against the demonstrators. The next morning, sleep deprived and frazzled, I took the metro to the University and missed my stop; suddenly I woke up surrounded by ugly buildings, big blocks of grey cement and I thought that Havana—through a kind of magical transportation—was in front of my eyes, but we were crossing a zone of East Berlin with buildings made in the same style as ours. The dream ended and my country of the future was the country of the past architecture, the somber, the dreadful, the surveillance, the repression, the lie.*

*Before the end of the Wall, I had heard of the Stasi on a few dispersed occasions. It was in the conversation with my friend where I heard, for the first time, the unthinkable range of surveillance that the Stasi had over the lives of ordinary people in the GDR. The combination of political structures and the perpetual work of the ideological apparatus elaborates a perpetual veil over reality, so it is almost impossible to see more than what it is permitted to see. In the summer of 1989, I saw the popular protests in East Germany and the placards on TV, at least in the beginning, showed only two petitions to the authorities: freedom of the press and the right to travel freely. This was just the same anguish that my country has had during all these years of socialism, the most evident examples of the structural weakness of the system. A system that, in other points, is strong even now as it is living its deepest crisis.*

*In a society like the Cuban, where cultural circulation is centralized in the hands of the state as the solitary owner of the media, of the editorial system, and of a monopoly on imports, to enter another culture is an act that depends on a combination of personal will and the opportunities of knowledge that this same state offers. In this world order, cultural production fuses with political discourses, travelers' tales, and things that arrive from the country that one is trying to know. Economic conditions and political work manufacture an ideological construction. The visited culture is doubly filtered: by the conditions of development from which the travelers leave and for all that it is chosen for them not to see in the place in which they arrive. Even the most reliable source, people, introduce their most quotidian desires into their travelers' tales and so offer deformed and sweet memories, without repression or conflicts. At the same time, we Cubans saw many sectors of our industry working with enormous and modern machinery manufactured in the Germany of the East, so the representation that we had of that country was determined by the perfect, the modern, and the monumental. No doubt, especially at that time, ideology was a strange game of mirrors in which, when looking at ourselves, we saw mostly a blurred image of the Other.*

• • •

**Hosek:** *Das Leben der Anderen,* the Stasi-centered drama that may go down as *the* canonical feature film about the GDR, appeared publicly in Cuba only at the Havana Film Festival. In 2007 it screened at the large cinema Acapulco, to which the increasingly well-attended Muestra Alemana had migrated.[22] Photos in the German media showed crowds pressing into the theater, whose capacity was just adequate to receive them. In front of the cinema, DPA/ Reuters undertook exit interviews with the public, including known dissidents, without police interference. Perhaps unsurprisingly, *Das Leben der Anderen* was treated with caution by the authorities because of concerns that viewers would compare Cuban structures to those of the diegetic society. Members of Cuba's intellectual elites who commented on the film both saw these continuities and many differences in its celluloid dreamwork.[23]

The story, written and directed by the Western German Florian Henckel von Donnersmarck, focuses on secret police surveillance of artists and intellectuals. In 1980s East Berlin, agent Gerd Wiesler is put on the case of the playwright Georg Dreyman by the Minister of Culture, who has designs on Dreymann's partner Christa-Maria Sieland, an actress who suffers from substance addiction and insecurity. The film details mechanisms of state and social control and surveillance throughout the robust psychological narrative in which Wiesler becomes disenchanted with the State and his role in it as he is converted by German literature, comes to identify with Dreymann, and falls in love with Sieland. At the final hour, he saves Dreymann from arrest and is demoted, while Sieland dies in an accident precipitated by her weak character. Shortly after unification, Wiesler finds Dreymann's new novel displayed prominently in a Berlin bookshop. Its thankful dedication to his agent code name demonstrates that, after reading his own Stasi files, Dreymann knows the truth. Thus the two men who had been at such odds in the GDR are reconciled in the new, seemingly more transparent Germany.

The fiction feature did not appear in Cuba as part of the German film week although it made the circuit of many other international German cultural institutions. Both the Goethe Institute/Embassy and ICAIC found this to be the best choice. As with *Good Bye, Lenin!* and most popular and problematic films in Cuba, *Das Leben der Anderen* had quite a broad informal dissemination; de-encrypted copies passed from hand to hand and thumb drive to thumb drive. Among Habaneros, the feature is often dubbed *La vida de nosotros* (The Lives of Ourselves). It is said that this label was coined in Miami and percolated across the 90-mile water wall into the Cuban capital. In my experience, this origin story emerges nearly every time that *Das Leben der Anderen* is referred to by its nickname. It seems that the comparison resonates for Cubans living on the island and that they prefer to distance themselves from it by stressing an international source.

The generalized commentary encapsulated in this moniker is an important part of the story of *Das Leben der Anderen*. As a point of evaluation, consider the 2009 sculpture by partially Cuba-based Cuban artist Carlos Garaicoa, *Las joyas de la corona* (*The Jewels in the Crown*), which consists of eight silver miniatures of buildings representing state power: the national stadium in Chile that Augusto Pinochet used in 1973 as a concentration camp to hold, torture, and kill; the Pentagon, headquarters of the United States Department of Defense; Argentina's ESMA, the foremost penitentiary during its "dirty war"; the Soviet headquarters of the KGB central intelligence agency; the naval base in Guantánamo, Cuba, used by the United States for imprisonment and torture; the Cuban DGI headquarters for external intelligence gathering, particularly against the United States; the German Democratic Republic's Stasi headquarters of the secret police and the central intelligence agency; and Cuba's Villa Marista, part of the intelligence section of the Ministry of the Interior, hence the organization most closely involved with surveilling Cuban nationals and in this way that with the closest parallel to the Stasi. By grouping and representing all of these centers of power similarly, the work suggests that their differences are insignificant. Perhaps cast more carefully than easy reiterations of the slightly tweaked, perhaps ironic, and neatly rhyming phrase, *la vida de nosotros, Las hoyas en la corona* similarly places Cuba's system of state regulation in parallel with what can be seen as very different frameworks and environments.

Consider also how to understand the statements of two thirty-something male viewers quoted in the Spanish newspaper *El País* that compare the GDR diegetic in *Das Leben der Anderen* with life in Cuba. One says, "Aquí han habido momentos también muy duros, en los 70 y en los 80" ("Here there have also been very hard moments, in the 1970s and 1980s"). The other contends, "Aquí ha pasado también lo mismo y algún día se sabrá, cuando se abran los archivos de la Seguridad del Estado" ("Here the same has happened and one day it will be known, when the archives of the state security are opened").[24] These remarks made during exit interviews that were clearly destined for public consumption may be read as self-censored, in which case their comparison of the GDR solely with the Cuban *past* would be expedient. Alternatively, these viewers may indeed consider the GDR situation comparable only with the times in which Cuba was under the protective, regulatory umbrella of the Soviet Union, particularly from 1968, and then later under national strictures as the Cuban state veered from Perestroika in the 1980s until the Special Period.

In contrast to the broad parallels that inform the above examples, my interlocutors stressed distinctions above similarities in the onscreen daily life in the GDR and the lived situation in Cuba. With what I read as ambivalent confidence, they understood the Cuban secret service and police to be very informed about all types of activity. Yet they emphasized that the Cuban system of surveillance is not as professionalized in terms of systematized protocol and specialized technology as was the Stasi. To them, perhaps especially in a land whose architecture features flat roofs, the notion of minute surveillance from an attic seemed fantastic and they were often struck by what they saw as comprehensive control. For instance, many were alienated by the classroom scene in which the instructor marks the name of the student who protests that the interrogation method is inhumane. Many referred to limitations on technology in poorer countries such as Cuba. Many also referenced, often with a sort of national pride, what is termed *socialismo tropical,* a notion according to which Cuba never attained nor strove to achieve the extensive social controls present in some other state socialist countries.

Among the Cuban interviewees there were also particular ways of understanding modes and functions of surveillance. The double lives of the characters, in which communication varies distinctly according to the degree of interpersonal trust and specific context, resonated with the lived experience of many. However, to the Cubans with whom I spoke, the events in *Das Leben der Anderen* would not have warranted such actions in their country, as they did not directly threaten the nation or the state apparatus. This begged the question of what constitutes dissent and led to the question of the role of art in society. Cubans pointed to the strictures of the Grey Decade of the 1970s as a period of censure imposed by the Soviet Union, while suggesting that revolutionary Cuba's own relationship to artistic production has tended toward acceptance of a broader range of expression than that shown in *Das Leben der Anderen.* Some proposed that the success of the playwright's book in the West should be understood as just as much engendered by politics as the sanction of his work in the East. Certainly Cubans abroad experience various types of success for similar reasons.

The extremely heated debates in Germany about how *Das Leben der Anderen* depicted Stasi practices suggested that more was at stake than putative melodramatic verisimilitude. As I have already hinted, the contest involved postmortem interpretation of the GDR, particularly revelations about and interpretations of its closeted skeletons. Cubans are interested in these accounts due to a rich tradition with Germany and felt correlations with the GDR. As Victor considers below, for instance, at issue is how to understand narratives that emerge within seismic geopolitical shifts such as the creation of the larger FRG and of Cuba after 1990 and into the future.

• • •

**Fowler**: *What is Germany for me now and how do I relate with the country and its people, history, and culture? It has been a process. Now I can once again integrate Brecht, Mann, Benn, Celan, Heidegger, Enzensberger, Arendt, Wolf, Böll, Grass and many others into a big nation, history, problems, questions, pain, struggles, defeat, sorrow, victories, expressions, voices. I've read about the infamous episode of the St. Louis, the ship with 936 Jews escaped from Nazi Germany whose landing was rejected by the Cuban government of Federico Laredo Brú. History is a spider's web and the desire for knowledge is hungry; you read and read and read, you discover your own country again, you find things that you don't want to. Now I know that most of those Jews returned to Europe and many were killed in concentration camps, that Cuban politician Ramón Grau San Martín organized an anti-Semitic public meeting to support the return voyage in the name of nationalism and the defense of the right to secure employment for the Cuban working class: only five days later the ship set sail from Havana harbor with a crowd of 40,000 in attendance. How was it possible? How is fear used to disarm solidarity? As the years passed, and it became known that many of the passengers of the St. Louis died in Nazi concentration camps, how did those protestors feel?*

*How many people remember today that we had a Partido Nazi Cubano (Cuban Nazi Party), founded on 13 October 1928 and officially dissolved on 27 September 1940? Not only the Partido Nazi Cubano, but also others in the orbit of the same ideology, sympathizers of Franco and Mussolini: Partido Fascista Nacional, Legión Estudiantil de Cuba, Legión Nacional Revolucionaria Sindicalista, Fondo de la Campaña de Invierno, Asociación Alemana de Beneficencia and Falange Española. They controlled a significant number of Cuban journals ("Pepín" Rivero, the owner of* Diario de la Marina, Avance, *and* Alerta *was supporter of falangism and Juan Prohías, the President of the Partido Nazi Cubano had a radio program named Hora Liberal Independiente). Enrolled in a fight against communism, they were anti-Semitic at the same time. Batista's government, in his first period as president (the second ending with the coup d'état in 1952) dissolved all the Cubans' fascist organizations in 1940. How many people know about the foundation of a Cuban cell of the Ku Klux Klan in 1928 under the government of Gerardo Machado, quickly dissolved by the authorities?*

*What I'm trying to show is that, in asking about Germany, I'm obliged to see Cuba and myself in a different way. Our idea about the Other is made up of pieces: oral memories, readings, events in which we could take part, movies, songs, cultural consumption, and life. We were not there. We need to learn, to reconstruct every moment, we progress, filling the hollows of the different "official" narratives and hearing the statements of the witnesses. We had the only Nazi spy who was captured in Latin America, Heinz August Kunning, sentenced to death and executed in 1942 (responsible for the sinking of six Cuban ships and the death of more than eighty Cuban sailors). We could not enjoy the stay of Walter Benjamin, whose escape from Hitler's order was supposed to have its first stop in Havana with employment as professor at the University (in the last letter to his friend, on 15 July 1940, T. W. Adorno promises to make all the necessary arrangements). The Cuban Revolution frustrated our opportunity to have a building designed by Mies van der Rohe, the "office without walls," which was to have been the head office of Bacardí; the work was to have begun when the rebel movement triumphed and ten years later, the original designs were the inspiration of the Neue Nationalgalerie inaugurated in West Berlin in 1968. In 1972 the Cuban government, in honor of the GDR and as part of its political ceremonies, renamed a small Cuban island (previously known as Cayo Blanco de Sur) Cayo Ernesto Thälmann. Located in the south Bay of Pigs, Cayo Blanco de Sur is a site without relevance. In the world of diplomacy, renaming a place is a gesture signifying nothing in terms of sovereignty. But, in a sort of cunning trick, some people contend that technically—since Cayo Ernesto Thälmann was not included in any of the Unification treaties—it is the current territory of the nonexistent GDR, a space worthy of a great sci-fi novel.*

*When I look at the country and its people, I look at mine. The questions turn back against themselves and I'm confronted by much of my uncertainty and emptiness. I love this country: its idealistic philosophy, its somber drift to the most terrible of authoritarian models, the long fight for democratic values into the grizzly days of socialism. I know Nackt unter Wölfen, directed by Frank Beyer, Die Legende von Paul und Paula, by Heiner Carow, and Solo Sunny, by Konrad Wolf and Wolfgang Kohlhaase, all from the East, but I also have the films of Herzog, Fassbinder, Wenders, von Trotta, and many others, coming from the West. I heard Tangerine Dream, Nico, Scorpions, Karlheinz Stockhausen, Kraftwerk, Silver Convention, Boney M blended with Puhdys and Karat. In real life, East and West are together (again). In my mind I'm a conciliator dealing with opposing tendencies. The Unification process, from the most obscure roots in the past to the present, with all its lights and shadows, is a constant presence in my thoughts. Germany is a question because we, the Cubans, are divided too and I live the Wall: my wall. Let me quote the German novelist Peter Schneider to express what happens: my Mauer im Kopf (Wall in the Head).*

• • •

**Hosek:** Christian Petzold's *Barbara* (2012) was the headliner in the Muestra Alemana of the 2013 Havana Film Festival, where it was shown three times in Cine Acapulco.[25] The theater was about three-quarters full at the premiere and the film did not provoke significant audience reaction. There was no significant presence of journalists after the screening, nor did the exiting public gather in large groups for discussion in front of the theater.

What tale had the audience seen? In the eponymous film, the professionally engaged and politically disengaged medical doctor Barbara arrives at a small-town medical facility in 1980, having been demoted from the prestigious Charité Hospital in Berlin. The film sets up her new boss, the similarly engaged and physically compatible André, as her perfect match. Their slow coming together involves a sea change in Barbara. Her boyfriend Jörg, a businessman from the Federal Republic, is planning her escape over the Baltic. Yet, as she waits, Barbara becomes increasingly rooted, for example in her work with the young, pregnant rebel Stella, who is frantic to leave the GDR, keep her baby, and escape the youth penitentiary where she is interned. Barbara and the attentive, respectful André have many interests in common, while Jörg brings her nylons and women's magazines, has furtive sex with her, and expects that, once in the West, she will give up her productive career and become his consuming woman. At the final hour, Barbara decides for the GDR with André; she sends Stella in her place, as per Stella's preference.

My questions to various interlocutors revealed difficulties in understanding and connecting with the film's plot. Most importantly to me, *Barbara* was read as a story about the GDR and seldom compared with Cuba except in response to explicit queries. Audiences appreciated what they saw as the opportunity to learn more about the GDR but they found the Berlin School–style filming and story line rather alienating. To them, the film depicted a country in which the only good is to be found in interpersonal and professional relations, not the state or societal structures. As in my earlier interviews regarding *Das Leben der Anderen,* interlocutors readily stated that Cuban secret service and the neighborhood watch organizations (*Comités de Defensa de la Revolución,* Committees for the Defense of the Revolution (CDR)) involve surveillance. At the same time, they were aghast at the totality of the observational network depicted in the film, from the fact that André was an informant on Barbara's case to the invasive cavity searches and the juvenile detention center depicted in the film. *Barbara* was seen as a work largely about the past not the present and about the GDR, not about Cuba.

These readings were surprising as, for me, *Barbara* resonates with the Cuban situation in at least two explicit ways: the decision around and the manner of flight and the position of women in relation to consumerism. A goodly number of more recent Cuban features include teary, dramatic scenes of beach departures, for instance Humberto Solás's *Miel para Oshún* (*Honey for Ochún,* 2001) and more recently Benito Zambrano's *Havana*

*Blues* (2005). Departures by sea vessels en route to Miami mark revolutionary Cuban history. The fact that early feature films avoided such depiction strongly suggests their divisiveness. Yet, the sole person who mentioned this scene talked of its lack of suspense. To him, Barbara would obviously send Stella. His insight may be informed by a standard migrant practice by which the perceived future of the next generation instigates the actions of the older generation. At the same time, neither this commentary nor any other incorporated explicit comparisons with Cuba or migration.

Similarly, none of my interlocutors talked about Barbara's decision to remain in the GDR in terms of her rejection of an impending altered positionality in the FRG. At first this struck me as odd. Despite patriarchal structures typical of state socialism and so-called Latin culture in Cuba, women are recognized for and identify with their professions. One might expect that Cubans would notice and take a stand on this womanist topic, which is a primary and popular success of the revolutionary government. For me, two recent shifts are key to understanding what may seem to be an uncritical take on Barbara's decision. One is the situation of Cuban migrants today, most of whom will not practice their trained profession once abroad. The career transfer opportunities that were open to East Germans in the FRG and Cubans in the United States in particular have declined radically. The second change involves employment circumstances on the island. While most Cubans continue to recognize the value of formal education and professions, the wage differential between specialized careers and well-paid private sector service jobs are giving rise to *nouveau riche* that are increasingly admired independently of how they obtained their wealth. For Cubans today, it may seem both a usual and utilitarian choice that a practicing, engaged doctor who migrates gives up her career to become a stay-at-home wife.

Indeed, the circumstances of Barbara's new hotel room confidante map onto the situation of many Cuban migrants today. The young, naïve opportunist revels in the Western commodities and a pledged marriage ticket to the West obtained through her sexual liaison with Jörg's FRG business colleague. This relational foil of Barbara's intimate association reverberates transnationally. And, although such arrangements are famously common in post-1990 Cuba, none of my interviewees paralleled them with migration between the two Germanys in *Barbara*. I believe its articulation touches an increasingly sore spot in national-foreigner bonds: its asymmetry.

• • •

**Fowler:** *I have been talking and joking about the problem of nonsymmetrical relations, the ways of experiencing "the before" (they are huge, we only a small island), the death of mother Russia, and the lies behind my country of the future.*

• • •

**Hosek:** Captured as they were over the course of nearly a decade, Cuban takes on these three films also reflect changes within their country, which has been moving toward more pluralistic organization and self-conceptualization. In some ways, twenty-five years after the GDR, it may stand to reason if Cubans see fewer connections between this German nation and their country today. In particular, although only time will tell, the dramatic and sudden end of the GDR seems not to have been a structural foreshadowing of the character of changes on the island. At the same time, the GDR and Germany continue to shape Cuba. This collaborative essay emphasizes that the GDR-Cuban relationship is part of a larger fabric of German-Cuban relations; its analysis also intends to encourage understanding the GDR as intrinsically part of national and transnational paradigms and to caution against the excision of material or ideational entities and forces out of analytic or ideological convenience.

## *The Idea of Carlos Marx*[26]

*Victor Fowler Calzada*

*Carlos Marx's idea about the State must not have been*
*Engels' companionship,*
*even though he was a great friend and collaborator,*
*in a pair of statues embodying them*
*in Berlin Alexanderplatz.*

*Lovers climb Marx's bronze shoulders,*
*strong enough to endure eternity,*
*and they have written revealing names*
*(probably from erotic pleasure)*
*on the titan's back.*

*Even I, a passing tourist*
*trying to overcome,*
*through laughter, past demons,*
*climbed that mountain of time that only then*
*and that way—when that world collapsed—*
*has permitted me to grasp:*
*bronze with the air imprisoned in its interior.*

*But in Havana on the corner of Carlos III and Infanta*
*yesterday afternoon,*
*two young people were talking, certainly just having left*
*some lecture hall at the nearby University*
*and one argued:*
*"Carlos Marx's idea about the State was..."*

*I admit that I care about it in a different way,*
*but, watching them, it was as if it were I who would return*
*to places I abandoned,*
*to polish the statue, covered with graffiti*
*written in the name of love,*
*dressed under the Caribbean heat with an overcoat as*
*long as the one Engels wears,*
*below the knee.*

*But in Alexanderplatz, Berlin, in the midst*
*of the new madness, I swear I only thought*
*of my lover's name.*

**Jennifer Ruth Hosek** is an Associate Professor of German Studies at Queen's University, Ontario, where she is also affiliated with Film and Media Studies, Cultural Studies, and the U. Havana-Queen's exchange. She is author of *Sun, Sex, and Socialism: Cuba in the German Imaginary* (University of Toronto Press, 2012), and her current larger projects are a monograph on urban movement and cinema in Berlin, Havana, and the San Francisco Bay Area and www.LinguaeLive.ca, a free, open access eTandem platform.

**Victor Fowler Calzada** is one of Cuba's most important contemporary writers. Born in 1960 to an Afro-Cuban family, he belongs to the first generation of the Revolution. Fowler has published extensively, with more than ten poetry and five essay volumes as well as anthologies and other collaborations. He has broken new ground in Cuban letters and cultural critique with his work on racialization, sexuality and the body.

## Notes

1. The authors would like to thank Carmen Beringuer, Cuban National Library; Mario Naito, Mediateca of ICAIC; Nathalie Soini of Queen's Library; Alberto Ramos; Petra Röhler, and all those interviewed for their immense assistance with this contribution.

2. Discussions with several cinemagoers. See also J. Schulz-Ojala, "Welcome to the Time Machine: The Success of Good Bye, Lenin! at the Havana Film Festival." http://www.fipresci.org/festivals/archive/2003/havana_2003/havana2003_jsojala .htm (accessed 22 February 2014). During the tense Special Period of the 1990ies, public screenings of politically challenging films were frequently confrontational. In Cuba, property is generally treated with care due to law enforcement and a common recognition of limited resources.

3. Assia Djebar, *Femmes d'Alger dans leur appartement: nouvelles* (Paris: Des femmes, 1980), viii.

4. Dipesh Chakrabarty, *Provincializing Europe: Postcolonial Thought and Historical Difference* (Princeton: Princeton University Press, 2000).

5. 9 April 1840. *Aphorisms, 700.*

6. José Martí, "A Enrique Estrázulas," in *José Martí. Obras Completas* (Havana: Editorial de Ciencias Sociales, 1991).

7. Jennifer Ruth Hosek, *Sun, Sex and Socialism: Cuba in the German Imaginary* (Toronto: University of Toronto Press, 2012). For a temporally more extensive documentation of the presence of German film in Cuba, see P. Noa, "Apuntes sobre la presencia alemana en el cine cubano," unpublished manuscript.

8. The English translation provided is from the Spanish version of the book, titled *Regresé siendo otra persona. Cubanas y cubanos en la RDA.*

9. Wolf-Dieter Vogel and Veronica Wunderlich, *Abenteuer DDR: Kubanerinnen und Kubaner im deutschen Sozialismus* (Berlin: Karl Dietz Verlag, 2011), 125–26.

10. Ibid., 76.

11. Ibid., 178.

12. For an overview of politico-cultural relations from the German side see Steffen Niese, *La política alemana hacia Cuba a partir de 1990: Balance y perspectivas* (Cologne: PapyRossa Verlag, 2012).

13. These paragraphs are based in discussions with Petra Röhler, coordinator of programming and educational cooperation in the cultural branch of the German Embassy/Goethe Institute in Havana, several in 2005 and one on 20 February 2014, all in Havana, and email exchange with Alberto Ramos Ruiz, Programmer and Catalogue Editor of the Havana Film Festival, 22 February 2014.

14. R. Gowland, "Protecting Che's Image," *The Guardian,* 2001. http://www.zip.com .au/~cpa/garchve4/1048cult.html. See also Wolfgang Kraushaar, *1968: das Jahr, das alles verändert hat* (Munich: Piper, 1998); and Ariana Hernández-Reguant, "Copyrighting Che: Art and Authorship under Cuban Late Socialism," *Public Culture* 16, no. 1 (2004): 1–29.

15. Email discussion with Alberto Ramos Ruiz February 2014.

16. For instance, the *Bundeszentrale für politische Bildung* has prepared school lesson plans for the film on this topic. http://www.bpb.de/shop/lernen/filmhefte/34162/ good-bye-lenin.

17. The end of the Soviet Union's support of Cuba began slowly in the 1980s, but 1990–91 suddenly ushered in the *Periodo especial en tiempo de paz* (*Special Period in Times of Peace*) in which Cuba arguably still finds itself today. To get a sense of this rupture: sources generally agree that in the most severe period from 1990 to 1993, the GDP fell 36 percent and average calorie consumption hovered around at one thousand calories a day.

18. Schulz-Ojala, "Welcome to the Time Machine."
19. Elizabeth Boa, "Telling It How It Wasn't: Familial Allegories of Wish-Fulfillment in Postunification Germany," in *Germany's Memory Contests and the Management of the Past,* ed. Anne Fuchs and Mary Cosgrove (Rochester: Camden House, 2006); Gary Schmidt, "Motherhood, Melodrama, and Masculinity in Wolfgang Becker's Good Bye Lenin!," *West Virginia University Philological Papers* 52 (2005); Jennifer Creech, "A Few Good Men: Gender, Ideology and Narrative Politics in The Lives of Others and Good Bye, Lenin!," *Women in German Yearbook* 25 (2009).
20. Jennifer Ruth Hosek, "Postcommunist Spectacle: Germany, Commodity, Comedy," in *Postcommunism, Postmodernism, and the Global Imagination,* ed. Christian Moraru (New York: Columbia University Press, 2009). Although it was not possible to include them in this chapter, many of my arguments there are indebted to my research on German film in Cuba, as are two papers, one given at the German Studies Association Conference (San Diego, CA, October 2007) entitled "Leveraging Cuban Perspectives on Choice in the Film *Good Bye, Lenin!*" and one presented at the Cinema and Social Change in Germany and Austria Conference (University of Waterloo, O.N., May 2008) entitled "Will the Bona Fide Experts Please Stand Up? Experiments in Film Analysis Method." I am extremely pleased that the appearance of this volume and the collaborative spirit of Quinn Slobodian have made it possible to publish explicitly on my research in Cuba.
21. Martin Blum, "Club Cola and Co.: Ostalgie, Material Culture and Identity," in *Transformation of the New Germany,* ed. Ruth Starkman (New York: Palgrave, 2006), 131–49.
22. Based on the Festival program, *Das Leben der Anderen* screened Saturday, 8 December 2007 at 8 and 10:30 P.M. at Cine Acapulco and Friday, 14 December 2007 at 10:30 P.M. at Cine Acapulco. http://www.habanafilmfestival.com/. See also "'La vida de los otros' será proyectado en el Festival de cine de La Habana." Hemeroteca > 16/11/2007 > http://www.abc.es/hemeroteca/historico-16-11-2007/abc/Internacional/la-vida-de-los-otros-sera-proyectada-en-el-festival-de-cine-de-la-habana_1641363384022.html
24. "'La vida de los otros' impacta en el Festival de La Habana." 10 DIC 2007 - 00:29 CET http://cultura.elpais.com/cultura/2007/12/10/actualidad/1197241201_850215.html
25. From the Festival program *Barbara* screened Wednesday, 5 December 2012 at 8:00 and 10:30 P.M. in Cine Acapulco and Friday, 14 December 2012 at 8:00 P.M., Cine Acapulco, http://www.habanafilmfestival.com/.
26. This poem has been published in Spanish and German as "La idea de Carlos Marx" and "Karl Marx' Vorstellung" in *Alba.* No. 3 (März) 2013. Trans. Léonce W. Lupette, 7.

# Bibliography

Blum, Martin. "Club Cola and Co.: Ostalgie, Material Culture and Identity." In *Transformation of the New Germany,* ed. Ruth Starkman, 131–49. New York: Palgrave, 2006.

Boa, Elizabeth. "Telling It How It Wasn't: Familial Allegories of Wish-Fulfillment in Postunification Germany." In *Germany's Memory Contests and the Management of the Past,* ed. Anne Fuchs and Mary Cosgrove, 67–86. Rochester: Camden House, 2006.

Chakrabarty, Dipesh. *Provincializing Europe: Postcolonial Thought and Historical Difference.* Princeton, NJ: Princeton University Press, 2000.

Creech, Jennifer. "A Few Good Men: Gender, Ideology and Narrative Politics in The Lives of Others and Good Bye, Lenin!." *Women in German Yearbook* 25 (2009): 100–126.

Djebar, Assia. *Femmes d'Alger dans leur appartement: nouvelles.* Paris: Des femmes, 1980.

Hernández-Reguant, Ariana. "Copyrighting Che: Art and Authorship under Cuban Late Socialism." *Public Culture* 16, no. 1 (2004): 1–30.

Hosek, Jennifer Ruth. "Postcommunist Spectacle: Germany, Commodity, Comedy." In *Postcommunism, Postmodernism, and the Global Imagination,* ed. Christian Moraru, 169–92. New York: Columbia University Press, 2009.

———. *Sun, Sex and Socialism: Cuba in the German Imaginary.* Toronto: University of Toronto Press, 2012.

Kraushaar, Wolfgang. *1968: das Jahr, das alles verändert hat.* Munich: Piper, 1998.

Martí, José. "A Enrique Estrázulas." In *José Martí. Obras Completas,* 349–53. Havana: Editorial de Ciencias Sociales, 1991.

Niese, Steffen. *La política alemana hacia Cuba a partir de 1990: Balance y perspectivas.* Cologne: PapyRossa Verlag, 2012.

Schmidt, Gary. "Motherhood, Melodrama, and Masculinity in Wolfgang Becker's Good Bye Lenin!." *West Virginia University Philological Papers* 52 (2005): 123–32.

Vogel, Wolf-Dieter, and Veronica Wunderlich. *Abenteuer DDR: Kubanerinnen und Kubaner im deutschen Sozialismus.* Berlin: Karl Dietz Verlag, 2011.

# Index

# Protest, Culture, and Society

General editors:
**Kathrin Fahlenbrach,** Institute for Media and Communication, University of Hamburg
**Martin Klimke,** New York University Abu Dhabi
**Joachim Scharloth,** Technical University Dresden, Germany

Protest movements have been recognized as significant contributors to processes of political participation and transformations of culture and value systems, as well as to the development of both a national and transnational civil society.

This series brings together the various innovative approaches to phenomena of social change, protest and dissent which have emerged in recent years, from an interdisciplinary perspective. It contextualizes social protest and cultures of dissent in larger political processes and socio-cultural transformations by examining the influence of historical trajectories and the response of various segments of society, political and legal institutions on a national and international level. In doing so, the series offers a more comprehensive and multi-dimensional view of historical and cultural change in the twentieth and twenty-first centuries.

Lightning Source UK Ltd.
Milton Keynes UK
UKHW021831030919
349133UK00005B/234/P

9 781785 337376